Econ   *u*

EASTERN AFRICAN STUDIES

Abdul Sheriff
Slaves, Spices & Ivory in Zanzibar
Integration of an East African Commercial Empire into the World Economy
1770–1873

Tabitha Kanogo
Squatters & the Roots of Mau Mau 1905–1963

David W. Throup
Economic and Social Origins of Mau Mau 1945–1953

Bruce Berman & John Lonsdale
Unhappy Valley
Clan, Class & State in Colonial Kenya*

Bethwell A. Ogot & Christopher Ehret
A History of Early Eastern Africa

* *forthcoming*

Economic & Social Origins of Mau Mau 1945–53

David Throup
Bye-Fellow
Magdalene College, Cambridge

James Currey

LONDON

Heinemann Kenya

NAIROBI

Ohio University Press

ATHENS

James Currey Ltd
54b Thornhill Square
Islington
London N1 1BE, England

Heinemann Kenya
Kijabe Street, PO Box 45314
Nairobi, Kenya

Ohio University Press
Scott Quadrangle
Athens, Ohio 45701, USA

British Library Cataloguing in Publication Data

Throup, David
Economic & social origins of Mau Mau,
1945-1953. —— (Eastern African studies).
1. Kenya —— Politics and government
I. Title   II. Series
967.6'203   DT433.575
ISBN 0-85255-023-5
ISBN 0-85255-024-3 Pbk

Library of Congress Cataloging-in-Publication Data

Throup, David.
Economic & social origins of Mau Mau.
Bibliography: p.
Includes index.
1. Agriculture and state —— Kenya —— History —— 20th century.
2. Kenya —— Economic conditions —— To 1963. 3. Kenya —— Social
conditions. 4. Kenya —— Politics and government —— To 1963. 5. Squatters
—— Kenya —— History —— 20th century. 6. Mau Mau —— History.
7. Kikuyu (African people) —— History —— 20th History. I. Title. II. Title:
Economic and social origins of Mau Mau.
HD2126.5.T48   1987   307.3'36   87-12387
ISBN 0-8214-0883-6
ISBN 0-8214-0884-4 (pbk.)

Typeset in 10/11pt Baskerville by Colset Private Limited, Singapore
Printed and bound in Great Britain

To my parents

Contents

Contents

Four
The Problems of Kikuyu Agriculture
63

Five
The Kikuyu Squatter Problem
91

Six
Olenguruone
120

Seven
The Peasant Revolt: Murang'a, 1947
139

Contents

Eight
Outcast Nairobi
171

Nine
A Change of Direction:
The Agricultural Department's Abandonment of Communalism
203

Ten
The Drift to Mau Mau
224

Eleven
Conclusion
237

Maps, Graphs and Tables

MAPS

GRAPHS

TABLES

Preface and Acknowledgements

One of the pleasures of historical research is the debt one incurs to people in all walks of life – many of whom will probably never read the finished book that they have helped to produce. That is particularly true in the case of a book like this on the social and economic origins of the Mau Mau movement in Kenya, which has taken eleven years to produce and which has involved research in both Britain and Kenya.

In October 1976, I first arrived in Nairobi with the vague idea of doing research while teaching at the *Banda* school. I am grateful to the late J.A.L. Chitty and to Douggie and Patricia Dalrymple for employing a totally inexperienced master and for introducing me to Kenya, while providing time for me to visit the archives. When I returned to Cambridge in September 1979, my research was funded by a grant from the Department of Education and Science and the Smuts Memorial Fund helped to finance another visit to Kenya from July 1980 to September 1981. In 1982–83 I was the holder of the Holland Rose Studentship in Commonwealth History of the University of Cambridge and in January 1984, I was elected to a Bye-Fellowship at Magdalene College, while the Leverhulme Trust awarded me a post-doctoral Study Abroad Studentship which enabled me to return to Kenya from February 1984 to January 1986 to undertake more research. I would like to express my gratitude to all these bodies.

During the last decade many friends have provided accommodation and intellectual sustenance. For their help in Nairobi I would especially like to thank Hugh and Jo Cowie, who welcomed me into their home for twelve months in 1980 to 1981; Glyn Davies, who did the same in 1984; and David and Margaret Pearson and Jan de Graaf, who solved my housing problems for shorter periods on several occasions. Richard and Jenny Davenport-Hines looked after me when I was working in the Public Record Office in Kew in 1979–80 and have done so on several occasions since, while Dave and Angie Anderson, Edward Chandler, James Thorne and Joanna Innes – old undergraduate friends – have sustained my endeavours. More recently, Joe and Janet Miller have welcomed me to the University of Virginia as Visiting Assistant Professor.

Various friends in Nairobi helped to retain my sanity by diverting me from the archives or have provided stimulating company in them. I would particularly like to thank my neighbours – Mary Anne, Tara and Petra Fitzgerald and Kate Macintyre – who used to ferry me in to town; and Susanne Mueller, Simon Myambo, Robert Bates, Michael Schatzberg, John Nordin, Barbara Grosh, Luise White and Jennifer Widner for their company in the archives. Jennifer Widner shared with me not only her knowledge of modern Kenyan politics and a 'hunt for Kimathi' in Nyeri but also introduced me to the charms of New Haven, Washington D.C. and New York on my first visit to America. She and the others have endured far too many of my monologues on Kikuyu history.

The staff of the Public Record Office at Kew; the Kenya National Archives, especially Mr Richard Ambani, who has an amazing ability to find misplaced files; and the Cambridge University Library have made this work possible. Janet Seeley and her colleagues at the African Studies Centre in Cambridge have introduced me to the delights of word processing and have kept me supplied with a steady stream of books and articles on Mau Mau which had escaped my attention. I would also like to take this opportunity to thank my colleagues in the History Department at the University of Nairobi to which I was attached as a research associate in 1980–81 and 1984–86 for showing such an interest in my research, especially Godfrey Muriuki, A.I. Salim, Atieno Odhiambo, Karim Janmohammed and Mwangi wa Githumo. I would also like to pay tribute to the memory of Dr Neville Chittick, the former Director of the British Institute in Eastern Africa, who encouraged me to use the Institute's facilities and always welcomed me to Nairobi, despite my strange interests in twentieth century Kenya instead of the *Shirazi* coast.

The Master and Fellows of Magdalene College, Cambridge, by electing me to a Bye-Fellowship provided me with a perfect home, where I could work in a friendly, productive and humane environment. For the privilege of being a 'Magdalene man', I am most grateful. I would particularly like to thank my fellow historians – Ronald Hyam, Eamon Duffy, Julian Hoppet, John Patterson and Jonathan Scott – for their encouragement and friendship.

Many people have read earlier drafts of chapters in this book – and indeed of some chapters which have been discarded, perhaps to appear in a second volume on *The Political Origins of Mau Mau* – and have offered valuable comments. I would like to thank Polly Bide, Ronald Hyam, John Iliffe, John Overton who also helped to produce the maps, Anne Thurston, Nicholas Westcott and the undergraduate members of the 1985–86 Saturday morning Mau Mau seminar, who over the course of forty hours forced me to change many of my opinions. David Fieldhouse and Richard Rathbone have followed my work with interest for many years and were incisive examiners of my doctoral thesis on 'The Governorship of Sir Philip Mitchell in Kenya, 1944 to 1952'. Selina Cohen has been a far more efficient editor than I have been author and has provided me with information on Kenyatta's Moscow period.

I am also most grateful to three participants – Sir Michael Blundell, who became the leader of the European Elected Members in the Legislative Council in 1952; Desmond O'Hagan, who served as District Commissioner in Murang'a from 1945–47, and then in the Secretariat before returning to Central Province as Provincial Commissioner in 1952 at the onset of Mau Mau; and Bildad Kaggia, the leader of the Clerks' and Commercial Workers' Union and member of the Mau Mau *Muhimu* – for reading and commenting at length upon my manuscript and for their kind hospitality during my frequent visits.

My debts – intellectual and personal – to David Anderson, Richard Waller and John Lonsdale, who began to supervise my work more years ago than he would care to remember, are beyond number. Their knowledge and enthusiasm for Kenya history have been an inspiration and their encouragement and patient criticism of my work has shown me how history ought to be written although I am acutely aware how far I have fallen short of their example. It should perhaps be emphasised here that there is no such thing as a 'Cambridge interpretation' of Kenya's history or a 'Cambridge school'. David, Richard and John have been my strongest critics. As such they have helped to produce this book and are largely responsible for any virtues it may have, but they should not be held responsible for its failings.

Finally, I would like to thank my long suffering parents, who have endured my protracted absences from home and who have sustained me with encouragement throughout this lengthy enterprise. This book is dedicated to them.

Charlottesville
Virginia

Abbreviations

PRO	*Public Record Office*
Cab.	Cabinet
CO	Colonial Office
WO	War Office

KNA	*Kenya National Archives*
Ag.	Department of Agriculture
C&I	Department of Commerce and Industry
CNC	Chief Native Commissioner
CP	Central Province
CS	Chief Secretary
DC	District Commissioner
DO	District Officer
FH	Fort Hall (Murang'a)
GH	Government House
KBU	Kiambu
Lab.	Department of Labour
MAA	Member for African Affairs
MAC/KEN	Murumbi Archive Collection/Kenya deposit
MKS	Machakos
NKU	Nakuru
NRK	Narok
NYI	Nyeri
PC	Provincial Commissioner
RVP	Rift Valley Province

Other abbreviations	
ADC	aide-de-camp
Afr.	Africa
Brt.Emp.	British Empire
CBE	Commander of the British Empire

CID	Criminal Investigation Department
CIGS	Chief of the Imperial General Staff
CMG	Companion of the Order of St Michael and St George
CMS	Church Missionary Society
CSM	Church of Scotland Mission
CVO	Commander of the Royal Victorian Order
DSO	Distinguished Service Order
EACA	East Africa Court of Appeal
FCS	Fellow of the Chemical Society
FRIC	Fellow of the Royal Institute of Chemistry
GBE	Knight Grand Cross of the British Empire
GCMG	Knight Grand Cross of St Michael and St George
KBE	Knight Commander of the British Empire
KC	Kings Counsel
KCB	Knight Commander of the Order of the Bath
KCVO	Knight Commander of the Royal Victorian Order
Kt.	Knight
LND	Land Number
LO	Land Office
MBE	Member of the Order of the British Empire
MC	Military Cross
MRCVS	Member of the Royal College of Veterinary Surgeons
Mss.	Manuscripts
OBE	Officer of the Order of the British Empire
PC	Privy Councillor
RAF	Royal Air Force
RH	Rhodes House
RMA	Royal Military Academy
RMC	Royal Military College

Glossary of African Words

K = Kikuyu   Sw. = Swahili

Agikuyu na Worjoria Wao	a co-operative of licensed egg exporters
ahoi	tenants at will, plural of *muhoi* (K)
Anake a Forty	the Forty Group, a criminal gang
askari	soldier (Sw.)
athamaki	elders of the *mbari* (K)
baraza	meeting/title of a newspaper (Sw.)
bibi	wife, wives (Sw.)
Dini ya Jesu Kristo	Church of Jesus Christ (Sw.)

Glossary of African Words

Dini ya Kaggia	Church of Kaggia (Sw.)
Dini ya Msambwa	Church of Msambwa/ancestral spirit of the Bukusu (Sw.)
duka	shop (Sw.)
githaka	plot of land belonging to a sub-clan (K)
itura	land (K)
karing'a	pure, strict, orthodox (K)
kiama	council (K)
Kifagio	broom – 'times of troubles' (K)
kipande	labour pass (Sw.)
liguru	land authority (Luhya)
majengo	shanty town (Sw.)
mbari	sub-clan (K)
Mihiriga	nine main Kikuyu clans or agricultural supervisory committees, plural of *Muhirig'a* (K)
Muhimu	Mau Mau Central Committee
Muhirig'a	one Kikuyu clan, or agricultural supervisory committee
muhoi	tenant-at-will, singular of *ahoi* (K)
murumati	trustee of *mbari* land (K)
muthoni	relation-in-law (K)
mwathi	ancestor (K)
ndungata	in-law (K)
ngwatio	communal labour (K)
njahi	pigeon pea
Njuri Ncheke	land authority (Meru)
nyimbo	hymns (K)
pombe	beer (Sw.)
posho	maize meal (Sw.)
Sauti ya Mwafrika	newspaper of the Kenya African Union, literally Voice of Africa (SW.)
shamba	cultivated plot, smallholding (Sw.)
tembo	kind of beer (K)
Uhuru	independence, freedom (Sw.)
utui	land authority (Kamba)
wananchi	people, citizens, the masses (Sw.)
Watu wa Mungu	False Prophets, lit. Men of God (Sw.)
wimbe	finger millet (Sw.)

One

The Economic and Social Origins of Mau Mau

Rather than attempting to identify a metropolitan grand strategy for the end of empire in Africa, in this book I try to argue that it would be more rewarding to abandon such Euro-centric blinkers and to place the policy makers of the Colonial Office within the context of Africa, the continent with which they have to deal despite their limited knowledge of the complex social, economic and political context which confronted administrators in the front line. This study, therefore, seeks to investigate the process of policy formation through the eyes of the local policy makers – the colonial governors, the Secretariats, the field administrators, and the various technical departments which dealt directly with Africans. These men were far more important for the future of Africa than the remote theorists in Whitehall. Recent studies of the Colonial Office in the 1940s have over-emphasised the importance of the 'Official Mind' for the history of decolonisation. This concentration on Whitehall has distorted our understanding of the process of colonial administration and decolonisation by concealing the different, often conflicting, aims of the various layers of the 'colonial state'.[1]

This story of Kenya in the decade before the outbreak of the Mau Mau Emergency attempts to present a more integrated view of imperial government as well as to examine the social and economic causes of the Kikuyu revolt. It is a contribution not only to the historiography of Kenya but also suggests that it is only by investigating the various strands of the interwoven historical processes of decolonisation that we can hope to comprehend its true complexity. The historiographical triptych of imperial policy, the international context, and the peripheral experience has to be reassembled and analysed as a unified whole. All three parts of the picture were important. No one strand alone can begin to portray the process of decolonisation for it is the linkages between these political arenas which provided the crucial element in the story.

In order to understand the process of decolonisation one must start with a discussion of the specificity of the colonial state. This study, therefore, begins with an investigation of the ambitions and policies of the various layers of the colonial state in Kenya. Whitehall, colonial governors and their Secretariats all had a profound impact on Africa, but the men in the field from lowly District Officers to senior Provincial Commissioners, not to mention the often forgotten technical services (particularly the agricultural, veterinary and labour departments) were often more important and frequently in conflict with the colonial administrative cadre.

The mandarins of the Colonial Office or governors and their Secretariats may have believed they ruled Africa, but in reality District Commissioners, agricultural officers and chiefs were far more important. They embodied the colonial state to most Africans – not the remote, unknown figures in the territorial or metropolitan capitals. It must also be remembered that the subconscious prejudices of these grassroots' administrators were often as important, as far as Africans were concerned, as the conscious policy decisions taken higher up the colonial hierarchy. Frequently, policies devised in Whitehall or Nairobi made little impression on the ingrained prejudices of policy implementers in the field. This study will attempt to justify these sweeping statements by examining the evolution of post-war policies in Kenya. It seeks to show how the aims of the Colonial Office, which were largely determined by the international climate and Britain's weak economic position in the late 1940s, were transformed by the political realities of Kenya. By combining traditional 'imperial' history, with its emphasis on the high politics of the official mind in the Colonial Office or in Government House, with the new peripherally focused African historiography, one can appreciate more fully the complexity of the problems which confronted not only British administrators but African politicians as they sought to construct their nationalist coalitions.[2]

The Kenyan settlers had made substantial economic and political advances during the last years of the war when Britain's African colonies were called upon to maximise production following the Japanese conquest of South East Asia. Whitehall, for example, had been alarmed in 1942 at the spectre of South African hegemony in East Africa, particularly in Kenya. Consequently, as the allied forces advanced towards victory, the Colonial Office reconsidered its pre-war policies and determined to reassert metropolitan authority in Kenya by instilling new life into the Duke of Devonshire's moribund 1923 declaration of African paramountcy.[3]

The new governor, Sir Philip Mitchell, was selected to undertake this task. He had secured a reputation as a pro-African administrator in Tanganyika and Uganda during the 1920s and 1930s. Mitchell's governorship was a failure for two reasons. First, he was reluctant to antagonise the settlers because he considered that any attempt to reduce their newly secured power would damage the colony's ambitious development plans. The future of East and Central Africa after 1945, under the Colonial Office's strategy of multiracialism, was posited upon the continued presence of a thriving European community, which would guarantee political stability, attract metropolitan investment into the region, and also act as the economic dynamo for industrial expansion since in the immediate future the settlers would provide the main consumers for the new secondary industries which, it was hoped, would absorb landless Africans from the reserves into wage employment.

Secondly, Mitchell was a proconsul of the old, pre-war school. He was an ardent defender of 'indirect rule'. Indeed his reputation had been founded upon his skilful introduction of the system into Tanganyika as Sir Donald Cameron's energetic adviser on African affairs. The new governor therefore had little sympathy for the Colonial Office's post-war plans to co-opt African politicians. Thus, despite the fact that in Kenya's acephalous, segmentary, lineage societies chiefs were British appointees, during Mitchell's eight years in office, the Kenyan government became dependent upon such antiquated allies. With little political legitimacy or influence, the chiefs became increasingly dictatorial, thereby further alienating their people. In contrast, the emerging African politicians remained excluded from the decision-making processes. Without any influence on official policy, they became increasingly intemperate. In consequence, their hopes of incorporation became even more remote. Their followers became disillusioned and abandoned advocates of constitutional politics, turning in desperation to the militants who became influential inside the nationalist movement.[4]

It was against this background of stymied African political advance and growing militancy that the colonial administration in Kenya evolved the policies that are examined here. The problems of Kikuyu agriculture both in the reserves and among the squatter communities on settler farms in the Rift Valley preoccupied Mitchell and his colleagues. We shall examine the development of agricultural policy in the Kikuyu reserves and follow the fate of the squatter farm labourers in the European enclave of the 'White Highlands' with particular attention since the government's failure to solve these problems lay at the heart of Mau Mau. The squatter communities, in particular, were confronted after the war by a drastic reduction in their cultivation and stock-holding rights without any commensurate increase in wages.[5]

The government's agricultural policies and political grand strategy, formulated partly by Mitchell and partly in Whitehall, were transformed by the field administration and the chiefs into an attack on those members of the emerging African élite who had not secured incorporation. These rivals of the chiefs for power and access to the pork-barrel of the colonial state had perforce turned to politics (in the 1930s to the Kikuyu Central

3

Association and after 1946 to the Kenya African Union) to force open the doors to the corridors of power. Their attempts to attract attention on both occasions backfired and ensured that their ambitions were denounced as illegitimate, subversive of the moral economy of 'Merrie Africa'. These attacks after the war on the political ambitions of the emerging proto-capitalists among the Kikuyu marked a return to the policies of the 1920s, when the settlers had also been politically influential.

The depression of the early 1930s, however, had created a fiscal crisis for the colonial state in Kenya, which forced the government to promote African peasant production in order to finance its bureaucracy and to ensure the survival of the settler farming community through subsidies until international commodity prices rose in the late 1930s. This encouragement of African individualism progressed even further during the war, when Kenya's exports were required to reduce the dollar deficit. Schemes for soil conservation and cattle destocking in the reserves were postponed and African entrepreneurs were encouraged to increase production regardless of the long-term effects on soil fertility. This decade, denounced after the war as an era of 'land-mining', came abruptly to an end when the Kenyan government began in 1944 to formulate its post-war policies in consultation with European settler leaders. The danger of erosion provided Kenya's settlers with a potent weapon with which to persuade the government in Nairobi and the Colonial Office to move against the economic base of their rivals, the emerging African capitalists and their representatives in the Kenya African Union and the banned Kikuyu Central Association.[6]

Policies formulated in the Colonial Office were subtly transformed by the local district administration and the chiefs into an attack on their political rivals in the Kenya African Union, who were struggling to emerge as an alternative indigenous élite. This belated attempt to forestall the emergence of African capitalism generated fierce resistance among the African élite, especially in Kikuyuland where these processes were most advanced. It coincided, moreover, with the disruptive effects on the peasantry of what Lonsdale and Low have described as 'the second colonial occupation'. For the first time ordinary Africans, cultivating their maize *shambas*, encountered administrative interference. Agricultural instructors and the chiefs ordered them to cultivate cassava and millet as security against famine, instead of the multi-purpose cash crop wattle, or maize which was more easily grown and prepared than the drought resistant new crops.[7]

Three mornings every week, peasant women were compelled to labour on communal terracing or grass-planting campaigns. Frequently they had to neglect their own plots in order to provide unpaid labour on the holdings of the chiefs and their wealthy supporters. Compulsion, not persuasion, was the hallmark of the first phase of the post-war agricultural betterment campaign, despite the Nairobi Secretariat's attempts to revive traditional land authorities such as the *Mihirig'a* among the Kikuyu, the *Njuri Ncheke* in Meru, or the Kamba *utui*. In fact, despite the advice of anthropologists, these bodies had never held executive power over the peasantry and their prestige had atrophied during 50 years of colonial rule.[8]

This second colonial occupation of the reserves was spearheaded by the chiefs, whose position became increasingly invidious. The colonial régime began to assess the loyalty and efficiency of its intermediaries by calculating the miles of terracing constructed in each location. The communal terracing campaign rapidly came to be perceived as the key indicator of social and economic progress. In the more advanced reserves, such as Kikuyuland, a new generation of chiefs were appointed after the war – school teachers, agricultural instructors, district headquarters' clerks. Long serving chiefs with established support among their people were replaced by younger men, willing to follow unquestioningly the orders of District Commissioners and agricultural officers. These new men had few claims to political power and were to prove less effective as intermediaries than the previous generation of African 'collaborators'. By 1947 peasant resistance was widespread.[9]

Following the Peasant Revolt, the agricultural department belatedly realised that compulsory terracing had alienated the rural population. Gradually the department adopted a new policy which sought to reward those who co-operated and built broad-based terraces, with permission to grow high-value cash crops such as coffee, tea and pineapples. By 1952, considerable areas had already been planted to such crops in Meru and Embu, but in Nyeri less than two per cent of peasant families had established coffee trees and in Murang'a fewer than one in 200 households were cultivating these remunerative new crops, which had hitherto been reserved for the European settlers. In Kiambu, in contrast, pineapple cultivation had been sponsored and sisal cultivation encouraged by the Agricultural Officer and the Administration in Machakos. Elsewhere, the field administration was reluctant to abandon compulsory labour and to return to the free enterprise policies of the 1930s and the war years, which it considered had increased social differentiation and threatened the traditional moral economy and, therefore, the fabric of peasant society. Officials consequently refused to switch once more to encouraging Kikuyu entrepreneurs, many of whom were enthusiastic supporters of the Kenya African Union or the Kikuyu Central Association, which were in conflict with the paternalist traditions of the district administration. The agricultural department's new strategy, therefore, made the least progress in those areas where the second colonial occupation had aroused the strongest African opposition, such as the Kikuyu heartlands of Murang'a and Nyeri. It was in these areas that communal terracing had most seriously eroded the authority of the chiefs and had alienated the peasantry. Thus although agricultural officers, such as Jack Benson in Meru and Leslie Brown in Embu, had recognised the need to secure African support for the betterment campaign by rewarding them with valuable cash crops, the field administration in the Kikuyu reserves remained reluctant to foster greater individualism, which they feared would exacerbate the problems created by increasing social differentiation. Individualism, they considered, would further undermine the cohesion of Kikuyu society and destroy customary social controls. Compulsion, therefore, continued to dominate the agricultural campaign in Kiambu, Murang'a and Nyeri, because the administration failed to recognise the need to broaden the colonial régime's narrow collaborative base. Thus, by 1952 the colonial order had become dangerously exposed in the Kikuyu reserves and the new generation of chiefs, appointed after the war, had squandered their political legitimacy.[10]

In many respects, of course, these new chiefs were very similar in education and background to the local leaders of the Kenya African Union and the Kikuyu Central Association, who were their strongest critics. Yet, despite Andrew Cohen's strategy of political incorporation, devised for the Gold Coast and Nigeria, African politicians in a settler colony such as Kenya, particularly at the district level, remained as firmly excluded from political and economic influence as before the war. They had, however, greater expectations. The field administration in Kenya (the infantrymen of the Colonial Service) failed to respond to the uncertain hints which percolated from Whitehall. African criticisms, however well founded or moderate, were deemed to be disruptive; subversive of the established order in the reserves. Some politicians deliberately attempted to stir up opposition to the chiefs, but official intransigence ensured that the district administration's fears became self-fulfilling. African politicians in Kenya, unlike their West African counterparts, or Kenya's settlers, could not break into the colonial corridors of power. Not all Africans, however, were excluded. The chiefs were securely entrenched at the local level, but the epithet 'politician' aroused the enmity of the administration and precluded the incorporation of Kenyatta and the Kenya African Union.[11]

The disruptive effects of the second colonial occupation enabled the activists of the Kenya African Union, under Kenyatta's leadership, to mobilise a popular constituency among the peasantry in opposition to the chiefs and communal terracing. The development of this confrontation is examined in detail in Murang'a District, the historic heartland of the Kikuyu, where Local Native Councillor James Beauttah, the chairman of the district branch of the Kenya African Union, clashed with Chief Ignatio Morai, the government's leading supporter. During the second half of 1947, the terracing campaign was disrupted throughout Murang'a.

d much support after the detention of the trade
Kibachia, and the shooting two weeks later by the
ers at Uplands.[16]

tion of legislation to allow for tighter control over
o the capital and to remove unemployed labourers
s, and new measures to increase the presence of the
stration in the African locations, there was little
uation. Those who were expelled from the city soon
he Kikuyu street gangs remained firmly in control
this date, they had established close links with the
ians and trade unionists who had risen to promi-
notably Fred Kubai and Bildad Kaggia. Encou-
gh, a self-avowed although rather undogmatic
ai and Kaggia organised the general strike of May
upted the capital. Armoured cars patrolled the
ar gas was used for the first time in Kenya to dis-
owds of strikers on the streets of Pumwani and
rt of the African residential area. When the strike
ays and the strike leaders, including Kubai and
l, the Nairobi militants had to reassess their syn-
ter careful deliberation, decided to switch from
ntation and trade unionism to one of political
f the constitutional nationalist movement, the
and the mass oathing of the capital's Kikuyu
, prostitutes, taxi drivers, vagrants and casual

control of the Nairobi branch of the Kenya
constitutionalists and had ousted Tom Mbotela,
the branch chairmanship, the trade union mili-
alliances with other radicals in the reserves and
September 1951, they felt strong enough to chal-
hip and when their attempt to capture control of
's national executive committee was thwarted,
the movement and establishing a more radical
had done two years earlier in the Gold Coast.
ntil the declaration of the Emergency by the
20 October 1952, the militants, secure in their
hallenged Kenyatta's authority and became
aising the stakes in the political contest. Unlike
f the banned Kikuyu Central Association, who
t supporters, the Nairobi militants and their
tion younger, were prepared to use force to
gemony.[18]

nt, as it was called by the government, was an

Several attacks were made on Chief Ignatio and Beauttah was arrested. Similar opposition to terracing and compulsory cattle dipping developed in Kiambu and Nyeri, the two other Kikuyu districts, until by September 1947, the government's authority appeared to be about to collapse throughout Kikuyuland.[12]

Meanwhile, the 200,000 Kikuyu squatters on settler farms had also been antagonised by the spate of post-war district Council orders, which regulated their stock and cultivation rights. Led by the Naivasha District Council, the main settler dairy and beef farming areas had introduced rules to end the disease threat posed to their grade cattle by squatter-owned stock. Settler cereal farmers and the large plantations were more cautious. They depended heavily upon squatter labour for sowing and harvesting their crops and feared serious disruption of their labour supply if draconian new restrictions were introduced. All settler farmers, however, were united in the fear that African resident labourers might secure squatters' rights under English law to the land they occupied on European-owned farms. Many squatter families had resided on the same farm since before the First World War, when they had been enticed by European farmers, short of capital and labour to develop their properties, to work in return for as much land as they wanted to graze their stock and to cultivate, in contrast to conditions in the already crowded reserves, where they were also subject to the exactions of the chiefs and their headmen and to taxation.

The Second World War had been a period of prosperity, as much for the squatters as for the peasants in the Reserves. Many settler farmers had been absent in the armed forces and the European district councils in the White Highlands had been cautious about antagonising their African labour in the midst of the hostilities once the British government, in December 1941, had urged Kenya to maximise production and had provided financial incentives to break new land and guaranteed prices. During the war, therefore, the squatters had been largely left alone and had been able to increase their own production for the black market at inflated war-time prices. Until the post-war squeeze, squatter family incomes had compared favourably with those in the Kikuyu reserves and the squatter option had enjoyed one last brief period of comparative prosperity. With the end of the war the situation changed. Squatter cultivation was restricted to two and a half acres per wife, while the number of sheep and goats they were permitted was drastically reduced, and all males over the age of sixteen were required to work 270 days per annum – virtually a full working year. During 1946, these new measures provoked fierce opposition, particularly in the Naivasha, Aberdares and Nakuru district council areas. The following year, discontent spread to the Uasin Gishu and Trans Nzoia, and to Abaluhya and Elgeyo squatters as well as to the Kikuyu, following the introduction of compulsory destocking of squatter cattle. In these western districts of the White Highlands, Elijah Masinde's Dini ya Msambwa provided a potent focus of resistance and was a portent of things to come among the Kikuyu – Mau Mau, which was to secure a strong following among dispossessed Kikuyu squatters.[13]

Relations between the former Kikuyu resident labourers at Olenguruone, the prototype African settlement scheme on the Mau escarpment above the White Highlands, and the remaining Kikuyu squatters in Naivasha and Nakuru were extremely close. In theory, the settlement had been designed to accommodate former Kikuyu squatters, who had been forced out of the White Highlands by the 1937 Resident Native Labour Ordinance, but in practice most of the residents of Olenguruone had been forcibly repatriated from Maasailand by the district administration in Narok during 1940–41. Most of them had, indeed, once been squatters, but they had arrived at Olenguruone in a belligerent mood, having been expelled from the more attractive ecological environment at Il Melili and Nairage Ngare. Thus, when the government attempted to enforce the settlement's agricultural rules in 1943, it encountered fierce resistance. Eventually, in September 1946, the residents had to be threatened with eviction and, after a three-year legal battle, were finally expelled in January 1950. Olenguruone was a running sore for the Kenyan government throughout the 1940s. Its Kikuyu residents introduced a new oath in 1942–43, which was administered to young men, women and children and not simply to the leaders, as with traditional Kikuyu oaths to ensure communal solidarity. This rapidly spread to the Kikuyu squatters on neighbouring farms, who were resisting the new district council regulations. Olenguruone thus became the centre of political subversion throughout the Rift Valley and established close ties with discontented squatters at Soysambu, Naivasha and Limuru. This chain of radical contacts provided the organisational framework for the development in the White Highlands, where one in four of the total Kikuyu population lived, of what came to be known as Mau Mau.[14]

The capital, Nairobi, was the other seed-bed of political militancy. While many squatters and peasants had prospered from the high commodity prices during the war, Kenya's urban population, particularly in Mombasa and Nairobi, lived on, or in many cases below, the official poverty line. Wages trailed behind inflationary price increases. Yet thousands of new migrants flocked to the capital and Mombasa throughout the 1940s. Between 1941 and 1948, Nairobi's population grew by 17 per cent each year. Many of these urban migrants after 1945 were former squatters, who had been squeezed off European farms, or Kikuyu *ahoi* (tenants) from Central Province, who had lost their small plots with the commoditisation of production and land. Senior lineages, like the settler farmers, cast off their dependent junior lineages and tenants and intensified their own commercial cultivation. Reinforced by increasing popula-

alliance between three groups of discontented Kikuyu: the urban unemployed and destitute; dispossessed squatters from the White Highlands; and poor peasants, tenants and members of the junior lineages of *mbari* (sub-clans) in the Kikuyu reserves who had endured the second colonial occupation, particularly the communal terracing campaign, at the moment they were being transformed into a landless rural proletariat as the senior lineages attempted to establish their exclusive access to land. The post-war agricultural betterment campaign, as it was conceived by Whitehall and the Secretariat in Nairobi, disrupted Kikuyu rural society and helped to destroy the political legitimacy of the chiefs, the essential intermediaries of the colonial system of control. Under the leadership of the Nairobi militants, who had established close links with the armed bands of Kikuyu thugs, these desperate elements among the Kikuyu, in the Reserves and on the European farms in the Rift Valley as much as in Nairobi, accepted violence as their last resort. They were convinced that they had nothing to lose and much to gain from a campaign of terror.[19]

By January–February 1952, violence had already reached serious proportions. Cattle on settler farms were hamstrung in large numbers and standing crops and haystacks were set on fire, particularly in the Nanyuki area immediately to the north of the Nyeri Reserve. Chiefs were attacked and agricultural instructors and police informers locked in their huts and burnt to death. Six months before the declaration of the Emergency, Othaya Division in Nyeri had become, like the African locations of Nairobi, a virtual Mau Mau republic where African officials and tribal police rarely went alone. The situation deteriorated rapidly after the retirement of Sir Philip Mitchell as governor in May 1952, during the four-month interregnum before his successor, Sir Evelyn Baring, arrived in Kenya at the end of September. Pressure from the settler community on the interim Governor, Henry Potter, to declare an Emergency and to detain those African political leaders who were considered to be behind the campaign of violence, became intense. Late in August, Potter sought permission from Whitehall to ban meetings of the Kenya African Union and to introduce legislation to control the vernacular press and freedom of movement in the Kikuyu areas. The Chief Native Commissioner and the Attorney General were despatched to London for consultation early in September to persuade a doubtful Colonial Office that the situation in Kenya was as bad as Potter's despatches had portrayed and to reinforce the case for drastic measures. The rapid deterioration in the political situation in Kenya during August and September 1952 astounded Whitehall. Under Mitchell, they had been given little inkling of the depth of Kikuyu alienation and, consequently, Potter's first warnings outlining the growing crisis had been dismissed as alarmist.[20]

When the new governor, Sir Evelyn Baring, arrived on 30 September, he was confronted by Potter and the Secretariat with extremely pessimistic reports and with carefully prepared plans for the declaration of an Emergency and the detention without trial of the colony's nationalist politicians. The assassination of Chief Waruhiu on 7 October, on his way home from a meeting with the governor, when Baring had been in the colony for only nine days, seemed to confirm the warnings of Potter and the district administration in Kikuyuland and compelled the new governor to accept their ill-considered solution. Like Mitchell, his predecessor, who had been captured in 1945 by his advisers in the Secretariat and had abandoned the Colonial Office's co-optive strategy for multiracialism, Baring in his first three weeks was persuaded to accept the Secretariat's interpretation of events. Denied time to consider the crisis, he failed to perceive the political divisions inside the Kenya African Union and the wide gap between Kenyatta and the militants, and denied himself the opportunity of incorporating Kenyatta, the moderate constitutional politician, and the chance to isolate the Nairobi militants and their rural allies from the peasantry. The remaining seven years of his governorship were to be spent paying for this error.[21]

Notes

1. Such an approach has already been attempted by several authors. R.F. Holland, *European Decolonization, 1918–1981*; J.A. Gallagher, *Decline, Revival and Fall of the British Empire*; J.M. Lee, *Colonial Development and Good Government*, pp. 1–206; J.M. Lee and M. Petter, *The Colonial Office, War and Development Policy*, pp. 49–256; R.D. Pearce, *The Turning Point in Africa, passim*, and R.F. Holland and G. Rizvi, (eds), *Perspectives on Imperialism and Decolonization*, particularly the essays by Holland, pp. 165–86 and J. Darwin, pp. 187–209. The following articles suffer from the same weakness, J.M. Lee: 'Forward Thinking and War', pp. 64–79; R.D. Pearce, 'Governors, Nationalists and Constitutions in Nigeria, 1935–1951' pp. 289–307; R.E. Robinson, 'Sir Andrew Cohen', pp. 353–63; and R.E. Robinson, 'Andrew Cohen and the Transfer of Power in Tropical Africa', pp. 50–72.
2. For a detailed assessment of Whitehall's strategy, see R.D. Pearce, *The Turning Point in Africa*, pp. 132–205; R.E. Robinson, 'Sir Andrew Cohen', pp. 353–63; and 'Andrew Cohen and the Transfer of Power in Tropical Africa', pp. 50–72. A more critical view of Cohen can be found in J.W. Cell, 'On the Eve of Decolonisation', pp. 235–57. The views of the field administration have been investigated by B.J. Berman in his unpublished thesis, 'Administration and Politics in Colonial Kenya', pp. 57–71, 113–60, 217–404. See also Berman, 'Bureaucracy and Incumbent Violence', pp. 143–75; and his unpublished paper, 'Provincial Administration and the Contradictions of Colonialism'.
3. G. Bennett, 'Settlers and Politics in Kenya, up to 1945', pp. 265–332, remains the standard account of European settler influence in Kenya. For a more radical critique of settler power, see E.A. Brett, *Colonialism and Underdevelopment in East Africa*; or R.M.A. van Zwanenberg, *Colonial Capitalism and Labour in Kenya, 1919–39*, pp. 1–35. B.J. Berman's thesis, 'Administration and Politics in Colonial Kenya', pp. 163–204 assesses settler pressure on the administration and Secretariat.

4. CO 533/543/38086/5 (1945–47), 'Kikuyu Petitions', Mitchell to Gater, November 1946; CO 533/543/38086/38 (1948), 'Kikuyu Petitions: Kikuyu Central Association', Rankine to Creech Jones, 28 December 1948; CO 533/543/38086/38 (1949), 'Kikuyu Petitions: Kikuyu Central Association', Mitchell to Creech Jones, 28 February 1949; and CO 533/537/38672 (1947–48), 'Memorandum from the Kenya African Union', Mitchell to Creech Jones, 11 February 1947.

5. CO 533/549/38232/15, 'European Settlement: Squatters', Wyn Harris, 'A Discussion of the Problem of the Squatter', 21 February 1946; KNA Lab 9/309, 'Resident Labourers General: Report of the Ad Hoc Committee, 1946–50', Hyde-Clarke's 'Policy on Resident Labour' for Cavendish-Bentinck, 5 March 1947; and Lab 9/1071, 'Resident Labourers Ordinance: The Problem of the Squatter: Ad Hoc Committee, 1946–48', draft statement of policy for Cavendish-Bentinck's committee, prepared by E.M. Hyde-Clarke and J.H. Martin.

6. Mitchell's views on the Kenya African Union and the Kikuyu Central Association can be found in CO 533/543/38086/5 (1945–47), 'Kikuyu Petitions', Mitchell to Creech Jones, 1 December 1945, November 1946, and 20 January 1947; CO 533/540/38032 (1949), 'Legislative Council', Mitchell to Creech Jones, 11 December 1948; and CO 533/543/38086/38 (1948), 'Kikuyu Central Association', Rankine to Creech Jones, 28 December 1948.

7. J.M. Lonsdale and D.A. Low, Introduction in Low and Smith, *History of East Africa*, pp. 1–63.

8. KNA DC/NYI 2/1/20, 'Mr Humphrey's Report on South Nyeri, 1944–47'; CO 852/662/19936/2 (1945–46), 'Soil Erosion: Kenya', H.E. Lambert and P. Wyn Harris's memorandum on 'Policy in Regard to Land Tenure in the Native Lands of Kenya'; and CO 852/557/16707/2 (1946), 'Land Tenure Policy: Kenya', especially the report of the Soil Conservation Committee to the District Commissioner Central Kavirondo, 18 August 1945; and H.E. Lambert, 'Policy in Regard to the Administration of the Native Lands – Note for Discussion', 10 July 1946.

9. See Chapter 7 *infra*.

10. B.J. Berman's thesis, 'Administration and Politics in Central Kenya', p. 361–7, 372–98; KNA DC/FH 1/26, 'Fort Hall Annual Report, 1947', pp. 2–6 and DC/FH 4/6, 'Chiefs and Headmen, 1937–54', for attacks on the Murang'a chiefs; and MAA 8/68 'Chief Waruhiu, 1948–52', *passim*, for Kiambu.

11. KNA MAA 7/49, 'Chiefs and Headmen: Discipline, 1942–46'; MAA 7/320, 'Chiefs Engaged in Commerce, 1948'. For examples of chiefs who became successful businessmen, see G. Kitching, *Class and Economic Change in Kenya*, pp. 297–311, where nine of the fourteen case studies were chiefs. See also J.M. Lonsdale's unpublished paper, 'African Elites and Social Classes in Colonial Kenya' pp. 10–13; and B.E. Kipkorir, 'The Educated Elite and Local Society', pp. 255–68.

12. KNA DC/FH 1/26, 'Fort Hall Annual Report, 1947', p. 6: Ag 4/451, 'Fort Hall Safari Diaries, 1948–51', entries for 2–6 March and 6–10 July 1948; and MAA 8/106, 'Intelligence Reports: Mumenyereri, 1947–50', extract for 1 December 1947.

13. T.M.J. Kanogo's, 'The History of Kikuyu Movement into the Nakuru District of the White Highlands, 1900–63', pp. 245–379; F. Furedi, 'The Social Composition of the Mau Mau Movement in the White Highlands', pp. 492–504; M. Tamarkin, 'Mau Mau in Nakuru', pp. 228–37; B.A. Ogot, 'Politics, Culture and Music in Central Kenya', pp. 277–86; KNA Secretariat 1/2/2, 'Nyanza Province, 1949–50', P. Wyn Harris to the Executive Council, 12 October 1949; and A. Wipper, 'Elijah Masinde', pp. 157–81.

14. C.G. Rosberg and J. Nottingham, *The Myth of Mau Mau*, pp. 243–4, 248–59; and F. Furedi's unpublished paper, 'Olenguruone in Mau Mau Historiography'.

15. KNA DC/FH 1/26, 'Fort Hall Annual Report, 1947', pp. 1–6, 15; DC/FH 1/27, 'Fort Hall Annual Report, 1948', pp. 1–2, 4–5, 11; MAA 8/68, 'Chief Waruhiu, 1948–52'; and CO 852/557/16707/2 (1946), 'Land Tenure Policy: Kenya', H.E. Lambert's

memorandum on 'Policy in regard to Administration of the Native Lands – Note for Discussion', 10 July 1946.

16. KNA Secretariat 1/12/8, 'Labour Unrest: Intelligence Reports, Central Province, 1947', C. Penfold to P. Wyn Harris, 29 August, 3, 24 and 25 September and 10 October 1947; and M. Singh, *History of Kenya's Trade Union Movement*, pp. 154–60.

17. J. Spencer *KAU*, pp. 202–32; B. Kaggia, *Roots of Freedom*, p. 79; KNA Lab 9/87, 'Labour Troubles: Nairobi, 1950'; and *East African Standard*, 17 February 1951.

18. Interview with Bildad Kaggia, 21 January 1985; KNA DC/FH 1/31, 'Fort Hall Annual Report, 1952', pp. 1–6, 11–18; Ag 4/410, 'Central Province and Districts: Annual Agricultural Reports, 1952', G. Gamble's Nyeri District Report; and F.D. Corfield, Historical Survey of the Origins and Growth of Mau Mau, Cmd. No. 1030 (London and Nairobi, 1960), pp. 124–6.

19. B. Kaggia, *Roots of Freedom*, pp. 113–15; and KNA Mss. 324.296762, Eliud Mutonyi Wanjie, 'Mau Mau Chairman', pp. Ii–J4.

20. CO 822/437, 'Proposals to Deal with the Disturbances Arising from the Activities of the Mau Mau Secret Society: Kenya', J. Whyatt to P. Rogers, 2 September 1952; CO 822/436, 'Activities of the Mau Mau Secret Society: 29 July–25 October 1952', H.S. Potter to P. Rogers, 17 August 1952 and Press Office Handout 203, 29 August 1952.

21. CO 822/443, 'Proclamation of a State of Emergency', E. Baring to O. Lyttelton, 10 October 1952; and CO 822/447, 'Reports on the Mau Mau Situation by the Commissioner of Police, Kenya', 16 October 1952–1 April 1953.

Two

The Metropolitan Perspective and the View from Nairobi

The official mind

During the scramble for Africa, Whitehall had perhaps responded coherently to the disintegration of informal empire once the imperialism of free trade had proved only too successful for the continued stability of Britain's allies on the periphery, but by the time the formal empire began to disintegrate, the Colonial Office had spawned a host of local sub-imperialists in every Secretariat with their own ambitions and rivalries. Superficially, the aims of the old official mind in Whitehall and the new ones in the colonies appeared to be the same. Both agreed that they should attempt to ensure that the colonies attracted as little international attention as possible. This study of Kenya from the war to the outbreak of Mau Mau in 1952, however, will show that the centre and the periphery had different policies. Consequently, although the Colonial Office and the Kenyan government considered that they were working together, by the time policies reached the district level they bore little resemblance to Whitehall's strategy for incorporating Africans into the political process.[1]

The prisms through which the Colonial Office, the Nairobi Secretariat and the field administration viewed Kenya produced different impressions of reality. No one image was correct; all contained elements of truth. While the Colonial Office had to withstand the pressures of world opinion and the reproofs of the Treasury, and recognised that Britain's diminished status required that African nationalism should be directed into constitutionalist paths before it attracted adverse attention to Britain's imperial trouble spots, the field administration, by contrast, looked at events from a local, not an international, perspective. The Secretariat and Sir Phillip Mitchell, the governor, stood mid-way between these extremes and tried to reconcile the contradictions between their instructions from Whitehall and the daily political pressures from the settlers, the African chiefs and the field administration against their rivals, the African politi-

15

cians. In Kenya and the other colonies in which there were large settler communities, the metropolitan and peripheral official minds had contradictory priorities and consequently the Kenyan state, which enjoyed considerable autonomy, did not always carry out Whitehall's instructions.[2]

The world from Whitehall

Britain in 1945 was exhausted; the United States seemed about to retreat into economic, if not military, isolationism; India and South East Asia were in turmoil; and the Russians had advanced deep into central Europe. World opinion had also moved sharply against the imperial powers since the 1930s. The new United Nations provided an arena for Britain's critics to condemn colonialism. Moreover, Britain's economic decline meant that she could no longer afford to carry the burden of a major power. Even if delusions of grandeur remained in the Foreign Office, she did not have the economic resources to compete with the new superpowers, both of which were ideologically hostile to the British empire. Although the spectre of American interference in colonial affairs had receded since the anxious days of 1942 and the dispute over the Atlantic Charter, the future did not bode well. Even Australia could not be relied upon to oppose plans for the internationalisation of the colonies under the suzerainty of the United Nation's Trusteeship Committee. The collapse of Malaya, Singapore and Burma and the acquiescence of the people of South East Asia to Japanese rule irreparably damaged Britain in the eyes of American opinion, But perhaps even more important, this debacle had destroyed the imperialists' own self-confidence. Britain's psychological commitment to empire was never quite the same.[3]

After the war the metropolitan mind wanted to keep the colonies quiet. The West Indies in the late 1930s; South East Asia during the post-war battles for independence in the Dutch East Indies, Vietnam and Malaya; and India almost continuously, showed a distressing inability to keep out of the world's headlines. Race riots, the catastrophic famine in Bengal and military disaster had all embarrassingly exposed Britain's imperial pretensions. It seemed that Africa was about to follow, unless the Colonial Office learnt from its lessons in the West Indies and the uninspired example of the India Office, and moved decisively to institute social and constitutional reforms. Thus, Lord Hailey, O.G.R. Williams and finally Andrew Cohen, attempted to devise plans for controlled political devolution which, it was hoped, would incorporate the emerging African nationalists into the colonial state. The Colonial Office was preparing to make a pre-emptive bid to direct African nationalism, unlike Indian, into constructive constitutionalist activity. In India, Whitehall had lagged behind events; in Africa, the Colonial Office was determined to lead the way. In addition, Whitehall was deeply influenced by the social welfare

16

ethos of Beveridge's Britain, especially as it seemed to provide a new weapon with which to keep the 'natives' quiet.[4]

Professor Robinson has called this growing self doubt and reluctance to carry the white man's burden in Africa 'the moral disarmament of African Empire'. He has observed that:

> By 1947 the trustees in the person of Arthur Creech Jones and officials like Andrew Cohen had come to believe that the tropical African empire should be dismantled in stages within the next two decades . . .[since] colonial governments during the inter-war years had proved incapable of supplying the necessary dynamic and therefore in their opinion, 'self-government was better than good government'. . . . They prepared to hand over their tasks to nationalists and achieve the purpose of trusteeship by other means. The long frustration in defending the ethic contributed much to the fall of African empire, in changing the mind of the imperial bureaucracy. The generation of consuls between the wars remoralised the empire so far beyond their capacity to live up to expectations that they demoralised the belief in empire of the post-war generation to come.[5]

This is an arresting interpretation of decolonisation in Africa, but was it quite so simple? Did the inter-war years really destroy Britain's will to rule in Africa as Robinson has suggested or was it, as Berque has suggested for the Maghreb and Iliffe for Tanganyika, that Africans became increasingly disillusioned with the economic advantages of colonialism? And in Britain's case was not the decision to withdraw as quickly as possible primarily determined by the blow the imperial psyche had suffered in Malaya and India, when subjugated peoples had shown themselves to be indifferent in the struggle between Britain and Japan rather than by any moral disarmament in the African colonial service?[6] Robinson has also failed to recognise the paradox that the lessons Whitehall had learnt in the white settler colonies of central and eastern Africa during the 1920s and 1930s had only undermined Whitehall's will to rule in the settler-less colonies of West Africa. The effects of any moral disarmament of African empire were not as straightforward as he would have us believe. The Colonial Office's co-optive strategy was essentially devised for colonies like the Gold Coast and Nigeria, where an educated élite had existed for many years and vigorous political movements had clearly emerged. In the east and central African colonies, such as Kenya, the future was less clear.[7]

In the dark days of May 1943, when American criticism of empire had been at its height, a Cabinet Committee pondering the fate of the colonies had declared that:

> Many parts of the Colonial Empire are still so little removed from their primitive state that it must be a matter of many generations before they

17

are ready for anything like full self-government. There are other parts inhabited by people of two or more different races, and it is impossible to say how long it will take to weld together these so-called plural communities into an entity capable of exercising self-government.[8]

This does not sound like moral disarmament. The Cabinet clearly did not envisage any rapid withdrawal. Moreover, the late Jack Gallagher has shown that the Second World War intensified rather than weakened Britain's commitment to empire. The war years did not produce any mass conversion to anti-imperialism, even in the rank and file of the Labour Party, while among the leadership, Attlee and Bevin, and even Cripps, proved to be just as sound defenders of Britain's imperial heritage as Churchill and Eden.

Ronald Hyam has pointed out that, before 1914, the Colonial Office had been well aware that it was impossible to translate the political decisions of the metropolitan mind into political practice in the colonies. In the age of the telegraph, Whitehall had simply acted as 'the final arbiters of empire, but they knew that they had no executive or enforcing power'. By 1945, this awareness of their limitations had disappeared and the metropolitan official mind attempted directly to control the periphery and to dictate policy. The colonies were to be bound together and a grand strategy of decolonisation implemented. This had disastrous consequences when the second colonial occupation disrupted Africa after the war. Now disturbances in one area, mediated through the official mind in Whitehall, had profound effects throughout the empire. Thus even Kenya could not remain completely untouched by Andrew Cohen's reactions to the Accra riots of February 1948.[9]

Cohen's five-phase strategy of decolonisation sprang from the same roots as Professor Robinson's wider moral disarmament. Despondent at the lack of development in the colonies, both economic and political, and alarmed at the spectre of nationalist protests which would attract international condemnation of British imperialism, the Colonial Office wanted to incorporate African political activists into the constitutional process. In West Africa it was apparent that the 'native' rulers would have to be ditched, except perhaps in the backwaters of northern Nigeria where the emirs seemed to be as powerful as ever, and a new alliance established with the educated élite of the towns and the primary school graduates of the provinces.[10] In east and central Africa, the settlers stood in the way of any attempt to incorporate the emerging African politicians, who represented the interests of a less well-established group of traders, commercial farmers and teachers. These men, it was believed, were not a serious challenge to colonial rule, unlike the lawyers and established cocoa farmers of the west, with their university degrees and tradition of active politics. In the east, the Colonial Office was more concerned that the settlers would destroy the present calm with their demands for self-government of dominion status. Such provocative suggestions would arouse African opposition and attract unfavourable attention to the settler colonies, where racial discrimination and the privileged status of the settlers invited condemnation. Whitehall was only too acutely aware that in Kenya and the Rhodesias, Africans were living in over-crowded reserves while their former land was being farmed by a small number of British settlers. If American and Russian anti-imperialists were not to have a field-day at Britain's expense, with untold consequences for the alliance with America, metropolitan authority had to be reasserted and the settlers reduced to a less powerful position inside the colonial corridors of power.[11]

The metropolitan mind, however, was divided between the colonialists and the 'little Englanders'. While the Colonial Office wanted to promote African interests and to use the new Colonial Development and Welfare Act to increase social welfare, the Treasury and the domestic ministries were concerned that the colonies should serve British interests. With an uncovered external debt of £2,879 million in 1945, Britain's economic position was unprecedentedly difficult. It quickly emerged that Creech Jones was a political lightweight in the Cabinet and could not defend the interests of the colonies against the exactions of the Board of Trade and the Ministry of Food. Africa was a world far removed from the usual preoccupations of government ministers and evoked little interest. Even Cripps and Strachey, who had held advanced views on colonial affairs, became preoccupied with domestic British politics. The government's electoral survival after all depended on the British voter. Thus, the British housewife's margarine supply was more important than the plight of the Tanganyikan peasant.[12]

The empire had emerged from the war over-stretched, much criticised and, above all, economically vulnerable. To finance the campaign, £1,118 million of overseas investments had been sold, but during the last year of the war Britain's food and raw material imports had amounted to over £2,000 million, of which only £800 million had been covered by exports. Existing gold and convertible currency reserves covered only one-sixth of her short-term debts. These problems were exacerbated by the sudden cancellation of land–lease by the United States on 21 August 1945. Throughout the immediate post-war years Britain's economic position remained perilous. The premature decision under American pressure to restore free convertibility in September 1947 cost Britain one-quarter of her hard-earned foreign reserves in only three weeks. Consequently the demands upon the colonies to maximise their hard currency earnings were intensified, fuelling further discontent.[13]

Despite the rhetoric of the Colonial Development and Welfare Act, these harsh economic realities dictated the Attlee government's colonial policies. Paradoxically, the theories of 'capitalist imperialism' only reflected British rule in most of tropical Africa when the Christian

Socialist, Stafford Cripps, was Chancellor of the Exchequer and the former Marxist, John Strachey, Minister of Food. Ostensibly the second colonial occupation was couched in the language of humanitarian social welfare thinking, but Britain's economic position prevented the Labour Party from fulfilling its promises of welfare state colonialism as had been advocated by the party's Imperial Advisory Committee and Creech Jones when he had been head of the Fabian Colonial Bureau. In fact, Africa was increasingly forced to subsidise the expansion of the welfare state in Britain, and the development measures which were undertaken were carefully devised to serve Britain's immediate interests.[14]

The correspondence of the Colonial Office's Economic Department clearly shows how Britain's perilous financial position, particularly her serious deficit on trade with the United States, was throughout the immediate post-war years a crucial determinant of plans for African economic and social development. As far as the Treasury, the Board of Trade or the Ministry of Food were concerned, the Colonial Office was Sydney Caine, not Creech Jones or Cohen. Caine was an economist and carried into the Colonial Office the inflexible *laissez-faire* ideology of a Treasury mandarin. It was hardly surprising that he clashed with the social welfare humanitarianism propounded by Arthur Lewis, Evan Durbin and Sir Bernard Bourdillon on the Colonial Economic Advisory Committee, and with Sir Philip Mitchell in Nairobi. As the economic crisis deepened, Caine's judgement became increasingly influential, if only because he could assuage a ruffled Treasury. His *laissez-faire* policies were cheap and did not commit the British taxpayer to endless subventions to colonial social welfare projects, or promote secondary industrialisation and commodity processing, which might have conflicted with established British industries. Moreover, this free market approach to economic development ensured that the flow of cheap raw materials continued unabated for Britain's post-war reconstruction and to reduce the dollar deficit.[15]

After the war Britain continued to hold sterling balances in London and used them to fund her trade deficit with the United States and to finance Britain's recovery. David Fieldhouse has estimated that between 1946 and 1951, while the colonies received a mere £40.5 million under the Colonial Development and Welfare Act, colonial sterling balances in London rose from £760 million to £920 million, and another £93 million was held for the West African marketing boards. Throughout the Attlee government's period in office funds flowed from the dependent empire to Britain as the periphery was exploited to serve metropolitan interests. Thus Fieldhouse points out, when international demand for tropical commodities was buoyant for the first time since the 1920s, when colonial governments were clamouring for increased investment in direct production as well as social welfare schemes, and when there was a pent-up demand for British exports among ordinary Africans following seven

20

years of war, the metropole could not deliver the goods. Africa would have to wait until her resources had enabled the British economy to recover. Only then would Africans receive their cotton piece-goods and the benefits of their increased production. Until then inflation and continued neglect would be their only reward. Britain not Africa came first.[16]

The Colonial Office and the Kenyan settlers

The Cabinet and the Colonial Office considered Kenya to be one of the empire's plural communities. Europeans, Asians and Arabs had all settled in the colony and considered themselves to have as much right to live in Kenya as the Africans. In 1945, it appeared to be unthinkable that these immigrant populations would be abandoned within less than two decades to African rule. Rather, the war-time Cabinet and its Labour successor hoped that European settlers would provide the 'steel frame' or 'cornerstone' of a new multiracial Kenya, in which the settlers would exert an influence incommensurate with their small numbers.[17]

South East Asia, especially French Indo-China and the Dutch East Indies, however, were soon to show that European settlers, even large-scale plantation capital, were a political nuisance, complicating the process of nationalist co-option.[18] This proved to be equally true in Kenya and the Rhodesias. It was already evident that settlers were less efficient than African cash-crop cultivators, and were always demanding preferential rights; while, politically, they represented the unacceptable face of imperialism, with their plans for self-government. They did, however, have the ability to appeal to a residual patriotism, particularly among the unreconstructed imperialists of the Tory right. This was to prove a great political asset.[19]

During the war, the settlers in Kenya had prospered as never before from the increased demand for their agricultural exports. By 1942, a major transformation had occurred in the world economy, ending the long years of restricted demand for East Africa's produce and marking the beginning of a new era of commodity shortages. Even the internal market expanded as the European population of the three mainland colonies trebled with the arrival of Italian prisoners of war and Polish refugees. The allied forces in the Middle East were also fed Kenyan wheat, maize and vegetables. Moreover the Japanese advance into the Philippines and Java benefited the sisal plantations (Kenya's most important export crop) by reducing British and American supplies of hard fibres from 530,000 to 245,000 tons, half of which came from East Africa. The prosperity of the European farming community was ensured by the preferential terms they were guaranteed by the settler-controlled Agricultural Production and Settlement Board which organised the war-time campaign for maximum production. The high guaranteed prices for settler maize and new breaking and clearing grants to encourage production resulted in a dramatic increase in maize cultivation from 80,000 acres in 1941 to 131,563 acres four years later, while wheat production rose from 103,000 to 184,500 acres by 1945.[20]

This economic security coincided with a period of greater settler political influence. During the 1930s, the Kenyan administration had suffered a decade of retrenchment and, on the outbreak of war; one-third of the field administration were absorbed into the armed forces and a mere skeleton force was left to police the reserves.[21] These military demands upon an already stretched administrative cadre forced the Kenyan government to incorporate settler agencies, such as the Kenya Farmers' Association, into the colonial state, especially in the economic sector. This use of settler organisations to oversee the marketing mechanism meant that by 1945 the settlers had become much more powerful. The reason why Kenya proved so difficult to control during the 1940s was that Mitchell found it virtually impossible to dislodge the settlers from their newly secured political and constitutional redoubts. Even after the war the field administration was called upon to supply men to help the army administer Somaliland and Eritrea and had insufficient staff to operate the new production and supply agencies which were left in the control of the local settlers. After the war, therefore, they were firmly entrenched in these positions and had been conceded far more authority over the economy than they had ever enjoyed in pre-war Kenya.[22]

As early as 1942 the Colonial Office had perceived that the presence of an over-mighty settler community was the fundamental problem in Kenya. The settlers, it was feared, would hinder African political and economic development and distort the colony's economy. Even if Whitehall had not yet realised that settlers and Kikuyu were on a collision course, it had, unlike the Kenyan Secretariat, recognised that their rival ambitions might soon become a dangerous source of conflict. In June 1942, Viscount Cranborne, the Secretary of State, had recorded his

> Extreme disquiet about the situation that is developing in East Africa. Since the formation of the Supply and Civil Defence Council in April, a step which was taken by the Government of Kenya without any consultation with the Colonial Office, things seemed to have moved at an increasingly rapid rate. There is ample evidence that the white inhabitants, both official and unofficial, are taking matters into their own hands, and that the Council is taking the form of a Cabinet, arrogating to itself the power to take decisions without any reference home, and increasingly intolerant of any guidance from the Colonial Office . . . It seems to me that immediate action is necessary if the position is to be held. If we dally, we shall be faced with what is in effect a white self-governing Dominion, backed by the whole force of white public opinion.[23]

22

His sentiments were echoed throughout the Colonial Office. Sir Arthur Dawe, one of the Assistant Under-Secretaries, for example, was prompted to contrast the settlers to twelfth-century barons who had 'constructed strong bulwarks against the power of the central government' in their campaign to secure effective control over Kenya. Whitehall was so concerned about the advances which the settlers had secured that they reassessed their policies during the inter-war years.[24]

When one analyses the history of Kenya during these years it is difficult not to conclude that the Devonshire declaration of African paramountcy of 1923 had been fatally undermined by a succession of secretaries of state and governors who had allowed the settlers to have their way throughout the 1920s and 1930s. The one exception was Sir Joseph Byrne, who had been governor during the depression, from 1931 to 1937. Dawe lamented that

> The policy of the home authorities has been one of appeasement and conciliation. With the lesson of 1923 in mind they, i.e. we, appear, in general, to have avoided any head-on clash with the settlers. . . .The fitful advocacy of the native point of view in England does not appear to have opposed any effective obstacle, to the steady pressure, which, quietly upon the spot, the settlers have been able to bring to bear on the local Government.[25]

It is striking that the governors of Kenya had been singularly subservient to settler aspirations and correspondingly unsuccessful in asserting metropolitan authority. Part of their failure was rooted in the fact that Nairobi, more than any other African governorship, was a political appointment. Of the fourteen governors, only five were appointed from inside the Colonial Service and, during the inter-war years, this ratio had fallen to one in five. Northey and Brooke-Popham were military men; Grigg was a politician; while Coryndon had worked for Rhodes's British South Africa Company in the Rhodesias and Swaziland. Of the governors of Kenya, only Byrne had been willing to stand up to the settlers, much to the dismay of his Chief Secretary, Henry Moore, who had been caught in the cross-fire. Throughout his term as governor from 1940 to 1944, therefore, Moore had been determined to avoid a confrontation with the Kenyan Europeans.[26]

Dawe and Cranborne were particularly concerned that 'the move towards settler domination has been much speeded up by the war'. Although the Colonial Office recognised that it was inevitable that settler farmers and businessmen would have to be enlisted to operate the network of boards and controls which were required for the war effort, Whitehall was alarmed that the Kenyan settlers would

> . . . look beyond these immediate necessities and see in the war a chance of quickening up the processes which, for a generation, have

been working in the direction of the White Dominion . . . To the settlers these events must appear as a further example of the beneficient working of evolution in their affairs. They must hope that this desirable piece of war-time machinery will prove to be the engine of policy which by its unobtrusive working will make the White Dominion an accomplished fact, beyond the power of the British Government to modify.[27]

South African expansion also concerned the Colonial Office. The presence of white South African troops in Kenya during the Ethiopian campaign and their continued passage through Kenya to the Libyan front, it was feared, had made a marked impression on the settlers. There were, it was believed in London, 'strong elements among the British in Kenya, who see in South Africa the ally which will enable them to break away from the trammels of Westminister and Downing Street. They are turning to this powerful ally to safeguard themselves against the rising black tide and the menace of British native policy'.[28] Undoubtedly the South African government was cautiously fostering this attitude and General Smuts seized every opportunity to improve contacts with East Africa where South African representatives became increasingly active. The Johannesburg mining interests were also keen to establish closer control over the mineral and agricultural wealth of central and eastern Africa. Certainly many settlers in Kenya looked to South Africa as a counterweight to the new Labour government in Britain. Alfred Vincent, the leader of the European elected members of the Kenyan Legislative Council and a prominent Nairobi businessman, was an admirer of Smuts and was eager that South Africa should establish closer economic ties with Kenya. Although the spectre of South African expansionism was exaggerated, it did arouse serious concern in Whitehall. Indeed one of the reasons for Mitchell's appointment as governor was that he had close ties with South Africa through his wife and had a farm near Grahamstown where he spent his holidays. Mitchell's contacts, it was thought, among the Cape Town and Durban liberal establishment might be useful if pressure had to be brought discreetly upon Smuts to divert South African ambitions from Kenya.[29]

In 1945 the Colonial Office was determined to recapture some of the ground that had been lost since Sir Joseph Byrne's departure in 1937. Settler power was becoming an embarrassment. Although it had been possible in 1923 to allow the Europeans in Southern Rhodesia to gain control over an overwhelmingly African country, this was impossible in the new international environment. The settlers' demands for self-government were becoming a diplomatic embarrassment. Organisations such as the Fabian Colonial Bureau and the Anti-Slavery Society had been particularly critical of the continued exclusion of Africans from the European enclave of the White Highlands despite the crisis of ovecrowding in the reserves. No-one in Whitehall, except Harold Macmillan, was willing to grasp the thorn. In 1942, after only a few months at the Colonial Office, and unencumbered by any previous knowledge of Africa, he had reached the radical conclusion that the settlers would have to be bought out and the Kikuyu allowed to settle on collective farms in the White Highlands. This went too far for the Whitehall establishment. The cautious Colonial Office chose instead to 'sandbag' the settlers from behind and to sap their strength by using their overweening ambitions to pull them down.[30]

The view from Nairobi

The official mind in Nairobi, however, was little influenced by the global problems which preoccupied the metropolitan mind. American and Russian condemnations cut little ice in 'darkest Africa' and were easily dismissed as meddling interference. Ostensibly the Nairobi Secretariat also wanted to keep things quiet, but while the Colonial Office saw Kenyan settlers as the essential problem, the Secretariat and the field administration were preoccupied by the Kikuyu. These pre-war administrators, conditioned by Kenya, necessarily did not have the global view of Whitehall or possess Andrew Cohen's ability to devise bold strategies, bordering on genius. The only problem with Whitehall's plan was that Mitchell, whom they had selected to become governor because they thought he shared their broad vision, having so sucessfully disarmed American criticism of British rule in the Pacific, proved to have a limited imagination. He was quickly converted to the myopic concerns of his Secretariat and showed little zeal for a confrontation with the settlers. Mitchell abandoned Whitehall's bold innovations and side-stepped the fundamental problem of settler hegemony.

After the war the sheer scale of the colonial presence increased dramatically, particularly in Kikuyuland. Between 1945 and 1957 the number of administrative officers increased from 117 to 213, while another 30 temporary District Officers and 150 district assistants were recruited during the Emergency. The expansion of the technical departments was even more dramatic. The agricultural department increased from 298 in 1945 to 2,519 in 1958 and the veterinary department grew from 291 to 892. The effect of this second colonial occupation upon the African cultivator was profound. Between 1945 and 1952 the total staff employed in the agricultural campaign in Central Province grew more than tenfold and, by the declaration of the Emergency, numbered more than 3,000. By 1952, the colonial state was stronger than ever before and was penetrating to new depths.[31]

The field administration's commitment to the preservation of a mythical, egalitarian, communal Africa, which had been the basis of indirect rule, the official ideology of British Africa during the 1920s and

1930s, had been strengthened by modern anthropological research, emphasising the communal solidarities of pre-colonial Africa. Indirect rule had initially emerged as much from fiscal constraint as administrative design, since neither the Colonial Office nor the territorial governments had the funds to intervene in African life. African progress, therefore, had necessarily had to be 'organic'. Increasingly, however, it appeared as though this administrative expedient was in fact a valuable mechanism of social control. After 1945, many members of the field administration in Kenya were alarmed that the traditional social linkages were being destroyed by the growth of 'irresponsible' individualism as the forces of economic competition undermined the power of the elders and the chiefs and increased pressure on the soil. By 1945, anthropological research had given these prejudices against African entrepreneurs a veneer of scientific respectability, which enabled the administration to justify resistance to Whitehall's plans to incorporate the emerging traders and school teachers, who were in the vanguard of increasing social differentiation. The field administration transformed the second colonial occupation from a social welfare campaign into an outright attack, designed to hinder these proto-capitalists. Social engineering was to be undertaken more blatantly than ever before to bolster the existing rural order and to entrench the authority of the chiefs and 'traditional' elders.[32]

The African proto-capitalists, however, were also stronger than before the war, and the new Kenya African Union provided them with leaders to present their case to the Secretariat and, if necessary, the Colonial Office and the United Nations. During the depression of the 1930s, the government actively encouraged African production to preserve the fiscal base of the colonial state and, during the war, to supply the allied forces in the Middle East, regardless of the long-term consequences on soil fertility or African communalism. Although Spencer has pointed out that Africans received lower prices for their crops than the settlers, and squatters were supposedly forced to sell their produce to their employers who then resold it to the government marketing board at a higher rate, in fact, African cultivators bypassed the official purchasing mechanism and sold their crops on the Black Market. Official returns, the historian should be aware, provide little guide to the quantities of African produce sold. Most lay concealed from view.[33]

The African proto-capitalists after 1945 were clamouring to enjoy the rewards of government patronage. These demands, of course, clashed with the determination of the field administration to obstruct the development of individualism because of the dangers of increasing social differentiation in the reserves. After the war, however, neither side was willing to back down and a clash between the paternalist administration and the emerging African entrepreneurs, especially in Central Province among the Kikuyu where this process was most advanced, was perhaps inevitable, as in the Gold Coast.[34] District Commissioners were determined to support their allies, the government-appointed chiefs, and to bolster their authority whenever it was attacked by the emerging African politicians. The politicians represented the traders and cash-crop cultivators who resented the preferential treatment bestowed upon the chiefs and their supporters when wattle and trading licences were issued. They were simply dismissed as irresponsible 'agitators' by the administration, which refused to recognise that they had widespread support.[35]

With the growth of a ramifying bureaucracy, the field administration had become isolated from African opinion and spent more and more time preparing reports and memoranda. Provincial Commissioners' meetings, which in the 1920s provided the vital link between policy and action, became increasingly anodyne and restricted to approved topics based on prepared memoranda. No longer were they rent by bitter disputes between Provincial Commissioners defending 'their people'. This bureaucratisation of the Colonial Service also isolated the District Commissioners and lowly District Officers.[36] Increasingly the administrative system ruled out direct consideration of what was happening in the reserves in favour of abstract policy, formulated in the Secretariat, despite the warnings of Shirley Victor Cooke and Clarence Buxton that they were becoming dangerously divorced from African reality.[37] During the 1940s, the Secretariat became obsessed with the technical aspects of its job. This retreat into theory was reinforced by Mitchell, who saw himself as a social technician who wanted to interfere in African society to preserve what he believed to be its surviving egalitarianism, and to prevent the emergence of an exploitative clique of capitalist accumulators. Unfortunately, given the administration's limited understanding of pre-colonial Africa, this social engineering was extremely dangerous, especially as the administration had become isolated from ordinary Africans. This bureaucratisation was only reversed after 1952, when manpower was rushed into Kikuyuland to contain Mau Mau and a belated attempt was made to return to the more primitive, but effective, grassroots administration. But by then it was far too late.[38]

Notes

1. R.F. Holland, *European Decolonization, passim*, provides the most useful example of this genre but see also J. Gallagher, *The Decline, Revival and Fall of the British Empire*, pp. 141–3. J.M. Lee and M. Petter, *The Colonial Office, War and Development Policy*, pp. 49–256 and R.D. Pearce, *The Turning Point in Africa*, pp. 132–205 are the most notable examples of this historiographical pre-occupation with the official mind of Whitehall. A more critical view of Cohen can be found in J.W. Cell, 'On the Eve of

Decolonisation', pp. 235-57. The attitude of the field administration has been investigated in B.J. Berman's thesis, 'Administration and Politics in Colonial Kenya,' pp. 57-71, 113-60, 217-404. See also Berman, 'Bureaucracy and Incumbent Violence', pp. 143-75, and his unpublished paper, 'Provincial Administration and the Contradictions of Colonialism'.

2. G. Bennett, 'Settlers and Politics in Kenya'. pp. 256-332, remains a standard account of European settler influence in Kenya. For a more radical critique of settler power see E.A. Brett, *Colonialism and Underdevelopment in East Africa, passim.*

3. W.R. Louis, *Imperialism at Bay*, pp. 512-73; C. Thorne, *Allies of a Kind*, pp. 202-48, 596-604; and J.M. Lee and M. Petter, *The Colonial Office, War and Development Policy*, pp. 101-14, 231-42. See also R. Storry, *Japan and the Decline of the West in Asia*, pp. 1-13; and B.W. and L.Y. Andaya, *A History of Malaysia*, pp. 247-54. Even the Kenyan settlers noted the Colonial Office's loss of morale after the fall of Malaya and Singapore: see the editorial in *East African Standard*, 16 July, 1943. The metropolitan political mind reacted swiftly to the blow and determined to replenish lost supplies from the Far East by developing Africa, while the African Colonies were kept quiet with promises of increased political participation after the war. See especially the following debates: 6 May 1942, *Hansard*, House of Lords, vol 122, cols. 889-940; 24 June 1942, *Hansard*, House of Commons, vol 380, cols. 2004-2119 (this was the first debate in the Commons on colonial affairs since June 1939) and 13 July 1943, *Hansard*, House of Commons, vol 391, cols. 48-151. Copies of these debates were sent to the Kenya Secretariat; see KNA CS2/7/36, 'Colonial Office: Reorganisation of Administration of the Colonial Empire'.

4. First the Morley–Minto constitution of 1909, then the Montagu–Chelmsford proposals of 1918, and finally the 1935 India Act and the 1937 Indian Provincial elections had been designed to incorporate 'moderate' Indian nationalists into the political processes of the colonial state and to transform them into collaborators. In India, at the centre at least, this had failed, and the Congress had remained intact, if not untarnished. A similar strategy had also been attempted in Egypt; J. Darwin, *Britain, Egypt and the Middle East*, pp. 49-137.

5. R.E. Robinson, 'The Moral Disarmament of African Empire', p. 101.

6. J. Berque, *French North Africa*, pp. 232-80; J. Iliffe, *A Modern History of Tanganyika*, pp. 342-80; and J. Forbes Munro, *Africa and the International Economy*, pp 150-74. See also N.J. Westcott's unpublished thesis, 'The Impact of the War on Tanganyika', pp. 107-86, and R. von Albertini, *Decolonization*, pp. 158-75.

7. R.E. Robinson, 'Non-European Foundations of European Imperialism', p. 122. There were a series of suggestions after the war to transform Kenya into a major military base to safeguard British interests in the Middle East, Africa and the Indian Ocean, and to treble the settler population. For the progress of these schemes see CO 537/1233/13012/24 (1945-46), 'Defence East Africa: The Development of Mombasa as a Major Port and Base'; CO 537/1230/13011 (1946) (Part II), 'Bases for British Forces in Kenya: Road Construction in Equatorial Africa'; CO 537/1883/94023/3 (1946), 'Defence of East Africa: Construction of a Base'. The Kenyan government also spent £1.6 million during these years attracting Europeans to settle in Kenya, CO 533/534/38232 (1944) and (1945), 'European Settlement Scheme'.

8. Quoted in J. Gallagher, *The Decline, Revival and Fall of the British Empire*, pp. 142-3.

9. R. Hyam, 'The Colonial Office Mind', p. 31 and R.D. Pearce, *The Turning Point in Africa*, pp. 188-202, outline Cohen's reaction.

10. D. Austin, *Politics in Ghana*, pp. 1-102 for a detailed account. R. Rathbone, 'The Government of the Gold Coast after the Second World War', pp. 209-18; R.E. Robinson, 'The Progress of Provincial Councils in the British African Teritories', pp. 59-62, 63-4. M. Crowder, *West Africa Under Colonial Rule*; and J. Miles, 'Rural Protest in the Gold Coast' provide useful insights into politics in British West Africa during the inter-war years. See also J.B. Bell, *On Revolt*, pp. 72-9, 92-106, which contrasts decolonisation in the Gold Coast and Kenya.

11. Mitchell's views on the Kenya African Union and the Kikuyu Central Association can be found in CO 533/543/38086/5 (1945–57), 'Kikuyu Petitions'; CO 533/540/38032 (1949), 'Legislative Council' and CO 533/543/38086/38 (1948), 'Kikuyu Central Association'. See also CO 967/56 (1942), 'Memorandum and Record of meetings with Sir Henry Moore to discuss the war effort in East Africa and the Political and Economic Situation in Kenya as a Result of the War', Cranborne to Gater, 18 June 1942.

12. H. Thomas, *John Strachey*, pp. 245–6; Scott Newton, 'Britain, the Sterling Area and European Integration', pp. 163–80; and P. S. Gupta, *Imperialism and the British Labour Movement*, pp. 309–25. A most useful overview is to be found in P. Kennedy, *The Realities Behind Diplomacy*, pp. 315–69.

13. D.J. Morgan, *The Official History of Colonial Development: Developing British Colonial Resources*, pp. 177–308. Morgan, however, underestimates Britain's exploitation.

14. KNA Secretariat 1/11/41, 'Balance of Trade with USA, 1947–49', and Secretariat 1/4/3, 'Trade and Commerce: The Colonial Empire and the Economic Crisis, 1948'. The centralisation of the marketing of colonial produce is evident from CO 852/650/19879/65 (1946). 'Marketing of Colonial Produce: British Colonial Exports 1939–45', Memorandum by F.V. Meyer. For Mitchell's opinions see CO 852/650/19879/62 (1944). 'Marketing of Colonial Produce – Primary Produce: Note by Sir P.E. Mitchell' and Caine's memorandum of 4 July 1944, in the same file. See also CO 852/650/19879/64 (1944), 'Marketing of Colonial Produce: Future of Agricultural Prices'; CO 852/650/19879/64 (1945), 'Marketing of Colonial Produce: Future of Agricultural Prices'; and J.M. Lee and M. Petter, *The Colonial Office, War and Development Policy*, pp. 78–84.

15. CO 852/588/19260 (Part 1) (1944). 'Planning of Economic and Social Development'; for Caine's exasperation with Mitchell, see CO 852/608/19643/1 (1944), 'Sisal: East Africa', memorandum from Caine to Clauson, 8 June 1945; and CO 852/650/19879/62 (1944), 'Marketing of Colonial Produce and Primary Produce Markets: Note by Sir P.E. Mitchell', minutes by Caine and Clauson on 4 July 1944. RH Mss. Afr. r. 101 entry for 29 November, 1944, contains Mitchell's account in his diary of his first meeting with Caine.

16. Review article by D. K. Fieldhouse of 'The Official History of Colonial Development' in the *English Historical Review*, vol. 97 (1982), pp. 386–94.

17. CO 533/534/38232 (1945), 'European Settlement Scheme' and RH Mss. Afr. r. 101, 1 November 1944, for Mitchell's advocacy of multiracialism.

18. M.C. Ricklefs, *A History of Modern Indonesia*, pp. 200–21; and R. Jeffrey (ed.) *Asia, The Winning of Independence, passim.*

19. G. Wasserman, *Politics of Decolonization*; and E.A. Brett, *Colonialism and Underdevelopment in East Africa*, for the inter-war years. D.K. Kennedy's unpublished thesis, 'A Tale of Two Colonies' and P. Mosley's thesis, 'The Settler Economies' provide some interesting insights and contrasts. For Mitchell's reactions to settler political demands, see CO 533/558/38688 (1947), 'Local Political Developments', Mitchell to Cohen, 26 February and 8 March 1947; and CO 822/114/46523 (Part 1) (1946), 'Closer Union', Mitchell to Gater, 19 March 1946, when he observed: 'If . . . the Elected Members can get it into their heads once and for all, first, that this (Col 191) is not a wicked plot by the present Government to destroy them, and secondly, that nobody of any party in the United Kingdom will for one moment tolerate a state of affairs in which a handful of European politicians, with an electorate of a few thousand voters, have over-riding political power in this or any other African Colony, then I think they will talk sense. Francis Scott, of course, still goes about talking of self-government for Kenya, or at least for the Highlands, by which he means of course, self-government based on an electorate composed only of those members whose names are in Debrett, if one might put it so. But he is, to be quite frank, a very prejudiced man.' For the reactions of the Tory right-wing in a slightly later period, D. Goldsworthy, *Colonial Issues in British Politics*, pp. 24–35, 169–202, 279–316; D. Horowitz, 'Attitudes of British Conservatives Towards

Decolonization in Africa', pp. 9–26; and his unpublished thesis, 'Attitudes of British Conservatives Towards Decolonization in Africa during the Period of the Macmillan Government'.

20. N.J. Westcotts's unpublished paper, 'The Politics of Planning and the Planning of Politics', pp. 4–9; and his thesis, 'The Impact of the Second World War on Tanganyika', pp. 62–3; and KNA Secretariat 1/1/12, 'Maize Control and Food Shortage, 1942–44'; CO 852/641/19785/1 (1944), 'East African Maize'; CO 533/535/38551/1 (1944–46), 'Food Shortage Appointment of Commission of Enquiry'; and Food Shortage Commission Evidence, p. 84; and Kenya Department of Agriculture Annual Report (1944) p. 11. See also I.R.G. Spencer, 'Settler Dominance, Agricultural Production and the Second World War in Kenya', p. 503, and D.M. Anderson and D.W. Throup, 'Africans and Agricultural Production in Colonial Kenya'; pp. 327–45.

21. A.H.M. Kirk-Greene, 'The Thin White Line', p.27; and B.J. Berman's unpublished thesis, 'Administration and Politics in Colonial Kenya', p. 68. Between 1931 and 1939 the Kenyan administration fell from 140 to 114, and the total European staff of the Kenyan government declined from 1,531 to 1,398, with a low of 1,252 between 1933 and 1935. The largest cutback was in the Public Works' Department where the number of Europeans fell from 207 to 87. See also KNA Defence 9/88, 'Analysis of Man Power, 1940–45', Sir H. Moore to Legislative Council, 13 November, 1940.

22. The notion of 'incorporation' is taken from K. Middlemas, *Politics in Industrial Society*, pp. 18–23. For its application to Kenya see J.M. Lonsdale's unpublished paper, 'The Growth and Transformation of the Colonial State in Kenya', p. 8, where he observes: 'The problem of competition between private interests could be solved only by extending the principle of delegated authority from production and marketing to supply as well, so that farmers and businessmen rationed themselves. The new functions of government passed, if for no other reason than that the apparatus of control was too large for the colony's slender Secretariat, into the hands of those who lived by making commercial assumptions about the future. By the end of the war, and in imitation of the British organisation of the war economy, settler farmers had captured the whole apparatus of production quotas and credit on the Highlands.' For acknowledgements of the administration's loss of control see CO 967/56 (1942), 'Memorandum and Record of Meeting with Sir Henry Moore to Discuss the War Effort in East Africa and the Political and Economic Situation in Kenya as a Result of the War', and CO 533/536/38598 (1945–46), 'Kenya: Staff Position', Mitchell to Creasy, 30 December 1944.

23. CO 967/56 (1942), 'Memorandum and Record of Meeting with Sir Henry Moore to discuss the War Effort in East Africa and the Political and Economic Situation in Kenya as a Result of the War', especially Cranborne to Gater, 18 June 1942.

24. CO 967/57/46709 (1942), 'Sir Arthur Dawe's Memorandum on a Federal Solution for East Africa and Mr Harold Macmillan's Counter-Proposals'.

25. *ibid.* Dawe, however, also observed that 'the main point to be kept in mind by the British Government is the difficulty that they would be in if matters were carried to the ultima ratio of physical force. The lesson of 1923 is always there and the settlers would be a much sterner proposition now than they were at that time. It is possible now that many of the British officials would come out on their side, which would not have happened in 1923.'

26. A.H.M. Kirk-Greene, 'The Progress of Pro-Consuls'; pp. 190–1; and his *A Biographical Dictionary of the British Colonial Governor*, p. 51. For details of a governor's duties and selection, see A.H.M. Kirk-Greene, 'On Governorship and Governors in British Africa', pp. 210–57. A brief assessment of Kenya's inter-war governors can be found in the Biographical Appendix *infra*. See also CO 967/56 (1942), 'Memorandum and Record of Meeting with Sir Henry Moore to Discuss the War Effort in East Africa and the Political and Economic Situation in Kenya as a Result of the War' and RH Mss. Afr. r. 101, Mitchell's diary entry 24 November 1944, for his view of Moore's relations with Oliver Stanley.

27. CO 967/57/46709 (1942), 'Sir Arthur Dawe's Memorandum on a Federal Solution for East Africa and Mr Harold Macmillan's Counter-Proposals', Sir Arthur Dawe to Sir George Gater, 27 July 1942.

28. *ibid.*

29. CO 537/5922 (1950), 'Liaison with the South African Government by Kenya Unofficials'. See also Legislative Council Debates, 2nd Series, vol. xx (1944–45), third Session, 4 January 1945, cols. 472–500 and *East African Standard*, 5 January 1945.

30. CO 822/114/46523 Part 1 (1946), 'Closer Union', Mitchell to Gater, 19 March 1946. R.E. Robinson, 'The Moral Disarmament of African Empire', pp. 86–102 analyses this transition. CO 533/537/38608 (1944–46), 'Land Policy': Memorandum by the Anti-Slavery Society'; and CO 533/558/38690 (1947), 'Fabian Society.'. For Macmillan's proposal see CO 967/57/46709 (1942), 'Sir Arthur Dawe's Memorandum on a Federal Solution for East Africa and Mr Harold Macmillan's Counter-Proposals'.

31. A.H.M. Kirk-Greene, 'The Thin White Line', p. 32. and B.J. Berman's unpublished thesis, 'Administration and Politics in Colonial Kenya', pp. 415–52.

32. C. Cagnolo, *The Akikuyu*; A.C. Hollis, *The Nandi*; J.G. Peristiany, *The Social Organization of the Kipsigis*; and W.S. and K. Routledge, *With a Prehistoric People*, to mention only the most well known. For a critique of western anthropology see T. Asad (ed.), *Anthropology and the Colonial Encounter*; J. Tosh, *Clan Leaders and the Colonial Chiefs in Lango*, pp. 1–6. L.S.B. Leakey's most recently published three-volume work, *The Southern Kikuyu before 1903*, (London, 1977), suffers from the same weaknesses. For an anthropologist's view see L. Mair, 'Anthropology and Colonial Policy', pp. 191–5.
     The concept of 'indirect rule', which was introduced from its Lugardian fastness in Nigeria during the 1920s and 1930s into Tanganyika, Sierra Leone, Nyasaland and Northern Rhodesia should perhaps be seen as the ex-centric counterpart to Gallagher's metropolitan retreat to informal empire; see J. Gallagher, *The Decline, Revival and Fall of the British Empire*, pp. 99–129; and R.D. Pearce, *The Turning Point in Africa*, pp. 7–11 and 154–9.
     The District Administration's attitude towards social engineering in Kikuyuland can be discerned from KNA DC/FH 1/24, 'Fort Hall Annual Report, 1945', pp. 13–16; DC/FH 1/25, 'Fort Hall Annual Report, 1946', pp. 7–9, 19–24; and DC/FH 1/26, 'Fort Hall Annual Report, 1947', pp. 5–6, for a few examples from one district out of many. See also B.J. Berman, 'Bureaucracy and Incumbent Violence' pp. 143–77.

33. Although the term 'proto-capitalist' may be inelegant, it captures the contest between the settlers and the Kikuyu élites to become Kenya's first local capitalists. See J.M. Lonsdale's unpublished paper, 'The Growth and Transformation of the Colonial State in Kenya' and E.A. Brett, *Colonialism and Underdevelopment in East Africa*, pp. 165–212. G. Kitching, *Class and Economic Change in Kenya*, pp. 297–311 provides 14 brief biographical case studies.
     G. Kitching, *Class and Economic Change in Kenya*, pp. 70–3, has some sensible observations on the difficulty of using district agricultural production figures. These crude totals mislead perhaps more than they reveal. For one example see KNA DC/FH 1/23, 'Fort Hall Annual Report, 1944', pp. 6–7. Only 1,400 bags out of an estimated surplus of 30,000 were sold to the Maize Control.

34. J.M. Lonsdale's unpublished paper, 'The Growth and Transformation of the Colonial State in Kenya' pp. 13–14. For the Gold Coast see R. Rathbone, 'Businessmen in Politics', pp. 391–401.

35. CO 533/54 38086/5, 'Kikuyu Memorials and Petitions' (1945–47). For the reaction of the field administration see KNA DC/FH 1/26, 'Fort Hall Annual Report, 1947' pp. 1–5.

36. KNA Secretariat 1/2/2, 'Nyanza Province, 1949–50', Memorandum by P. Wyn Harris, 13 July 1949, about arson in Trans Nzoia. This report by the Chief Native Commissioner followed complaints by two Legislative Councillors, Major Keyser and S.V. Cooke that the North Nyanza administration had lost control in Kitosh and had

allowed the *Dini ya Msambwa* to mount an anti-European campaign. Wyn Harris pointed out that North Nyanza with a population of over 600,000 was twenty times the size of the Seychelles, and twice that of Zanzibar, or of Mitchell's former governorship in Fiji. Every day the District Commissioner received fifty letters, and twenty more as chairman of the Local Native Council. The district's European staff consisted of one District Commissioner, three District Officers, one district welfare officer and one district revenue officer. There were three African assistant administrative officers, eight Asian and forty African clerks. Each month the cashiers' office made over 500 payments, amounting to 150,000 shillings, and received 420 payments quite apart from the Local Native Council, which had an annual revenue of £107,000 and an expenditure of £104,000. The District Commissioner was burdened by the following administrative tasks: policy; secret correspondence; government circulars and publications; political records; agriculture; public health; veterinary affairs; education; buildings and roads; control of revenue; African local government; chiefs and headmen; mines; monthly and annual reports; staff discipline and establishment. He acted as the chairman of the district team and the local legislation committee, prepared the estimates; supervised postings; forests; and the registration of births, deaths and marriages.

The District Officers were equally busy. One of them had the following duties: secretary of the district team; liquor licences; furniture; transport licences; plots in townships and trading centres; supervising the African location; applications for motor vehicles; arms and ammunition; the issuing of *kipande*; meteorological records; trading licences; control of commodities; food rationing; sugar distribution; wildlife; and also acted as the secretary of the township committee and supervised the local cooperative societies. By the late 1940s, life as an administrator in Africa was almost as desk bound as in Britain.

37. *ibid* and RH Mss. Brit.Emp. s. 390, Box 3, File 4, Item 3, ff.1–4, C.E.V. Buxton to Mitchell, 15 August 1948; and KNA MAA 8/102, 'Intelligence and Security: Miscellaneous Press Cuttings, 1948–50'. *East Africa News Review*, 22 January 1948.

38. B.J. Berman's unpublished thesis, 'Administration and Politics in Colonial Kenya', pp. 415–52.

Three

The Character and Policies
of Sir Philip Mitchell

The Colonial Office and Sir Philip Mitchell

Mitchell was chosen to become governor because of his vast experience of East Africa. He seemed to be the ideal choice to reassert metropolitan authority. A blunt, unattractive, fat, little man, without any social graces, Mitchell was on paper the best man for the job and had a wide knowledge of the problems he would find in Kenya. He had served as Chief Native Commissioner and Chief Secretary in Tanganyika, as governor of Uganda and, for the first two years of the war, was based in Nairobi as deputy chairman of the East African Governors' Conference, where he co-ordinated the war effort against the Italians in Ethiopia and Somalia. His brief tour of duty as governor of Fiji and High Commissioner in the Western Pacific from 1942 to 1944 confirmed his high reputation in Whitehall. He had been appointed at a difficult moment when Anglo–American relations had been strained. Many Americans had wanted to establish international or regional trustees to administer the recaptured territories rather than return them to their former colonial rulers. Mitchell had quickly resolved these problems and had demonstrated such a zeal to promote economic development in Fiji that the Americans had become reconciled to British imperialism in the area.[1] The Colonial Office hoped that he would reproduce these successes in Kenya and heal the bitter racial divisions. Ever since the visit of the young Margery Perham to Tanganyika in 1929, Mitchell's reputation as the able administrator who had implemented Sir Donald Cameron's plans for 'native authorities' in the most successful implanting of the ideology of 'indirect rule', had been high. As Miss Perham's influence in the Colonial Office grew, Mitchell's career flourished. In 1944, her authority was at its zenith, overriding the muted opposition of Sir Arthur Dawe and of the discredited Colonial Office establishment of the 1930s to his appointment.[2]

Whitehall wanted a forceful personality not only to reassert metropolitan authority, but also to implement new development policies to promote African production. Throughout the empire, since the West Indian disturbances of the late 1930s, there had been a new emphasis on development as the essential prerequisite for political advance. Under the influence of Malcolm MacDonald and Lord Moyne, the old trusteeship tradition had been transformed into a positive programme to ensure economic diversification, which would enable 'the agricultural slums of the colonial empire' to finance improved social services from a sound economic base. Whereas the inter-war ideology of indirect rule, or in Kenya the more direct supervision of the prefectoral field administration, had emphasised the need for organic, evolutionary development in the reserves, the new philosophy required a shift towards positive administration and a more interventionist role for both the technical departments and the District Officers.[3]

In Kenya, the Colonial Office's strategy to reassert metropolitan authority and to encourage African economic and political advance, failed and ended in the debacle of Mau Mau for three reasons. First, the settlers were more securely entrenched than the Colonial Office had considered possible. Secondly, African problems, both in the reserves and in the towns, were much more serious than had been anticipated and, thirdly, Mitchell failed because he was not up to his job. He was an indirect ruler of the inter-war years, ill-equipped to cope with the complex rivalries between settler, Asian and Kikuyu accumulators. The Colonial Office was trying to fight post-war problems with pre-war weapons. Mitchell's panicky despatches from the field simply played into the hands of the settlers and the Nairobi Secretariat, whose aims were different from those of Whitehall.

Mitchell's governorship can be divided into three distinct periods. This periodisation, however, is more a reflection of how Mitchell wanted to be perceived by the Colonial Office and of his changing relationship with metropolitan policy makers, than of the situation in Kenya. From his first year in office until his breakdown in December 1945 Mitchell was a clever alarmist, constantly bombarding the Colonial Office with lengthy despatches about the dreadful conditions he had discovered and the appalling disorganisation of the Kenyan administration. His spate of proposals was, of course, designed to convince Whitehall that he was fulfilling their instructions and thoroughly shaking up the moribund Secretariat and field administration.[4]

The second period overlaps slightly with the first, beginning in mid-1945 with Mitchell's proposals for the reorganisation of the Secretariat and of the agricultural department and continuing until the end of 1947. These were the years of 'Mitchell the doer'. Preparatory planning had been completed, the Secretariat had been mobilised for action and extension services had been expanded. The government's deck had been cleared for action. Resistance, he warned Whitehall, was inevitable. Until ordinary cultivators had perceived that terracing and the agricultural betterment campaign were for their benefit, the local agitators would gain considerable support for a brief period. The depth of opposition to compulsory cattle dipping in South Nyeri in 1946 and to terracing in Murang'a and Kiambu during 1947, clearly suprised Mitchell, but his confidence did not wane. After 1948, he was confident that the measures were beginning to be accepted and that peasant agriculture would soon be transformed. During his last four years as governor, Mitchell became a 'passive optimist'. Tenacity would see the government through. Eventually the militants would be discredited and ordinary Africans would be convinced that the administration, not the rabble-rousers of the Kenya African Union, had their best interests at heart.[5]

Mitchell was an intensely ambitious man. He knew that he was at the peak of his career and desperately wanted to perpetuate his reputation as a distinguished colonial ruler. His speedy diagnosis, which events later proved to be seriously flawed, was carefully designed to make the maximum impression in Whitehall. While Sir John Hathorn Hall quietly got on with a similar task in Uganda, Mitchell was acutely conscious of his political image and won all the plaudits. By 1948, he had successfully convinced himself, as well as the Colonial Office, that his strategy was working. He therefore agreed, in 1949, to accept another term as governor and turned down the opportunity of a retirement festooned with honours. This passive optimism, however, was itself a reflection of Mitchell's declining powers. Mentally, physically and spiritually he was exhausted throughout his last term, from which he emerged as an administrative dinosaur, a remnant from the era of indirect rule, increasingly out of touch with the Colonial Office's plans for local government reform and controlled African political advance.[6]

After 1947, isolated in Government House, Mitchell lost touch with reality. As peasant discontent and urban unrest were politicised, he refused to acknowledge that the administration was losing control, obstinately insisting that a few alarmist reports were untypical and unduly exaggerated. Meanwhile, the government lost its sense of direction and ultimate purpose and increasingly came to react simply on a day-to-day basis without any overall strategy. As the district administration's fire brigade rushed from crisis to crisis, Mitchell and the Secretariat failed to realise that the conflagration was getting out of control and that their attempted social engineering was fanning the flames.

Mitchell's policies for Kenya

When Mitchell arrived in Nairobi on 12 December 1944, the problems seemed rather different than when assessed in Whitehall. The field

administration and the Secretariat insisted that unrestrained individualism in the reserves was producing serious erosion, undermining the
authority of the chiefs and destroying the traditional moral economy.[7]

The settlers were also demanding that the squatters in the White Highlands be converted into a passive agricultural labour force, tied to the
European farms and deprived of their cattle and smallholdings. Only then
would the squatter threat to the safety of the White Highlands disappear.
Meanwhile, in Nairobi and Mombasa, urban Africans were becoming
increasingly restless and were showing alarming signs of resorting to
crime and politics. The official mind in Nairobi was preoccupied with
these issues rather than with reducing the influences of the settlers.[8]

The new governor found an exhausted, understaffed administration
both in the provinces and the Secretariat. Within three weeks of his
arrival, as the Colonial Office had hoped, he had embarked upon a fundamental reorganisation of the government machine. Before the end of 1944
he had decided that the financial secretary, the conservator of forests, the
director of public works, the commissioner for lands and settlement, three
of the four Provincial Commissioners and the directors of agriculture and
veterinary services would all have to retire. At the same time, many men
lower down the bureaucracy were told that they could not expect to rise
any higher under Mitchell. The governor informed Whitehall that men
over 45 were exhausted in the tropics and needed replacing if Kenya was
to embark upon the drastic development needed to solve its problems.[9]

These draconian measures created much resentment inside the government. In the short term they confirmed Mitchell's reputation in the
Colonial Office; but in the longer term they were to have disastrous consequences on his understanding of the deteriorating situation in the
Kikuyu areas. No-one in the Secretariat or field administration had
the courage to oppose Mitchell's social engineering or to warn about the
dangers of growing administrative isolation. In fact, no Kenyan governor
since Girouard (1909–1912) had had such an easy time with the Secretariat.[10] In the 1930s, the anti-settler Joseph Byrne had faced considerable
opposition, but throughout Mitchell's governorship neither Rennie nor
Rankine, his two Chief Secretaries, had the guts or the ability to stand up
to him. Whereas Rennie, who had already spent six years in office under
the 'settlers' nominee' Brooke-Popham and the cautious Moore, simply
wanted to escape to a governorship of his own,[11] Rankine was a Mitchell
protégé and his rise in Uganda occurred under Mitchell's patronage as
governor. He had accompanied him in 1939 to Nairobi as assistant secretary to the Governors' Conference and followed him to Fiji as assistant
Colonial Secretary. Apart from a two-year term as Colonial Secretary in
Barbados, from 1945 to 1947, Rankine's career from cadet in Uganda to
Resident in Zanzibar progressed under the watchful eye of his benign
patron, Philip Mitchell. From 1947 to 1952, therefore, as the situation in

Kikuyuland and Nairobi deteriorated, the crucial position of Chief Secretary, which involved vetting all information that reached the governor and serving as head of the Development and Reconstruction Authority, was occupied by a Mitchell acolyte who was completely overawed by his chief.

The settlers capture Mitchell

When he had been in the colony for only 18 days, Mitchell reported to Oliver Stanley that the war-time advances in settler power would have to be acknowleged and proposed that the most prominent of the settler politicians, Ferdinand Cavendish-Bentinck, become an official member of the Legislative and Executive Councils. Mitchell explained that the 'processes which have brought about the present state of affairs in respect of Cavendish-Bentinck are of a kind which I do not think it would be either wise or practicable to put into reverse'.[12] He was already functioning virtually as Minister of Agriculture. During the war he had come to dominate the agricultural sector of the economy and had served as a member of the East African Supply Council, as well as on its executive board and production executive committee. He had also been chairman of the Kenya Agricultural Production and Settlement Board, Controller of Stock Feed and Fertilisers, a member of the Highlands and the Land Advisory Boards, Timber Controller, and chairman of the Kenya and East African Publicity Associations. He was also a member of both the Kenya Legislative and Executive Councils and was leader of the European Elected Members. To oust Cavendish-Bentinck from his war-time positions, Mitchell warned, would provoke vociferous settler opposition and seriously damage Whitehall's multiracial strategy. The governor argued that there was no alternative but to institutionalise Cavendish-Bentinck and to temper his anti-African sentiments with government responsibility, although he had to confess to Whitehall that 'I would have been happier if he had emerged straw in hair and dung on boots from a farm and had no political past'. Cavendish-Bentinck's appointment as member for Agriculture and Natural Resources, Mitchell realised, was bound to provoke African and Asian criticism.[13]

Cavendish-Bentinck's appointment was part of a major reorganisation of the Secretariat to prepare it for the demands of the post-war development campaign. Mitchell proposed reducing the excessive burden on the Chief Secretary by introducing a member system into the Executive Council, whereby members would be responsible for specific departments in an embryonic ministerial structure. The volume of work and its increasingly technical nature, he informed the Colonial Office, made it impossible for even the most industrious Chief Secretary to control the expanding government machine. The present arrangement, whereby all problems in the Secretariat had to go through the Chief Secretary before they reached the governor or the Executive Council, was creating a serious bottleneck in the government not only of Kenya but of many other large colonies. Mitchell's appointment of Cavendish-Bentinck as Member for Agriculture and Charles Mortimer, the former Commissioner for Local Government, as Member for Health and Local Government, was hailed by Andrew Cohen in the Colonial Office as the first attempt to restructure colonial governments. It confirmed Whitehall's belief that Mitchell was a dynamic reformer, especially as he suggested that Rennie, the Chief Secretary, should be appointed director of the Development and Reconstruction Authority and should oversee the second colonial occupation in Kenya. Whitehall's fascination with government efficiency, however, obscured the crucial fact that Mitchell had effectively conceded the settlers' war-time gains and had abandoned the Colonial Office's plans for a metropolitan invasion, which would reduce the settlers to a subordinate position, and allow greater African participation in political affairs.[14]

In reality, Mitchell had quickly been captured by the local administration and the settlers. This meant that African advance would be conditional upon settler agreement. Although Mitchell still hoped to create a multiracial society, he had nothing to offer Africans except increased government interference in the reserves and modest social reforms in the cities, and they were soon alienated from colonial rule. His policies were merely palliatives, since his early concession to the settlers precluded any root and branch reforms.

Mitchell's agricultural policies in Kikuyuland and the White Highlands

Humanitarian and mission organisations in Britain had for many years been critical of the exclusion of Africans from the White Highlands. The Aborigines Protection Society, for example, protested to Oliver Stanley in 1944 that the Africans in Kenya were crowded into 30 million acres, while a mere 1,890 Europeans occupied nearly 11 million acres, of which they actually cultivated only half a million. The Colonial Office, however, rejected these estimates of land distribution. Three years later the Communist Party's colonial expert, Sam Aaronovitch, alleged that during the 1930s, on settler farms of over 2,000 acres, on average only 269 acres were actually cultivated. In support of his statement he quoted the Kenya Land Commission's report which noted that, in 1934, only 11.8 per cent of the alienated White Highlands, which had an area of 10,345 square miles, was under cultivation, while 40.7 per cent was grazing land for stock, 20 per cent occupied by African squatters, and 27.5 per cent was completely unused. Similar criticisms were often made by left-wing opinion in Britain, which condemned the fact that the settlers, who formed less than

0.25 per cent of the population, should control nearly one third of the best agricultural land, while Africans were crowded into the exhausted reserves, which were suffering from continuous cultivation and overstocking.[15]

These problems had been exacerbated by the war-time drive to maximise production, regardless of the effects on the reserves. Many agriculturalists and members of the field administration feared that the damage to the soil structure and the organic harmonies of 'tribal' life had been irreparable. Sir Harold Tempany, the Colonial Office's chief agricultural adviser, shared these fears and recommended a drastic remedy. He reported in July 1946, after a brief visit to Kenya, that 'to put the matter quite plainly, from what I saw of the position, Kenya will never be able to solve its land problems satisfactorily until the findings of the Carter Commission have once more been thrown into the melting pot'.[16]

After protracted deliberations, the Kenya Land Commission had decided, in 1934, that the area of the Kikuyu reserves should be increased by a mere 21,000 acres. The Commission also recommended that the restored land should not be distributed among the *mbari*, which had been dispossessed at the beginning of the century, but handed over to the British-created Local Native Councils, which were controlled by the District Commissioner and used to benefit the whole district.[17] This, of course, had meant that the only people who had really benefited had been the collaborators of the local élite – the chiefs, Local Native Councillors and their supporters. The dispossessed *mbari* had remained uncompensated. As a final insult, the Commission also confirmed the sanctity of the European enclave in the White Highlands and excluded Africans from ever owning land in this vast area of eleven million acres. Two million Africans in overcrowded Central Province, therefore, looked with mounting anger upon the 2,000 settlers who occupied so large a proportion of the best farming land in the colony.[18]

Mitchell, the social engineer, felt confident that he could solve these problems, especially as the new Colonial Development and Welfare Act seemed to have removed the financial limitations which had hindered previous governments. The war, however, had exacerbated rather than healed Kenya's divisions and the new confidence and prosperity of both settlers and African cultivators had increased political expectations and rivalry. Social engineering alone could do little to diminish the frustration of many Africans. The agricultural crisis in the reserves and the squatter problem in the White Highlands were symptoms, not causes, of Kenya's divisions.

The Colonial Office's plan to reassert metropolitan authority and to create a tolerant multiracial society satisfied no one. The divisions were already too great; settlers and Africans could not be reconciled. The settlers, for example, demanded immediate self-government and insisted

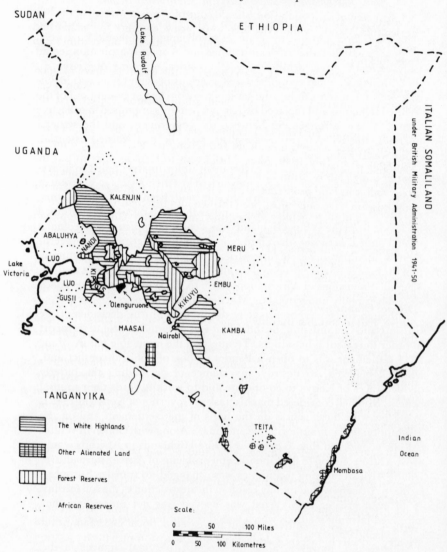

Map 3.1: *Kenyan Tribes and Alienated Areas*

on the White Highlands remaining a European enclave, while Africans demanded land and greater political involvement. It should have been evident to Mitchell that African political and economic aspirations could only be met by overturning the whole political economy of Kenya. In 1942, Macmillan had recognised that a serious peasant revolt was inevitable within ten years unless the settlers were ditched or bought out of the White Highlands and replaced by Kikuyu peasants organised in collective farms. A new arrangement between the government and the settlers' enemies, the Kikuyu proto-capitalists, was, he had warned essential. Time was running out.[19]

Whitehall and the Nairobi government unfortunately failed to appreciate that, for the landless Africans who had lost their *githaka* in Kiambu or Nyeri at the beginning of British rule and been forced to become squatters, sometimes on the same land as they had occupied, continued exclusion from the White Highlands was a constant indictment of colonial rule. Political activists, therefore, were able to undermine the government's attempts to restructure African agriculture simply by claiming that the land was being prepared for alienation to another wave of settlers. The full dimensions of African opposition to the White Highlands policy were never really understood by Mitchell and his advisers.[20]

Although the governor privately disagreed with the decisions of the Carter Land Commission, he thought it was essential to defend its report in order to reassure the settlers. To question the inviolable nature of the 1934 settlement was to open a Pandora's box of political conflict and, Mitchell believed, to destroy any chance of persuading the bitterly divided races of Kenya to co-operate and to work towards their mutual benefit. Mitchell considered that his 'task as Governor of Kenya in 1945 is to get on with the business on the basis of that settlement and on the assumption that it is authoritative and final'. Along with Cohen in Whitehall, he considered that to open the White Highlands to Africans would prove a false solution to the fundamental problems of African agriculture. Unless African farming techniques were changed, to transfer European farms to Africans would merely result in the destruction of the soil fertility of an even greater area. What was needed was not more land, but improved farming methods which would restore nutrients to the soil and land consolidation, particularly in Central Province.[21]

Mitchell did, however, hope that certain marginal changes in the delineation of the White Highlands might be negotiated without antagonising the settlers or undermining their faith in the integrity of the government. Creech Jones, who became the Secretary of State in October 1946, invariably adopted a more critical view of the settlers than either his advisers in the Colonial Officer or the governor. When he first heard of Mitchell's decision to defend the Carter Land Commission settlement he had insisted that:

I think . . . that while it may be expedient to build the case on the Carter Commission it would be unfortunate from my point of view if the impression were conveyed that this was a final and inflexible allocation of lands which could not permit of any adjustment either as a result of population needs or subsequent political development. I want to avoid any suggestion that the European Highlands are absolutely reserved when later it may be necessary to make room for some forms of African settlement.[22]

Yet this was exactly the suggestion Mitchell wished to give the settlers. Slowly, the governor and his ally in the Colonial Office, Cohen, persuaded Creech Jones to accept their view. It took them less than a year. When the Secretary of State's former colleagues in the Fabian Colonial Bureau complained, in 1947, that they 'were unaware that the present British Government stood by the findings of this Commission . . .', he replied that the continued presence of a large settler community was essential if African development was rapidly to progress. Creech Jones informed them that:

The African land problem is less one of the distribution of existing land . . . than of the use to which the lands are being put . . . It is hardly a case that a solution to the Africans' large and complex problems can be found in the Highlands marked for European settlement . . . The African land problem needs primarily to be attacked by the great campaign of resettlement, improved agriculture and water supplies.[23]

Cohen and Mitchell had won; Creech Jones, completely captured by the official mind, abandoned his opposition to the Kenya Land Commission's settlement. Kenyan Africans, however, did not.

Despite his reputation in Tanganyika and Uganda as an advocate of peasant production and a critic of the settlers, in Kenya it had required little persuading by the settler politicians and the Secretariat to convince Mitchell that European farming offered the most effective means to develop the colony and to increase production to meet the world's commodity shortages. He was soon convinced that the threat of erosion was so serious that any attempt to increase peasant production would irreparably destroy the fertility of the soil with disastrous consequences for rural Africans. In fact the reverse happened. By foreclosing the peasant option and by evicting the squatters from the settler farms in the Rift Valley, Mitchell destroyed any chance of creating a multiracial society in Kenya.

The continued dominance of the settlers, however crucial they were for financing African development and enticing foreign investment to Kenya, effectively hamstrung the government's agricultural campaign in the Kikuyu reserves. The colonial authorities were entrapped in an impossible situation. To open up the White Highlands would destroy political stability (the essential prerequisite for economic development in both the settler and the African sectors of the economy) by provoking settler opposition; whereas failure to abandon the Kenya Land Commission would merely provoke peasant protest and destroy, by another means, the political equilibrium needed if Kenya was to attract new investment.[24]

With the exception of Macmillan, no-one in the Colonial Office or Kenyan government realised that, in the long run, the seemingly more dangerous option of ditching the settlers and accommodating moderate African leaders afforded the greater assurance of Kenya's future stability. Instead, post-war policies for Kenya were based on the fatal premise that it was politically impossible to ditch the settlers. Apart from Macmillan's flight of fancy, the alternative was never seriously considered. The settlers remained stronger than before the war. The government never seriously attempted to solve the problem of how it should reconcile the small, but politically powerful, European community's interests with the demands of the increasingly confident and articulate African élite.

Mitchell's paternalism

The governor misguidedly reassured the Colonial Office that settler and African interests were compatible. The harmonious mixing of Polynesians, Indians and Europeans in Fiji had made a profound impression on him and his diaries show that Mitchell had been inspired to attempt to recreate this tolerant atmosphere in Kenya.[25] This multiracial strategy in which the settlers were to provide the 'steel-frame' for African progress, lulled Whitehall into a false optimism and convinced them that a confrontation could be avoided. This was completely incorrect. Mitchell and the Secretariat, however, were convinced that their development plans were dependent upon British settlement. The settlers' presence would attract investment and demonstrate Britain's long-term commitment to the region. Moreover the settlers and local Asians would provide the stable internal demand for the new processing and import substitution industries the government hoped to encourage. These, in turn, would generate the economic expansion necessary to provide the revenue for the post-war social engineering projects in the reserves.[26]

Mitchell proved to be far less radical than many settlers had feared and shared the field administration's prejudices against African politicians and traders. He believed in the myth of the organic nature of African society. The governor, like his senior colleagues, was a second not third generation colonial ruler; a man of the indirect rule era. Mitchell had entered the Colonial Service in Nyasaland in 1913 and had served in the area disrupted by the Chilembwe rising; Rennie, the Chief Secretary, had entered the Ceylon service in 1920; Thornley had gone to Tanganyika in 1930; while Wyn Harris and Troughton had spent the whole of their careers in Kenya. Such men found it impossible to adjust, as Whitehall could, to the emergence of African nationalism and failed to respond to the growing demands for African paramountcy and the clamour for the abrogation of the Carter Land Commission and the opening up of the White Highlands.[27]

Mitchell was personally hostile to African politicians. Even a comparatively moderate figure like Kenyatta, he considered, was a dangerous demagogue, merely out to further his own career at the expense of the African masses, who needed the protection of many years of British rule before they could be safely entrusted with greater political power.[28] To paraphrase Churchill, he had not become a governor to preside over the dissolution of the British empire. Mitchell firmly believed that 'ignorant agitators' had to be kept in their place. Centuries would be required before the ordinary African could be entrusted to their unscrupulous mercy. Africa was only beginning the journey to civilization, which had taken 2,000 years in Europe. With British aid and direction, he considered, Africa could advance quickly along the path of civilization:

> I am not one of those who say because it has taken Europe two thousand years it must necessarily take that time for Africans; but it is barely two thousand weeks since Africans had not even an alphabet, let alone any means of writing, no transport except their wives' backs or heads; no plant except arrows, spears, hoes and digging sticks; no common language (they have not yet); no government other than small tribal authorities, and no industries – in fact, since they were in a condition of which, as far as I know, there is no record in England – for when Caesar landed 'The English' were centuries ahead of Africans in 1880 or '90. I have no doubt that it will be possible in much less than two thousand years to bring Africa to the condition of . . . Europe; but *some* sense of historical time values is surely not an unreasonable postulate.[29]

If Britain withdrew too soon, he prophesied that Africa would degenerate to the level of independent Liberia or Ethiopia. Mitchell had first-hand knowledge of conditions in Ethiopia, having served briefly as chief political adviser to the Middle East Command under Field Marshall Wavell, with responsibility for the administration of the areas recently captured from the Italians. Haile Selassie's régime had confirmed his opinion that Africa was not yet ready for independence and that to withdraw would be to betray Britain's duty and to leave the ordinary African to the exploitation of a corrupt élite. The 'white man's burden' still had its advocates in the late 1940s.

In consequence, the governor failed to satisfy rising African expectations and few concessions were made to their new economic importance. Although Eliud Mathu was appointed to the Legislative Council in October 1944 to represent African interests, this was a small advance.

Usually African opinion was not consulted or was provided by the chiefs. The administration knew little about the realities of rural African life and even less about the plight of the urban residents of Pumwani or the *majengo* of Mombasa.[30] The African traders and commercial farmers who wanted to share in government patronage were dismissed as middlemen, prospering on the backs of the peasantry, and were never acknowledged as legitimate representatives of indigenous capitalism.[31] The field administration and the Secretariat remained convinced that only the chiefs represented ordinary Africans. Their authority was, therefore, strengthened. A new generation of chiefs, more sympathetic to Mitchell's interventionist policies, was appointed to explain and enforce the agricultural campaign. Thus, while the settler-controlled district councils and farmers' associations were securing new powers and were being incorporated into the state's decision making to an extent they had never achieved before the war, the new African organisations, the Kenya African Union, the Central Province Wattle Growers' and Producers' Association and their political leaders, Eliud Mathu, and later Jomo Kenyatta, remained excluded from participation in the formulation of new policies because of the paternalist assumptions of the official mind about the structure and future coherence of African society.[32]

The continued neglect of the African politicians while popular political consciousness was growing transformed Mathu's client relationship with the government. From his nomination to the Legislative Council until Kenyatta's return from exile in Britain in September 1946, Mathu had been the leading African politician. To the government and chiefs he seemed a reliable representative of the new generation of constitutionalist politicians, who, it was hoped, would replace the discredited Kikuyu Central Association. Kenyatta's return, however, forced Mathu to become increasingly critical of the government and its allies, the chiefs, otherwise he would have lost his popular following and credibility as an independent political force. He had to move closer to Kenyatta and attempt to improve relations with the Kikuyu Central Association in order to ensure his political survival.[33] This move to the left, of course, discredited him in the eyes of Mitchell. Mathu had always had his critics. Carey Francis, the influential headmaster of the Alliance High School, for example, had earlier attempted to convince the Secretariat that Mathu was unreliable. During 1947, his critics became increasingly numerous; a host of police and field administration reports about Mathu's subversive contacts eventually persuaded Mitchell that he could not be trusted.[34] No African, therefore, was appointed to the Executive Council, which continued to be dominated by the settlers and their supporters inside the Secretariat. Counting Cavendish-Bentinck and Sir Charles Mortimer as settlers disguised as officials, five of the eleven members on the central body of the Kenyan state were settlers during the post-war years. Such a body could hardly be expected to challenge the settlers' privileged status in the political economy of Kenya.[35]

The Kenyan government saw the settlers, not as an obstacle to African advance but as the agents of further progress. Mitchell, for example, believed that:

> It is of the greatest importance . . . for the future well being and prosperity of the native people that there should be a vigorous and well established British settlement in these Highlands, for without it there is no hope of successfully overcoming the immense problems which confront us . . . The British people in East Africa are the key-stone of the arch.[36]

The governor reported that, 'so far from this state of agricultural slum existence being due to white settlement . . . the only known palliative is White Settlement, industry or mining', since 'an ignorant man and his wife with a hoe are a totally inadequate foundation for an enlightened state of society'.[37] Cohen in the Colonial Office concurred. He and Mitchell agreed that the proposed £1.6 million European settlement scheme was essential for Kenya's future and they reassured Creech Jones, persuading him that: 'Increased white settlement must be looked at not as a thing in itself, but as an integral part of the Kenya development programme and is necessary in order to provide the increased financial and economic resources without which African social development cannot proceed.'[38] Without Cohen's help, Mitchell would have found it extremely difficult to persuade the Colonial Office to approve this large grant, which marked the abandonment of Byrne's peasant strategy and increased the economic power of the settlers. Mitchell and Cohen, however, considered that this European presence would strengthen Kenya's stability and facilitate its development into a fully multiracial society and ally of Britain.

Mitchell's anti-Asian prejudices prevented him from recognising that small-scale Asian enterprises might have generated a larger multiplier effect on the Kenyan economy and absorbed a much larger unskilled workforce than the capital-intensive multinational corporations the government was attempting to attract. This would have enabled the government to resettle families from the reserves as urban employment opportunities expanded. Colin Leys has argued that Asian capital would have provided a more effective means of generating industrial expansion and has pointed out that, despite official disapproval, at the time of Independence Asians owned nearly three-quarters of the private non-agricultural assets of the colony, and over 67 per cent of locally-owned industrial concerns employing more than 50 people. By the early 1950s, there was no more room for expansion in real estate and trading, which had attracted Asian capital, and it began to invest in the secondary processing and manufacturing sectors, which the government wished to encourage.[39]

In contrast, multinational companies regarded their Kenyan interests as peripheral and reinvested their profits in Britain. Indeed these companies were only willing to invest in Kenya after they had received assurances of protection and special privileges.[40] The multinationals' presence, however, had a political as well as a purely economic purpose. The settlers had vociferously supported the government's attempts to attract them because they appeared to guarantee the continuation of the settler community and would provide jobs for the next generation. International capital offered the settlers their only opportunity to become Kenya's first national bourgeoisie. Without its support they would be squeezed between Asian and African entrepreneurs. The settlers believed that the multinationals would tighten the links between Britain and Kenya, guarantee Kenya's continued colonial status and protect their dominant position. Events, however, were to show that British capital, like the metropolitan official mind, had a global vision and was willing to sacrifice the dependent Kenyan settlers for a new world strategy of informal rather than formal empire, that would now be called neo-colonialism. This, however, only became apparent in the late 1950s. Ten years earlier, the settlers' position in Kenya had seemed secure. Kenya, it had appeared, was about to become the strategic centre of a retreating empire, with the settlers as the core.[41]

Thus, instead of being the bogey destroying every effort to improve race relations, the Kenyan settlers came to be seen as an essential element in the economic and political development of Kenya. Whitehall's commitment to African advance wavered. Advance there was to be, or so Whitehall hoped, but it was to be at a pace that would not unduly alarm the settlers. After 1946, following the planned British withdrawal from India and Palestine, the presence of a prosperous settler community was deemed essential for the strategic security of Africa and for the dollars the settler exports contributed to embattled sterling. The presence of the growing settler population, therefore, made the future of Kenya much more problematic than that of the Gold Coast or Nigeria. Indeed, with the withdrawal from India in 1947 and from Palestine in 1948, and with mounting Egyptian demands for British withdrawal from Suez, Kenya seemed likely to become the fulcrum of British defence strategy not only in Africa, but in the Middle East and Indian Ocean, providing a secure base for a British rapid-deployment force. The Cabinet, for example, seriously contemplated transforming Mackinnon Road near Mombasa into a major base. Stores began to be moved to Kenya. Creech Jones accepted, without any qualms, plans to quadruple the settler population in Kenya, and to transform it into a second Southern Rhodesia. More than £120 million was to be spent, mainly in Kenya, on these military preparations in East Africa.[42] Until Britain's financial problems and government retrenchment compelled a reassessment, the soldier settlement scheme had seemed likely to be only the first of many schemes to strengthen the

British presence in Kenya. The retreat from empire was not without its repercussions in the remaining colonies. British withdrawal from India and the Middle East clearly made the retreat from Kenya, in the long term, much more difficult and, in the short term, strengthened the settlers' bargaining position.

Closer union

Another political factor, which alienated African opinion, was the government's confusing behaviour during the Closer Union controversy. Mitchell and Whitehall had hoped to achieve four objectives with their proposals in 'Colonial 191'; Closer Union would improve inter-territorial co-operation, dilute settler influence in Kenya, enhance metropolitan power and point the way towards the evolution of a multiracial political system in Kenya and the other East African colonies. In consultations with the Colonial Office while *en route* from Fiji to Kenya, Mitchell revitalised the Closer Union proposals.[43] He began by increasing their scope while making them more acceptable to Africans and Asians and to the Labour Party at home. Instead of being a device to entrench settler power, Closer Union was redesigned to restore metropolitan authority and to create a bulwark against South African expansionism. Kenyan settlers, he hoped, would still support the new proposals because they fulfilled one of their old ambitions, but they would also prove acceptable to the other races who were to be given an equal number of seats as the settlers on the Central Assembly. This was the first example of Mitchell's attempts to obscure the racial divide and to appear as all things to all men.[44]

The new scheme was much simpler than his predecessor's plans for complete integration. It was also specifically designed not to antagonise opponents of Closer Union and was presented as 'a natural growth from the existing state of affairs'. Health, education, labour and African affairs – the issues that most interested Africans – were to remain territorial responsibilities. Industrial development, the railways, fiscal policy, research, agricultural investigations, Mitchell was convinced could only be effectively tackled on a co-ordinated East African basis. He also hoped that Kenya's racial divisions might be reduced under the moderating influence of the two other territories. The Closer Union proposals, therefore, were Mitchell's most important attempt to reduce the overweening influence of the Kenyan settlers.[45]

By the time of the Governors' Conference meeting in August 1945, Mitchell, who had taken careful soundings of settler opinion, was already beginning to doubt that the proposed equal racial composition of the Central-Assembly would prove acceptable to the Kenyan Europeans. He therefore attempted to make the Assembly more acceptable to them, not at the expense of African or Asian members, but by introducing an electoral college to select the Europeans. This would have enabled the Kenyan settlers to secure extra representation at the expense of Tanganyikan and Ugandan Europeans. After nine months in Nairobi, Mitchell realised that, as it stood, 'Colonial 191' would prove unacceptable and he struggled to make it more presentable without changing the vital principle of equal unofficial representation for the three major races.[46] He had the difficult task not only of reassuring Africans and Asians, but also of gaining the confidence of the vociferous European population in Kenya. This had proved more difficult than he had anticipated. Settler suspicion of the Colonial Office's new man, especially after the return of the Labour government, was deeply entrenched.[47] At the crucial moment, Mitchell fell ill and, from December 1945 until March 1946, the delicate negotiations were left in the hands of Chief Secretary Rennie, who was a much less subtle political operator than Mitchell.[48]

In December 1945, when 'Colonial 191' was finally published, settler opposition erupted against the proposals, although the hue and cry did have the advantage of ensuring unanimous African and Asian support. The settlers, however, feared that the Labour government was 'determined to take away the power of the Europeans in Kenya'. These suspicions undermined Mitchell's attempts to create a less racially divisive atmosphere. Alfred Vincent, the settlers' political leader, for example, demanded an immediate unofficial majority on the Kenya Legislative Council as 'the only means by which we can stop this fooling around by the Colonial Office'. Yet, despite this apparently irreconcilable divide, Rennie as acting governor still believed that:

> Equal territorial and unofficial representation on any East African Council form the only possible foundation on which post-war programmes of social, cultural and material development can be safely built, if these East African territories are to progress harmoniously . . .
> All three communities in East Africa as a whole are inter-dependent and no one of them can prosper without the co-operation of the other two. All must advance together.[49]

The settler politicians, however, were committed too deeply for them to extricate themselves without help.

After their visit to East Africa in August 1946, in an abortive attempt to solve the deadlock, Creech Jones and Andrew Cohen, as well as the three governors, became even more convinced that a scheme similar to 'Colonial 191' was essential.[50] The revised proposals embodied in 'Colonial 210', as far as the Colonial Office and the East African governments were concerned, maintained the principle of equal racial representation, although there was now to be one member from each racial group per territory instead of two.[51] In addition, the territorial Legislative Councils were to choose one extra unofficial member for the Assembly. The Colonial Office hoped that this would prove acceptable to all three races while it would enable the composition of the Central Assembly to be modified as Africans gained greater representation at the territorial level. Racial fluidity would replace rigidity.

'Colonial 210' was not devised, as has frequently been suggested, by the Colonial Office as a sell-out to settler pressure. The racial composition of the unofficials on the Central Assembly clearly proved that equal racial representation was preserved. 'Colonial 210' simply presented the Assembly in a more attractive way to Kenyan settlers by restricting the power of the High Commission and subordinating its revenue to the control of the territorial Legislative Councils. The Colonial Office and the governors never anticipated that this would arouse African and Asian opposition. Mitchell, indeed, still feared that the scheme had not gone far enough to appease the settlers.[52] Creech Jones was willing to take a hard line: 'I am not unduly alarmed at the danger of precipitating a major political crisis. It is the European settler method in Kenya of asserting their claim to a degree of political dominance and of showing resentment. Whatever privilege they may have had in the past cannot be perpetuated much longer.'[53] The Secretary of State was evidently less apprehensive of creating a political storm with the settlers than Sir Philip Mitchell.

The new proposals, however, encountered African and Asian opposition because the official announcement emphasised that four unofficial members were to be elected from each territory. Since Africans and Asians knew that they were only to be given one seat each, they jumped to the conclusion that the other two members were to be settlers. In contrast, 'Colonial 191' had made it appear as if there were to be equal unofficial representation of the three main races and had hidden the additional European members among the representatives to be nominated by the High Commission.[54] Thus 'Colonial 210' heightened African suspicions. Although '210' retained the essential core of '191', in the racially divided arena of Kenyan politics, myth proved to be more powerful than reality. By miscalculating in the original proposals how much reassurance the Kenyan settlers required before they would support Closer Union, both British and Kenyan governments appeared to have conceded the racial equality promised in '191' because of intense settler pressure, although they were simply seeking to reassure the settlers rather than to abandon their promises to the Africans and Asians. The Closer Union crisis, which lasted from December 1945 to March 1948, was the first of a series of cases of the Kenyan government trying to appeal to both Africans and settlers, but merely succeeding in arousing the suspicion of both communities and alienating the authorities even further from the Africans.

The Closer Union controversy also marked an important change in metropolitan attitudes to the settlers, particularly on the part of Creech Jones and Andrew Cohen. Creech Jones had the reputation, from his days as chairman of the Fabian Colonial Bureau, of being a noted sympathiser with African criticism of colonial rule. As Under-Secretary and, after October 1946, as Secretary of State for the Colonies, however, he seemed to be a completely different figure, totally subservient to his official advisers.[55] His East African journey in the summer of 1946 encouraged this dramatic change. This visit made an equally profound impression upon Andrew Cohen, his chief adviser on East African affairs, who, the following year, became Assistant Under-Secretary for Africa; a position of crucial importance not only for the future of Kenya but for decolonisation throughout British Africa. Cohen had the most creative mind in the Colonial Office and possessed a dynamic personality and willpower equalled by few other bureaucrats.[56] After a brief visit to Central Africa as private secretary to Sir John Maffey in the late 1930s, Cohen had returned to Whitehall disillusioned with the morality of empire. Like Creech Jones he was determined to transform the imperial relationship into a force for African development, but this did not mean African political power in the settler colonies. Cohen was concerned primarily to create self-sustaining nations with sound economic bases. He had, therefore, been quickly convinced by Mitchell that the settlers offered the most effective way of improving conditions for the African masses in colonies like Kenya. Thus, despite their initial distrust of the Kenya settlers, both Creech Jones and Cohen were more susceptible to their views than appeared at first sight. After prolonged discussions with Mitchell and the settlers' political leaders, they returned to London with a much more sympathetic appreciation of the settlers' role in Kenyan life and its future economic progress.[57] As had happened to Mitchell in the first months of 1945, the political and economic realities of Kenya forced them to modify their previous inclination to side with African demands. Although no-one realised it at the time, this was a vital turning point. The British government's new proposals on Closer Union, contained in 'Colonial 210', were significant not because of what they had to say about economic integration but because they marked a turning point in the subconscious assumptions of the two most influential men in the Colonial Office. The Kenya African Union's meagre chance of rewriting the rules of Kenyan politics had been lost before Kenyatta appeared on the scene. His return in September 1946 simply confirmed the settlers' dominant influence, not only in Nairobi but also in London. Exposed to the political situation in Kenya, Creech Jones's and Cohen's preconceived opinions had begun slowly to change.[58]

Their visit and several despatches from Mitchell over the previous 18 months highlight the reasoning of the official mind as it came to grips with the intractable political realities of settler intransigence. Slowly the Colonial Office realised that the reform of African empire would be extremely difficult to implement in those colonies that had actually provoked this reassessment – Kenya and the Rhodesias. By the end of 1946, any thoughts the Labour Party may have had of transferring some power to the African élite in Kenya in the same way as in the Gold Coast had been dispelled; the presence of the settler community precluded such a step. Indeed, the excesses of left-wing rhetoric had increased the settlers' intransigence. The price of abandoning the settlers appeared to be too high in terms of political uproar, economic chaos and lost confidence.[59]

Sir Philip Mitchell and the rationale of the Kenyan official mind

Within less than three years, the agricultural campaign in the three Kikuyu Districts, the attempt to remove the threat of squatter accumulation which was undermining the heart of the settler economy by expelling squatter cattle from the White Highlands, and the government's failure to tackle Nairobi's acute social problems, had all helped to alienate Africans from the colonial régime. The impact of Mitchell's policies was most acute upon the Kikuyu, the largest 'tribe' in the colony. The government's agricultural development programme was particularly disruptive in the three overcrowed Kikuyu reserves. The Kikuyu formed nearly two-thirds of the total squatter community, with an even larger proportion in the Naivasha, Nakuru and Aberdares district council areas, where the new anti-squatter rules were' most severe. In Nairobi, approximately 55 per cent of the total population were Kikuyu.[60] The Kikuyu and the government thus clashed over post-war Kenya's three most explosive problems. Moreover, it was the Kikuyu politicians who dominated the fledgling trade unions and the Kenya African Union, while Kikuyu businessmen and commercial farmers provided the greatest threat to the economic hegemony of the settlers.[61] When the Mitchell government failed to incorporate them into the political process, to reward them with a share in government patronage or to provide new economic opportunities, many Kikuyu were driven into militant opposition to the colonial order. By 1952, many of them had turned in desperation to open revolt in the Mau Mau rebellion. Why did the government fail to react and not attempt to prevent the development of violent opposition among the Kikuyu to colonial rule? Why was the situation allowed to deteriorate so far?

The Kenyan authorities and settlers placed the blame for these troubles on Jomo Kenyatta, whom they denounced as a communist agitator. It appeared inconceivable that anyone else could have masterminded the protests. After all, Kenyatta was the avowed leader of the main African political movement – the Kenya African Union. In 1960, the official Corfield report on 'the origins and growth of Mau Mau' still contended that Kenyatta had controlled Mau Mau. It declared:

Land had already become a political issues, but it did not become a burning issue until the return of Jomo Kenyatta to Kenya at the end of

1946 . . . Jomo Kenyatta and his associates saw all too clearly that the exploitation of land hunger was a sure way of furthering their own ends of uniting the Kikuyu against the Government in general, and the settled European farmer in particular.[62]

This campaign, Corfield alleged, had been organised through the Kikuyu Central Association and the Kikuyu Karing'a Educational Association which, he believed, Kenyatta controlled as part of the web of contacts centred on the Githunguri Teachers' Training College. This educational movement, with Githunguri and Kenyatta at the centre and the Karing'a schools and the African Orthodox Church in the localities, provided the organisation through which Kenyatta had allegedly fostered the spread of Mau Mau.

Kenyatta was thus seen as the evil genius in whom the various strands of Kikuyu subversion met. The independent schools, the Teachers' Training College, age-group organisations, ex-soldiers' associations, the trade unions, the Kikuyu Central Association and the Kenya African Union, all looked to him as their ultimate leader and, it appeared to the offical mind, only he could unite these movements into a formidable challenge to the colonial state. He appeared particularly insidious to many settlers because his long sojourn in Britain and his contacts with the Labour Party had made him as adept as themselves at bypassing the Kenyan government when he wanted to put pressure on the metropolitan state. Kenyatta refused to accept the rules of the Kenyan political game of the previous 50 years, whereby only the settlers had direct access to the counsels of Whitehall and Westminister.[63]

Kenyatta all too easily fitted the Kenyan government's need for a scapegoat; a brilliant, evil mastermind who could employ traditional witchcraft and modern anthropology to terrify the Kikuyu into revolt, while tying the colonial authorities' iron fist by skilful manipulation of the humanitarian sentiments of the Labour left and of missionary opinion in Britain. Corfield expressed this settler alarm when he castigated Kenyatta for manipulating British support with his references to

. . . the word democracy, as this word was dearly respected by left-wing sympathizers in the United Kingdom. He also had a full knowledge and understanding of the psychology of the Kikuyu and was able to blend the technique of revolution, undoubtedly learnt while he was in Russia, with an appeal to superstition and to the strong sense of tribal destiny which the Kikuyu possessed.[64]

Such views were not simply the product of Corfield's bilious view of Africans, but were typical of European attitudes in Kenya, not only among the settlers but also in the field administration and the Secretariat.

The Kenyan authorities never realised that they were out of touch with African opinion. The field administration, for example, had become desk-bound and was dependent on the colonial chiefs for most of its information about what people really thought. The chiefs, of course, used this control over government information to discredit their own political rivals in the Kenya African Union, who thereupon became increasingly disillusioned with constitutionalist politics. The Special Branch's concentration on preserving the political *status quo* also coloured the reports of African political activity that reached the Secretariat and prevented the central bureaucracy from understanding what was really happening in the reserves and the White Highlands.[65]

Both the White Highlands and African Nairobi were areas in which the colonial state was peculiarly weak, as power had been devolved to the settler-controlled district and municipal councils. This division of responsibility between settler institutions and the field administration had created a serious gap in the government's defences and reduced its ability to monitor and suppress opposition. The social transformation which followed the war was, however, especially acute in these same two areas where settler and African Kenya were inextricably interlinked.[66] The Kenyan government, therefore, failed not only to appreciate the depth of the discontent which simmered beneath the surface, but critically misread the warning signs of violence among the squatters on the settler farms, the urban unemployed in Pumwani and Shauri Moyo, and among the peasantry in the Kikuyu reserves. The problems were compounded by the field administration's prejudices against the emerging proto-capitalists and the Kenya African Union, which distorted the reports they forwarded to the Secretariat and the governor and obscured the complex struggles beneath the surface of popular African politics.

Mitchell and the field administration were convinced, until the end, that their strategy had worked. The year 1947 was one disaster, when the second colonial occupation began to provoke sustained resistance. But the administration saw this unpopularity as something that had to be endured for a brief period before Kikuyu society could be restructured. Ignorant protests from self-seeking politicians cut little ice.[67] They were inevitable in the short run, before the benefits of the agricultural development programme filtered down to the *wananchi*. Although 1948 was a difficult year, opposition seemed to be less vociferous. In 1949, when Mitchells's term as governor was renewed for another three years, it seemed to him and his advisers in the Secretariat that the tide had at last turned. By 1950 or 1951, the governor believed that his programme was on course, tackling land degradation and reducing social tension in the reserves. The soil had been saved from the depredations of the greedy land-miners, and was being protected and replenished for the future prosperity of the ordinary African.[68]

In fact by 1950, the grand design with which he had arrived in Nairobi in 1944, intending to wrest control of the colonial state from the settlers and to create in Kenya the contented multiracial society he believed he had governed in Fiji, had collapsed into chaos. Instead of striving to achieve set goals, the weary governor was reduced to responding on an *ad hoc* basis to every problem that passed over his desk. Grand strategy was dead; tactical survival was all that remained. His poor health made it impossible for Mitchell to maintain his original punishing régime of tours throughout the colony.[69] After his serious illness in the middle of the Closer Union furore over 'Colonial 191', when he was incapacitated from December 1945 to March 1946, his energies were noticeably diminished. Although the stream of correspondence to the Colonial Office continued in full spate, the constant round of district tours he had undertaken during his first year, was drastically cut. During his last three years as governor after 1949, he was virtually a prisoner in Nairobi, seldom venturing into the districts, tied to Government House by his heart condition and utter exhaustion.[70]

Instead of instilling enthusiasm into the field administration by his forceful presence, Mitchell became isolated; an aloof figure, little known to the new generation of District Commissioners. For example, while O'Hagan, who had been District Commissioner in Murang'a from 1945 to 1947 before moving to the Secretariat, remembers the dynamic governor of the first years, his friend and colleague Kennaway, who was the District Commissioner in Kiambu during the early 1950s, recalls a totally different man, devoid of any interest in the problems of the district.[71]

One abiding passion did, however, survive Mitchell's decline; his intense personal ambition. A solitary, unapproachable man, who found it difficult to make friends and extremely easy to provoke lasting personal enmity, Mitchell was driven by fiercely competitive instincts, whether at work or in his leisure. He had to be outstanding, whether it was governing Kenya or fishing for trout. Indeed it was reported that he had only married his wife, a South African open golf ladies' champion, because she was the first woman to have defeated him. Mitchell's constant desire was to excel and to leave his imprint upon what he believed to be the *tabula rasa* of Africa and the African mind.[72]

As the complexities of Kenya ground him down by their sheer intractability, Mitchell's nerve snapped and his health collapsed. Although he managed to conceal this from the Colonial Office when it renewed his appointment in 1949, the Kenyan governor between 1949 and 1952 was a mere shadow of his former self, but the ambition remained. If Sir Arthur Richards could get to the House of Lords, then so could he. Well aware of his reputation in the Colonial Office as the most dynamic of the African governors, Mitchell clung on, impervious to administration and settler warnings about the imminence of a widespread Kikuyu revolt. The governor became increasingly reluctant to heed advice as the political situation deteriorated and his energies were sapped. He showed a remarkable ability to ignore events and opinions that contradicted his preconceived view. While in 1948, when Clarence Buxton and Canon Capon had first warned him of the serious situation among the Kikuyu, it might have been true that the tensions were no more serious than an experienced governor like Mitchell had encountered many times before in his long career, this was no longer true after 1950.[73] But as Mitchell's term of office drew to a close, he became reluctant to contemplate the possibility of a widespread rebellion and closed his mind to all the evidence that was presented, obstinately refusing to acknowledge that the situation had changed in case it endangered his reputation and let slip the peerage. By 1952, he was already an exhausted, shuffling, ill figure; a remnant from the age of indirect rule. He had succeeded for too long and survived too well into an uncongenial time. This was his tragedy; and Kenya's.

Notes

1. C. Thorne, *Allies of a Kind*, pp. 259, 371–2, outlines the tensions in the Anglo–American alliance in the Pacific when Mitchell became governor of Fiji in 1942. For Mitchell's view of Nimitz and the American commanders see RH Mss. Afr. r. 101, Mitchell's diary entry for 29 August 1944, the day before he received the cable from the Colonial Office offering him the governorship of Kenya.

2. CO 822/114/46523 (1944), 'Closer Union', minute by Dawe, 4 December 1944 for his unenthusiastic response to Mitchell and his proposals. For Margery Perham's view of Mitchell see her *East African Journey*, pp. 17, 42, 56; and her *Colonial Sequence*, vol. 1, pp. 12–33 for an account of his work in Tanganyika. A.H.M. Kirk-Greene, 'Margery Perham and Colonial Administration', pp. 122–43 provides a brief introduction to her career.

3. D.J. Morgan, *The Official History of Overseas Development*, vol. 1, pp. xiv–xvii, 23–34, 64–99, 185–239; and J.M. Lee, *Colonial Development and Good Government*, pp. 13–18, 41–53, 111–39, 172–88. See also J.M. Lee, 'Forward Thinking and War', pp. 64–79; and CO 852/588/19260 (Part 1) (1944), 'Planning of Economic and Social Development', Economic Advisory Committee questions to Oliver Stanley and memorandum by W.A. Lewis, 14 September 1944.

4. CO 533/536/38598 (1945–46), 'Kenya: Staff Position', and CO 533/537/38628 (1945), 'Grouping of Agricultural Departments', for a host of examples.

5. CO 533/557/38672 (1947–48), 'Memorandum from the Kenya African Union', Mitchell to Creech Jones, 11 February 1947; and CO 533/556/38664 (1946–47), 'Land Policy', Half Yearly Report on Soil Conservation in Fort Hall, June 1946, and T. Hughes Rice to A.B. Cohen, 3 August 1946; and P.E. Mitchell's published despatch, *Agricultural Policy in African Areas*, 1951.

6. CO 533/557/38672 (1947–48), 'Memorandum from the Kenya African Union', P.E. Mitchell to the Kenya African Union, March 1948; CO 533/543/38086/38 (1949), 'Kikuyu Petitions: Kikuyu Central Association', Mitchell to Creech Jones, 28 February 1949; CO 533/557/38678/1 (1947–48), 'African Land Settlement: Olenguruone', A.B. Cohen, 14 July 1947; CO 533/557/38678/1 (1949) 'African Land

Settlement: Olenguruone', I.D. Robertson, 28 November 1949; and P.E. Mitchell, *Agricultural Policy in African Areas, passim*. See also CO 533/537/38646 (1945), 'Proposals for the Reorganization of the Administration', A.B. Cohen, 10 August 1945.

7. KNA Secretariat 1/1/12, 'Report of the Joint Agricultural and Veterinary Services Sub-committee of the Development Committee', pp. 6–15; CO 852/662/19936/2 (1945–46), 'Soil Erosion: Kenya', N. Humphrey, 'The Relationship of Population to the Land in South Nyeri'; and H.E. Lambert and P. Wyn Harris, 'Memorandum on Policy in Regard to Land Tenure in the Native Lands of Kenya'; and Legislative Council Debates, Second Series, vol. xx, 1944–45, 3rd Session, 30 November 1945, speech by Cavendish-Bentinck, columns 328–330.

8. KNA Lab 9/97, 'Association of District Councils, 1941–53', conference 12–13 September 1944; Lab 9/10, 'Labour: Squatters in Forest Areas, 1944–50', Agricultural Production and Settlement Board to Chief Secretary, 17 March 1945; and Lab 9/316, 'Resident Labour: Naivasha Country Council, 1941–59', meeting 27 October 1945. For an African view see K.J. King and R.M. Wambaa, 'The Political Economy of the Rift Valley', pp. 201–8.

9. CO 533/537/38628 (1945), 'Grouping of Agricultural Departments'; and CO 533/536/38598 (1945–46), 'Kenya Staff Position', Mitchell to Creasy, 30 December 1944. This is also based upon conversations with Desmond O'Hagan, 24 April and 10–11 June 1981 in Nairobi; and T.H.R. Cashmore, 21 and 28 October 1982 in London.

10. G.H. Mungeam, *British Rule in Kenya*, pp. 208–73. See also R. Hyam, '*The Colonial Office Mind*', p. 47, which provides another parallel between Girouard and Mitchell: 'The need for a stronger governor in the Kenya trouble-spot was obvious; the new man must not be swayed by the settlers. The office thought it had found one who met all its requirements for grip and capacity, energy and pro-African enthusiasm – Sir Percy Girouard, who had upheld African interests well in Nigeria and shown aversion to military adventurers and swashbucklers. His appointment proved to be a colossal miscalculation. It was a major turning-point in the wayward evolution of Kenya, enabling the settlers to entrench themselves in a way far removed from official intention.' This was to be equally true of Mitchell.

11. Interviews in Nairobi with M.H. Cowie, 8 July 1981; H. Kennaway, 4 September 1979; and Clive Salter, 11 March 1981. See also RH Mss. Brit.Emp. s. 390, Box 3, File 4, Item 3, ff. 32–9, C.E.V. Buxton's memoranda on the Emergency. These are undated, but internal evidence suggests that they were probably written in February or March 1953. Interview in Ferndown, Dorset, with C.O. Oates, 20 June 1983.

12. CO 533/536/38598 (1945–46), 'Kenya: Staff Position', Mitchell to G. Creasy, 30 December 1944; and CO 533/537/38628 (1945), 'Grouping of Agricultural Departments'. C.O. Oates, who was acting deputy director of agriculture in 1944, recalled that the agricultural department lost more than half its manpower during the war and had to recruit settlers as agricultural officers, (interview 20 June 1983).

13. CO 533/537/38628 (1945), 'Grouping of Agricultural Departments' Mitchell to Creasy, 18 February 1945.

14. CO 533/537/38646 (1945), 'Proposals for the Reorganisation of the Administration', Cohen's minute, 10 August 1945. For his earlier opposition to Mitchell's proposals see his note of 2 March 1945.

15. CO 533/537/38608 (1944–46), 'Land Policy: Memorandum by the Anti-Slavery and Aborigines Protection Society', letter to Stanley, 5 May 1944. See also S. and K. Aaronovitch, *Crisis in Kenya*, p. 74.

16. CO 533/534/38313 (1946), 'Alienation of Crown Land outside Townships', Tempany's minute, 27 July 1946.

17. R.M. Breen's unpublished thesis, 'The Politics of Land', pp. 81–91.

18. C.G. Rosberg and J. Nottingham, *The Myth of Mau Mau*, pp.153–5, 223–5; and B.A. Ogot, 'Politics, Culture and Music in Central Kenya', pp. 277–86. See also Maina wa

Kinyatti's controversial collection of Mau Mau *nyimbo* (hymns), *Thunder from the Mountains*, pp. 14–46, for various songs lamenting the lost lands.

Harold Macmillan's warnings of a peasant revolt if the Kikuyu were not given more land are in CO 967/57/46709 (1942), 'Sir Arthur Dawe's Memorandum on a Federal Solution for East Africa and Mr Harold Macmillan's Counter-Proposals', dated 15 August 1942.

19. CO 822/114/46523 (1946), 'Closer Union', Vincent's opening speech at the Electors' Union Conference, 24 January 1946; and Mitchell to Creech Jones, 11 May 1946.

20. C.G. Rosberg and J. Nottingham, *The Myth of Mau Mau*, pp. 223–5; and B.A. Ogot, 'Politics, Culture and Music in Central Kenya', pp. 227–82. See also CO 533/534/38232 (1945), 'European Settlement Scheme', Mitchell to George Hall, 11 September 1945.

21. *ibid*, Mitchell to Creasy, 30 May 1945. See also CO 533/536/38557 (1945), 'Development and Welfare Schemes', Sessional Paper no. 2 of 1945, Interim Report on Development, 4 June 1945; and CO 533/553/38557/8 (1947–48), 'General Aspects of the Agrarian Situation in Kenya', Despatch 44 of 1946 to Hall, 17 April 1946. The constitutionalist leaders of the Kenya African Union, Gichuru and Mathu, also initially accepted this view: see CO 533/537/38672 (1946), 'Memorandum by the Kenya African Union', forwarded by the Secretariat, 17 August 1946.

22. CO 533/534/38232 (Part II) (1945), 'Land Use and Settlement in Kenya', Creech Jones's comments, 26 September 1945.

23. CO 533/558/38690 (1947), 'Fabian Society', Creech Jones to Hinden, 22 May 1947; and CO 533/557/38678 (1948–49), 'African Land Settlement', Creech Jones to Hinden, 16 August 1949.

24. Mitchell considered that a confrontation with the settlers would be politically and economically disastrous: CO 533/558/38678/2 (1949), 'African Land Settlement–Kamba', Mitchell to Cohen, 7 September 1949. See C.G. Rosberg and J. Nottingham, *The Myth of Mau Mau*, pp. 198–203, for their assessment of Mitchell's multiracialism.

25. RH Mss Afr. r. 101, Mitchell's diary, 1 November 1944; P.E. Mitchell, *African Afterthoughts*, p. 211; and R.A. Frost, 'Sir Philip Mitchell', pp. 535–53, and his book, *Race against Time*, pp. 45–64. For Mitchell's optimistic hopes see CO 533/537/38628 (1945), 'Grouping of Agricultural Departments', Mitchell to Stanley, 9 March 1945.

26. CO 533/534/38232 (1945), 'European Settlement Scheme', Mitchell to Stanley, 19 March 1945. By 1948 non-African direct taxation was producing 18 per cent of Kenya's government revenue, compared to only 7 per cent from African hut and poll tax. Twenty years earlier these proportions had been reversed with 2 per cent from non-African and 31 per cent from African sources; see D.A. Low and A. Smith, *History of East Africa*, vol. 3, pp. 603–4.

27. Mitchell had served briefly in July 1914, in the area which was at the centre of the Chilembwe rising the following year, and had been confronted with a serious famine. See P.E. Mitchell, *African Afterthoughts*, pp. 27, 248–50. G.A. Shepperson and T. Price, *Independent African*, provide a definitive account.

28. CO 533/540/38032 (1949), 'Legislative Council', Mitchell to Creech Jones, 11 December 1948; CO 533/543/38086/5 (1945–57), 'Kikuyu Petitions and Memorials', Mitchell to Gater, November 1946; CO 533/543/38086/38 (1949), 'Kikuyu Central Association', Mitchell to Creech Jones, 28 February 1949; and CO 533/545/38091/10 (1944–47), 'Labour Registration and Identification', Rennie to Creech Jones, 11 May 1947.

29. CO 533/549/38232/15 (1946–47), 'European Settlement: Squatters', Mitchell to Creech Jones, 14 April 1947.

30. KNA MAA 7/491, 'Administration Policy: Urban Areas Nairobi, 1945–47'; MAA 8/22, 'Municipal African Affairs Officer: Correspondence, 1947–50'; and CO 533/558/38715 (1948), 'Municipal African Affairs Annual Report', reveal all too

clearly the Administration's ignorance of urban Africa. KNA Lab 9/1775, 'Survey of African Housing in Mombasa, 1946–47'; and Lab 9/1751, 'African Housing: General', provide grim evidence of the appalling housing conditions in the African locations of Mombasa and Nairobi. For details of the cost of living for urban Africans see the evidence in Lab 9/1841, 'Trade Disputes Tribunal, 1947'.

31. KNA MAA 7/14, 'Fort Hall African Merchants' Association, 1950'; C&I 6/782, 'Trading by Africans, 1946–50'; and Ag 4/77, 'Wattle Cooperative Societies, 1947–51'. For the administration's attitude to African commercial farming, see CO 852/662/19936/2 (1945–46), 'Soil Erosion: Kenya', N. Humphrey's report on South Nyeri, pp. 19–20; and KNA MAA 6/13 and 14, 'Committee on Agricultural Credit for Africans, 1949–50'.

32. CO 533/543/38086/5 (1945–47), 'Kikuyu Petitions', Mitchell to Gater, November 1946, and to Creech Jones 20 January 1947; CO 533/545/38091/10 (1944–47), 'Labour: Registration and Identification', Rennie to Creech Jones, 11 May 1947; CO 533/543/38086/38 (1949), 'Kikuyu Central Association Petitions and Kikuyu Grievances', Mitchell to Creech Jones, 28 February 1949; CO 537/3588/38696 (1947–48), 'Activities of Mathu', shows the government's increasing suspicion of Mathu and the Kenya African Union following Kenyatta's return in September 1946.

33. CO 537/3588/38696 (1947–48), 'Activities of Mathu'; and J. Roelker, *Mathu of Kenya*, pp. 89–106.

34. KNA MAA 8/8, 'Intelligence Reports: Confidential Information', C.M. Johnston to Provincial Commissioner, Central, 18 May 1947; and Director of Intelligence to the Chief Native Commissioner about Mathu's contacts with Kenyatta, 7 August 1947.

35. The Executive Council consisted of seven ex-officio members, including Cavendish-Bentinck as member for Agriculture and Natural Resources and Sir Charles Mortimer as member for Health and Local Government; three Europeans nominated 'unofficials' including the missionary, Archdeacon L.J. Beecher, who was appointed to represent African interests, and A.B. Patel, the senior Asian Legislative Councillor. In 1952 Mathu was finally appointed the first African member of the Executive Council, although the first African to be appointed a minister was B.A. Ohanga in 1954. See G. Bennett, *Kenya*, p. 137; and D.A. Low and A. Smith (eds), *History of East Africa*, vol. 3, pp. 558–9 for a brief outline of the evolution of the Kenya Legislative and Executive Councils.

36. CO 533/534/3823A (Part 1) (1945), 'European Settlement Scheme', Mitchell to Stanley 19 March 1945.

37. CO 533/553/38557/8 (1947–48), 'General Aspects of the Agrarian Situation in Kenya', despatch no. 44 of 1946, Mitchell to Hall, 17 April 1946.

38. CO 533/534/38232 (Part II) (1945), 'Land Use and Settlement in Kenya', draft despatch prepared by Cohen, February 1946, to Anti-Slavery and Aboriginal Protection Society.

39. C. Leys, *Underdevelopment in Kenya*, pp. 44–5, 119–21.

40. N. Swainson, *The Development of Corporate Capitalism in Kenya*, pp. 116–24, 130–69. See also KNA C&I 6/331, 'East African Industrial Council, 1942–60'; C&I 6/418, 'Kenya Canners Ltd., 1948–51'; C&I 6/457, 'British Standard Portland Cement Co. Ltd., Bamburi, 1951–56'; C&I 6/333, 'Agenda and Papers: East African Industrial Council, 1948–53'; C&I 6/332, 'East African Industrial Council, 1942–49'; C&I 6/638, 'Secondary Industries: Committee to Advise on Industrial Siting, 1949–50'; C&I 6/683, 'Secondary Industries: Fiscal Policy Committee on Drawbacks of Custom Duty, 1949–50'; and C&I 6/374, 'Secondary Industries: Allocation of Industrial Plots, 1946–49', for various disputes over protection, siting and government guarantees.

41. CO 537/1233/13012/24 (1945–46), 'Defence East Africa: Mombasa as a Major Port and Base', Bevin to G. Hall 21 January 1946; CO 537/1883/94023/3 (1946), 'Defence of East Africa: Construction of a Base', East Africa as a Base (501 Mission) 26 November 1946; CO 537/4711 (1948–49), 'African Conference: Address by

Montgomery'. Three files of the East African High Command also contain interesting information, WO 276/251 'Visit C.I.G.S.: Defence Policy Discussions'; WO 276/9, 'East African Command: Defence Services Sub-committee'; and WO 276/10, 'East African Governors' Conference, 1947'. See also CO 968/94/6/13023/24 (1945), 'Defence Middle East: Imperial Security and Location of British Troops', Cabinet Paper, Minister Resident in the Middle East, 2 July 1945.

42. CO 537/1883/94023/3 (1946), 'Defence of East Africa: Construction of a Base'. The expenditure was to be spread over six years. The War Office was to provide £64 million; the RAF £22 million; the Admiralty £20 million; and the three mainland colonial governments a total of £24 million.

43. RH Mss. Afr. r. 101, Mitchell's diary, 23 November to 5 December 1944; and CO 822/114/46523 (1944), 'Closer Union', minutes of Mitchell's meeting with Stanley, Gater, Devonshire and Creasy, Seel and Edmonds on 29 November 1944; and Dawe's minute on Constitutional Questions in East Africa.

44. *ibid*, and CO 822/114/46523 (1945), 'Closer Union', Memorandum from East African Governors' Conference, 14 February 1945; and Mitchell to Stanley, 15 March 1945. For Mitchell's private commitment to multiracialism see CO 533/536/38599/4 (1945 and 1946), 'Education: Admission of Mixed Blood Children to European Schools'.

45. CO 822/114/46523 (1944), 'Closer Union', minute of meeting in Colonial Office with Mitchell on 28 November 1944; and CO 822/114/46523 (1945), 'Closer Union', Mitchell to Creasy 7 September 1945; and meeting with Creech Jones 24–25 October 1945.

46. CO 822/114/46523 (1945), 'Closer Union', Mitchell to George Hall, 6 September 1945; and meeting with Creech Jones, 24–25 October 1945. See also Vincent to Gater 17 October 1945, for Kenya settler opinion.

47. CO 822/114/46523 (Part I) (1946), Rennie to Gater, 6 February 1946, enclosing Vincent's speech at the opening of the Electors' Union Conference on 24 January 1946. For the Labour Party's opposition to Closer Union during the war, see CO 822/114/46523 (1944), 'Closer Union', Note on the Position as at 1 March 1944; Edmonds's memorandum of 4 April 1944; and Stanley to Moore 12 April 1944. Contrast these with Creech Jones's minute of 4 October 1945 in CO 822/114/46523 (1945).

48. RH Mss. Afr. r. 101, Mitchell's diary 2 December 1945, and 9 to 14 December 1945, for the governor's physical exhaustion and eventual collapse. The White Paper on Closer Union was published on 12 December. See CO 822/121/46523 (1947), 'Closer Union', Mitchell to Creech Jones, 18 April 1947, for an example of Rennie's lack of subtlety as a politician.

49. CO 822/114/46523 (1946), 'Closer Union', Rennie to Hall, 6 March 1946.

50. *ibid*. Cohen to Gater, 10 September 1946, about the meeting with the three mainland governors at Dar-es-Salaam on 11 August 1946, and with the Kenyan Secretariat on 22 August, to discuss 'The Necessity for the Early Establishment of Constitutional Backing for East African Inter-Territorial Machinery'.

51. CO 822/121/46523 (1947), 'Closer Union', especially M.J. Davies to the India Office, 19 May 1947; and Cohen's note to the Indian government in June 1947. A more orthodox interpretation of the controversy can be found in N.J. Westcott, 'Closer Union and the Future of East Africa', pp. 83–4.

52. CO 822/114/46523 (1946), 'Closer Union', Cohen to Gater, 10 September 1946 for his views on the public reaction to the proposed composition of the Central Assembly; and CO 822/121/46523 (1947), 'Closer Union', C.D.W. Anderson, proprietor of the *East African Standard* to Cohen, 10 June 1947.

53. CO 822/114/46523 (1946), 'Closer Union', Creech Jones's minute, 20 September 1946.

54. CO 822/121/46523 (1947), 'Closer Union', Cohen's memorandum, June 1947.

55. Mbiyu Koinange was becoming increasingly critical of the Labour government; see

CO 533/547/38132/465, 'Visit of Mr Koinange to the United Kingdom', especially Koinange to Creech Jones, 24 June 1947.

56. RH Mss, Afr. r. 101, Mitchell's diary, 20 July to 22 August 1946 and CO 822/114/46523 (1946), 'Closer Union', especially European Elected Members' meeting with Creech Jones in August 1946; and Cohen's long report to Gater of 10 September 1946. Favourable appraisals of Cohen are R.E. Robinson, 'Sir Andrew Cohen', pp. 353–63; and his 'Andrew Cohen and the Transfer of Power in Tropical Africa'. See also R.E. Robinson, 'The Journal and the Transfer of Power', pp. 255–8 and A.B. Cohen's own *British Policy in Changing Africa*. Unfortunately this says nothing about his visit to East Africa in 1946, but pp. 51–3 provide some insights into its effect on his thinking.

57. CO 822/114/46523 (1946) 'Closer Union', and CO 822/121/46523 (1947), 'Closer Union', provide evidence for this gradual 'mellowing' of Creech Jones and Cohen towards the Kenyan settlers. It is apparent, of course, that the Colonial Office was giving something away to assuage the fears of the Europeans in Kenya in 'Colonial 210'. It should, however, be emphasised that this was not, as has hitherto been believed, the principle of equal racial representation on the Central Assembly. '210' instead attempted to reassure the Kenyan settlers by reducing the powers of the central bureaucracy in the High Commission, and by granting a veto on the expansion and funding of the High Commission to the territorial Legislative Councils, where, of course, in Kenya there was a strong settler lobby.

58. CO 533/558/38690 (1947), 'Correspondence with Fabian Society', Creech Jones to Hinden 22 May 1947; and CO 533/556/38664/2 (1947), 'Land Policy: Memorandum by the Labour Party on Land Utilization and Settlement'. These all show how far Creech Jones's opinions had been changed by his journey to East Africa. This had been his first visit to Kenya, and only his second to Africa. He was also slowly being 'captured' by the Colonial Office.

59. R.D. Pearce, *The Turning Point in Africa*, pp. 177–9, for a brief discussion of Mitchell's attempt to persuade the Colonial Office that their West Africa strategy would fail in the settler colonies. See also CO 533/534/38232 (1945), 'Land Use and Settlement in Kenya', Mitchell to Stanley, 19 March 1945, for an early defence of the Kenyan settlers.

See also RH Mss. Afr. r. 101, Mitchell's diary, 29 October to 14 November 1947, for his account of the African Governors' Conference in London, especially the entry for 10 November, where he recorded: 'We conferred all day, largely on dry theoretical ideas of Colonial self-government, totally divorced from the realities of the present day. The C.D. has got itself into a sort of mystic enchantment and sees visions of grateful, independent Utopias beaming at them from all round the world, as if there was – yet – any reason to suppose that any African can be cashier of a village council for three weeks without stealing the cash. It is uphill work, but we bludgeoned them pretty severely from both sides, although the West Africans, other than Milverton, are a silent lot. There is really no understanding whatever of contemporary realities in the C.O. – Creech blathered a good deal.'

60. CO 533/549/38232/15 (1946–47), 'European Settlement: Squatters', J.H. Martin's report, 'The Problem of the Squatter: Economic Survey of Resident Labour in Kenya', 24 February 1947.

61. N. Swainson, *The Development of Corporate Capitalism in Kenya*, pp. 173–82; and J.M. Lonsdale's unpublished paper, 'The Growth and Transformation of the Colonial State in Kenya', pp. 6–14.

62. F.D. Corfield, *The Origins and Growth of Mau Mau*, pp. 18 and 51.

63. RH Mss. Brit.Emp. s. 390, Box 3, File 4, Item 3, ff. 1–4, C.E.V. Buxton to Mitchell 15 August 1948; and Mss. Afr. s. 596, 'European Elected Members' Organisation', File 38 (A)/1, 'Mau Mau 1947–55', Executive Committee of the Electors' Union, 26 October 1946; and memorandum by Major C.E.V. Buxton on Kikuyu Associations,

February 1947, and Kendall Ward, 'The Rise of Mau Mau: European Warnings', 17 March 1953.
64. F.D. Corfield, *The Origins and Growth of Mau Mau*, p. 52.
65. N.S. Carey Jones, *The Anatomy of Uhuru*, p. 84.
66. See Chapters 4 and 6 *infra*.
67. CO 533/543/38086/5 (1945–47), 'Kikuyu Petitions', Mitchell to Gater, November 1946; CO 533/543/38086/38 (1948), 'Kikuyu Petitions: Kikuyu Central Association', Rankine to Creech Jones, 28 December 1948; CO 533/543/38086/38 (1949), 'Kikuyu Petitions: Kikuyu Central Association', Mitchell to Creech Jones, 28 February 1949; and CO 533/557/38672 (1947–48), 'Memorandum from Kenya African Union', Mitchell to Creech Jones, 11 February 1947.
68. P.E. Mitchell's published despatch, 'Agricultural Policy in African Areas' (1951); and CO 533/5/38678, 'African Soil Improvements, 1948–50'.
69. Interviews with Sir Michael Blundell, Noel Kennaway, Clive Salter and Mervyn Cowie, and N. Farson, *Last Chance in Africa*, p. 45.
70. Sir Michael Blundell and Mervyn Cowie. See also RH Mss. Afr. r. 101, Mitchell's diary for regular references to exhaustion and ill health. KNA CS 2/5/6, 'Speeches Miscellaneous by Governor, 1940–49'; CS 2/5/37, 'Addresses by Governor Mitchell, 1947–48'; and RH 4/346, 'Governor Mitchell's Speeches, 1948–52' show that Mitchell made most of his speeches to Europeans in Nairobi and rarely ventured into the African reserves. CS 2/5/7, 'Addresses by the Governor in Central Province, 1940–49' contains only one entry for the Mitchell era, when the governor visited Meru in May 1949. It should, however, be pointed out that Mitchell continued to go fishing in the trout streams of the Aberdares and Mount Kenya.
71. Interviews with Noel Kennaway and Desmond O'Hagan.
72. For a more sympathetic portrait see N. Farson, *Last Chance in Africa*, pp. 18–19, 28–35, 47–52, which Mitchell had persuaded him to write. RH Mss. Afr. r. 101, Mitchell's diary, 1 September 1947, contains Mitchell's account of a meeting to arrange Farson's trip to Kenya later that year.
73. RH Mss. Afr. s. 596, 'European Elected Members' Organisation' File 38(A)/1, Kendall Ward, 'Mau Mau, 1947–55'; Mss. Brit.Emp. s. 390, Box 3, File 4, Item 3, ff. 1–4, Buxton to Mitchell, 15 August 1948; and two memoranda about the Emergency by Buxton, ff. 32–9. See also (cont.) KNA DC/FH 1/30, 'Fort Hall Annual Report, 1951', pp. 1–2, 14; MAA 8/102 'Intelligence and Security: Press Cuttings, 1948–50'; MAA 8/106, 'Intelligence and Security: Mumenyereri, 1947–50'; MAA 8/109, 'Intelligence and Security: Daily Chronicle, 1947–49'; and MAA 8/68, 'Intelligence: Chief Waruhiu, 1948–1952' for a series of warnings from the Special Branch and settlers about the deteriorating position in the reserves and for militant African attacks on the colonial régime.

Four

The Problems of Kikuyu Agriculture

In the 1930s, the Kenyan government became concerned by reports of serious land degradation in the reserves. The agricultural department had begun closely to follow the anti-erosion measures which were being devised in the United States and South Africa. In 1938, for instance, Colin Maher, the head of the recently established soil conservation unit in the department, was sent to America to study their techniques and South African experts were asked to advise on the worst affected areas, Ukambani and Baringo.[1]

During the depression and even more so during the war, however, regardless of its effects on soil fertility, Africans were encouraged to maximise production to bolster the finances of the colonial state and to supply the troops. Norman Humphrey's report on South Nyeri in 1944 and the arrival of Mitchell, who considered himself an expert on African agriculture, marked another shift in the Nairobi official mind as the Secretariat became alarmed once again about the situation in the reserves, especially in Machakos, where there were serious food shortages between 1942 and 1944. Humphrey's alarmist report reinforced the administration's opposition to African individualism and strengthened its commitment to defending a mythical, egalitarian 'Merrie Africa' against the encroachment of cash-crop cultivators and small traders who supported the Kenya African Union. This was a futile strategy which not only attempted to reverse a process of increasing differentiation, dating back at least to the late nineteenth century, but also failed to recognise that the second colonial occupation was encouraging individualism and social differentiation. The administration and initially the agricultural department, however, after the war ignored these African realities and attempted to bolster communal authority by reviving the traditional power of the *Muhirig'a* elders among the Kikuyu, and by strengthening the *Njuri Ncheke* in Meru. These supposedly traditional institutions, it was planned, would supervise the post-war agricultural campaign in the reserves.[2]

The Problems of Kikuyu Agriculture
Official perceptions of crisis before 1945

In the late 1930s, several reports warned the Kenyan authorities that the African reserves faced a serious ecological crisis. The most obvious damage could be seen in Ukambani and Baringo, but the problem was not confined to the semi-arid pastoral reserves. The situation was even more serious in the densely-populated Kikuyu districts where once fertile land was being destroyed by constant cultivation and grazing following the abandonment, through population pressure, of shifting cultivation. Already the population density in the central zone between 4,500 and 6,000 feet was over 500 to the square mile.[3]

For five months every year, from March to May during the long rains, and again during the short rains in November and December, torrential downpours cascaded down the steep ridges and washed away the precious topsoil into the overflowing rivers. Streams and rivers became dark brown as the floods swept the soil downstream. The agricultural department warned that resolute action was immediately required to stem the loss or the Kikuyu reserves would soon be destitute. These reports convinced the Secretariat that the ecological crisis of the Kikuyu reserves was the most crucial issue facing the Kenyan government.

When the depression began to recede in the late 1930s, the government became increasingly concerned about land degradation in the pastoral reserves. Colin Maher prepared a series of reports on Baringo, Machakos and East and West Pokot, which emphasised the rapid growth of erosion and ecological collapse. In Machakos and the agricultural reserves, pasture land was being reduced, destroying the balance between arable and pastoral elements in the economy, as population growth and the demand for cash crops increased pressure on the commonage. But while arable land expanded at the expense of the pastoral commonage, the number of cattle using the commonage for grazing also expanded dramatically. This pressure on the various sectors of the rural economy exacerbated the ecological problems in the more arid reserves.[4] In 1929, the Hall Agricultural Commission had already recognised that erosion in Machakos was extremely serious. A decade later Maher and Barnes estimated that between 37 and 75 per cent of the land in Machakos needed to be closed to grazing and, in 1938, the South African agriculturalist, Professor I.B. Pole-Evans had reported that: 'The reserve as shown to me was a most distressing sight. It was a shambles . . . most of the topsoil had gone and the subsoil was rapidly following suit. Sheet erosion and gully erosion were eating the land away in almost every direction. The grass cover had almost entirely disappeared.'[5] Machakos attracted the most concern because of its large population. The spectre of a major famine in the pastoral reserves haunted the government in Nairobi, following the serious food shortages which had occurred in the pastoral reserves in the early 1930s.

The Problems of Kikuyu Agriculture

After the dislocation during the conquest and the First World War, the population of Kenya had grown rapidly after the early 1920s. By the late 1930s, the Kenyan government was convinced that the situation in Kikuyuland and in certain pastoral areas had reached crisis proportions. The first attempts to combat the problem were ill advised, beginning with the Machakos destocking campaign in 1938. Against the advice of the administration, compulsory culling was introduced and the stock was disposed of at the nearby Liebigs processing factory at Athi River. This merely united African opposition and undermined the reputation of the local administration and the Kamba chiefs. A few years earlier, in Baringo, the agricultural department's grass-planting scheme had proved equally ineffective because of lack of investment and supervision during the depression.[6]

These measures to prevent erosion, however, clashed with the government's need during the depression to encourage African production (regardless of the ecological effects on the reserves or on African communalism) to offset the declining fiscal returns from the settler sector. This process was carried further during the war. Kikuyu wattle and vegetable growers and Abaluhya maize cultivators prospered; the war was not a period of increasing African disillusionment with colonial rule, despite the grumblings about import shortages and discriminatory crop prices. Funds were available for the larger producers to acquire new land at the expense of the marginal lineages and poor peasants, who lacked the resources to increase commodity production.[7]

The quantitative evidence for increased African production is less clear than for the settlers. The district export figures are haphazard and African production fluctuated considerably with the weather. But official figures unduly exaggerate the variations. African cultivators did not attempt to compete with the settlers but restructured the local terms of trade to their own advantage by producing not for the settler-controlled marketing boards but for the black market where prices were far above those offered by the Maize Control. The Kikuyu, for example, during the droughts of 1942–45, switched their sales from official channels to the more remunerative black market in Ukambani. District Commissioners lamented that only a fraction of Kikuyu production appeared at the marketing boards' inspection centres. In Murang'a only 1,400 out of an estimated 30,000 surplus bags of maize were sold to the Government Control.[8]

Black market goods from South Nyeri followed three main routes: into Murang'a via Karatina and then into Ukambani; through the Aberdares forest to Nanyuki; and to Rumuruti and Thomson's Falls. These were pre-colonial trade routes. The black market was in fact organised on a similar basis to local inter-tribal trade in the late nineteenth century, which continued underground throughout the colonial era. The field administration had only come near to controlling this hidden trade network in the late 1920s, but with the depression it had once again become an extremely important adjunct to the maintenance of the peasant option against settler pressure. It allowed African accumulators to circumvent the restrictions imposed on them by their settler rivals and to consolidate their own position in the reserves. Even when the rains failed, as in May 1944, and Murang'a needed to import maize, large quantities were still exported at high prices to Machakos, while cheap imports were bought from Embu and Nyeri. As the District Commissioner observed: 'Viewed by the cold light of business morals the Kikuyu had brought off a notable and meritorious coup – he had sold in the highest and bought in the lowest market.'[9] When the movement of maize was banned in 1945, large quantities were transported by lorry at night to Ukambani. These shipments far outnumbered the mere 1,169 bags which were sold to the Maize Control for £4,000. In Kambu, supposedly a grain deficit area, the assistant agricultural officer complained in 1947 that 'the urban population are living entirely on Kiambu maize and buying but little of their rationed mixed meal and the farm labour forces augment their rations as they like. It is a traffic that is impossible to stop owing to our network of roads'.[10] Every day Kikuyu women carried their loads into the African locations of Nairobi where they fetched higher prices than if sold to the government. In August 1945, an estimated 700 to 1,000 bags of charcoal a day were transported into the capital. These exports were so remunerative that wattle in southern Kiambu was rarely permitted to reach maturity but was chopped down to sell as charcoal and firewood in Nairobi, Thika and Ruiru. Nairobi Africans depended on the black market for their supplies and, throughout the war, African traders thrived, accumulating funds to invest in new shops or lorries when these became available. The District Commissioner in Murang'a was convinced that greater changes had occurred in Kikuyuland during the war than ever before.[11]

The failure of the maize harvest in 1942, and the resulting famine in marginal Ukambani, focussed government attention once more on the agricultural problems of the reserves. The famine strengthened the opponents of African production and seemed to demonstrate the need to transform agricultural practices in the reserves. During the last two years of the war, new plans were devised for immediate application as soon as equipment and supervisors could be obtained. Meanwhile a few ameliorative measures were undertaken. During 1943–44, 23,000 acres were terraced in Central Province and 26,000 closed to grazing; but these were temporary palliatives. The agricultural department warned that more drastic action was required to prevent erosion. The 1944 Soil Conservation report, for example, warned that at the current rate of progress it would take 200 years to protect the province. Economic collapse was inevitable unless peasant incomes were increased and investment in agriculture facilitated. Land alienation, the demarcation of fixed Kikuyu reserves (in the 1920s) and population growth, had all destroyed the traditional system of shifting cultivation. Now the Kikuyu were unable to abandon their exhausted plots for virgin land; pressure on *shambas* was increasing; fallows were shorter and in the more heavily-populated areas were virtually nonexistent. Even when yields dropped because the soils were exhausted, the old plots were not abandoned; instead new areas on steep hillsides were opened for cultivation to fill the deficiencies created by the declining fertility of the main *shambas*. These slopes in the bracken zone were particularly susceptible to erosion. The problem was compounded by the fact that the land had to provide school fees, clothing and government taxes in the changing world of rural Africa.[12]

Medical evidence showed that Kikuyu health was deteriorating as the intake of animal protein declined. During the war, 90 per cent of recruits for the army had had to be rejected because they were suffering from malnutrition. The army's medical advisor, Dr T.F. Anderson, considered that much less milk and meat were being consumed than in 1900 and the calcium-rich traditional crops, *wimbe* and *njahi*, had become scarce and expensive. He reported, 'the loss of *wimbe* is a grave misfortune. It could have been offset only by the introduction of milk into the diet, but that has not occurred . . . As a result calcium deficiency is a fact'. The administration blamed the spread of individualism at the expense of communal values for the abandonment of these traditional crops for more easily cultivated and remunerative crops like maize and wattle, which were now the main sources of income for most Kikuyu families.[13]

Both maize and wattle had been introduced 20 years earlier by the colonial authorities and had been eagerly adopted because they were easy to grow.[14] But after 1945 the agriculturalists denounced them for exhausting the nitrogen content of the soils. Maize, it was belatedly discovered, was an unsuitable crop for most of Central Province, where uncertain rainfall guaranteed a good harvest in only one year in three. The agricultural department, therefore, attempted to restrict cultivation to the long rains, especially in Machakos and Kitui where the rainfall averaged less than 30 inches per annum, and strenuous efforts were made to popularise the traditional Kikuyu food crop, *wimbe*, whose once dominant place in African diets had been usurped by maize.[15] Yet, despite these endeavours, maize remained the staple food crop during both harvests and provided considerable income in Kikuyuland from black market sales to Ukambani. Although the rainfall in Machakos was unsuitable for maize, successive harvest failures merely ensured that even greater acreages were planted in a desperate attempt to ensure that at least some food would be harvested.[16] This desire for edible crops with a secure market value for the surplus had also resulted in the French bean replacing cow peas and *njahi* and English potatoes being grown instead of the more resilient sweet potato. The agricultural department bemoaned that 'once again an exportable crop has advanced at the expense of an older one, grown solely for food'. Despite attempts by the Local Native Councils to enforce compulsory planting of famine reserve crops such as cassava and yams, the acreages declined.[17]

The field administration blamed the emerging commercial cultivators and small traders rather than population growth and the collapse of shifting cultivation for the ecological crisis. Greed, it was suggested, and the spread of selfish individualism at the expense of the communal solidarities of pre-colonial Africa had undermined the harmonious balance between Africans and their land. Only by restoring the authority of the indigenous land authorities could the land-miners be checked and the people's long-term interests in the soil be protected.[18]

Sir Philip Mitchell shared this distaste for the proto-capitalists in the reserves, whom he denounced as exploiters of ordinary Africans. He too sought to restore 'the organic balances' of African society, although he recognised that there was an urgent need to transform agricultural practices. Shortly after his arrival, Mitchell had gone on a tour of Ukambani and had returned deeply perturbed. The eroded hillsides, failed crops and malnutrition had so disturbed the governor that he had proposed an agricultural 'D Day'. He informed Oliver Stanley, the Secretary of State, that Kenya faced serious problems because of the declining fertility of the land after continuous cultivation. The colony was 'heading for a really shocking disaster. Unless we get onto the job in a really large scale [way] with a determination and consistency, in ten years time there will be a million landless people'.[19] The governor castigated his predecessors for their failure to devise a coherent agricultural policy. Action seemed to have been left to the idiosyncracies of individual District Commissioners without any continuity or co-ordination. He complained, 'I can't think how they can have existed all these years without having thought out their land administration at all, and without any attempt at getting the Administration and the Departments to shoot at the same target.'[20] This was symptomatic of Mitchell's alarmist strategy to convince Whitehall that he was energetically tackling Kenya's problems. During this first year, he bombarded the Colonial Office with a barrage of proposals, warning that Kenya's stability could only be assured by resolute action to solve the problems created by peasant cultivation. He was confident that, as an expert on peasant agriculture, he could transform the situation.[21]

The Problems of Kikuyu Agriculture
Norman Humphrey's proposals

The most influential agriculturalist in Kenya during the first years after the war was Norman Humphrey. His writings, which were typical of the gloomy pessimists, exerted a profound influence on the government. During 1944, Humphrey and Hughes Rice had studied South Nyeri in the north of Kikuyuland. They discovered that since the last detailed agricultural survey by Fazan in 1931, the population density had increased from 463 to 542 per square mile; average smallholdings had fallen from 8.09 to 6.71 acres; and Humphrey predicted that they would decline to 5.22 acres by 1955, when only half the land would be under crops. Mathira Division, the most densely-populated part of the district, already only just managed to grow enough maize to feed its population and there was no surplus for export. The area was seriously overstocked because grazing land was being used for cultivation. There would have been a serious food shortage but for the money earned from selling crops to the dried-vegetable factory at Karatina, and for the remittances from *askari* and migrant workers in Nairobi and the White Highlands, which amounted to £250,000 a year. If these conditions spread, the government would face social collapse in Kikuyuland.[22]

Humphrey's report reflected contemporary thinking about the low carrying capacity of Africa's soils. Investigations by agriculturalists in Northern Rhodesia, based on careful analyses of soil types and vegetation, had instilled this belief into agriculturalists throughout British Africa. Humphrey adopted their excessively strict criteria for assessing carrying capacity and consequently underestimated how many people could stay in Nyeri without exacerbating land degradation.[23]

He wanted to ensure that Africans enjoyed an adequate diet and a household income of not less than £20 per annum, compared to a mere 60 shillings. Humphrey calculated that this target income could only be generated on holdings over twelve acres, more than double the size of most existing *shambas*.[24] After 1948, Leslie Brown proved that household incomes could be raised to £100 per annum on smallholdings of between seven and ten acres by growing high-priced cash crops such as coffee and tea. Unfortunately, until peasant opposition became evident in 1947, the agricultural campaign was based on Humphrey's reports, which had failed to appreciate that the only way to tackle rural immiseration was to challenge the settlers' monopoly on the cultivation of the most remunerative crops. The Swynnerton Plan in the 1950s showed that Brown's scheme offered the only chance to restructure peasant agriculture without provoking serious opposition. Humphrey, however, accepted that only European farmers should grow tea and coffee and accepted the differentiated price structure for African-grown cereals. Thus, instead of encouraging the government to continue with its peasant production strategy of the 1930s, which had promoted commercial cultivation in the reserves, Humphrey proposed that many Africans should be moved to new settlement areas, which the government had neither the time, the land, the money, nor the manpower to develop. Nyeri, he argued, was incapable of providing a subsistence standard of living for its present population. According to his calculation, one in two families would have to move because the land could only accommodate 15,360 families compared to the existing 29,271. A mass exodus was required to rest the land and to restore soil fertility in order to avert social collapse.[25]

Humphrey's temporary solution to Nyeri's problems was to undertake a massive reafforestation programme – planting over 350,000 acres. This was to provide employment for those whose *shambas* were being left to regenerate for three years. A search was also to be conducted to find suitable settlement sites. Attention was, therefore, diverted from persuading the peasantry to adopt new agricultural methods and drought-resistant crops. The government hoped that some magical panacea would be discovered for the problems of erosion and African discontent. The Tana and Juba Valleys, Trans Mara and Makueni were all carefully investigated as suitable resettlement areas, but only Makueni was deemed appropriate, although several smaller schemes were also approved. The alternative strategy of attempting to educate the population to follow approved techniques of 'sound' land use was dismissed as too slow, since it was considered that immediate action was essential. Consequently the palliative anti-erosion measures were introduced without the understanding or support of the peasantry. This was a fatal error.[26]

The settlements proved equally unsuccessful; even the largest at Makueni had absorbed only 664 families, at a cost of £18,340, by the end of 1952. This was only a small fraction of the people who supposedly had to be moved from Machakos. It had also quickly become apparent that African peasants with limited capital were incapable of developing the semi-arid lands on which all the new settlements were situated. In Makueni, for example, each family needed 120 acres compared with the five-acre plots they had cultivated in their former locations. It would, therefore, have required 1,680,000 acres (2,625 square miles) – the equivalent of 30 per cent of the alienated White Highlands – to accommodate the surplus families from South Nyeri on similar marginal land in Laikipia. The best farming land in Kenya was already occupied; Kikuyuland and Nyanza were densely-populated African reserves; the only uninhabited areas had irregular rainfall and were totally unsuited to intensive peasant cultivation. All the potential resettlement sites were in areas with an average rainfall of less than 20 inches per annum and needed extensive irrigation. Their soils were unsuitable, with low organic matter, slightly acid in reaction and low in bases and phosphates. The natural vegetation was a thorn and scrub grassland with much bare soil exposed for sheet and gully erosion. The optimistic expectation that thousands of African families could be resettled outside the reserves or the White Highlands was a complete fallacy. Even where suitable land was available, such as in the Shimba Hills near the coast, the overcrowded peasant cultivators of nearby Teita obstinately refused to leave their homes.[27]

Humphrey's alarmist reports, however, had reinforced the widely-held view that erosion had reached crisis proportions. He had warned that 'unless radical reforms are introduced, the land and the people of South Nyeri face disaster within the next decade'. Immediate action was needed to ensure that new systems of land tenure and cutivation were adopted. Even compulsion, he acknowledged, might have to be used as a last resort, although he recognised that 'used by itself, its lessons will be grudgingly learnt, and it must lead to still more compulsion over an ever-widening field, until by sheer excess it breaks down in utter failure'.[28] Humphrey himself had perceived that if the agricultural campaign was to succeed, then the people must understand what the government was doing and why. But at the same time he emphasised that immediate action was required and had conceded that force might have to be used. Thus was the seed of disaster planted.

The paternalist administration decided that the most effective way to gain popular support was to work through the traditional African land authorities – the *Muhirig'a* elders in Kikuyuland, the *Liguru* among the Abaluhya, the *Utui* in Kamba and the *Njuri Ncheke* in Meru. Osborne, the enterprising District Commissioner in Murang'a during the last years of the war, had dramatically increased terracing and anti-erosion work by using the local *Muhirig'a*. During the first six months of 1945, only 377 miles of narrow-based terraces had been constructed, but with the help of the *Muhirig'a* this increased to 3,051 miles during the second half of the year. The administration considered that this remarkable change of attitude towards soil conservation had been achieved by reviving the precolonial land authorities, which had been suppressed but not destroyed by 50 years of British rule. The successes of Murang'a, it was believed, proved that the traditional elders still exerted considerable influence, despite the supposed growth of unrestrained individualism among the Kikuyu.[29]

Humphrey proposed giving full recognition to these indigenous authorities so that support could be mobilised for the terracing and agricultural betterment campaign. This plan was considered by H.E. Lambert, the government's advisor on African land tenure, and Percy Wyn Harris, who was then Provincial Commissioner for Central Province and was therefore responsible for Kikuyuland and Ukambani. Their 'Memorandum on Policy in Regard to Land Tenure in the Native

Lands of Kenya' largely accepted Humphrey's assessment of the problems facing the reserves and endorsed his fear of individualism and increasing differentiation.[30] They also agreed that the traditional communal controls over the land should be strengthened as the basis for post-war development. Wyn Harris and Lambert explained that the advantage of the 'untouched native system' was that it preserved a stable equilibrium between the interests of the community and the rights of the individual. British rule, they declared, had disturbed this balance, weighting the scales in favour of individualism which had helped destroy the traditional controls. These, they feared, would soon be completely destroyed and it would then be impossible to use indigenous institutions to protect the land. Wyn Harris and Lambert therefore recommended that every effort should be made to preserve 'the spiritual conception of community'. Chiefs and the Local Native Councils were no real substitute for accepted African authorities because they were foreign impositions and did not command popular respect. By relying upon such arms of government, the possibilities of mobilising popular support, which were still provided by the traditional authorities, might be irredeemably lost.

The prejudices of the field administration and the Secretariat against the African 'proto-capitalists' blinded them to the fact that the indigenous land authorities' remaining power would vanish as soon as they became associated with the government's terracing campaign; they would soon become identified as merely another government-controlled institution like the supposedly traditional Tribunal Elders. The administration failed to recognise that anyone who supported the second colonial occupation and greater interference in African society would lose African support. It also failed to understand that the *Muhirig'a* elders were as much involved in the race for more land and struggle for economic resources as the rest of the Kikuyu people. They were not neutral observers of the development of capitalist relations of production, committed to the preservation of an egalitarian Kikuyu communalism, but active participants in the growth of individualism, which the administration so condemned.[31]

The official mind and the myth of 'merrie Africa'

These recommendations, of course, strongly appealed to Mitchell, the indirect ruler, striking deep chords in his experience. In Tanganyika in the 1920s, he had been instrumental in uncovering and reviving Native Authorities, which were to provide the new framework for British rule. The proposals of the Kenya Secretariat also accorded with the thinking of the Colonial Office's advisory committe on African land tenure. Its chairman, the arch-mandarin Lord Hailey, a former governor of the Punjab and of the United Provinces who, after his retirement from the Indian Civil Service had become an expert on African administration and land tenure, also considered that the essential problem was 'how to ensure that the community retains the power to guard against the harmful consequences of the growth of individual rights in land, while at the same time not impeding the development of such rights, under proper control by the community, to the extent that they are an essential concomitant of economic or social progress'.[32] Consequently, requests from 'progressive' African farmers for loans were refused. Both the Kenyan government and the Colonial Office were convinced that any concession to the mounting pressure for individual rights would be against the communal interest and would be bound to end in the disaster of peasant indebtedness as in India.[33]

In his secret war-time study, *Native Administration and Political Development in British Tropical Africa*, Lord Hailey had warned that certain developments could already be discerned in 'native' land ownership which would create a serious problem for governments throughout the continent. He observed that quite apart from the question of land alienation to Europeans which had aroused opposition in Kenya and Northern Rhodesia, there were:

. . . problems of another character connected with the land, which, though they have not yet been a source of friction, remain as a potential cause of trouble for the future. They are those which relate to the legal definition of title in the lands occupied by natives and of the tenures under which they are held. The treatment of these questions will demand decisions of general policy affecting most of the African dependencies. If individual land rights are allowed to grow up in a form which involves a system under which the relations of landlord and tenant are regulated only by market competition, we may have to face all the social and political evils consequent on the existence of large bodies of rackrented tenants. If, again, no legal restraint is placed on the use of the land as a basis of credit, the African Colonies may in time see the growth of widespread agricultural indebtedness, such as now constitutes so grave a menace in many of our Eastern dependencies.

No one can fail to regret that the British administration did not at an earlier date foresee the necessity for providing against the development of these conditions in rural India. Their existence has not only been inimical to agricultural progress, but has proved a potent source of social division and one of the main causes of political unrest. Those provisions could have been made with relative ease at an early period of our administration, before rights based on European conceptions of law and novel to Indian practice, had assumed the character of vested interests. But to-day it is estimated that no less than twenty-five million persons classified as agricultural workers are landless, and agricultural indebtedness is estimated to amount to £675,000,000.[34]

Thus the lessons of India weighed heavily on the official mind, not only in Whitehall but throughout Africa. For the best of reasons the field administration throughout British Africa had imbibed the orthodoxies of contemporary anthropology with the ideology of indirect rule and had adopted its commitment to the preservation of what were believed to be traditional African communal values. Under the influence of Malinowski and Evans-Pritchard and the British anthropological tradition of structural-functionalism, during the 1930s and 1940s the Kenyan administration saw itself as the defender of the egalitarian values of pre-colonial 'Merrie Africa'. This myth was to prove very difficult to destroy. Thus, as government intervention in African societies penetrated to greater depths and became increasingly demanding during the second colonial occupation after the war, the provincial administration earnestly believed that the campaign was a final attempt to prevent the collapse of African communalism and the disintegration of the traditional ordering of rural society.[35]

Both the Secretariat and the provincial administration were trapped within this stereotype of African life. African towns were regarded as an anomaly, dangerously disruptive of the hierarchy of communal Africa. So entrenched was this belief that urban Africans were categorised as 'detribalised'; selfish individuals who had abandoned the communalism of rural life. The peripheral official mind, especially the field administration, was resolutely opposed to the idea that urban expansion might provide the best way to ease the population burden on the reserves.[36]

There were also certain practical difficulties as well as ideological prejudices. The administration's control over the African locations of Nairobi was weak, partly because responsibility was shared with the settler-controlled Municipal Council.[37] In addition, Nairobi's African population was already expanding faster than the government could supply new accommodation or employment. When the first official census was taken in 1948, it was discovered that the population had increased nearly eightfold in the previous 25 years. Moreover, this rapid urban expansion had not noticeably eased the problems of rural overcrowding in the reserves. The southern locations of Kiambu, around Dagoretti, had indeed become suburbs of the capital. While Nairobi's workforce remained unskilled, wages were too low for them to bring their families to live in the capital. Wives and children were, therefore, left in the reserves to cultivate as best they could their small *shambas* without the advantages of male labour. Margaret Hay and Mike Cowen have shown that in Kowe in Central Nyanza and in South Nyeri, the families of migrant labourers had fallen behind in the rural scramble for more land and new resources, and had been forced to sell land and to seek work on the plots of their more prosperous neighbours. As rural differentiation increased, it was usually the families of low-paid migrant workers who formed the emerging 'class' of poor peasants with less than three acres of land. Nairobi and the smaller towns did not provide any panacea for the problems of the reserves while urban wages remained at subsistence levels.[38]

However, the Kenyan government's plans to transform African agriculture and to inculcate improved farming techniques in order to raise peasant standards of living were also flawed because the administration's commitment to change African society was halfhearted. Agricultural reform required a traumatic transition. To have ensured its success, the administration would have had to abandon its alliance with the chiefs and forge a new arrangement with the emerging 'class' of rich peasants and traders, who resented the privileged position the chiefs and their supporters enjoyed with preferential access to the resources of the Local Native Councils and government patronage. In the past, the more radical of these 'outsiders' had supported the now banned Kikuyu Central Association. Indeed, by the act of opposing the chiefs, they had identified themselves to the administration as untrustworthy 'agitators'.[39] Most District Commissioners, particularly in Kikuyuland where the divisions between the chiefs and the politicians had been acute since the days of Thuku's Young Kikuyu Association in the early 1920s, found it impossible to reconcile themselves to Whitehall's plans to incorporate the more moderate political 'outsiders'. Aspiring businessmen, like Andrew Ng'ang'a and James Beauttah in Murang'a, were often prominent leaders of the local Kikuyu Central Association and, therefore, stood condemned by their past indiscretions and could not be supported in preference to loyal chiefs who had performed such stalwart service.[40] Indeed, the administration was convinced that such men and their supporters, who were constantly pestering the district headquarters for new licences or seeking new business opportunities, were the people who were responsible for the increasing differentiation in the reserves, which was undermining Africa's egalitarian communalism. Young men, it was lamented, no longer showed respect for the elders, chiefs, or indeed the government.[41]

Only romantically inclined Englishmen, escaping from the pressures of life in industrial Britain, could have failed to realise that this idealised image of African communalism was a delusion and have attempted to foist upon the Kikuyu a system of land law that bore little resemblance to their traditions.[42] All levels of the peripheral official mind – District Commissioners, the Secretariat, even initially, the agricultural department – failed to perceive that the peasantry in Central Province had always been intensely independent, jealous of its neighbours and mindful of the chance to prosper at their expense. In particular, the administration failed to recognise that the second colonial occupation primarily benefited those who were closely associated with the colonial power structure, the chiefs and their supporters; while the 'outsiders' became increasingly frustrated at their exclusion. The prejudices of the field administration became more explicit when it had more resources with which to reward the collaborators than during the inter-war era.

Petty traders and commercial cultivators were denounced as disruptive 'agitators', insidiously undermining the fabric of peasant life. Thus, the supporters of the banned Kikuyu Central Association and the more cautious Kenya African Union were further alienated. The administration and the agricultural department also failed to recognise that their reliance on the chiefs and the Mihiriga elders to mobilise communal labour for the agricultural betterment campaign was antagonising the peasantry. There was a contradiction in government policy. Although the administration wanted to strengthen communalism, the second colonial occupation was also designed to transform African agriculture, the basis of rural life. As we have seen, Humphrey even wanted to remove thousands of people from the reserves. Such social engineering inevitably had a profound effect on ordinary Africans and seriously disrupted their lives.[43]

The chiefs and elders seized the new resources, which the government provided after the war, to enhance their own economic power. Increased funds became available; remunerative cash crops were supplied for them to grow and technical staff provided to advise on how to make the most of these new opportunities. Despite the administration's intentions, therefore, the second colonial occupation increased the disparities between the favoured few and the African masses. Whatever the government may have believed it was doing, the chiefs were active participants in the contest for resources in the reserves. During the 1930s, they had effectively discredited the Kikuyu Central Association and monopolised the political weapon of controlled access to the district administration to serve their own interests. After the war, they attempted to destroy the new challenge to their authority posed by the Kenya African Union and to undermine the economic independence of their rivals, the traders and commercial farmers, who supported the new movement. This attempt to intimidate the opposition backfired as the exactions of the second colonial occupation drove the peasantry into the arms of the political activists.[44] The field administration, however, remained oblivious of this conflict. The chiefs had only too successfully mesmerised it into believing that the aspiring 'men in trousers' were undermining the stability of the colonial state, when, in fact, most of them in the first years after the war desired to be co-opted. As events were to prove, the chiefs' monopolising of access to government patronage was a much greater threat to peace in the reserves. Nevertheless, until 1947 and the emergence of widespread opposition to terracing and the authority of the chiefs, the administration had pressed ahead with its communalist strategy, blind to the realities of Kikuyu society.[45]

As a result, the Kenyan government failed to consider other possible approaches. Harold Macmillan had proposed, in 1942, that Soviet-style collective farms should be established in the White Highlands, onto which

76

the 'surplus' population from the over-crowded reserves could be moved.[46] The provincial agricultural staff in Nyanza were also experimenting with the establishment of group farms from contiguous smallholdings, which were to be operated on a communal basis. This scheme, of course, fitted more closely than Macmillan's with the field administration's commitment to the preservation of African communalism and was thoroughly investigated. In marked contrast, any suggestions for harnessing African individualism, as the Kenya African Union demanded, such as introducing government loans for 'progressive' farmers, were dismissed with great hostility. In theory, the government remained totally opposed to the creation of a 'class' of rich peasants who could absorb the growing number of landless Africans as wage labourers.[47]

This opposition to peasant entrepreneurs was a decisive break with the government's strategy during the 1930s, when the agricultural department had encouraged African production in the face of a contracting settler economy. Then, small cultivators had not been regarded as a protected species and the extension services had actively encouraged large African cash-crop growers, whom they had hoped would subsidise the failing settlers, to emerge as a 'class' of proto-capitalists.[48] But after the war, these same large-scale African wattle and maize growers were attacked by their rivals for government patronage – the settlers and the chiefs – who convinced the field administration and the Secretariat that the proto-capitalists were merely irresponsible land-miners, destroying the fertility of the reserves, while exploiting their fellow Africans.[49] The administration therefore became committed to reviving the traditional land authorities. They were to supervise the use of *ngwatio* (communal) labour on terracing and other anti-erosion projects, which were designed to encourage improved farming while preserving the holdings of small-scale peasant cultivators. The problem with this approach was that the Kikuyu reserves were not static or changeless, but had undergone dramatic changes which had undermined the position of women in the household division of labour and had increased social differentiation. The clock could not be put back.[50]

African realities

Let us briefly investigate what had happend in Kikuyuland. Lineage ties had grown weaker and *mbari* had begun to question the rights of *ahoi* and their descendants to cultivate. It was argued that only members of the senior lineage, directly descended from the *githaka*'s founder, were entitled to occupy the land. During the first 50 years of British rule, Kikuyu attitudes to land had been transformed. With British examples of outright ownership before them, the status of the *ahoi*, who had traditionally had rights to the usufruct of the land, diminished while that of the *muramati* and the direct heirs of the *githaka* founder was strengthened. This process had been carried furthest in Kiambu. This district, immediately to the north of Nairobi, had attracted immigrants from Murang'a and Nyeri, who used it as a suburb for commuting to the capital. It was also the Kikuyu district in which the greatest proportion of land had been alienated for European settlement. The example, therefore, of British notions of individual ownership had been extremely strong. Another reason for the growth of individual land claims in Kiambu stemmed from the history of pre-colonial Kikuyu expansion into the area. This had created a distinctive attitude towards the control and cultivation of land among the southern Kikuyu, which had predisposed them to adopt British land law with its notion of individual ownership. Thus, by 1945, Kikuyu attitudes to land use were far removed from the field administration's belief in African communalism.[51]

In 1933, in their evidence to the Kenya Land Commission, the Kikuyu delegates from Kiambu claimed to have traditionally followed a system of individual land ownership. They claimed they had bought their land from the Ndorobo hunter–gatherers, who had lived in the forests into which the Kikuyu penetrated as they had moved south during the nineteenth century.[52] This was, perhaps, to overstate their case, but it was a more accurate view of Kiambu traditional land law than the field administration's obsession with egalitarian communalism. Since the colonial conquest there had gradually emerged new, more strictly-defined categories of land ownership and differentiation between the rights of *githaka* holders, who had developed an individualist conception of ownership, and the *ahoi* and *ndungata*, who had sunk to the status of mere tenants – a position entirely alien to pre-colonial Kikuyu land law.[53] In his discussion of the settlement of Kiambu by the southern Kikuyu in the last third of the nineteenth century and their relations with the original Ndorobo occupants of the land, Kitching has perceptively observed that:

. . . any attempt by the historian to determine whether the original transfers were 'really' a form of rent or a form of land purchase is based on a false premise. For in the pre-colonial situation, conditions were such that the people involved had no need of such concepts because the distinction they embodied was otiose. Land was abundant. People to work it and to defend the people and livestock upon it were scarce. Hence in the 'typical' situation there was no reason for second comers to suppose that they would be asked to leave and no incentive for first comers of pioneers to make such a request. The land which they all occupied was available to be put to the limited range of uses then open. This substantive situation would have been all that mattered to them. It only became necessary to distinguish between land 'owned' and land 'rented' when land became a commodity as a result of relative scarcity, and this itself came about through a change of land use . . .

and through the increasing commoditisation of agricultural production.[54]

Increasing social differentiation had already, therefore, been accepted by the Kikuyu and was reflected in the transformation of their traditional land law and the emergence of a concept of individual ownership.

Since the beginning of the century the elders of the *mbari*, led by the *athamaki*, had asserted control over the distribution of land. In these new conditions the sons of junior wives and the descendants of *ahoi* and *ndungata* felt increasingly insecure. Land their fathers had regarded as their own was taken away as the rewards of commodity production became evident. Wattle was an ideal crop for the aspiring Kikuyu entrepreneur since, once planted it required little cultivation and possessed a variety of uses. The leather industry wanted the tannin, or it could be sold for charcoal, or as wood for building. Members of *mbari*, therefore, who did not belong to the senior lineages were dispossessed and replaced by wattle plantations. When they protested to the Native Tribunals, they discovered that these were packed with the chiefs' and other prominent government supporters' friends. Thus the reputation of the courts deteriorated until by the late 1940s they had been totally discredited and were regarded as tools of the local élite.[55]

The field administration refused to co-opt this emerging group into a restructured patronage network and chose to depend upon its old allies, the chiefs and their clients. The settlers also encouraged the growing antagonism of the district officials to these African accumulators. Chiefs, settlers and the district administration all realised that the proto-capitalists of the Kenya African Union posed a serious challenge to their authority. Thus the requests of the African commercial farmers and traders, who were not supporters of the chiefs, for a greater share of government patronage were rejected. Kenya's post-war agricultural campaign was based upon the futile attempt to revive the traditional land authorities as a medium for government intervention. Instead of attempting to use the growth of individualism and the development of capitalist relations to promote new agricultural techniques and to engender support for the government-sponsored campaigns to prevent erosion, the administration vainly attempted to resist them by appeals to a mythical communal past.[56]

From 1945 until 1947 the policy seemed to have worked in Murang'a, where Osborne had first encouraged the *Muhirig'a* to organise terracing. The *ngwatio* communal-labour system was expanded dramatically during 1946 and constructed an astounding 7,086 miles of narrow-base terraces, protecting more than 24,000 acres. During the first six months of 1947, Murang'a produced 43 per cent of the total number of terraces completed in Central Province. Between July 1945 and July 1947, under

The Problems of Kikuyu Agriculture

Table 4.1: *Narrow-based Terraces Constructed in Central Province 1944 to 1947[57]*

	July–Dec 1944	Jan–June 1945	July–Dec 1945	Jan–June 1946	July–Dec 1946	Jan–June 1947	July–Dec 1947
Meru:							
Miles	212	95	503	130	208	20	306
Acres	2,650	n.a.	n.a.	550	2,095	n.a.	2,290
Embu:							
Miles	426	n.a.	802	978	555	663	827
Acres	5,321	4,344	3,362	5,514	1,975	2,596	4,565
Nyeri:							
Miles	200	184	453	100	554	888	977
Acres	2,493	n.a.	n.a.	692	1,385	2,220	3,420
Murang'a:							
Miles	42	377	3,051	3,448	3,620	2,611	918
Acres	527	n.a.	11,700	11,467	12,711	9,137	3,107
Kiambu:							
Miles	882	554	888	1,000	831	1,012	1,555
Acres	11,025	n.a.	n.a.	3,520	2,907	3,591	5,443
Machakos:							
Miles	228	220	367	567	939	762	1,233
Acres	2,800	n.a.	n.a.	2,851	4,885	3,835	6,222
Kitui:							
Miles	n.a.	25	768	97	104	125	246
Acres	n.a.	n.a.	n.a.	354	523	625	1,228

the direction of the District Commissioner, Desmond O'Hagan, and T. Hughes Rice, the local agricultural officer, Murang'a built more terraces than South Nyeri, Meru, Machakos and Kitui Districts combined.[58] Table 4.1 shows the total number of miles of terracing dug and the acreages protected from erosion in Central Province during the half-yearly periods from July 1944 to December 1947.

In contrast with several districts, Osborne and O'Hagan in Murang'a had collaborated closely with the technical departments and the local chiefs. A district team was established to organise the campaign. This consisted not only of the local administration but also of the representatives of the various technical departments, such as the local agricultural, veterinary and education officers, as well as several chiefs, African councillors and some nearby settler coffee farmers. Murang'a's successes had been helped by the fact that Hughes Rice, the local agricultural officer, had helped Humphrey prepare his report on conditions in South Nyeri in 1944 and had been instrumental in devising the new policy of using *ngwatio* labour and reviving the *Muhirig'a*. He energetically directed the agricultural aspects of the campaign, while

O'Hagan, who became the District Commissioner in 1945, ensured that the chiefs actively enforced the new soil conservation rules and kept a close watch on their location's progress at terracing. This close collaboration ensured that Murang'a did not suffer from the disputes over policy which disrupted progress in Machakos and Embu, where the local agricultural officers were dubious of the new approach.[59]

These successes simply confirmed the Secretariat in the belief that the *Mihiriga* elders were the best people to prevent land degradation in Kikuyuland. The strategy of 'indirect rule' seemed to have fulfilled their expectations. Creech Jones was greatly impressed by the progress that had been achieved in Murang'a when he toured the area in August 1946 and asked Hughes Rice to prepare a memorandum for him, outlining how this dramatic growth of 'popular' support for conservation had been achieved. Neither Creech Jones, nor the agriculturalists sent by Whitehall to investigate conditions in Kenya, had realised, any more than the Kenyan Secretariat or field administration, that they were sitting on a volcano of pent-up rural frustration and discontent. The figures of terraces dug, live wash-stop planted and acreages protected, blinded them to the realities of peasant opposition to the compulsory labour required for the agricultural campaign.[60]

Although the betterment programme was supposed to persuade the peasantry to adopt new crop rotations, more suitable for areas with uncertain rainfall and to build compost pits and cattle sheds, it appeared to many Kikuyu cultivators that the new agricultural strategy consisted of little more than compulsory terracing two mornings every week. Most people continued to plant maize rather than millet or cassava, which required a much higher input of labour and more land – both scarce resources among the overcrowded Kikuyu. For most people in 1947, the agricultural campaign had not produced any positive returns, such as high-value cash crops, which might have encouraged them to persevere with terracing. Disillusionment was spreading and centres of opposition were emerging in what the administration considered to be its most successful district – Murang'a.[61]

Notes

1. John Saul and Roger Woods, 'African Peasantries', pp. 103–13, have provided a useful working definition, which can be applied to the Kikuyu: 'Peasants are those whose ultimate security and subsistence lies in their having certain rights in land and in the labour of family members on the land, but who are involved, through rights and obligations, in a wider economic system which includes the participation of non-peasants'. See the recent special issue 'Kenya: the Agrarian Question', of the *Review of African Political Economy*, no. 20, January–April 1981, for the current debate between

Michael Cowen and Apollo Njonjo, and their supporters; and E.R. Wolf, *Peasants*, (Englewood Cliffs, New Jersey, 1966), for an interesting introduction to the question by a social anthropologist. For details of the ecological crisis in Baringo, Ukambani and Pokot see J.F. Munro, *Colonial Rule and the Kamba* pp. 189–246; D.M. Anderson's unpublished thesis, 'Herder, Settler and Colonial Rule pp. 217–60; KNA MAA 7/604, 'Surveys: Dr. Stanner: The Kitui Kamba, 1943–50'; and C. Maher's unpublished report, 'Soil Erosion and Land Utilisation in the Kamasia'.

2. DC/NYI 2/1/20, 'Mr Humphrey's Report on South Nyeri, 1944–47', C. Tomkinson to Information Officer, 3 July 1945; CO 852/662/19936/2 (1945–46, 'Soil Erosion: Kenya', H.E. Lambert and P. Wyn Harris's memorandum on 'Policy in Regard to Land Tenure in the Native Lands of Kenya'; and CO 852/557/16707/2 (1946), 'Land Tenure Policy: Kenya', especially the report of the Soil Conservation Committee to DC Central Kavirondo, 18 August 1945; and H.E. Lambert, 'Policy in Regard to the Administration of the Native Lands – Note for Discussion', 10 July 1946.

3. For details of population densities in Murang'a see DC/FH 5/1 (Dep 1) 'District Team Fort Hall, 1949–52'. See also DC/FH 1/27, 'Fort Hall Annual Report, 1948; Appendix D, to compare population estimates based on poll and hut tax returns and the actual returns of the first African census in 1948. A survey of locations 4, 5, 8, 11, 13 and 15 in Murang'a revealed that average-sized holdings varied with altitude: under 4,000 feet they were 13.5 acres; 4–5,000 feet – 10.4 acres; 5,000–5,500 feet – only 4.3 acres; 5,500–6,000 feet – 4.0 acres; 6,000–6,500 feet – 4.9 acres; and over 6,500 feet – 7.6 acres.

4. J.F. Munro, *Colonial Rule and the Kamba*, pp. 189–223; and D.M. Anderson's thesis, 'Herder, Settler and Colonial Rule', pp. 141–63.

5. DC/MKS 10A/29/1, Barnes's Memorandum on Soil Erosion, p. 6; C. Maher, 'Soil Erosion and Land Utilisation in the Ukamba Reserve', p. 16; and I.B. Pole-Evans, 'Report of a Visit to Kenya', p. 4.

6. J.F. Munro, *Colonial Rule and the Kamba*, pp. 225–46; R.L. Tignor, *The Colonial Transformation of Kenya* pp. 331–54; and J.R. Newman's *The Ukamba Members Association*, pp. 7–18; and KNA GH/505, 'Soil Erosion: Destocking, Liebigs, 1938–50'.

7. G. Kitching, *Class and Economic Change in Kenya*, pp. 108–30.

8. KNA DC/FH 1/23, 'Fort Hall Annual Report, 1944', pp. 6–7; DC/FH 1/29, 'Fort Hall Annual Report, 1950', p. 10. Andrew Ng'ang'a, first chairman of the district's Kenya African Union branch, led the opposition to the monopoly of the government marketing boards. See KNA PC/CP 8/5/4, 'Fort Hall Merchants', protest to Provincial Commissioner, 31 October 1950, 21 March 1951, and 11 May 1951, and reply from Cavendish Bentinck, 5 February 1951.

9. See KNA Ag 4/118, 'Provincial Agricultural Handing Over Reports, 1942–51', Nyeri Marketing Report, 15 January 1951 for complaints that agricultural officers had to spend far too much time overseeing local Maize Control and curtailing the black market; and Handing Over Report South Nyeri, 3 March 1947, for·details of smuggling and the black marketeers favoured routes.

10 KNA Ag 4/381, 'Kiambu Monthly Agricultural Reports, 1940–49', July–September 1947.

11 KNA Ag 4/220, 'Wattle Rules and Marketing, 1942–46', G.J. Gollop, Assistant Agricultural Officer, Kiambu, to acting Senior Agricultural Officer, Kiambu, 21 August 1945; and Ag 4/381, 'Kiambu Monthly Agricultural Reports, 1940–49', January–June 1948; C&I 6/782, 'Trading by Africans, 1946–50', T.C. Colchester, Municipal Native Affairs Officer to Rennie, November 1944; C. Tomkinson, PC Central, to Rennie, 6 October 1945; and F.R. Stephen to A. Hope-Jones, 23 August 1946. See also DC/FH 1/23, 'Fort Hall Annual Report, 1944', p. 2, and DC/FH 1/24, 'Fort Hall Annual Report, 1945', pp. 1–2, 34–6.

The Problems of Kikuyu Agriculture

12. CO 852/662/19936/2 (1945–46), 'Soil Erosion: Kenya', 1944 Soil Conservation Report.

13. *ibid.*, N. Humphrey, 'The Relationship of Population to the Land in South Nyeri', paragraphs 22 and 28; KNA Ag 4/488, 'Monthly Agricultural Reports Central Province, 1940–47', January–March 1945 and 1946; and Secretariat 1/1/13, 'Native Welfare in Kenya, 1944', A.M. Champion, 'Review of Present Conditions in the Native Areas', pp. 3–6 and 39; Dr Philip, 'Nutrition in Kenya'. In the main cash-crop areas of eastern Buganda household income and labour have also been invested in the cultivation of inedible cash crops. This has produced a decline in dietary standards and the population have become dependent upon cassava as their main source of protein. Humphrey's report on South Nyeri was excessively alarmist. The work of M.P. Cowen, especially his unpublished papers, 'Concentration of Sales and Assets' and 'Patterns of Cattle Ownership and Dairy Production' have recently shown that milk remained a staple element in the diet in Nyeri.

14. For a defence of controlled wattle growing see Ag 4/220, 'Wattle Rules and Marketing, 1942–46', Senior Agricultural Officer, Central, 26 July 1944. M.P. Cowen has argued that wattle was of crucial importance to the success of the peasant option because it enabled the middle peasantry to preserve a household mode of production and provided an antidote to the prohibition on African coffee planting. See Cowen's unpublished thesis, 'Capital and Household Production', pp. 189–99, 205–11.

15. KNA Ag 4/488, 'Monthly Agricultural Report Central Province, 1940–47, Lyne Watt to Director of Agriculture, October–December 1944 and January–March 1945; DC/FH 3/1, 'Reports on the Kikuyu by Miss J.M. Fisher, 1950–52', paragraphs 181–262; and CO 852/662/19936/2 (1945–46), 'Soil Erosion: Kenya', N. Humphrey, 'The Kikuyu Lands: the Relationship of Population to the Land in South Nyeri, (Nairobi, 1945), paragraphs 25–29; and B.D. Bowles, 'Underdevelopment in Agriculture in Colonial Kenya' pp. 195–213.

16. KNA Ag 4/125, 'Annual District Agricultural Reports, Central Province 1951', Machakos District Agricultural Annual Report, 1951.

17. CO 852/662/19936/2 (1945–46), 'Soil Erosion: Kenya', N. Humphrey, 'The Relationship of Population to the Land in South Nyeri', paragraph 27; and KNA Ag 4/118, 'Provincial Agricultural Handing Over Reports, 1942–51', Embu, August 1945; and Kitui, April 1951.

18. CO 852/662/19936/2 (1945–46), 'Shifting Erosion: Kenya', N. Humphrey, 'The Relationship of Population to the Land in South Nyeri', paragraphs 19–24; and KNA DC/NYI/2/1/20, 'Mr Humphrey's Report on South Nyeri, 1944–47', W. Lyne Watt to Director of Agriculture, 27 October 1944.

19. CO 533/537/38628 (1945), 'Grouping of Agricultural Departments', P.E. Mitchell to G. Creasy, 27 February 1945, and to O. Stanley, 15 March 1945. For Mitchell's comments on African agriculture, see CO 533/553/38557/8 (1947–48), 'General Aspects of the Agrarian Situation in Kenya', Despatch no. 44 of 1946 to Hall, 17 April 1946.

20. CO 533/537/38628 (1945), 'Grouping of Agricultural Departments', Mitchell to Stanley, 15 March and 26 May 1945.

21. CO 533/537/38646 (1945), 'Proposals for the Reorganization of the Administration'; CO 533/553/38557/8 (1947–48), 'General Aspects of the Agrarian Situation in Kenya', Despatch no. 44 of 1946 to Hall, 17 April 1946; and CO 852/662/19936/2 (1945–46), 'Soil Erosion: Kenya', for the most important correspondence files.

22. N. Humphrey's most influential reports were subsequently published as *The Kikuyu Lands* and *The Liguru and the Land*. For the 1931 survey, see S.H. Fazan, 'An Economic Survey of the Kikuyu Reserves'; Kenya Land Commission, Evidence and Memoranda, vol. i, paragraphs 971–1039. See also Fazan's minority recommendations in the 'Report of the Committee on Land tenure in Kikuyu

The Problems of Kikuyu Agriculture

Province, 1929'. G. Kitching, *Class and Economic Change in Kenya*, pp. 35–9, 115–20 has an interesting discussion of these reports. See also CO 852/662/19936/2 (1945–46), 'Soil Erosion: Kenya', N. Humphrey, 'The Relationship of Population to the Land in South Nyeri', paragraphs 1–10. Estimates of remittances from *askari* can be found in KNA DC/FH 1/23, 'Fort Hall Annual Report, 1944', p. 26 and DC/FH 1/24, 'Fort Hall Annual Report, 1945', p. 38. Murang'a contributed 1,806 men to the armed forces, who sent home the following sums: 1942 – 114,000 shillings; 1943 – 388,000 shillings; 1944 – 781,000 shillings; 1945 – 976,000 shillings. In 1944–45 remittances from African *askari* exceeded the total revenue of central government poll tax and Local Native Council rates in the district, or the total value of Murang'a's exports through official channels, excluding wattle, which in 1945 amounted to approximately £50,000 out of a total of £93,000. The money sent back to the reserves by migrant labourers is unknown, but probably considerably enhanced the sums received from *askari*.

23. These beliefs in the ecological fragility of African soils were not wrong, but the colonial agricultural departments institutionalised the reports and exaggerated the dangers involved. W. Allan, *Studies in African Land Usage in Northern Rhodesia*; C.G. Trapnell and J.M. Clothier, *The Soils, Vegetation and Agricultural Systems of North-Western Rhodesia* and C.G. Trapnell, 'Ecological Methods in the Study of Native Agriculture', pp. 491–4. J. McCracken, 'Experts and Expertise in Colonial Malawi', pp. 104–5, 108–14 has similar observations to make for the agricultural department in Nyasaland. For the pastoral reserves of Kenya, D.M. Anderson's thesis, 'Herder, Settler and Colonial Rule', pp. 141–64 and 'Depression, Dust Bowl, Demography and Drought', pp. 321–43, contain most useful assessments of official attitudes. I am grateful to Dr Anderson for many interesting discussions on this topic.

24. CO 852/662/19936/2 (1945–46), 'Soil Erosion: Kenya', N. Humphrey, 'The Relationship of Population to the Land in South Nyeri', paragraphs 9 and 41–7. Humphrey estimated that total export earnings amounted to only 57 shillings per family per annum. The Kenya Department of Agriculture's memoranda to the East African Royal Commission contain some useful insights into the evolution of official thinking: 'Report on Agrarian Policy for Dealing with Population Increase: Land Tenure and Fragmentation in Kenya' (1951); and 'The Agricultural Problems and Potential of the African Lands of Kenya', 23 February 1952. I am grateful to Dr J.M. Lonsdale for lending me xeroxes of these reports.

For the first signs of Brown's new approach see KNA Ag 4/419, 'Agricultural Development and Maintenance of Soil Fertility: The Growing of High Priced Crops, 1933–51', J.T. Moon to Director of Agriculture, 5 February 1948; and L.H. Brown to DC Embu, 6 February 1948; and Ag 1/1079, 'Soil Erosion Native Areas, 1946–54', L.H. Brown, Provincial Agricultural Officer to Director of Agriculture, 20 August 1951, for a discussion of the planning of arable areas for peasant farmers. See also Ag 4/502, 'Agricultural Reports Central Province, 1942–55'; Ag 4/328, 'Annual Agricultural Report Central Province, 1951'; Ag 4/125, 'Annual Agricultual Reports, Central Province Districts, 1951'; Ag 4/410, 'Central Province and Districts Annual Agricultural Reports, 1952'; and Ag 4/118, 'Provincial Agricultural Handing Over Reports, 1942–51', Embu Handing Over Report, February 1951.

Brown believed that it was possible in Central Province to establish balanced smallholdings which could carry 1,000 people to the square mile and perhaps 2,000 near Nairobi. Nevertheless, in 1952 he considered that only 5 per cent of the population followed 'sound agricultural' techniques, such as paddocking and rotational grazing and cultivation. See his letter to *East African Standard*, 17 April 1953; and RH Mss. Afr. s. 596, 'European Elected Members Organisation', 38(A)/1, 'Mau Mau 1947–55', for his views on Kikuyu agricultural practices.

25. R.J.M. Swynnerton, *A Plan to Intensify the Development of African Agriculture in Kenya*; and A. Thurston's draft manuscript, 'The Intensification of Smallholder Agriculture in

Kenya', pp. 38, 50–2, 97–104, 118–19. See also CO 852/662/19936/2 (1945–46), 'Soil Erosion: Kenya', N. Humphrey, 'The Relationship of Population to the Land in South Nyeri', Appendix A. For the official account of the rehabilitation and resettlement campaigns, African Land Development Board, *African Land Development in Kenya 1946–55*.

26. For estimates of the value of these new crops see KNA Ag 4/410, 'Central Province and District Annual Agricultural Reports, 1952', Appendix D.

27. African Land Development Board, *African Land Development in Kenya 1946–55*; pp. 38–44; KNA DC/MKS 14/3/2, 'Machakos Gazeteer, 1890–1957', pp. 31–50; and Ag 1/732, 'Land: African Settlement Board: Simba, Kibwezi, Chuyulu and Teita Areas, 1946–55', minutes of the meeting with the Provincial Commissioner, 10 April 1948, to discuss land and water conservation in the Teita Hills; and DC Teita–Taveta 3/32, 'Development in the Reserves: Teita Betterment Scheme, 1948–50', A.W. Thompson, Shimba Hills Survey, 24 January 1950. I am grateful to Simon Myambo for these references and for a tour of the terracing work in Teita.

28. CO 852/662/19936/2 (1945–46), 'Soil Erosion: Kenya', N. Humphrey, 'The Relationship of Population to the Land in South Nyeri', paragraph 55. See also CO 533/538/38005/29 (1947), 'Land Commission: Native Lands Trust Board', minute by P. Wyn Harris, 9 August 1947.

29. CO 852/557/16707/2 (1946), 'Land Tenure Policy: Kenya', especially the report of the soil conservation committee under Archdeacon Owen to DC Central Kavirondo, 18 August 1945. See also N. Humphrey, *The Liguru and the Land*; CO 852/662/19936/2 (1945–46), 'Soil Erosion: Kenya', H.E. Lambert and P. Wyn Harris, 'Memorandum on Policy in Regard to Land Tenure in the Native Lands of Kenya'; KNA DC/FH 1/24, 'Fort Hall Annual Report, 1945', pp. 7–8; and Ag 4/512, 'Fort Hall Monthly Agricultural Reports, 1940–49', reports for January–March 1945 and October to December 1945.

30. CO 852/662/19936/2 (1945–46), 'Soil Conservation: Kenya', H.E. Lambert and P. Wyn Harris, 'Memorandum on Policy in Regard to Land Tenure in the Native Lands of Kenya'. See also CO 852/557/16707/2 (1946), 'Land Tenure Policy: Kenya'. Lambert was the author of two noted books on the Kikuyu, *Systems of Land Tenure in the Kikuyu Land Unit* and *Kikuyu Social and Political Institutions*.

31. As late as 1954 the District Commissioner in Machakos was still defending communalism and hindering the emergence of African entrepreneurs and commercial farmers. See B.J. Berman's unpublished thesis, 'Administration and Politics in Colonial Kenya', pp. 308–27. The gradual evolution of official thinking can be followed in KNA MAA 7/842, 'Provincial Commissioners' Meetings, 1945–51'; MAA 6/13 and 14 'Reports of the Committee on Agricultural Credit for Africans, 1949–50'; and MAA 9/959, 'Credit to Africans Ordinance, 1941–59'.

   The rivalry between the chiefs and the alternative élite is evident in DC/FH 1/26, 'Fort Hall Annual Report, 1947', pp. 4–5, 17–18; Ag 4/77, 'Wattle Cooperative Societies, 1947–51'; Ag 4/220, 'Wattle Rules and Marketing, 1942–46'; and C&I 6/782 'Trading by Africans, 1946–50'.

32. Lord Hailey, *Native Land Tenure in Africa*, p. 13. For the attitudes of the Kenyan administration see M.P.K. Sorrenson, *Land Reform in the Kikuyu Country*, p. 56; and KNA MAA 6/13, 'Report of the Committee on Agricultural Credit for Africans, 1949–50', meeting 29 October 1949. Mitchell endorsed this view, and observed that '. . . in fact, outright ownership by ignorant and often avaricious small farmers is the most disastrous thing that can happen to land anywhere as examples all over the world prove.' LO/LND 30/2/2, Mitchell to Rennie, 25 April 1945. For similar comments in Whitehall see CO 852/557/16708 (1945), 'Land Tenure Panel', Colonial Office to the Colonial Social Science Research Council, 28 December 1944; and M. Perham, *East African Journey*, pp. 17, 42–6, 56; and her *Colonial Sequence, 1930–1949*, pp. 12–33.

33. KNA MAA 6/13 and 13, 'Reports of the Committee on Agricultural Credit for

The Problems of Kikuyu Agriculture

Africans, 1949–50'; MAA 9/959, 'Credit to Africans Ordinance, 1941–59'; and MAA 7/842, 'Provincial Commissioners' Meetings, 1945–51', 12 April 1945.

34. Lord Hailey, *Native Land Tenure in Africa*, p. 13.

35. L. Mair, 'Anthropology and Colonial Policy', pp. 191–5; D.H. Johnson, 'Evans-Pritchard, the Nuer, and the Sudan Political Service', pp. 231–46; and T. Asad (ed.), *Anthropology and the Colonial Encounter, passim*. For relations between anthropologists and the administration in Kenya, KNA MAA 7/604, 'Surveys by Dr W.E.H. Stanner: The Kitui Kamba, 1943–50'; and I. Schapera, 'Some Problems of Anthropological Research in Kenya Colony', p. 14, quoted in J.M. Lee, *Colonial Development and Good Government*, pp. 86–98. B.J. Berman's unpublished thesis, 'Administration and Politics in Colonial Kenya', pp. 119–39, analyses the attitude of the Kenyan field administration. See also P.E. Mitchell's foreword to R.O. Hennings, *African Morning*, p. 9; and J.M. Lonsdale, 'European Attitudes and African Pressures', p. 142.

36. For the opinions of the 'detribalised' élite in Nairobi see KNA MAA 2/5/223, 'Nairobi Advisory Council, 1946–49', especially T.G. Askwith's memorandum on the Advisory Council, 1 September 1948; and MAA 7/491, 'Administration Policy: Urban Areas Nairobi, 1945–47', F. Khamisi to Rennie, 10 September 1945; and meeting in Secretariat, 28 November 1945, when Khamisi, Mathu and Odede met the Deputy Chief Secretary, the Chief Native Commissioner, the Mayor, the Commissioner for Local Government and the Provincial Commissioner Central Province. For Mitchell's attitude, see CO 533/549/38232/15 (1946–47), 'European Settlement: Squatters', Mitchell to Creech Jones, 14 April 1947.

37. KNA Lab 9/99, 'Labour Efficiency Survey, Kenya and Uganda Railways and Harbours: Northcott Report, 1946–49'; and MAA /22, 'City African Affairs Officer: Correspondence, 1947–50', clearly show the depth of African discontent in Nairobi. This culminated in the general strike of May 1950, for which see Lab 9/87, 'Labour Troubles: Nairobi, 1950'. For Mombasa see CO 533/545/38091/6 (1947 and 1948), 'Labour: Strikes and Disturbances'; CO 533/534/38091/13 (1947), 'Labour: A Social and Economic Survey of Mombasa'; KNA Lab 9/1835, 'Mombasa Strikes, 1937–46'; Lab 9/1841, 'Trade Disputes Tribunal, 1947'; and Lab 9/1775, 'A Survey of African Housing in Mombasa, 1946–47'. A. Hake, *African Metropolis*, pp. 19–63, provides an account of African life in the capital. See also J. Bujra, 'Women entrepreneurs of Early Nairobi', pp. 213–34; N. Nelson, 'How Women and Men Get By'; and R.M.A. van Zwanenberg, 'History and Theory of Urban Poverty in Nairobi', pp. 165–203.

38. G. Kitching, *Class and Economic Change in Kenya*, pp. 82–94, 121–30; M.J. Hay's unpublished thesis, 'Economic Change in Luoland: Kowe, 1890–1945', pp. 204–32; J.M. Fischer, *Anatomy of Kikuyu Domesticity and Husbandry*, pp. 237–54, 261–85; and several unpublished articles by M.P. Cowen, especially, 'Differentiation in a Kenya Location', p. 20; M.P. Cowen and K. Kinyanjui, 'Some Problems of Class Formation in Kenya', M.P. Cowen and F. Murage, 'Notes on Agricultural Wage Labour in a Kenya Location'; M.P. Cowen and F.Murage, 'Wattle Production in the Central Province'; and M.P. Cowen's unpublished thesis, 'Capital and Household Production'.

39. KNA MAA 2/5/146, 'Kenya African Union, 1948–52'; Secretariat 1/12/8, 'Labour Unrest: Intelligence Reports Central Province, 1947'; and B.J. Berman's thesis, 'Administration and Politics in Colonial Kenya', pp. 378–404. See also DC/FH 1/26, 'Fort Hall Annual Report, 1947', pp. 1–6; DC/FH 1/27, 'Fort Hall Annual Report, 1948', pp. 1–5; and DC/KBU 1/43, 'Kiambu Annual Report, 1952', pp. 1–4.

40. KNA DC/FH 1/26, 'Fort Hall Annual Report, 1947', pp. 1–6; DC/FH 1/27, 'Fort Hall Annual Report, 1948', pp. 1–5; and DC/FH 1/30, 'Fort Hall Annual Report, 1951', pp. 1–2.

41. CO 852/557/16707/2 (1946), 'Land Tenure Policy: Kenya', H.E. Lambert, 'Policy in Regard to Administration of the Native Lands – Note for a Discussion', 10 July 1946; CO 852/662/19936/2 (1945–46), 'Soil Erosion: Kenya', H.E. Lambert and P.Wyn Harris, 'Policy in Regard to Land Tenure in the Native Lands of Kenya'; and CO

86

852/557/16708 (1945), 'Land Tenure Panel', Colonial Office to Colonial Social Science Research Council, 28 December 1944.

42. H.E. Lambert's *Systems of Land Tenure in the Kikuyu Land Unit*, should be compared with L.S.B. Leakey, *The Southern Kikuyu before 1903*, vol. 1, which shows an acute consciousness of the differences between the Metume (the Kikuyu from north of the River Chania) and the Karura (those from the south, in Kiambu).

In his thesis Berman has characterised the administration's views as those of an aristocratic conservative élite: '. . . an anti-urban, anti-materialist and anti-bourgeois response of the traditional landed rural class to modern industrial society'. He claims that these views were preserved in the Kenyan administration 'long after their influence had begun to wane in Britain', pp. 105–6. Berman adopted these ideas from S. Barrington Moore, *The Social Origins of Dictatorship and Democracy*, pp. 491–6, and C.F. Behrmann's unpublished thesis, 'The Mythology of British Imperialism', which he cites.

The most influential advocate of such ideas was Lord Hailey; see his four-volume survey of *Native Administration in the British African Territories*. For a discussion of Hailey's influence see R.D. Pearce, *The Turning Point in Africa*' pp. 42–67; and his secretary, Sir Frederick Pedler's account, 'The Contribution of Lord Hailey to Africa', pp. 267–75.

43. C.G. Rosberg and J. Nottingham, *The Myth of Mau Mau*, pp. 188–234; and KNA MAA 2/5/146, 'Kenya African Union, 1948–52', for many examples of the Kenyan government's refusal to incorporate African politicians.

44. KNA MAA 7/320, 'Chiefs Engaged in Commerce'; and complaints in Ag 4/77, 'Wattle Cooperative Societies, 1947–51', James Warrego, Secretary of the Central Province Wattle Growers' Association to the Agricultural Officer, Kiambu, 20 August 1948; and the meeting at Ruiru with the District Commissioner, 2 March 1949. For opposition to terracing, Secretariat 1/12/8, 'Intelligence: Mumenyereri, 1947–50', letter from Mrs M.W. Gathaku, published in Mumenyereri, 29 September 1947, about events in Location 13 in Murang'a; and the letters from B.K. Ruhia, 27 October 1947; and Benjamin Mang'uru, 3 November 1947.

45. KNA DC/FH 1/25, 'Fort Hall Annual Report, 1946', pp. 3–7; and DC/KBU 1/36, 'Kiambu Annual Report, 1945', pp. 13–15. See also Ag 4/118, 'Provincial Agricultural Handing Over Reports, 1942–51', South Nyeri, 12 February 1945; and T. Hughes Rice to C.D. Knight in Murang'a, March 1947; Ag 4/147, 'Fort Hall Agricultural Annual Report, 1945'; Ag 4/381, 'Kiambu Monthly Agricultural Reports, 1940–49'; Ag 4/512, 'Murang'a Monthly Agricultural Reports, 1940–49'; and Ag 4/539, 'Reconditioning: Central Province, 1934–48'.

46. CO 967/57/46709 (1942), 'Sir Arthur Dawe's Memorandum on a Federal Solution for East Africa and Mr Harold Macmillan's Counter-Proposals', Macmillan to Gater, 15 August 1942. For other collectivisation schemes, see C. Maher, 'Peasantry or Prosperity?' and KNA Ag 1/1065, 'Soil Erosion Native Areas, 1943–46', C. Maher's 'Agricultural Changes as Alternatives to Disaster in the Native Reserves'; Secretariat 1/1/13, 'Native Welfare in Kenya', A.M. Champion's 'Review of Present Conditions in the Native Areas, 1944', pp. 42–44. Champion, a former Provincial Commissioner, considered that collective farming was more 'in keeping with native communal ideas of land cultivation . . . and also it is only by some such method that optimum production can be obtained from the soil. The possibility of introducing such a system with a minimum disturbance to native society should be one of the prime considerations of the social anthropologists', whom he wished the government to appoint.

Mitchell also favoured collective farming and considered that African peasant societies needed 'some form of organization which will do what the peasant cannot do for himself . . . In the two greatest areas where the peasant system survives, e.g. in India and China, the picture is one of extreme poverty and recurring economic disasters. There is no reality behind the belief that the African peasant farmer can do for himself what other (and often better) farmers have done elsewhere, if only he is given more land and help with communications and markets'. For Hailey's comments on this despatch, see CO 852/557/16707/2 (1946), 'Land Tenure Policy: Kenya', 13 May 1946.

47. African Land Development Board's report on African Land Development in Kenya, 1946-55, pp. 6-7; KNA Ag 1/1065, 'Soil Erosion Native Areas, 1943-46', especially C. Maher, 'Notes on a Visit to South Kavirondo and to Nyakatch, Central Kavirondo', 3 January 1945; and 'Agricultural Changes as Alternatives to Disaster in the Native Reserves'. See also Maher's 'Notes on Estimates for the Development of the Native reserves' to D.L. Blunt, 1 June 1945, in the same file. For A.M. Champion's report see Secretariat 1/1/13, 'Native Welfare in Kenya', A.M. Champion, 'Review of Present Conditions in the Native Areas, 1944'; and DC/NYI/2/1/20, 'Mr Humphrey's Report on South Nyeri, 1944-47', Lyne Watt to Director of Agriculture, 27 October 1944; and C. Tomkinson's interim comments on development to Rennie, 14 May 1945.

Lyne Watt blamed the uncontrolled spread of wattle cultivation for the growth of rampant individualism, and favoured a communal development programme to reverse this trend. He was completely opposed to encouraging a few selected progressive smallholders. Tomkinson also considered that 'unless it is to be Government policy to encourage the evolution of the big landowner and employer of labour, it will be necessary for such men to be made to realise that they must reorientate themselves on clan lines sufficiently to ensure their conformation to sound land usage'. This, of course, marked the escalation of the conflict between the administration and its allies, the chiefs, in their political and economic struggle with those aspiring entrepreneurs who supported the Kenya African Union and the Kikuyu Central Association.

48. C. Leys, *Underdevelopment in Kenya*, pp. 33-62; E.A. Brett, *Colonialism and Underdevelopment in East Africa*', pp. 288-95, 300-5; and J.M. Lonsdale's unpublished paper, 'African Elites and Social Classes in Colonial Kenya', pp. 10-14.

49. KNA Ag 4/77, 'Wattle Cooperative Societies, 1947-51', G.J. Gollop to DC Kiambu, 18 December 1948; Ag 4/80, 'Agricultural Conferences and Meetings, 1933-51', Conference of Senior Agricultural Officers, 10-11 June 1946; Secretariat 1/1/12, 'Report of the Joint Agricultural and Veterinary Services Sub-Committee of the Development Committee'; and Secretariat 1/1/13, 'Native Welfare in Kenya', A.M. Champion, 'A Review of the Present Conditions in the Native Areas, 1944'. By 1949 the district team in Murang'a contained three settlers, see DC/FH 5/1 (Dep 1), 'District Team Fort Hall, 1949-52'. See also DC/NYI/2/1/20, 'Mr Humphrey's Report on South Nyeri, 1944-47'; DC/NYI 2/2/4, 'Mr Humphrey's Report on Agriculture in South Nyeri, 1945'; and DC/NYI 2/1/16, 'Development and Welfare Planning, 1944-48' for further examples of the post-war commitment to preserving African communalism. These topics were debated in the Legislative Council in November 1944; see Legislative Council Debates, Second Series, vol. 20, (1944-45), Third Session, Mrs V. Watkins, 23 November 1944, cols. 139-49; D.L. Blunt, Director of Agriculture, cols. 203-17; R. Daubney, Director of Veterinary Services, cols. 217-22; W.F.O. Trench, cols. 238-49; and F.W. Cavendish-Bentinck, who six months later was appointed Member for Agriculture, 30 November 1944, cols. 323-36.

50. KNA DC/FH 3/1 'Reports on the Kikuyu by Miss J.M. Fisher, 1950-52', paragraphs 181-262; and G. Kitching, *Class and Economic Change in Kenya*, pp. 82-94 and 121-130.

51. G. Kitching, *Class and Economic Change in Kenya*, pp. 282-97. See also L.S.B. Leakey, *The Southern Kikuyu before 1903*, vol. 1, pp. 105-27; and KNA DC/NYI/2/1/20, 'Mr Humphrey's Report on South Nyeri, 1944-47', C. Tomkinson to Information Officer, 3 July 1945. Calculations of average-sized landholdings revealed that these had fallen to 4.83 acres per family, plus 3.87 acres of communal grazing, compared to the agricultural department's estimated minimum of 8 acres arable and 6 acres grazing. Maher considered that there were 11,500 too many families in Kiambu. The *ahoi*

The Problems of Kikuyu Agriculture

system of clientage had collapsed and many people were already being employed at low wages by large landowners. See Ag 4/392, 'District Agricultural Annual Report, Kiambu, 1948'. In the 'suburban' area, population densities were over 1,000 to the square mile. Gollop, the Assistant Agricultural Officer, reported that in this area the Kikuyu 'are largely parasitical on Nairobi. They have no interest in the land other than as a dwelling place for their families and there they leave their wives to scratch what they can from the soil by methods both primitive and destructive, while they themselves, ply their multifarious trades, often dishonest, in Nairobi . . . Here is needed stern and drastic action to stop a rape of the land that is criminal to the highest degree, and what is worse must to future generations spell poverty and bankruptcy. No doctor's diagnosis is needed here but the surgeon's knife and that quickly before the patient dies. These locations should receive firm handling in 1949'. By 1948, in contrast to when Fazan had done his report in 1929, both the actual and available cultivated land per household was less than in Nyeri or Murang'a, and over these years the population increase in Kiambu was double that of Murang'a (4.4 per cent), and treble Nyeri's (3.0 per cent). See G. Kitching, *Class and Economic Change in Kenya*, pp. 199–20 for a detailed assessment of these changes.

52. G. Kitching, *Class and Economic Change in Kenya*, pp. 288–97; H.E. Lambert, *Systems of Land Tenure in the Kikuyu Land Unit*, pp. 23–5, 79, 87, 95–109, 152–3; and L.S.B. Leakey, *The Southern Kikuyu before 1903*, vol. 1, pp. 89–104.

53. L.S.B. Leakey, *The Southern Kikuyu before 1903*, vol. 1, pp. 105–27, outlines the *githaka* system and the circumstances under which *mbari* land could be divided, the rights of a *muthami* or resident tenant, a *muhoi* or tenant-at-will, and a *muthoni* or a relation-in-law. Basically the *githaka* was the land cleared by one individual, who left his home *mbari* or sub-clan to seek more land on the Kikuyu frontier. These landholdings varied in size from 50 acres to perhaps 20 square miles. The man who cleared the land or 'bought' it from the Dorobo became the *mwathi* or *githaka* controller, with absolute rights to the land. When he died the *githaka* continued to be named after him and became the property of all his male descendants, who formed a new *mbari*, under the leadership of a trustee, the *murumati*, who was usually the eldest son of the former *mwathi*. Sometimes the *mwathi* had come from one of the wealthier families in his original *mbari* and sought more land for his stock, but normally it was members of the junior lineages who left either to search for land to establish their own *githaka* or to become *ahoi* or tenants-at-will of richer landholders. In either case once they had left their *mbari* and had relinquished their cultivation rights, the *murumati* and the *kiama*, or council, would allocate their land to another member of the *mbari*. The *muhoi* originally merely cultivated the land of a neighbouring *mwathi* in exchange for a portion of his crops, but did not actually live on the new *githaka*; while the *muthami* or resident tenant was required to pledge his services to the landowner but did not pay any rent, and could only be evicted under Kikuyu law if the land was needed for the *mwathi*'s own family. Often he hoped to consolidate his position and to marry a member of the *mwathi*'s family or to have one of his sons or daughters do so. He would then become a *muthoni* or relation-in-law, who could only be evicted with great difficulty. All tenants were traditionally safeguarded from unreasonable eviction by the custom that the land a tenant had cleared and cultivated had to be allowed to lie fallow and to revert to bush before it could be used for cultivation by the *mwathi*. G. Kitching, *Class and Economic Change in Kenya*, pp. 288–97 provides an extremely lucid assessment of the effects of the development of capitalist relations upon Kikuyu land law and concept of 'ownership'.

54. G. Kitching, *Class and Economic Change in Kenya*, p. 290; see also M.P. Cowen and F. Murage's unpublished paper, 'Wattle Production in the Central Province, p. 63.

55. A. Thurston's draft manuscript, 'The Intensification of Smallholder Agriculture in Kenya', p. 75. For an African view see KNA MAA 8/102, 'Intelligence and Security: Press Cuttings, 1948–50', letter from E.N. Samson published in *Mucemanio*, 3 July 1948.

56. For a detailed study of the formation of the anti-Kikuyu Central Association coalition see D.M. Feldman's unpublished thesis, 'Christians and Politics', pp. 202–301; and J.M. Lonsdale's unpublished paper, 'African Elites and Social Classes in Colonial Kenya', pp. 7–13.
    The administration's attitude to individualism can be found in CO 852/662/19936/2 (1945–46), 'Soil Erosion: Kenya', H.E. Lambert and P. Wyn Harris, 'Policy in Regard to Land Tenure in the Native Reserves of Kenya'; CO 852/557/16707/2 (1946), 'Land Tenure Policy: Kenya', Soil Conservation committee to DC Central Kavirondo, 18 August 1945; and H.E. Lambert, 'Policy in Regard to Administration of the Native Lands – Note for Discussion', 10 July 1946; KNA Ag 4/491, 'Nyeri Reconditioning Report, 1944–46', Secretariat circular no. 64, 22 May 1946; Ag 4/80, 'Agricultural Conferences and Meetings, 1933–41', conference of Senior Agricultural Officers 10–11 June 1946; Ag 4/330, 'Provincial Agricultural Newsletters, 1939–51', September 1949, Group Farming in Nyanza; and Hughes Rice on Youth Conference in Central Province, in February 1950 issue; and Ag 4/539, 'Reconditioning Central Province, 1934–48', PC Central to Chief Native Commissioner, 7 March 1945; and Secretariat circular no. 3 on 'Soil Conservation in the Reserves', 24 April 1945.

57. Table 4.1 was compiled from the following sources: KNA Ag 4/147, 'Fort Hall Agricultural Annual Report, 1945'; Ag 4/358, 'Monthly Agricultural Report, Embu, 1945–49'; Ag 4/381, 'Kiambu Monthly Reports, 1940–49'; Ag 4/512, 'Fort Hall Monthly Agricultural Reports, 1940–49'; Ag 4/539, 'Reconditioning Central Province, 1934–48'.

58. KNA Ag 4/539, 'Reconditioning Central Province, 1934–48', Soil Conservation reports, July–December 1945; January–June 1946; July–December 1946; and January–June 1947. See also Ag 4/512, 'Fort Hall Monthly Agricultural Report, 1940–49'; Ag 4/147, 'Fort Hall Annual Agricultural Report, 1945'; DC/FH 1/24, 'Fort Hall Annual Report, 1945', pp. 7–9; DC/FH 1/25, 'Fort Hall Annual Report, 1946', pp. 6–7; and DC/FH 1/26, 'Fort Hall Annual Report, 1947', pp. 1–4, 15.

59. CO 533/537/38628 (1945), 'Grouping of Agricultural Departments', Mitchell to Creasy, 18 February 1945; CO 533/537/38646 (1945), 'Proposals for the Reorganization of the Administration', Mitchell to Stanley, 5 June 1945; DC/FH 5/1 (Dep 1), 'District Team Fort Hall, 1949–52'; and DC/FH 2/1, 'Fort Hall Production Sub-Committee Meetings, 1931–52'. A. Thurston's draft manuscript, 'The Intensification of Smallholder Agriculture in Kenya', pp. 66–9, provides some examples of dissension and departmental rivalry. Relations between the agricultural and veterinary departments were particularly strained according to C.O. Oates, the former Provincial Agricultural Officer in Nyanza and the Rift Valley; interview in Dorset, 20 June 1983. See also KNA Ag 4/80, 'Agricultural Conferences and Meetings, 1933–51', Agricultural Officer, Embu, 29 July 1947; Agricultural Officers' meetings, 11 August 1947, and 8–9 April 1948; L.H. Brown, 21 August and 26 October 1948 to Senior Agricultural Officer, Nyeri; and the Provincial Agricultural Officers' meeting on 9 June 1950; Ag 4/518, 'Reconditioning Central Province, 1948–51, Soil Conservation report, Central Province, January–June 1948, especially the entry for Machakos; and G.M. Roddan to F.W. Cavendish-Bentinck, 31 August 1948; and Ag 4/392, 'District Annual Agricultural Reports, 1948', the Embu report.

60. CO 533/556/38664 (1946–47), 'Land Policy', T. Hughes Rice to A.B. Cohen, 3 August 1946.

61. KNA Ag 4/125, 'Central Province Agricultural Annual Reports, 1951'; Ag 4/410, 'Central Province and Districts Agricultural Annual Reports, 1952'; and Ag 4/451, 'Fort Hall Safari Diaries, 1948–51', clearly demonstrate the continued emphasis upon terracing.

Five

The Kikuyu Squatter Problem

'I have received information that squatter labour is pouring into the forest reserve, where the conditions are probably so attractive as to make this a squatters' paradise, and a haven of refuge. Land; land; land; nice fresh virgin land, is their cry; little or no work for their *bibis*; sheep filling their bellies with good green luscious grass; firewood quite handy; *pombe* brewing galore – who will visit us in the forest at night . . . Utopia has been discovered; Bacchus reigns peacefully, or noisily; no horrid police to disturb us; very handsome profits from vegetables and potatoes; and enough to spare for our dear indolent brethren; thereby saving them the dreadful prospect of work.'[1]

This complaint from an Aberdares farmer was typical of the wave of anti-squatter feeling which swept the White Highlands after the war. It contained elements of truth; although squatter life was never so idyllic, it was better than staying in the reserves. Squatters during the previous 30 years had enjoyed access to more land, had owned more stock and cultivated larger *shambas* than their relatives in Central Province. According to official estimates, squatter household incomes of 1,000 shillings a year from wage labour, stock and crops, were not uncommon during the war. The peasant option seemed to be even more successsul among the squatters on European farms than in Central Province.[2]

This success explains why the settlers were so eager after the war to restrict squatter cultivation and small stock and to eliminate their cattle. The squatter option had become a serious threat to the privileged economic status of the settlers. The squatters seemed to be gaining ground, gnawing away from the inside of the settler enclave in the White Highlands. African accumulation was strongest among the Kikuyu, who dominated the squatter communities in Naivasha, Nakuru and the Aberdares. It was in these three district councils, on the borders of Kikuyuland, that the post-war confrontation between settlers and squatters was most intense.[3]

The Kenyan government was deeply divided over the squatter problem. Under pressure from the chiefs and the African Local Native Councils, the field administration strongly opposed any attempt to expel squatter stock into the reserves as the European district councils demanded, supported by the local government department. The labour department, under the able leadership of Wyn Harris and Hyde-Clarke, bcame a particularly forceful critic of the new anti-squatter orders. These divisions within the official mind ensured that the evolution of squatter policy was protracted and painful. By 1947, however, it appeared as though a five-stage policy for the controlled evolution of squatters into wage labourers over a generation had been agreed, but it was never introduced because of the opposition of Cavendish-Bentinck, the member for agriculture, and Mortimer, the member for health and local government, who were sympathetic to the settlers' cause. Until the declaration of the Emergency in October 1952, the settler-controlled district councils were allowed to devise their own policies with only minimal supervision from the Secretariat, despite the protests of Hyde-Clarke, the Labour Commissioner. In August 1950, the last semblance of control by the Nairobi government was abandoned and squatter policy was left to the Association of District Councils. Henceforth the district councils were to moderate themselves.[4]

Squatter versus settler accumulation

The squatters typified Kenya's problem – the clash between two forms of accumulation, Kikuyu and settler. Between 1905 and 1920 their interests had seemed compatible. Under-capitalised European farmers had needed cheap African labour to develop their farms. Squatter cattle provided milk and manure, helped to prevent bush regeneration and kept pastures sweet for European stock. In contrast to the early settlers, the first squatters were over-capitalised, that is they had too many stock to remain in crowded Kikuyuland. During the nineteenth century aspiring Kikuyu had abandoned the security of their *mbari* to search for more land on the frontier of Kikuyu expansion. The term *ahoi*, which has been used to describe many of the squatters, was not a social category for the landless poor but a legal concept, defining the terms on which they had gained access to the land of a different *mbari*. Often, therefore, the people who became *ahoi* were not the landless, but wealthy cattle owners who required additional grazing land beyond the resources of their *mbari*. After 1905, when expansion to the south was closed by the alienation of land to European settlers, the Kikuyu turned westwards into the sparsely-populated Rift Valley to work on the European farms which had been alienated from the Maasai.[5]

This arrangement worked well for both sides until the 1920s when high commodity prices enabled the settlers to diversify into cattle and sheep. For the first time, the interests of the two communities clashed and the settlers, fearful of the diseases carried by squatter stock began to force them off their farms. Squatter cultivators, however, had also increased cultivation during the First World War and, in Naivasha and Nakuru, had prospered. They too in the 1920s had bought cattle and small stock and did not wish to lose their grazing rights.[6]

During the 1920s the squatters encountered stringent new controls. 'Kaffir farming' agreements, whereby under-capitalised settlers had allowed squatters to rent land for cash or payments in kind, without requiring any labour, had been prohibited under the Resident Native Labour Ordinance of 1918. The 1920s provided both sides with a foretaste of what would happen 20 years later. Squatter stock were seized and Africans retaliated by maiming settler cattle and burning crops. But just when a clash appeared inevitable, the collapse of international commodity prices in the depression undercut settler prosperity. Many settlers had to abandon their farms and most had to retrench and go back to an earlier stage of accumulation and to a symbiotic relationship with their squatters. In contrast, the depression provided squatters with further opportunities as peasant production was encouraged to bolster the fiscal base of the state. As before the First World War, the race between settler and squatter accumulators once again favoured the squatters.[7]

The economic depression of the 1930s removed the threat of intensive European farming for more than a decade. Many settlers farming marginal land in areas such as Solai, Sotik and Machakos could survive only by resorting to illegal 'kaffir farming' agreements with squatters and Africans in the neighbouring reserves, who wanted to graze their cattle on less exhausted pastures. Along sections of the border between the Tugen Reserve and Nakuru District, 90 per cent of farms were abandoned at the height of the depression.[8]

Large parts of the White Highlands were 'colonised' by squatters. In 1931, the *East African Standard* reported that only 2,828,000 acres of a total area of 6,847,000 acres of land which had been alienated to settlers were actually under crops or being grazed. Another 1,850,000 acres were occupied by squatters. Other estimates suggested that the squatters were occupying an even larger proportion of the so-called White Highlands. Maasai cattle were grazing pastures on unoccupied farms on the Mau escarpment, and the Nandi were trespassing into the Uasin Gishu.[9]

At this crucial juncture the Kenyan government decided, after a certain amount of wavering, not to abandon the settlers to their fate. It hedged its bets and vainly attempted to help settler farming through the crisis, by providing loans from the government-controlled Land Bank, at the same time as it encouraged African production. The agricultural department also encouraged the settlers to diversify from maize monoculture into mixed farming with dairy and stock herds. This failure to choose between the settlers and the Kikuyu, although no one appreciated it at the time, was the beginning of the end for Kikuyu squatters. After 1935 a violent confrontation between settler and Kikuyu accumulators, both in the reserves and the White Highlands, was almost inevitable. In the late 1930s the settlers were already trying to claw back their advantages and to prevent the squatters gaining *de facto* rights to land in the White Highlands. They knew that if squatters' rights under English law were conceded then the game would be over, since during the depression the government had clearly shown its ambiguous commitment to Kenya as a 'White Man's Country' and its willingness to back the winning side, be it African or European.[10]

Thus in the late 1930s, when the depression had receded and agricultural prices had improved, the settlers once again moved against squatter stock and attempted to undermine the peasant option in the reserves by arousing fears among the administration that the irresponsible land-mining of their African competitors was exacerbating erosion and land degradation. By 1939, the rallying cry of 'the White Highlands in danger' and the conservation card had almost won the game. The settlers had secured the right to dictate their own rules in the contest with the squatters under the 1937 Resident Native Labour Ordinance, which transferred responsibility for controlling squatters to the settler district councils. Meanwhile the focus of the agricultural department's erosion phobia was successfully diverted from the White Highlands to the neighbouring African reserves.[11]

The war, however, intervened just as the squatters were beginning to feel threatened. The real reversal of fortunes in the late 1930s was thus masked until 1945, as both sides profited from the new demand for Kenya's products and the high prices they were able to command. Wartime prosperity, however, ensured that when the battle resumed the ensuing crisis would be even worse than had seemed likely in the late 1930s, since both the settler and African economies had expanded and both sides had more to lose than before the war.[12]

When the district councils moved against the squatters in 1945, eliminating small stock and reducing cultivation to two acres per family, the settlers encountered the opposition of a revamped labour department, which warned of the crisis that would be created in the reserves if thousands of squatter stock were forced out of the White Highlands. The labour department attempted to rewrite the terms of the 1937 Ordinance and to reassert central control over the autonomous district councils. It soon discovered, however, like the Colonial Office, that the settler-controlled institutions, such as the district councils, had become firmly incorporated into the colonial state during the war. Both the settlers and the Secretariat saw the department's campaign as a threat to the newly-established accord between state and settlers.[13]

Settler divisions

Settler farmers were deeply divided over the future of squatter labour. Under-capitalised settlers, struggling to survive on marginal land, often connived with their squatters to avoid the Resident Native Labour Ordinance, which had banned 'kaffir farming' at the insistence of the prosperous settlers who had the resources to develop their farms and who had invested on large herds of expensive high-grade cattle. This division became less important during the Second World War, when virtually all European farmers flourished under the guaranteed purchasing agreements with the Ministries of Supply and Food. In this transformed economic environment, settler confidence in Kenya's future as a 'White Man's Country' was restored. During the late 1940s, however, the division became acute once more. Even in the early days of European settlement, the interests of cereal farmers and the plantation sector, which depended on squatter labour, had conflicted with those of the dairy and stock farmers, who were determined to eliminate squatter cattle and small stock from the White Highlands, regardless of the possible disruption of the labour supply. As early as 1908, the stockmen had formed their own Pastoralist Association to represent their interests against those of the settler maize and wheat farmers. After 1945 the stock farmers and their supporters among the prosperous mixed farmers pushed through the district councils' new restrictions on squatter cultivation and stock, which were a source of tick-borne diseases, such as East Coast Fever, and Black and Red Water Fever. By the late 1920s, Rinderpest and Bovine Pleuro-Pneumonia had almost been eliminated in the White Highlands but remained enzootic in the surrounding reserves. Undipped squatter cattle, which were continually being moved between the reserves and the controlled settler areas, were undoubtedly a possible source of infection.[14]

The coffee, tea and pyrethrum plantations, and the commercial maize and wheat farmers, in contrast, all required large quantities of seasonal labour to help with planting and harvests. They encouraged squatters to remain on their farms and allowed them to cultivate small *shambas* and to graze their stock, so that a dependent labour force could easily be tapped when required. Initially the cereal farmers and planters endorsed the stricter post-war regulations. They also feared that their resident labourers might acquire 'squatters' rights' to the land they occupied under English law. But as squatter opposition became apparent and there was a spate of strikes and refusals to reattest on new contrasts, many maize, wheat and pyrethrum growers became increasingly concerned about their threatened harvests. These farmers began to reconsider and to doubt the wisdom of the stringent new regulations. Thus the survival of one group of settlers seemed to threaten the destruction of the other.[15]

This harsher attitude towards the squatters first became evident at a two-day conference of District Council Production Committee representatives in June 1944. Under the chairmanship of Cavendish-Bentinck, the delegates demanded an end to the recruitment of squatters and pressed for the adoption of an agreed policy. The government, they insisted, must take the initiative and put its own house in order by extending the new district council orders to cover the 19,000 squatters who lived in the forests and evaded local controls. Three months later, a conference of district council chairmen declared the existing orders too 'generous' and agreed to strive to eliminate all squatter stock from the White Highlands within five years. The resident labourer, they decided, should be replaced by 'properly paid labour which should not be bribed by allowing it to cultivate and keep stock for gain'. Despite the reservations of certain chairmen about the speed, a motion was adopted that they would begin to remove all squatter stock immediately. These conferences in 1944 marked the beginning of a new phase during which the district councils started to introduce more restrictive regulations under pressure from the dairy and stock interests.[16]

These new orders, however, soon revealed divisions in the settler community and ensured that intense political disputes over the future of squatters occurred in several districts in the decade after the war. Map 5.1 shows the complexity of district council politics and emphasises the varying importance of particular interests with their conflicting views of squatters. Previous historians have ignored these divisions within the settler farming community and have underestimated the labour department's difficulties in trying to co-ordinate the various local options into a coherent policy.[17]

Let us briefly investigate these conflicting economic interests among the settlers in three district councils; Nyanza, Naivasha and the Trans Nzoia. The Nyanza District Council was particularly plagued by the conflicting interest of its settler population. The district ranged from prosperous tea estates at Kericho, owned by metropolitan capital, to poor scrub farmers, surviving on maize monoculture in Sotik. Nyanza, therefore, lacked a unified attitude to squatters. There was always strong opposition to new regulations because the settlers lacked the homogeneous agricultural structure of Naivasha or Nakuru. In Nyanza particular interests could invariably be safeguarded by securing exemptions under the local option clause of the 1937 Ordinance.[18] Naivasha, by contrast, was relatively united. It was the one district which had attempted to impose new restrictions during the war and, over the next few years, consistently adopted the most intransigent attitude to the squatters. The settlers were a relatively homogeneous group of small mixed farmers. Situated on the borders of both the Kikuyu and Maasai reserves, many settlers were financially heavily committed to dairy and stock farming and had built up large herds of high-grade cattle, which were particularly susceptible to the diseases they believed were carried by squatter cattle. Whereas in most other districts the cereal farmers were a powerful lobby in support of squatter rights and opposed any measure that threatened to antagonise over half their labour force, in Naivasha the dairy and stock farmers completely dominated the council and were able to ride roughshod over the few defenders of the resident native labourers. In this European cattle-farming area the fear of diseased squatter stock proved far more powerful than the danger of disrupting the harvest by antagonising the squatters. The Naivasha District Council therefore provided the leadership, throughout the period, for the anti-squatter campaign and set the pace for the other councils to follow.[19]

Even in Naivasha, certain farmers in the semi-arid region on the floor of the Rift Valley considered the Council's 1945 proposal to reduce squatter sheep from 40 to 15 too drastic. It would force virtually all squatters to leave the area and seriously disrupt their labour supply. During the summer of 1945, while the new order was being considered in the Secretariat, several farmers warned of the dire consequences it would have. This opposition was centred on Elmenteita and the Kedong Valley, areas with low rainfall, where the squatters depended on their sheep in years of drought and crop failure. Crops had failed for the last three years and earlier, in 1945, famine relief had been distributed. Both the squatters and the local farmers complained that it was unfair that these areas, with an average rainfall of only 24 inches per annum, which was only enough to grow irregular crops of poor-quality maize, should receive the same regulations as in wetter parts of Naivasha. Squatters on Lord Delamere's feudal estate at Soysambu insisted on keeping 40 sheep. Both 1944 and 1945, they pointed out, had been bad years when they had been unable to reap any harvest and their families had survived only by selling sheep. Their continued existence was imperilled by the district council's limitation of squatter stock to a maximum of 15 sheep. These problems of survival were particularly acute on stock farms that provided little work for women or other opportunities to diversify squatter household incomes. Unfortunately stock farms were concentrated in exactly those semi-arid areas where squatter families most needed alternative sources of money or food. During 1944 and 1945 many squatters had left Soysambu to seek work on farms where they could be assured of harvesting enough food to satisfy their families, and the manager was extremely concerned that many more would leave if sheep numbers were reduced as proposed by the new order. The Naivasha Council, however, supported by the majority of dairy and stock farmers, refused to back down, despite pressure from the labour department and mounting squatter protests.[20]

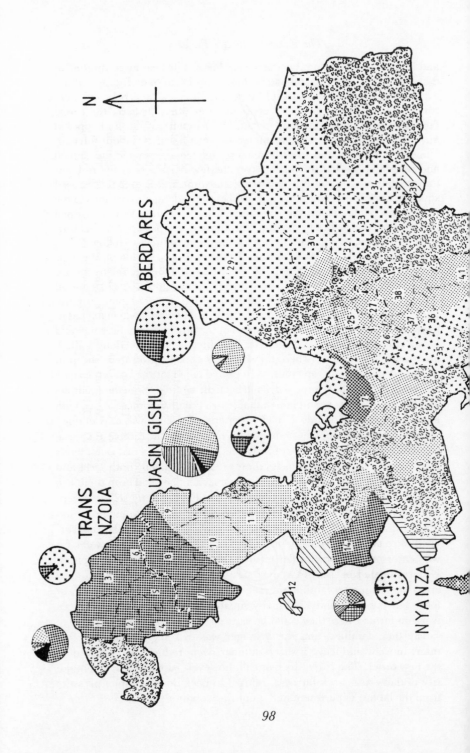

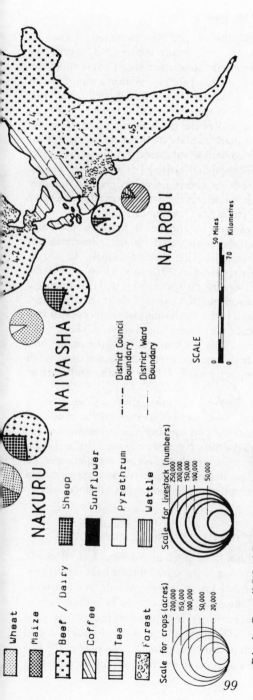

Wheat

Maize

Beef / Dairy

Coffee

Tea

Forest

Sheep

Sunflower

Pyrethrum

Wattle

– – – District Council Boundary

– ·· – District Ward Boundary

Scale for crops (acres)
200,000
150,000
100,000
50,000
20,000

Scale for livestock (numbers)
250,000
200,000
150,000
100,000
50,000

SCALE

0   50 Miles
0   70 Kilometres

NAKURU

NAIVASHA

NAIROBI

District Council Ward Production Committee Areas

1 NNW Trans Nzoia
2 NW Trans Nzoia
3 NE Trans Nzoia
4 WSW Trans Nzoia
5 SSW Trans Nzoia
6 SE Trans Nzoia
7 Turbo
8 Soy/Hoey's Bridge
9 Moiben
10 Eldoret
11 Elgeyo Border
12 Nandi
13 Kipkabus
14 Lumbwa/Songhor
15 Londiani
16 Eldama Ravine
17 Rongai
18 Sotik
19 Kericho
20 Mau/Molo
21 Njoro
22 Solai
23 Subukia
24 Thomson's Falls
25 Ol Joro Orok
26 Mereroni
27 Ol Kalou
28 Marmanet
29 Rumuruti
30 Leshau
31 Nanyuki
32 Aberdares
33 Moyo Ridge
34 Naro Moru
35 Elmenteita
36 Lower Gilgil
37 Upper Gilgil
38 Ol Bolossat
39 Nyeri
40 Naivasha
41 N. Kinangop
42 S. Kinangop
43 Nairobi
44 Thika
45 Machakos

Map 5.1: Settler Districts and Land Use

In Trans Nzoia, by contrast, the council was eventually forced to reconsider. By the beginning of 1946, many maize and pyrethrum farmers had already become seriously concerned about what effect the council's order would have on their labour supply. Within a month of the regulations being introduced, the district council found itself faced with strong opposition from the settlers as squatter resistance grew. A special meeting of the council failed to resolve the disagreements, as the hard-liners proposed that if the order made the labour situation impossible on certain farms, then the district council should insist on the government reintroducing conscription to ensure that the district's valuable food crops were harvested. The opponents of the order, however, insisted that any attempt to reduce squatter stock would seriously disrupt production since resident labourers provided 40 per cent of the labour force.[21]

This dispute was a struggle, as in the other districts, between cereal and dairy farmers. Of the 102 farmers who voted for the elimination of squatter stock in the poll organised by the district council, 42 did so primarily out of fear of the threat posed by African stock to their dairy herds, while of the 63 votes cast against the order, 38 stated that they saw the orders as guaranteed to exacerbate the existing shortage of labour. They proposed that the operation of the regulations be postponed for two years until the world food crisis had eased and Kenya's labour pool increased. Defeated in the council by six votes to five, the maize and pyrethrum farmers continued to protest and eventually forced the council to postpone the reduction of squatter cattle for 18 months until 1 June 1947.[22]

By 1946, maize and wheat farmers, the plantations and even some cattle ranchers in the more arid areas, were concerned by the repercussions of the new draconian limitations on squatter stock and cultivation, which had been pushed through the district councils by the dairy and stock lobby, which did not depend on squatter labour. A cleavage had emerged within settler ranks as African, particularly Kikuyu, opposition increased and the threat of large-scale disruption of production became increasingly apparent.[23]

The labour department and squatter policy

The Kenyan official mind did not have a squatter policy. Indeed as will become apparent, different sections of the colonial state held fundamentally opposed views. The member for local government, for example, soon emerged as a firm ally of the settler district councils in their fight to impose stricter controls. At the centre of this dispute inside the Secretariat stood the labour department. Throughout the war, although it had enforced the new orders, the department had taken little part in the formulation of policy. When bitter opposition emerged among the squatters in Naivasha and Nakuru, the department felt increasingly frustrated by the councils' utter disregard of its warnings.[24]

For the first five years after the Colonial Office had belatedly approved the new Resident Native Labour Ordinance in 1940, the reconstituted labour department had left the district councils to grope towards their different solutions to the squatter problem, but, as the anti-squatter lobby began to force the pace at the end of the war, the labour department felt compelled to intervene. As early as April 1945, Wyn Harris, the Labour Commissioner, had seen the dangers involved and had warned the Chief Secretary that 'the problem of the squatter is going to be one of the most serious problems of this country, and it has already assumed in certain areas unmanageable proportions'. The Labour Commissioner understood the fears of many settler farmers about squatters acquiring land rights inside the White Highlands and the disease threat posed by squatter stock, but he warned that the new district council orders would antagonise the resident labourers and their families and create violent opposition.[25]

The labour department was especially concerned about the draconian restrictions proposed in Naivasha. The department vigorously opposed the order inside the Secretariat and attempted to persuade the Council to reconsider and to allow squatters in the more arid zones to keep 30 or 40 sheep. When the Council rejected this advice, the Labour Commissioner informed the Commissioner for Local Government of his formal opposition to the proposed reductions. Wyn Harris urged a gradual reduction, which would enable the squatters and their employers to adjust and to increase the wage component of household incomes. Despite these protests from the department, which was responsible for enforcing the district councils' orders, the Standing Committee for Local Government in Rural Areas – a settler-dominated body – approved the restrictions on 27 October 1945.[26]

Following this rejection of its advice, the labour department began to devise its own squatter policy. This, however, proved to be an extremely difficult task, since the 1937 Ordinance had transferred power over resident labourers from central government to the district councils. The Secretariat was therefore extremely reluctant to interfere with council affairs in case this precipitated one of Kenya's famed political storms, since to tamper with settler privileges, especially those established by statute, was to play with fire. Settler power had been consolidated during the war. We have seen how the acute manpower shortage forced the government to co-opt settlers to serve in the state bureaucracy. This wartime acceptance of the district councils' responsibility for squatters meant that, after 1945, the labour department had to compete against accepted settler authorities for control over the policy. The war and the 1937 Ordinance had both fundamentally shifted the political balance of power and transformed the district councils into 'governing institutions' with a legitimate right to influence, and even sometimes to dictate, the direction of government action. By 1945 it was widely accepted within the Kenyan government that these settler institutions, rather than the labour department, should determine squatter policy. The department had become no more than the executive arm of the district councils and was expected simply to enforce their orders.[27]

Following the refusal of the district councils and the Standing Committee to heed its warnings, the labour department launched a campaign to force the Secretariat to reconsider or, if this could not be achieved, to transfer responsibility for controlling squatters from the department either to the field administration or to the agricultural department. The Labour Officer at Nakuru warned that if the Nakuru and Naivasha orders were introduced, they would have a catastrophic effect on squatter household incomes. While settlers had profited from the high commodity prices during the war, squatter wages had remained static at eight shillings per 30-day ticket, and they had relied upon selling their stock and vegetables from their *shambas* to satisfy their subsistence requirements. The new orders, he pointed out, were specifically designed to reduce this additional income but did not compensate the squatter families with higher wages or increased rations. Consequently, squatters who had been a comparatively prosperous group of Africans were being squeezed into destitution by the district council regulations.[28]

Wyn Harris was so alarmed by the growth of squatter resistance in Naivasha and the spectre of widespread food shortages among the squatters, who accepted new contracts, that he took independent action and instructed the attestation officers not to issue new contracts unless wages in the semi-arid zones were increased to at least twelve shillings per ticket and squatters given two pounds of *posho* for every day worked. These measures at least ensured that those who reattested were not threatened by starvation. The Labour Commissioner complained that the district councils did not realise the consequences of their restrictions. While their long-term aim to change the squatter into a wage labourer was correct, they were moving far too rapidly. Squatters would not disappear overnight if their stock and cultivation rights were removed. The only result would be chaos and serious resistance. Progress towards stricter control had to be slow, spread over perhaps one or two generations rather than one or two years as some district councils envisaged.[29]

Wyn Harris and his successor Hyde-Clarke both persistently reiterated that squatter wages must be increased to offset reductions in stock and crops. Squatters, Wyn Harris observed in November 1945, often made profits from selling stock of 50 shillings per month; 30 shillings was common. This vital source of income, one of the attractions that originally encouraged squatters to leave the reserves for the White Highlands, was being destroyed. The Nakuru order, for example, would reduce these earnings by half to 25 shillings per month, with the result that squatter family budgets would decline by one-third unless male wages were increased from between eight to twelve shillings per 30-day ticket to at least 30 or 40 shillings. Even this dramatic increase would merely preserve the *status quo*. Until the district councils realised this crucial fact and raised squatter wages in an attempt to offset the effects of their more stringent controls of land use, squatter opposition would continue. Wyn Harris therefore urged the government to assert its authority and to refuse to sanction further reductions in squatter rights.[30]

Eventually the Labour Commissioner persuaded Rennie, who was acting as governor during Mitchell's absence in South Africa, to agree to squatters being compensated with higher wages for reduced stock and crops. He also succeeded in obtaining a respite during which the Secretariat would reconsider the Naivasha order. Cavendish-Bentinck, the member for agriculture, was appointed chairman of an interim committee to consider squatter policy.[31]

Cavendish-Bentinck's committees on squatter policy

Cavendish-Bentinck recognised that the district councils had acted precipitately; after neglecting the squatter problem for years, he observed, the 'local authorities have now taken the bit in their teeth and are all vying with each other in passing regulations which are far too drastic and which do not in any way conform to any general plan'. The committee first met on 14 March 1946 to discuss a detailed report by Wyn Harris. Part one presented a factual review of the question and analysed squatter household incomes. The second part, entitled 'An Approach to the Solution', contained the dramatic statement that the 250,000 squatters simply could not be reabsorbed into the African reserves. Any discussion of the possible options, Wyn Harris declared, had to begin with the recognition that 'it must be accepted that the majority of these families are on the farms for good'. This, of course, was diametrically opposed to the settlers' desire to end the threat of resident labourers acquiring squatters' rights on their farms.[32]

The labour department reported that it had discovered that squatter household incomes were even higher than it had estimated. Wyn Harris explained that they should aim to create a contented wage labourer, 'who regards his labour as his main means of livelihood, but whose efficiency, and indeed, the general economy of the country makes it impossible to pay the wage we know to be necessary for his reasonable standard of living'.[33] Investigations in Naivasha had revealed that in the Kinangop, a high, wet area, where the settler dairy farms were concentrated, average squatter family incomes had amounted to 1,200 shillings per annum, and one household had even earned 3,700 shillings. In the lower zone, where the stock farms were situated, average annual incomes were still above 700 shillings. Indeed the lowest figure the labour department discovered in the whole district was 274 shillings. Average squatter household annual incomes in neighbouring Nakuru District could be broken down as in Table 5.1 below.[34]

Table 5.1: Squatter Household Earnings in Nakuru District in 1946

	Shillings per household per annum
Earnings from cultivation	374
Income from selling sheep	120
Male earnings from ticket labour	90
Earnings by women and children	46
Total earnings	630

This amounted to over 50 shillings per month per household which was more than many urban workers received. These figures, of course, were only estimates acquired in unsettled times when squatter distrust of government was at its height. Nevertheless, they provide the most detailed estimates available of squatter incomes and had a profound impact on the labour department's thinking. Both Wyn Harris and Hyde-Clarke realised that total squatter household earnings would have to be safeguarded and wages raised as quickly as possible. Few settlers had yet realised that squatters earned such considerable sums from their *shambas* and stock. The Labour Commissioner summed up the problem to the committee: 'Farmers regard the resident labourer as cheap labour. He is not, he receives in total wages far more than the ordinary monthly or migrant labourer.'[35] It was therefore inevitable that the district council orders, which had all failed to take account of squatter earnings apart from wage labour, would provoke unrest. Squatter households were earning far more from the black economy than they did by working for settlers. As occupation and stock rights were reduced, the squatters and their families, Wyn Harris emphasised, would have to be compensated. The question was how much could the settler economy afford?

The labour department proposed that total family incomes should not fall below 480 shillings per annum. According to its calculations, this could be assured without threatening the profitability of settler agriculture, since wages only needed to be raised to 12 shillings per month. This would amount to 120 shillings per annum, while earnings by wives and children from farm labour should produce another 150 shillings per annum. Produce grown on squatters' *shambas* would contribute another 90 shillings and food provided by employers would be equivalent to another 120 shillings. The department was optimistic that this 50 per cent increase in the basic wages could be offset by greater productivity.[36]

From this stage onwards progress became extremely slow as the forces of opposition gathered inside the Secretariat to resist the new policy. Cavendish-Bentinck's interim committee had first met to discuss Wyn Harris's statement of squatters on 14 March 1946. There was then a delay of a year while more precise information was gathered on squatter household incomes and, for the first three months of 1947, the Secretariat was preoccupied by the Mombasa general strike. It was therefore not until 3 March 1947 that Cavendish-Bentinck's committee reconvened. So far it had taken nearly a year to confirm Wyn Harris's memorandum.[37]

The new Labour Commissioner, Meredyth Hyde-Clarke, proposed that squatters should be seen as part of the interrelated agrarian problems confronting Kenya. The African reserves were already overpopulated and overstocked and were incapable of absorbing large numbers of dispossessed squatters with their stock. Settler farmers, he insisted, must be persuaded that it was in their interests to keep Africans in the White Highlands as a contented labour supply. Hyde-Clarke outlined a five-phase strategy for creating a contented African population in the White Highlands while ending its dependence on the land. According to this analysis, Africans in the reserves were still at phase one, being totally dependent on the land for their livelihood, while the squatters had advanced to stage two and were partially dependent upon wage labour although cultivation and stock still provided their main source of income. Stage three, which had now been reached, required a gradual continuation of this trend with squatters becoming less dependent on the land and more on wages, until they had reached a position similar to that of the Scottish crofter. Stage four carried this process even further, until the labourer received his income almost entirely in wages and had only a small vegetable plot akin to the cottage labourer. Stage five, the ultimate aim of the process, was the creation of completely dependent wage labourers, without any access to land.[38]

Essentially the move to stage three – the crofter – which was taking place in the White Highlands was the most difficult change, requiring the reduction of squatter cultivation and stock. The labour department considered that this transformation had been made more difficult than necessary by the precipitate action of certain district councils, which seemed to be attempting to jump straight from stage two – the squatter – to stage four without any increase in squatter wages. This foolhardy course inevitably provoked serious opposition and profoundly increased African suspicions of all attempts to wean them away from dependence on the land. According to the labour department, the crofter phase ought to last a generation, during which time the squatters' wives and children could be coaxed into working at least six months a year. The reduction of African holdings to one acre of cultivation and sufficient land to graze ten sheep or two cattle would enable large portions of the White Highlands to be returned to the settler for intensive occupation. This redistribution of land, it was believed, would itself enable the settlers to pay higher wages to their squatters. This would enable a further reduction in African plots and facilitate the progression to stage four. This evolution from the crofter to the cottage labourer phase should be gradual rather than precipitated by convulsive changes in African life. Workers would live on the settler farms and markets, schools, welfare centres and shops would be established in 'villages'. Increased efficiency would enable higher wages to be paid, which would further reduce reliance on land, until in the fifth phase Africans would live in these villages, working as craftsmen or farm labourers, without any access to land.[39]

When the squatter policy committee met on 7 May 1947 to consider Hyde-Clarke's proposals, it agreed that the squatter problem was primarily another aspect of Kenya's agrarian crisis. It also acknowledged that it was politically impossible to send large numbers of dispossessed squatters back to the reserves. Any such attempt would create grave social and economic distress. Squatters must, therefore, either remain 'under control' in the White Highlands or be absorbed in secondary industries in the towns. This statement was a decisive victory for the labour department over its settler critics. It was the first unambiguous assertion by the government that the squatter problem would not go away and could not simply be resolved by moving disgruntled Africans back to the over-crowded reserves. If the squatter was to disappear, he and his family would have to be transformed into fully-paid agricultural labourers, capable of living on their farm wages. The solution to the problem, it seems to have been acknowledged, lay in the White Highlands themselves, and with increased investment and modernisation by the settlers, rather than in new draconian restrictions. At last, it appeared, a policy had been agreed by the Secretariat. Provided the official mind remained united it would be able to force the district councils to moderate their moves against squatters.[40]

The retreat of the Trans Nzoia district council

Let us briefly examine how the combined opposition of the cereal and pyrethrum farmers, the labour department and the field administration in North Nyanza and Nandi was able to force one of the more divided district councils – Trans Nzoia – to reconsider its anti-squatter legislation. Trans Nzoia was the maize granary of East Africa, producing nearly half the settler crop in Kenya, while the neighbouring African reserve, North Nyanza, was the main African producer. During 1946 and 1947 there was a serious shortfall in maize supplies to the central Supply Board and, in February 1946, the Maize Controller had recommended that maize rations, the staple African diet, would have to be cut in the towns from two to one and a half pounds. When the government finally agreed in July, the supply position had become even more desperate. The Trans Nzoia's new restrictions upon squatters would have further disrupted supplies of maize, not only in Trans Nzoia, when the squatters refused to reattest under the new regulations, but also in North Nyanza, which would have had to reabsorb 20,000 cattle and thousands of squatter families, who would have consumed a large proportion of the district's surplus maize crop, which was usually exported. Any further reduction in maize supplies might have had serious repercussions in Nairobi and Mombasa where discontent was growing over the lack of food.[41]

The new Labour Commissioner, Hyde-Clarke, was extremely perturbed that the situation in Trans Nzoia and North Nyanza might become the same as in Naivasha, where the district council's restrictions had produced widespread strikes among farm labourers and mounting violence. He suggested that Trans Nzoia should follow the example of its neighbours in Uasin Gishu, who had introduced what the labour department regarded as the least oppressive of the spate of new orders. Like the labour department's own proposals, it was designed gradually to replace squatters with casual labour. Squatter cattle were gradually to be absorbed into the reserve over a five-year period. The ultimate aim of the Tranz Nzoia regulations was the same, but the labour department and the field administration felt that they were trying to move too quickly.[42]

As we have seen, widespread opposition from the maize and pyrethrum farmers won a postponement of the order until July 1947. This, however, compounded the dangers since the dairy farmers had insisted that, over the following 18 months, squatter cattle would not simply be reduced in number but completely eliminated from the district. This 'compromise' between the settler factions was guaranteed to provoke mass resistance by the squatters and was likely to create serious discontent in North Nyanza. The labour department and field administration protested that no regard had been given to the squatters' interests. The timing of the exodus, for example, had been fixed to serve the settlers rather than to diminish the plight of the squatters' families. The local Labour Officer insisted on the date of the moves coinciding with the African planting season. The end of June, proposed by the district council, was totally unsatisfactory; maize would be at the beginning of its growth cycle; there would be no crops in the reserves to tide the squatters over until they could break new land and secure their harvest. This would take at least six months.[43]

During July and August 1947, Vaughan-Philpott, the chairman of the Trans Nzoia District Council, held discussions with Hyde-Clarke and T.C. Colchester, the secretary for local government, to devise a more acceptable solution. The Labour Commissioner reiterated his view that a gradual reduction was the only way to avoid serious disruption of the labour supply and squatter resistance. He pointed to the situation in

Naivasha as a warning of the dangers of rapid destocking and cautioned that if the Trans Nzoia order were submitted to the governor, the labour department would vigorously oppose its passage through the Executive Council. The government, he informed the hardliners, would under no circumstances contemplate introducing conscription to solve the labour crisis which would ensue. He urged the council to reconsider and to follow its neighbours in the Uasin Gishu, who had adopted a policy of gradual destocking, whereby the number of squatters with cattle were to be reduced by 20 per cent per annum. If only one-fifth of squatters on every farm lost their stock each year, this would sufficiently limit the number of cattle flowing into the reserves to enable them to be absorbed. Equally, if some squatters refused to accept the new regulations they could be dismissed without totally disrupting the labour supply since only a proportion would have to leave every year, and the gaps could be filled with casual labour before the next stage of the controlled reduction began. Hyde-Clarke suggested that squatters' contracts should be allowed to expire rather than be terminated, as the council had suggested, at a specific time. This would further reduce the threat of disruption, since the movement of squatters back to the reserves would become a continuous flow. Serious dislocation in both the Trans Nzoia and the reserves would be prevented and a further fall in the colony's food supply circumvented.[44]

Eventually the council agreed to phase its elimination of squatter stock over a four-year period. It was also persuaded, at the prompting of the District Commissioner for North Nyanza, to meet the North Nyanza chiefs at Kakamega to discuss how they could minimise the effects of the expulsion on the reserves. The chiefs also agreed to encourage disgruntled squatters to remain as farm labourers in the Trans Nzoia without their cattle. Thus the labour department and the field administration, supported by a large number of apprehensive maize farmers, successfully forestalled the growth of squatter resistance and persuaded the district council to reconsider.[45]

Opposition in the Secretariat

Meanwhile the labour department's opponents in the Secretariat had become increasingly vocifeorus. Both Mortimer, the member for Health and Local Government, who was nominally responsible for district council affairs and therefore for squatters, and Cavendish-Bentinck, who was firmly embedded inside the government, were unwilling to antagonise the district councils. These key officials were both settlers in disguise. Mortimer's father had been a prominent settler politician and mayor of Nairobi, while Cavendish-Bentinck was a former leader of the European Elected Members in the Legislative Council and a settler nominee on the Executive Council. They had been extremely embarrassed by the labour department's campaign and feared that it would destroy the good relations between the government and the settlers, which they deemed essential if the government was to secure settler poli- tial support for its social engineering schemes in the reserves. The fight against the Labour Department's squatter policies, therefore, continued inside the Secretariat. Cavendish-Bentinck and Mortimer were parti- cularly adept at using delaying tactics to prevent further consideration of the department's proposals.[46]

It was now two years since Wyn Harris, exasperated by Cavendish- Bentinck's delaying strategy, had tried to shift responsibility for enforcing squatter controls to the agricultural department. It was, he had informed Cavendish-Bentinck, a problem 'concerned to a very much greater degree with the proper utilisation of land, which is your responsibility, rather than with the proper utilisation of man power, which is perhaps mine'.[47] Wyn Harris had argued that the labour department was destroy- ing its reputation among Africans by being identified as the enforcer of the hated new regulations. The agricultural department, however, had no desire to become associated with the anti-squatter orders while it was attempting to gain African support for its agricultural campaign in the reserves. Cavendish-Bentinck did not want to take over executive respon- sibility for squatter affairs or to be exposed to settler and squatter criticism. He realised that, as a former settler politician, he would have provided an ideal target for Kenyatta and for left-wing criticism in Britain if he appeared to be leading the anti-squatter campaign. He preferred instead to play a spoiling role, hamstringing the labour department's attempts to reduce the authority of the district councils from the anony- mity of the Secretariat. The labour department, therefore, remained trapped in the invidious position of having to enforce district council orders with which it wholeheartedly disagreed.[48]

By June 1949, relations between Hyde-Clarke and Cavendish- Bentinck had become so strained that the Labour Commissioner was not even consulted over the preparation of a new memorandum on squatters for the Executive Council discussions. When Hyde-Clarke discovered the meeting had taken place, he furiously demanded that responsibility for squatters be immediately transferred from his department. The squatters, he declared, were an agricultural problem which should be controlled as part of the proposed agrarian legislation. He pointed out that the Execu- tive Council's decision the previous day to approve raids to seize excess stock from squatters in Nairobi district clearly demonstrated the oppres- sive nature of squatter control and that this was undermining African trust in his department which was supposed to protect African interests. Since the Executive Councils's squatter sub-committee no longer con- tained any representative from the labour department, the situation was now completely ludicrous.[49]

Nothing, however, actually happened. The district councils'

dominance became even more entrenched with the formation of a resident labour sub-committee of the standing committee for Local Government in Rural Areas on 4 July 1949 and the announcement, in August, that resident labour inspectors, although members of the labour department, would henceforth come directly under the control of the district councils. Scrutiny of the memorandum on squatters, which was presented to the Executive Council in January 1950, clearly reveals how little progress had been made since 1946 in enforcing the labour department's strategy on the councils. Meanwhile squatter opposition had spread from Naivasha throughout the White Highlands. If anything, the department's influence was less than at the end of the war. In February 1950, the governor himself intervened to ensure that the authority of the settler-dominated Standing Committee for Local Government in Rural Areas should not be infringed. The settlers' infiltration into the heart of the colonial state had ensured that they had been able to block any proposals to reduce their power. The final *dénouement* came in August 1950, when the district councils unilaterally decided to seize complete control over squatter affairs. Major Sharpe, the chairman of the Aberdares Council, with the support of the six other district council representatives on the central co-ordinating committee successfully resolved to disband this consultative committee and to transfer discussion of resident native labour regulations to the Association of District Councils. Henceforth the district councils were to scrutinise their own orders. The attempt to formulate a uniform squatter policy acceptable to different sectors of settler agriculture, the field administration in the reserves and the labour department, was abandoned. After 1950, each district council was allowed to devise its own squatter policies according to the relative strength of the pastoral and arable interests in each particular area. Soon there was a proliferation of local options as the councils abandoned the attempt to reconcile these conflicting interests; by 1952 there were no less than 14 local options in the Nyanza District Council area alone. This plethora of local variations made the labour department's task of enforcement virtually impossible, while the constant alteration of regulations inflamed the squatters.[50]

The growth of squatter resistance

By November 1946, more than 3,000 Kikuyu squatters in Naivasha, Nakuru and the Aberdares had refused to reattest and had been forced to leave the White Highlands.[51] Many of them congregated at Limuru just inside the Kikuyu reserve. On 21 and 22 November 1946, large numbers of them travelled to Nairobi and demonstrated outside the Secretariat, insisting that they would not go away until they had seen the Chief Native Commissioner, the head of the field administration. When a meeting eventually took place at Kiambu on 30 December 1946, with the Provincial and District Commissioners and Hyde-Clarke, the dispossessed squatters protested against the settlers having seized their land at the beginning of the century and demanded that they be resettled on their original *githaka* in Kiambu. The squatters' campaign continued. On the evening of 1 February 1947, for example, a group of 30 squatters broke into the grounds of Government House and confronted a startled Mitchell. They complained that their wives and families in Limuru were starving and insisted on knowing why they had been forced off their small *shambas* when the settlers already had such large farms. Many of their families, they declared, had worked on settler farms for 30 years, had completely lost contact with Kikuyuland and had nowhere to go. The governor, of course, refused their demand for land in Kiambu and urged them to reattest, if only for 12 months, until the authorities could investigate the problem. They had, the governor declared, brought their troubles upon themselves, by abandoning their homes and *shambas* when the new district council regulations were introduced, without any thought of how they would survive.

Throughout 1947, petitions flowed from the Kikuyu Highlands Squatters' Association in Limuru to the Secretary of State, complaining about the Kikuyu's plight and urging the Colonial Office to intervene to save them from the settler-controlled Kenyan government. Mitchell, however, advised Whitehall that they must not waver since 'any weakening in this attitude at the present time would inevitably lead to the belief that Africans could occupy the European lands with impunity and a very dangerous situation would be created'.[52] In other words, the sanctity of the White Highlands must remain inviolate and the authority of the Kenyan government and the settler-controlled district councils upheld.

In Naivasha, Nakuru and the Aberdares, where the vast majority of squatters were Kikuyu, the labour department could do little to protect them from the onslaught of a united settler community after the war. We have noted that these three districts were comparatively homogeneous communities of heavily capitalised dairy and stock farmers, who were determined to get rid of all squatter-owned stock from their farms. Between 1945 and 1947 the settlers successfully fought and defeated their Kikuyu economic rivals, using their privileged access to the corridors of power to manipulate the colonial state.[53]

During the first months of 1947, squatter discontent spread. Abaluhya, Elgeyo and Nandi squatters, as well as the Kikuyu, had realised that the district council orders threatened their continued prosperity and, in desperation, had turned to violence as a final act of resistance. Arson and cattle maiming enabled the politically powerless to voice their opposition to the new restrictions which were destroying their way of life. By the end of 1947, the intransigent behaviour of the district councils had irreparably damaged the labour department's gradualist strategy to transform the squatter into a contented and productive wage labourer. September 1947 had seen the virtual collapse of Mitchell's original policies. The government's agricultural campaign in the reserves, based on terracing, had alienated the Kikuyu peasantry and Nairobi seemed to be on the verge of a general strike. Meanwhile, in the White Highlands squatter discontent was causing acute alarm not only in Naivasha and Nakuru, where many were still refusing to reattest under the new regulations, but also in the Uasin Gishu and the Aberdares, where within six weeks there were strikes on 14 farms. Many Trans Nzoia settlers, such as S.H. Powles and A.C. Hoey, two of the district's largest landowners, were also extremely concerned about the possibility of the troubles spreading to their area when the new district council order, reducing squatter cattle by one-third, came into operation on 1 January 1948. If all squatter stock were to be removed in a three-stage operation by 1 April 1950, the overcrowded Nandi and North Nyanza reserves would have to absorb large numbers of squatter-owned cattle. It was estimated, for example, that the total number of cattle in the Nandi reserve would increase by more than 50 per cent, from 175,000 to 275,000, with disastrous consequences for the ecological balance of the reserve.[54]

By the end of 1947, Kikuyu squatters from the Naivasha, Nakuru, Aberdares and Nairobi district council areas had been forced to admit defeat. Unlike the Kalenjin or Abaluhya squatters, they could not pressurise the settler farmers by threatening to return to the reserves, since most had abandoned their *githaka* land three decades earlier when they had moved to the White Highlands. The Kikuyu squatters therefore had three options. Some began to move into the Uasin Gishu and Trans Nzoia, where the squatter option was still possible. Others returned in frustration to Central Province, where they became a focus of discontent. The vast majority, however, realising that a return to Kikuyuland was pointless, remained on the settler farms, embittered and waiting to be politicised. Once again the settlers seemed to have got their way and had forced the government to approve measures about which many members of the administration and the labour department had serious reservations. It appeared to many squatters that constitutionalist African politicians of the élitist Kenya African Union made little headway against the entrenched influence of the settlers. The moderates became increasingly discredited as their constituents turned in desperation to the militant advocates of violent resistance to what they denounced as 'settler rule'.[55]

After 1947 the Kikuyu squatters waited, preparing to get their own back on their settler overlords. By 1949/50, the situation was already very tense. Those squatters who had reattested were being attacked and large numbers of the radicals were abandoning the farms and vanishing into the forests. The deteriorating labour supply was already beginning to concern the Naivasha resident labour committee. In the neighbouring Aberdares

District Council, Major L.B.L. Hughes complained that when squatters refused to reattest 'it is a very rare occurrence that new labour applies to take their place, unless first class land, usually the very best on the farm is made available for their cultivation'.[56]

Squatter resistance in the area was led by Mwangi Mukea and, until his arrest, the administration seemed on the verge of losing control. As in the Uasin Gishu, where Elijah Masinde's *Dini ya Msambwa* was active, resistance took the form of religious millenarianism. Former squatters in Naivasha joined the *Dini ya Jesu Kristo*, with its message that the White Highlands belonged to Africans and its prophecy that the Europeans would soon be driven out of Kenya. Rumours of a secret organisation called Mau Mau, which would unite the Kikuyu and drive out the settlers, began to circulate. The District Commissioner, R.D.F. Ryland, was so concerned that he held six anti-Mau Mau *barazas* in Naivasha during August 1950, which were attended by hundreds of squatters. Between 1950 and 1952, physical intimidation increased among the squatters with the spread of oathing from Olenguruone on the Mau escarpment, an area radicalised by a ten-year conflict over the government's agricultural regulations. Oath administrators from Nairobi had also been active around Limuru, where many former Naivasha squatters had taken refuge. Oathing had also spread to the resident labourers on the settler farms in North and South Kinangop. Underground opposition was gaining strength. Africans opposed to Mau Mau were attacked and several mutilated bodies were discovered. Beneath the surface calm of the White Highlands discontent seethed.[57]

The district councils' policies of compulsory destocking and drastic reductions in squatter cultivation had produced a violent backlash. By 1952, the labour department's squatter inspectors had been completely discredited in African eyes, because of the district councils' intransigence, and had become identified as the oppressive arm of the settler-controlled state. Mau Mau support was strongest exactly where the reductions in squatters' rights had been most severe – among the Kikuyu resident labourers of the Aberdares, Nakuru and, above all, Naivasha areas.[58]

Notes

1. KNA Lab 9/320, 'The Resident Labourers' Ordinance: Aberdare District Council, 1944–51', Major L.B.L. Hughes to DC Naivasha, 16 March 1949.
2. Contrast the estimates of squatter household incomes in CO 533/549/38232/15 (1946–47), 'European Settlement: Squatters', Wyn Harris's 'A Discussion of the Problem of the Squatter', 21 February 1946; and J.H. Martin, 'The Problem of the Squatter: Economic Survey of Resident Labour in Kenya', 24 February 1947; with CO 852/662/19936/2 (1945–46), 'Soil Erosion: Kenya', N. Humphrey, 'The Relationship of Population to the Land in South Nyeri', paragraph 9.

The Kikuyu Squatter Problem

3. KNA Lab 9/316, 'Resident Labour: Naivasha County Council, 1941–59'; Lab 9/320,' The Resident Labour Ordinance: Aberdares District Council, 1944–51; Lab 9/317, 'Resident Labour: Nakuru, 1945–53'.

Ethnic Orgins of Squatters in the White Highlands in 1945

	Luo, Gusii & Luhya	Kipsigis	Nandi	Kikuyu	Kamba	Others	Total
Nairobi	252	nil	nil	11,675	18,620	96	30,643
Naivasha	24	166	50	22,136	79	227	22,682
Nakuru	687	929	106	36,383	87	300	38,492
Aberdares	24	392	5	19,622	11	218	20,272
Uasin Gishu	3,843	898	16,723	3,709	4	4,907	30,084
Trans Nzoia	8,946	431	1,800	754	nil	5,811	17,742
Nyanza	822	9,582	4,295	6,754	nil	24	21,477
Forests	66	52	nil	21,143	8	114	21,383
Total	14,664	12,450	22,979	122,176	18,809	11,697	202,775

The table is based on information from CO 533/549/38232/15 (1946–47), 'European Settlement: Squatters', J.H. Martin, 'The Problem of the Squatter: Economic Survey of Resident Labour in Kenya', 24 February 1947.

4. KNA Lab 9/310, 'Resident Labourers' General: Ordinance Committee, 1949–50', meeting of the central co-ordinating committee, 9 August 1950; and minute by the Secretary of Health and Local Government, 28 August 1950.

5. F. Furedi, 'The Kikuyu Squatters in the Rift Valley', pp. 179–83; K.J. King and R.M. Wambaa, 'The Political Economy of the Rift Valley', pp. 193–209; and T.M.J. Kanogo's unpublished thesis, 'The History of Kikuyu Movement . . .', especially pp. 74–87, 113–17. See also her unpublished articles, 'The Kikuyu Squatter Phenomenon in the Nakuru District of the Rift Valley', and 'Comparative Analysis of Aspirations of the Kikuyu, Luo and Luhya Workers in the White Highlands', pp. 3–9; G. Kitching, *Class and Economic Change in Kenya*, p. 294; and Report of the Kenya Land Commission: Evidence and Memoranda, vol. 1, (London, 1934, Cmd. 4556), pp. 167–70, 589–92, 885–7.

6. T.M.J. Kanogo's thesis, 'The History of Kikuyu Movement . . .', pp. 149–224; and R.M.A. van Zwanenberg, *Colonial Capitalism and Labour in Kenya*, pp. 210–74.

7. KNA Lab 9/594, 'Resident Native Labour Ordinance: Operation and Application of Ordinance, 1940–48'; and CO 533/549/38232/15 (1946–47), 'European Settlement: Squatters', P. Wyn Harris, 'A Discussion of the Problem of the Squatter', 21 February 1946; and J.H. Martin, 'The Problem of the Squatter: Economic Survey of Resident Labour in Kenya', 24 February 1947.

8. D.M. Anderson's unpublished thesis, 'Herder, Settler and Colonial Rule', pp. 130–1, 202.

9. *East African Standard*, 11 and 12 September 1931, quoted in R.M.A. van Zwanenberg, *Colonial Capitalism and Labour in Kenya*, p. 216; CO 533/537/38608 (1944–46), 'Land Policy: Memorandum by the Anti-Slavery and Aboriginal Protection Society', note to Oliver Stanley, 5 May 1944; and CO 533/556/38664/2 (1947), 'Land Policy: Memorandum by the Labour Party on Land Utilization and Settlement', Morgan Philips to Creech Jones, 4 March 1947.

10. P. Mosley's thesis, 'The Settler Economies', pp. 178–80. For the Land Bank's role in the post-war years see CO 533/542/38071 (1945–47), 'Land and Agricultural Bank'; and CO 533/534/38232 (1945), 'European Settlement Scheme', Mitchell to Creasy, 30

May 1945; and meeting of B.F. Macdona and A.B. Cohen, 11 May 1945; J.M. Lonsdale's unpublished paper, 'The Growth and Transformation of the Colonial State in Kenya', pp. 1–8. The campaign by the settlers to foreclose the squatter option paradoxically, in the long term, brought the end of European farming in Kenya.

11. M.G. Redley's unpublished thesis, 'The Politics of a Predicament', pp. 175–202, 239; Y.P. Ghai and J.P.W.B. McAuslan, *Public Law and Political Change in Kenya*, pp. 130–1, 202.

12. S. Stichter, *Migrant Labour in Kenya*, pp. 128–9; K.J. King and R.M. Wambaa, 'The Political-Economy of the Rift Valley', pp. 201–2; and T.M.J. Kanogo's unpublished thesis, 'The History of Kikuyu Movement . . .', pp. 294–338.

13. KNA Lab 9/309, 'Resident Labour General: Report of Ad Hoc Committee, 1946–50', Hyde-Clarke's memorandum on Resident Labour Policy, undated, but probably March 1947; Lab 9/316, 'Resident Labour: Naivasha County Council, 1941–59', P. Wyn Harris to T. Colchester, Commissioner for Local Government, 29 September 1945; and to Rennie, Chief Secretary, 16 February 1946; and Resolution of the Council, 21 February 1946; Lab 9/326, 'Resident Labour: Trans Nzoia, 1945–57', P. Wyn Harris to the acting Chief Secretary, 12 November 1945, Chairman Trans Nzoia Council's letters, 14 August 1946 and 14 May 1947; Lab 9/749, 'Nyeri Production and Manpower Committee, 1946–52', Kenya Information Office, release no. 435, on the Labour Commissioner's speech at Naro Moru on 28 August 1946; Lab 9/1071, 'Resident Labourers Ordinance: The Problem of the Squatter: *Ad Hoc* Committee, 1946–48', E.M. Hyde-Clarke to the Member for Labour, 16 June 1949 and E.M. Hyde-Clarke to Rennie, 17 September 1946; and MAA 8/124, 'Central Coordinating Committee for Resident Labour, 1947–51', minutes of the meeting on 7 May 1947; Lab 9/598, 'Resident Labour: Trans Nzoia, 1943–56'; Lab 9/326 'Resident Labour: Trans Nzoia, 1945–57'. See also Lab 9/310, 'Resident Labour General: Ordinance Committee, 1949–50', Cavendish-Bentinck to Assistant Secretary for Agriculture, 28 June 1950.

14. KNA Lab 9/316, 'Resident Labour: Naivasha County Council, 1941–59', Soysambu Estate to P. Wyn Harris, 26 April 1945; Lab 9/326, 'Resident Labour: Trans Nzoia, 1945–57', Council minutes, 23 October 1946; and F.R. Bancroft to Commissioner for Local Government, 7 November 1946; and Lab 9/598, 'Resident Labour: Trans Nzoia, 1943–56', A.C. Hoey to F.W. Cavendish-Bentinck, 12 February 1946; and protest from R.W. Buswell, February 1947 and Council minutes, 23 October 1946; and R.L. Tignor, *The Colonial Transformation of Kenya*, pp. 310–23.

15. This was especially true in Trans Nzoia. Lab 9/326, 'Resident Labour: Trans Nzoia, 1945–57' and Lab 9/598, 'Resident Labour: Trans Nzoia, 1943–56' contain a large number of petitions from cereal and plantation farmers against the district council order, and reports of bitter meetings of the divided council.

16. KNA Lab 9/97, 'Association of District Councils, 1941–53', report of the Councils' conference on 26–27 June 1944; and the meeting on 12–13 September 1944. See also Lab 9/10, 'Labour: Squatters in Forest Areas, 1944–50', S.J. Pinney to the Conservator of Forests, 11 October 1944.

17. Furedi, Kanogo, King and van Zwanenberg have largely ignored these important divisions among the European settler farming community and have treated them as an undifferentiated conglomerate. In fact, settler farmers were extremely divided and had diametrically opposed attitudes towards squatters.

18. KNA Lab 9/331, 'Resident Labour: Nyanza District Council, 1946–53'; and Lab 9/304, 'Resident Labour: General Correspondence', provides a detailed list of the various district council orders as of 21 June 1949.

19. KNA Lab 9/316, 'Resident Labour: Naivasha County Council, 1941–59'.

20. *ibid*, Manager of Soysambu Estate, Elmenteita, to the Secretary for Local Government, 26 April 1945; W.O. Townsend to C.E. Mortimer, 22 December 1945 and P. Wyn Harris to C.E. Mortimer, 31 December 1945.

21. KNA Lab 9/326, 'Resident Labour: Tranzs Nzoia, 1945–57', debate of the Trans

The Kikuyu Squatter Problem

Nzoia District Council, 27 February 1946; and Lab 9/598, 'Resident Labour: Trans Nzoia, 1943–56', A.C. Hoey to F.W. Cavendish-Bentinck, 12 February 1946.

22. KNA Lab 9/326, 'Resident Labour: Trans Nzoia, 1945–57', T.L. Bolton, Chairman of the Council, to the Commissioner for Local Government, 14 May 1947; and the minutes of the special meeting of the district council and the Trans Nzoia Association with Hyde-Clarke, 26 May 1947, for subsequent developments in the battle.

23. KNA Lab 9/1071, 'Resident Labourers Ordinance: The Problem of the Squatter: Ad Hoc Committee, 1946–48', Hyde-Clarke to Rennie, 17 September 1946; and Hyde-Clarke's memorandum on squatters, dated 7 May 1947.

24. KNA Lab 9/309, 'Resident Labourers' General: Report of Ad Hoc Committee, 1946–50', Hyde-Clarke to the Member for Labour, 16 June 1949; Lab 9/316, 'Resident Labour: Naivasha County Council, 1941–59', P. Wyn Harris to T. Colchester, Commissioner for Local Government, 29 September 1945; W.O. Townsend to C.E. Mortimer, 22 December 1945; and P. Wyn Harris to C.E. Mortimer, 31 December 1945; Lab 9/326, 'Resident Labour: Trans Nzoia, 1945–57', P. Wyn Harris to T. Colchester, 12 April 1946; and Hyde-Clarke to T. Colchester, 2 July 1946; Lab 9/598, 'Resident Labour: Trans Nzoia, 1943–56', Marchant, the Chief Native Commissioner to C.E. Mortimer, 29 July 1946; and Lab 9/1071, 'Resident Labourers Ordinance: The Problem of the Squatter: Ad Hoc Committee, 1946–48', Hyde-Clarke to Rennie, 17 September 1946.

25. KNA Lab 9/304, 'Resident Labourers: General Correspondence', Wyn Harris to Rennie, 12 April 1945; Lab 9/97, 'Association of District Councils, 1941–53', P. Wyn Harris to Rennie, 3 November 1945; Lab 9/316, 'Resident Labour: Naivasha County Council, 1941–59', Wyn Harris to the Commissioner for Local Government, 29 September 1945; and to C.E. Mortimer, 31 December 1945; and to Rennie, 16 February 1946; Lab 9/326, 'Resident Labour: Trans Nzoia, 1945–47', Wyn Harris to acting Chief Secretary, 12 November 1945; Lab 9/331, 'Resident Labour: Nyanza District Council, 1946–53', Wyn Harris to the Attorney General, 7 November 1945; and CO 533/549/38232/15 (1946–47), 'European Settlement: Squatters', P. Wyn Harris, 'A Discussion of the Problem of the Squatter', 21 February 1946.

26. KNA Lab 9/316, 'Resident Labour: Naivasha County Council, 1941–59', P. Wyn Harris to the Commissioner for Local Government, 29 September 1945; protest from Soysambu Estate, 26 April 1945; W.O. Townsend to C.E. Mortimer, 22 December 1945; and Wyn Harris to Mortimer, 31 December 1945. See also Lab 9/97, 'Association of District Councils, 1941–53', Wyn Harris to Rennie, 3 November 1945; Lab 9/97, 'Association of District Councils, 1941–53', Wyn Harris to C.E. Mortimer, the Commissioner for Local Government, 29 September 1945; and the memorandum prepared for the Executive Council, dated 5 February 1946.

27. KNA Lab 9/594, 'Resident Native Labour Ordinance: Operation and Application of the Ordinance, 1940–48'. See also Y.P. Ghai and J.P.W.B. McAuslan, Public Law and Political Change in Kenya, pp. 95–6. Lab 9/316, 'Resident Labour: Naivasha County Council, 1941–53'; Lab 9/326, 'Resident Labour: Trans Nzoia, 1945–57'; Lab 9/317, 'Resident Labour: Nakuru, 1945–53' provide many examples of district councils taking independent action against the advice of the labour department.

28. KNA Lab 9/1071, 'Resident Labourers Ordinance: The Problem of the Squatter: Ad Hoc Committee, 1946–48', Hyde-Clarke to Rennie, 17 September 1946; and Hyde-Clarke to the Committee, 7 May 1945; Lab 9/749, 'Nyeri Production and Manpower Committee, 1946–52', Kenya Information Office, release no. 435, about the Labour Commissioner's speech at Naro Moru on 28 August 1946; Lab 9/317, 'Resident Labour: Nakuru, 1945–53', W.O. Townsend to Wyn Harris, 11 November 1945; and Hyde-Clarke to Rennie, September 1946. See also CO 533/549/38232/15 (1946–47) 'European Settlement: Squatters', Wyn Harris, 'A Discussion of the Problem of the Squatter', 21 February 1946; and J.H. Martin, 'The Problem of the Squatter:

Economic Survey of Resident Labour in Kenya', 24 February 1947, for detailed estimates of squatter household incomes.

29. KNA Lab 9/316, 'Resident Labour: Naivasha County Council, 1941–59', Wyn Harris to Rennie, 16 February 1946; and to the Labour Officer, Nakuru, 20 March 1946; and CO 533/549/38232/15 (1946–47), 'European Settlement: Squatters', Wyn Harris, 'A Discussion of the Problem of the Squatter', 21 February 1946.

30. KNA Lab 9/317, 'Resident Labour: Nakuru, 1945–53', Hyde-Clarke to Rennie, September 1946; and Lab 9/749, 'Nyeri Production and Manpower Committee, 1946–52', Kenya Information Office, release no. 435, 28 August 1946; and Lab 9/316, 'Resident Labour: Naivasha County Council, 1941–59', Wyn Harris to Rennie 16 February 1946; and C.H. Thornley to Marchant, the Chief Native Commissioner, 22 February 1946. See also the protest from the Naivasha district council at the decision, 21 February 1946.

31. KNA Lab 9/1071 'Resident Labourers Ordinance: The Problem of the Squatter: *Ad Hoc* Committee, 1946–48', Hyde-Clarke to Rennie, 17 September 1946; and MAA 8/124, 'Central Coordinating Committee for Resident Labour, 1947–51', Hyde-Clarke to Cavendish-Bentinck, 3 March 1947, for the campaign behind the establishment of the *Ad Hoc* Committee.

32. KNA Lab 9/598, 'Resident Labour: Trans Nzoia, 1943–56', Cavendish-Bentinck to A.C. Hoey, 15 February 1946; and CO 533/549/38232/15 (1946–47), 'European Settlement: Squatters', Wyn Harris, 'A Discussion of the Problem of the Squatter', 21 February 1946.

33. CO 533/549/38232/15 (1946–47), Wyn Harris, 'A Discussion of the Problem of the Squatter', 21 February 1946.

34. CO 533/549/38232/15 (1946–47), 'European Settlement: Squatters', Wyn Harris, 'A Discussion of the Problem of the Squatter', 21 February 1946. For other estimates of squatter household earnings, see KNA 9/309, 'Resident Labourers General: Report of *Ad Hoc* Committee, 1946–50', Hyde-Clarke's Policy on Resident Labour for Cavendish-Bentinck, 5 March 1947.

35. CO 533/549/38232/15 (1946–47), 'European Settlement: Squatters', Wyn Harris, 'A Discussion of the Problem of the Squatter', 21 February 1946. See also KNA 9/749, 'Nyeri Production and Manpower Committee, 1946–52', Kenya Information Office, release no. 535, 28 August 1946.

36. KNA Lab 9/1071, 'Resident Labourers Ordinance: The Problem of the Squatter: *Ad Hoc* Committee, 1946–48', draft statement of policy for Cavendish-Bentinck's committee, prepared by Hyde-Clarke and J.H. Martin, dated 5 March 1947.

37. For the origins of the *Ad Hoc* Committee, see KNA MAA 8/124, 'Central Coordinating Committee for Resident Labour', Hyde-Clarke to Cavendish-Bentinck, 3 March 1947.

38. KNA Lab 9/309, 'Resident Labourers General: Report of *Ad Hoc* Committee, 1946–50' Hyde-Clarke's 'Policy on Resident Labour', 5 March 1947; and Lab 9/1071, 'Resident Labourers Ordinance: The Problem of the Squatter: *Ad Hoc* Committee, 1946–48', draft statement of policy discussed by Cavendish-Bentinck's committee, 7 March 1947.

39. *ibid.*

40. KNA Lab 9/1071, 'Resident Labourers Ordinance: The Problem of the Squatter: *Ad Hoc* Committee, 1946–48', draft statement of policy discussed by Cavendish-Bentinck's committee, 7 March 1947.

41. KNA Lab 9/748, 'Naivasha District Council Labour Committee, 1944–47', meeting 14 May 1946; Lab 9/598, 'Resident Labour: Trans Nzoia, 1943–56', PC Rift Valley to the Chief Native Commissioner, 2 March 1945; and Wyn Harris to the acting Chief Secretary, 12 November 1945; and Lab 9/1835, 'Mombasa Strikes, 1937–46', Mombasa Monthly Intelligence Report, September 1942; and P. de V. Allen to the

acting governor, Rennie, 15 October 1942.

42. KNA Lab 9/598, 'Resident Labour: Trans Nzoia, 1943–56', Chief Native Commissioner to C.E. Mortimer, 29 July 1946; and Wyn Harris to Mortimer, 19 February 1947. See also Lab 9/326, 'Resident Labour: Trans Nzoia, 1945–47', Labour Officer, Kitale to Hyde-Clarke, 2 August 1946; and Hyde-Clarke to the Commissioner for Local Government, 30 August 1946; and to C.E. Mortimer, 25 November 1946.

43. Lab 9/326, 'Resident Labour: Trans Nzoia, 1945–47', Wyn Harris to Colchester, 12 April 1946; Hyde-Clarke to Commander Vernon of the Trans Nzoia District Council, 26 July 1946; the Labour Officer, Kitale to Hyde-Clarke, 2 August 1946; and T. Colchester, the Commissioner for Local Government to Hyde-Clarke, 21 August 1946.

44. Lab 9/326, Vaughan-Philpott's memorandum on resident labour, 14 August 1946; and the minutes of the special meeting between Hyde-Clarke and the district council and the Trans Nzoia Association, 26 May 1947.

45. Lab 9/326, minutes of the special meeting between Hyde-Clarke, the District Council and the Trans Nzoia Association, 26 May 1947. For petitions to be excluded from the council order by cereal farmers see KNA Lab 9/598, 'Resident Labour: Trans Nzoia, 1943–56'.

46. KNA Lab 9/1071, 'Resident Labour Ordinance: The Problem of the Squatter: *Ad Hoc* Committee, 1946–48', Hyde-Clarke to Rennie, 17 September 1946; Hyde-Clarke to Cavendish-Bentinck, 18 March 1948 and 2 July 1948.

47. KNA Lab 9/309, 'Resident Labour General: Report of *Ad Hoc* Committee, 1946–50', Labour Department to Cavendish-Bentinck, 3 March 1947.

48. *ibid*, Hyde-Clarke to Member for Labour, 16 June 1949. See also Lab 9/310, 'Resident Labourers General: Ordinance Committee, 1949–50', Cavendish-Bentinck to the Assistant Secretary of Agriculture, 28 June 1950.

49. KNA Lab 9/310, 'Resident Labour General: Report of *Ad Hoc* Committee, 1946–50', Hyde-Clarke to Member for Labour, 16 June 1949. For further details see Lab 9/1071, 'Resident Labour Ordinance: The Problem of the Squatter: *Ad Hoc* Committee, 1946–48', memorandum to the Executive Council on the disposal of surplus stock in the Nairobi District, 8 June 1949; and Lab 9/309, 'Resident Labour General: Report of *Ad Hoc* Committee, 1946–50', Hyde-Clarke to Member for Labour, 16 June 1949.

50. KNA MAA 8/124, 'Central Coordinating Committee for Resident Labour, 1947–51', Cavendish-Bentinck's 'Resident Labour in Kenya: Outline of Policy', drafted 15 February 1949. This should be contrasted with CO 533/549/38232/15 (1946–47), 'European Settlement: Squatters', Wyn Harris, 'A Discussion of the Problem of the Squatter', 21 February 1946; and KNA Lab 9/1071, 'Resident Labour Ordinance: The Problem of the Squatter: *Ad Hoc* Committee, 1946–48', Hyde-Clarke's proposals, discussed on 7 May 1947. See also Lab 9/310, 'Resident Labourers General: Ordinance Committee, 1949–50', F.W. Cavendish-Bentinck to the Assistant Secretary for Agriculture, 28 June 1950; and KNA Lab 9/304, 'Resident Labour General Correspondence', provisions of District Councils' Orders; Lab 9/312, 'Resident Labour Provincial Coordinating Committees, 1950', the second meeting of the Nyanza Coordinating Committee, 6 May 1950; and the first meeting of the Kericho committee, 20 February 1950. See also Lab 9/331, 'Resident Labour: Nyanza District Council, 1946–53', comprehensive order, 5 October 1951.

51. KNA DC/NKU 1/5, 'Nakuru–Naivasha–Ravine District Annual Reports', (1946) pp. 3, 7–8; and (1947) Annual Report, pp. 25–6. F. Furedi, 'The Social Composition of the Mau Mau Movement in the White Highlands', pp. 492–7; and T.M.J. Kanogo's thesis, 'The History of Kikuyu Movement . . .', pp. 360–8.

52. CO 533/549/38232/15 (1946–47), 'European Settlement: Squatters', Mitchell to Creech Jones, 19 February 1947; and CO 533/543/38086/38 (1946–47), 'Petitions: Kikuyu Grievances', Samuel K. Gikami to Creech Jones, 16 July 1947; and Kikuyu Squatters to the Chief Justice of Kenya, 2 September 1947.

53. KNA Lab 9/316, 'Resident Labour: Naivasha County Council, 1941–59'; Lab 9/320, 'Resident Labourers Ordinance: Aberdare District Council, 1944–51'; Lab 9/317, 'Resident Labour: Nakuru, 1945–53'; and Lab 9/10, 'Labour: Squatters in Forest Areas, 1944–50'.

54. KNA Lab 9/1071, 'Resident Labourers Ordinance: The Problem of the Squatter: *Ad Hoc* Committee, 1946–48', Labour Officer, Eldoret, to the Labour Commissioner, 29 January 1948. See also Lab 9/325, 'Reduction of Resident Labour Stock, 1950–57', PC Nyanza to Cavendish-Bentinck, 3 April 1952.

55. Lab 9/320, 'Resident Labourers Ordinance: Aberdare District Council, 1944–51', A.R. Swift, Labour Officer at Thomson's Falls, to Hyde-Clarke, 18 October 1946; and Lab 9/317, 'Resident Labour: Nakuru, 1945–53', J.D. Stringer to the Chief Native Commissioner, 25 November 1946; and the reports by W.O. Townsend, dated 12 September 1946, and A.R. Swift, dated 13 November 1947; RH Mss. Afr. s. 1121, S.H. Powles's diary 10 July 1947. KNA Lab 9/598, 'Resident Labour, Trans Nzoia, 1943–56' contains complaints from other settlers, especially A.C. Hoey to F.W. Cavendish-Bentinck, 12 February 1946; and Lab 9/771, 'Labour Control: Agricultural, 1946–47', G. Walker to Hyde-Clarke, 15 October 1946. See also Lab 9/1071, 'Resident Labourers Ordinance: The Problem of the Squatter: *Ad Hoc* Committee, 1946–48', Labour Officer, Eldoret, to the Labour Commissioner, 29 January 1948; and Lab 9/325, 'Reduction of Resident Labour Stock, 1950–57', PC Nyanza to Cavendish-Bentinck, 3 April 1952.

56. KNA MAA 8/125 'Reports Principal Labour Officer, 1947–48', report for February 1947, quoted in F. Furedi's unpublished paper, 'Olenguruone in Mau Mau Historiography', p. 4; Lab 9/320, 'Resident Labourers Ordinance: Aberdare District Council, 1944–51', A.R. Swift to Hyde-Clarke, 18 October 1946. See also Lab 9/317, 'Resident Labour: Nakuru, 1945–53'; and Lab 9/316, 'Resident Labour: Naivasha County Council, 1941–59', and MAA 8/124, 'Central Coordinating Committee for Resident Labour, 1947–51', A.T. Wise, Registrar of Native Societies, to Hyde-Clarke, 13 March 1947; Secretariat 1/12/8, 'Labour Unrest: Intelligence Reports, Central Province, 1947', report 20 February 1947; and CO 533/543/38086/38 (1946–47), 'Petitions: Kikuyu Grievances', Samuel K. Gikami to Creech Jones, 16 July 1947; and the government's reply, dated 14 November 1947; and Lab 3/41, 'Resident Labour: Squatters', police report, September 1946; and F. Furedi, 'Social Composition of the Mau Mau Movement in the White Highlands', pp. 492–7, for details of the gathering at Naivasha. Lab 9/317, 'Resident Labour: Nakuru, 1945–53', A.T. Wise to the Labour Commissioner, 25 July 1946, reports the attempt at mediation with discontented squatters by Joseph Kinyua, the Secretary of the Kenya African Union branch at Nakuru, and recounts the hostile treatment he received. Lab 9/337, 'Resident Labour: Forest Areas, 1947–50', Hyde-Clarke to Wyn Harris, 5 April 1949; and F.J. Hart, Labour Officer, Thomson's Falls, to Divisional Forest Officer, 25 August 1949, contains details of plans to reward Johnson Kaya, the President of the local branch of the Kenya African Union, for mediating in squatter disputes. See also F. Furedi, 'The Development of Anti-Asian Opinion among Africans in Nakuru District', pp. 347–58.

57. KNA Lab 9/320, 'Resident Labourers Ordinance: Aberdare District Council, 1944–51', Major L.B.L. Hughes to DC Naivasha, 16 March 1946, for protest about the lax supervision of forest squatters employed by the Forest Department and private sawmills.

58. KNA Lab 9/1071, 'Resident Labourers Ordinance: The Problem of the Squatter: *Ad Hoc* Committee, 1946–48', Hyde-Clarke to Rennie, 17 September 1946; and Hyde-Clarke to the Member for Labour, 16 June 1949; F. Furedi, 'The Social Composition of the Mau Mau Movement in the White Highlands', p. 499; and T.M.J. Kanogo's thesis, 'The History of Kikuyu Movement . . .', pp. 337–8, 366–75.

Six

Olenguruone

The fate of the prototype African settlement at Olenguruone on the western Mau escarpment was of profound importance for the development of Mau Mau. The 4,000 people who were moved into the area in 1941 were mainly former Kikuyu squatter families who had left the White Highlands to pursue the peasant option as 'interpenetrators' in Maasailand. By 1944, they had already created a centre of militant opposition to the government's agricultural campaign and transformed the traditional Kikuyu oaths into a powerful device for guaranteeing communal solidarity. They are credited with having introduced what subsequently became the first Mau Mau oath. Throughout the 1940s Olenguruone provided inspiration to Kikuyu militants in the White Highlands and set an example of unconditional resistance to the colonial régime, which has been celebrated in several Mau Mau *nyimbo*.[1]

From the beginning Olenguruone had little chance of success. This was because the majority of the people who were moved into this prototype settlement were not squatters who had refused to accept the new restrictions imposed by the district councils, but Kikuyu cultivators who had been farming in Maasailand where they had discovered new opportunities for the peasant option. They loathed having to move to the bleak environment, high on the Mau escarpment, where they realised they would be unable to grow their normal crops.[2]

By October 1946, the Olenguruone residents were locked in battle with the colonial state, which was trying to evict them for failing to follow the settlement's agricultural rules. They developed close contacts with the Kikuyu squatters in the Nakuru and Naivasha districts and with the Kikuyu Highlands Squatters' Association in Limuru.[3] The new oath of unity, which had been introduced in 1944, quickly spread among the Kikuyu squatter communities throughout the White Highlands. Meanwhile, as the eviction plans became bogged down in legal technicalities in the Kenya Supreme Court and the Court of Appeal for Eastern Africa, the administration and the legal department began to blame each other for their respective failures to deal with the Olenguruone 'agitators'.[4] The Olenguruone Kikuyu insisted that they were *githaka* rightholders and that the government was not entitled to interfere with their *shambas*. After eight years of resistance morale in the settlement was very low; by 1949 it had become apparent that the government intended to expel all the dissidents. The evictions and mass arrests at Olenguruone between January and March 1950 were, however, counter-productive and merely confirmed the Olenguruone resistors' position in the pantheon of Kikuyu heroes and provided further ammunition to the militants.[5]

The foundation of the settlement

Much of the agricultural department's post-war development programme, we have noted, was based upon Norman Humphrey's contention that vast numbers of people would have to be resettled on newly-cleared land or absorbed with their families into permanent urban employment, before land degradation could be tackled. During the first three years after the war a series of ecological and geological surveys were undertaken and several potential settlements were scrutinised. It was hardly surprising, therefore, that the progress of the prototype African settlement at Olenguruone, high on the western slopes of the Mau escarpment, was closely watched and considered of vital importance to the success of the new strategy.[6]

The Colonial Office had initially refused to sanction the transfer of responsibility for resident labour legislation to the settler-controlled district councils, as proposed in the 1937 Resident Native Labour Ordinance, until the Kenyan authorities established a settlement for those squatters who refused to accept the tighter restrictions imposed on squatter cultivation and stock during the *Kifagio* in the late 1930s. After a three-year delay, the Secretary of State reluctantly approved the Ordinance, but only when he was assured that the Kenyan government had excised 33,000 acres from the Maasai Reserve and the South West Mau Forest, on which to establish a settlement for former Kikuyu squatters who had refused to reattest and had been expelled from settler farms.[7] Such families, who had often been away from the Kikuyu reserves for 30 years, had lost their *githaka* rights and were now completely landless and threatened with destitution. Many had left Kikuyuland voluntarily to search for better conditions in the White Highlands; others had been forced off their land when it had been alienated to Europeans. In moving to the Rift Valley they had abandoned their lineage ties in the reserves to take advantage of the new opportunities that opened up in the White Highlands between 1904 and 1913,when the British removed the Maasai from their traditional northern grazing grounds and opened the area for European and, unwittingly, Kikuyu settlement.[8]

The Colonial Office believed that Olenguruone would serve two purposes. Firstly, it would enable the Kenyan government to minimise squatter opposition to the new regulations governing squatter contracts (which was anticipated once the new Ordinance transferred squatter legislation to the district councils) because Olenguruone would absorb the more obdurate squatters who refused to accept the new regulations without causing trouble in Kikuyuland. But secondly, and more importantly, the settlement at Olenguruone was designed to enable Whitehall to assuage humanitarian criticism in Britain about another concession to Kenya's settlers.[9] Events, however, turned out very differently. Once reassured and armed with information to withstand left-wing criticism, Whitehall quickly lost interest in Olenguruone and turned its attention to the pressing problems of mobilising the colonies' war effort. The Kenyan government was therefore able to use Olenguruone for other purposes.

Instead of resettling squatter families that had been evicted from European farms during the *Kifagio*, Olenguruone was used to accommodate those Kikuyu who had settled in Maasailand. During the 1920s and 1930s more than 4,000 Kikuyu had abandoned the White Highlands and began to cultivate at Il Melili and Nairage Ngare in north Narok. They established economic alliances with prominent local Maasai, who, as pastoralists, were willing to allow these enterprising Kikuyu cultivators as much land as they wanted in return for food and labour.[10] By 1937, many settler farmers around Elburgon, on the other side of the Mau escarpment, were already becoming concerned in case this new settlement in Maasailand provided a more attractive option to their squatters and encouraged others, whose stock rights were being curtailed in the White Highlands.[11] This would have severely impaired the settlers' supplies of labour. By the late 1930s, these farmers' protests and complaints about Kikuyu interpenetration relayed by the field administration in Maasailand, had persuaded the Secretariat to remove these 'undesirables' and to resettle them at Olenguruone with other former Kikuyu squatters who had come directly from European farms.[12]

The concept of interpenetration had a long and tarnished history, but, by the late 1930s, the field administration had begun to discuss it in a more constructive manner. The administration in Maasai, however, had remained resolutely opposed to the idea. When, in the late 1930s, it recognised that interpenetration would soon become official policy, it was determined to undertake one last drive to expel the Kikuyu interlopers. In 1936, Clarence Buxton, who was then Officer-in-Charge in Maasai, had attempted to clear Il Melili and Nairage Ngare. Olenguruone provided his successor with one last opportunity to clear Narok before interpenetration became accepted and the Maasai administration was stuck with unwanted Kikuyu interlopers.[13]

The choice of Olenguruone as the site for the new settlement was there-

fore a compromise between the forestry department and the Maasai Rift
Valley administration. It was an isolated place that nobody wanted where
discontented Kikuyu could be 'abandoned' without, it was thought, any
danger of spreading dissent. It soon, however, proved to be a singularly
inauspicious site for the first African settlement, becoming notorious as
the 'Sherwood Forest' of western Kenya and an important staging post on
the stock-theft routes.[14]

The situation was made even worse when the Kikuyu refused to leave
their smallholdings in Maasailand.[15] Consequently the first families were
not moved into Oleguruone until 1941, by which time the administration
was being stretched by the war against the Italians in Ethiopia and was
unable to assert its authority. The ex-squatters were able to disregard the
settlement's rules when they were belatedly promulgated in 1942. By then
many families had already started to cultivate large acreages and refused
to obey the new regulations.[16]

The geographical and administrative roots of failure

Olenguruone was completely unsuitable for a settlement of peasant cultivators. The four main valleys all had extremely steep slopes covered with
dense bamboo and trees. The ridges between the main rivers were broken
by deep ravines, densely covered with bamboo, and swift streams. Any
cultivation or movement was extremely difficult. The climate was equally
unsuitable for peasant agriculture. The rainfall appeared to be good,
averaging more than 80 inches per annum, but it fell unevenly in violent
downpours between April and October, often turning into hailstorms
which damaged the crops. Frost also hindered cultivation and night tem-
peratures averaged only 40°F. Sunshine in the rainy months was confined
to a brief spell in the early morning. Consequently, in contrast to most of
Central Province and the White Highlands, only one crop a year could be
grown at Olenguruone.[17]

The hilly terrain was another major obstacle to the development of the
settlement and made the construction of internal roads financially pro-
hibitive. During the rainy season, from May to September, most of the
slopes in the cultivated area were too steep and slippery for the
ex-squatters' mules and donkeys to move about. All communication to
the north-west and south-east was virtually impossible throughout the
year because of the difficulty of crossing the ridges and four main rivers,
which all flowed from the north-east to the south-west. These long radial
lines of communication added considerably to the cost of marketing
produce. Even the two main roads out of Olenguruone were usually
impassable during the rainy season. The official line of access ran over the
Maasai Mau and through the Elburgon Forest Reserve, along a sawmill

road to Elburgon. Although some attempts were made to improve it, in bad weather it was impassable since it climbed to 10,000 feet and meandered over several hills. The alternative route, along district council and farm roads through the Marindas and Keringet estates, took a better alignment and avoided steep hills, but was not chosen as the official road to Olenguruone because the local settlers feared that diseased stock would constantly be moving across their land.[18]

When cultivation regulations were finally introduced in 1942, the Olenguruone Kikuyu refused to accept any attempt to restrict their *shambas* to a maximum of eight acres per family or to limit their stock to seven cattle.[19] Their leader, Samuel Koina Gitebi, insisted that the Officer-in-Charge in Maasai had assured them, in the presence of Senior Chief Koinange and Chief Josiah Njonjo, that they could hold Olenguruone on *githaka* terms without any restrictions or agricultural regulations, as compensation for their *githaka* in Kiambu, which had been alienated to European settlers. If this was untrue, he asked, why had everyone allowed into Olenguruone been carefully vetted by the Kiambu Local Native Council's representative, Chief Njonjo, to ascertain which of the Kikuyu in Maasailand had originally been *githaka* holders and were, therefore, eligible for land in the settlement?[20]

By attempting to restrict Olenguruone to former *githaka* holders and by refusing to accept the claims of former *ahoi* and other 'tenants' the government had in fact created the impression that this land was being given to them without any conditions in compensation for their alienated *githaka* and was to be held on *githaka* terms. The Olenguruone Kikuyu, therefore, refused to accept the belated settlement rules. Gitebi defended this interpretation in a petition to the King and alleged that:

> A totally new set of laws was introduced in 1943 based on the Government's failure to honour the previous agreed terms . . . The Kenya Government alleged that we have refused to obey the laws of the settlement but have never been shown precisely what clause of the said laws we have violated. We were admitted to Olenguruone Settlement on the terms and conditions agreed upon and satisfactory to Government in January 1940.[21]

As early as June 1942, three months before the promulgation of the Native Settlement Areas (Olenguruone) (No 2) Rules, Gitebi had complained that the administration was attempting to regulate cultivation on the *shambas* which, he insisted, were held on *githaka* terms and, therefore, should not be subject to any kind of government interference.[22] When the settlement rules were eventually issued and translated into Kikuyu, discontent escalated. The dispute over whether they held *githaka* rights of exclusive ownership, or were *ahoi* and merely occupied the land under conditional tenure, became so serious that the Chief Native Com-

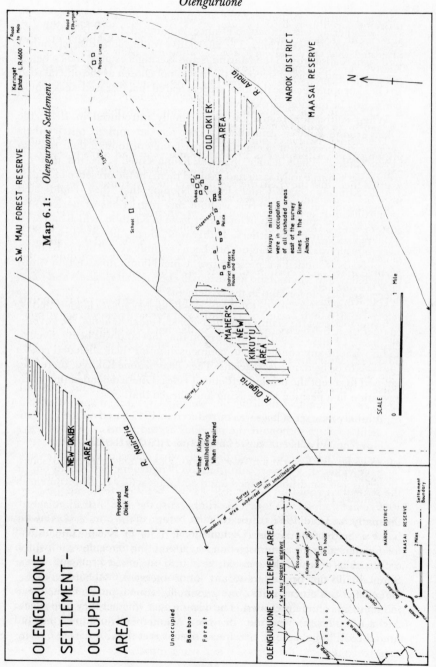

Map 6.1: *Olenguruone Settlement*

missioner eventually held a *baraza*, on 21 June 1943, to resolve the disagreement. This was attended by 200 Kikuyu and 20 Okiek elders who protested that they were not *ahoi*, as they had been described in the Kikuyu version of the settlement rules. They demanded to be treated like the Kikuyu who had been moved to Lari and Kerita and who had been compensated for their lost land with new *githaka*, insisting that Bailward, the Officer-in-Charge in Maasai, had promised them in 1940 that Olenguruone would be held on *githaka* terms.[23]

The Chief Native Commissioner, however, remained adamant, arguing that as trespassers in Maasailand they had already received extremely generous treatment by being allowed to go to Olenguruone. He warned them that they held their *shambas* on the government's terms: they were in fact *ahoi* and would be dispossessed if they did not obey the settlement rules and the instructions of the Settlement Officer. When their own customs were incompatible with the regulations, they would have to give way. They would be required to conserve soil fertility, and the eight-acre plots which had been allocated could not be subdivided, according to the partible inheritance customs of the Kikuyu, but would have to be passed intact to one heir.[24]

Following this declaration of the government's hard line many Kikuyu refused to sign their occupation permits and started a policy of active non-co-operation.[25] All orders from the Settlement Officer and Agricultural Department staff were ignored; experimental agricultural work was hindered; and rules about crop rotation and maize cultivation were disregarded, as was the prohibition against burning grass to clear new *shambas*. This campaign of disobedience continued throughout 1944 and 1945; government threats of eviction were met by virulent opposition and communal oathing to ensure unity.[26]

Maher's agricultural regulations

Meanwhile, the government was becoming extremely concerned about the rapid decline in soil fertility. By 1944 this had become so serious that the settlement could no longer feed itself.[27] Between 1943 and January 1946, conditions were allowed to drift because the administration lacked the manpower to enforce the rules. With the end of the war, as plans were being prepared for other new settlements, it suddenly became imperative for Olenguruone to be brought under control and the cultivation rules enforced, in order to demonstrate to future settlers at Makueni or the Shimba Hills that opposition would not be tolerated.[28] Robertson in the Colonial Office observed that 'the present agitation is purely for political motives and . . . if the Government gives way in this case, the large scale African Settlement Schemes which are planned for the future will be prejudiced'.[29] His superior, Andrew Cohen was even more determined to reassert control at Olenguruone, and warned that:

There is a vital issue at stake here – the willingness . . . of Africans to accept conditions of proper land control in schemes for settlement . . . A determined campaign is being coordinated in Kenya at the moment, under the leadership of Jomo Kenyatta, to encourage Africans everywhere to resist attempts to improve the condition of the land. If this campaign succeeds the bad consequences will be incalculable.[30]

Early in 1946, therefore, Colin Maher, the head of the Soil Conservation Unit, was despatched to investigate conditions and to suggest how the administration could regain control. Able though he undoubtedly was, Maher had little sympathy for traditional African agricultural practices; he strictly adhered to his 'scientific' preconceptions about tropical agriculture and completely disregarded Kikuyu land-use practices. In his zeal to propagate the gospel of soil conservation, Maher based his programme on what he believed was agriculturally desirable rather than on what was possible in the face of outright opposition. Like many agricultural officers, Maher had been greatly impressed by Allan and Trapnell's work in Northern Rhodesia and was obsessed with the belief that, through close investigation of the vegetation, soils and climate, it was possible to determine the exact human and stock-carrying capacities of specific areas.[31] Maher was the most vociferous advocate of this approach in Kenya and, like Humphrey, obstinately refused to recognise that, even in relatively small areas like Olenguruone, it was exceedingly difficult to determine with any precision the fertility of the soil or its powers of regeneration. Indeed, given the climatic conditions and the nitrogen-deficient soils at Olenguruone, Maher's recommendations were probably more destructive than the Kikuyu's shifting cultivation he so condemned. The Olenguruone Kikuyu in fact utilised their land in a highly efficient manner, well adapted to meet the difficult conditions of their inhospitable *shambas* high on the Mau escarpment. After their experiences in the White Highlands and among the pastoral Maasai, they concentrated primarily on stock keeping rather than on growing poor crops of maize and wheat. Unlike Maher, who remained inflexibly committed to his preconceived views about sound agricultural practice, which bore little resemblance to the realities of Olenguruone, the Kikuyu were willing to adapt to fit in with the environment. By turning to pre-colonial Kikuyu practices of shifting cultivation in a mixed farming rotation of stock and crops, the Olenguruone Kikuyu maximised the economic potential of the area and minimised the danger of land degradation. The government, however, failed to recognise this simple fact and endorsed Maher's recommendations.[32]

Maher proposed a radical reorganisation of the settlement, with every household having five acres of arable land on slopes of less than 20 per cent, a further three acres under permanent grass and four acres of communal grazing for every smallholder. This total of 12 acres, he pointed out, was 'considerably in excess of that available in the Kikuyu Reserves'.[33] This formula, however, failed to take account of the fact that only one crop a year could be grown in the harsh environment at Olenguruone. Maher also recommended that no more than two and a half acres per household be allowed under cultivation at any given moment, that initially land should be cultivated continuously for no more than four years and then, after three years complete rest under planted grass, for no more than three years at a stretch. These two and a half acres, he considered, could supply both cash and food crops. The remaining five and a half acres and the four acres of communal grazing should be used to keep eight or nine high-grade cattle or the equivalent number of sheep. All the grassland, temporary and permanent, private or communal, Maher suggested, ought to be divided into paddocks and grazed in rotation using grazing permits. He even suggested building all the houses in the settlement on a single contour. Everyone at Olenguruone was to be compelled to follow this new agricultural plan and the settlement was to be dramatically reformed. Every plot was to be resurveyed and those on steep slopes closed within two years. Once the new *shambas* had been demarcated, the Olenguruone Kikuyu would have to build terraces and follow agricultural regulations. During this interim period, however, Maher made a fatal concession to expedite the clearing of bamboo from the proposed smallholdings. He agreed to let those who were to be moved cultivate as large an area as they wished. This undermined all the attempts to enforce his recommendations, for once settled and allowed to cultivate as much land as they could clear, the Kikuyu refused to reduce their *shambas* to eight acres.[34] The government resorted to force and opposition escalated.

The growth of Kikuyu opposition

On 16 October 1946, Major F.W. Carpenter, the District Commissioner in Nakuru, who had taken over responsibility for Olenguruone from the Maasai administration the previous month, held another *baraza* attended by over 700 Kikuyu, at which he reiterated the government's interpretation of their status.[35] He did, however, announce two new major government concessions. Junior wives of polygamous households were to be granted their own *shambas* and married sons of Olenguruone residents, who had illegally entered the settlement, were to be allowed to remain, to be treated as separate families and to be given their own five-acre *shambas*. These concessions were warmly welcomed, but the crowd angrily refused to accept impartible inheritance on the grounds that it would leave younger sons landless and with a bleak future. Carpenter then presented them with the blunt alternative of either accepting the conditions or being evicted. The District Commissioner remained optimistic that the new arrangements and the threat of eviction would win the majority

over to the government's side and undermine the authority of the militants. The concessions, however, had come too late to reduce the
Olenguruone residents' determination to uphold their *githaka* rights.[36]

Meanwhile the troubles had attracted widespread attention throughout
the White Highlands and in Central Province. Messengers left the settlement to seek support or to hide on neighbouring farms and they spread
their new oath to Kikuyu Central Association activists throughout the
Rift Valley, using Lord Delamere's Soysambu estate as a staging post on
their journeys to Kiambu. Close ties were created between the settlement
and the Kikuyu squatters, who were fighting the new district council
regulations and were already in a militant mood.[37] Gitebi, the
Olenguruone leader, was well known among the squatter political activists as one of the founders of the Kikuyu Central Association in the Rift
Valley, which he had joined at Limuru in 1928. He was particularly well
known at Soysambu where he had opened a Kikuyu *Karing'a* school in the
1930s.[38]

In April 1946, when nearly the whole settlement had taken the
oath – and not simply the elders as is traditional for Kikuyu
oaths – Gitebi led several hundered supporters on a 150-mile march from
Olenguruone to Kiambu to discuss their problems with Senior Chief
Koinange and Eliud Mathu and to spread the new oath among discontented squatters in Nakuru and Naivasha. Resistance to the district
council's new regulations spread rapidly throughout the White
Highlands.[39] The day before Creech Jones, then Under Secretary of State
for the Colonies, was due to arrive in the district in August 1946, the
Soysambu squatters went on strike and refused to reattest under the new
Naivasha resident labour rules.[40] The District Commissioner explained
that, in taking 'full advantage of the power of oath-swearing, many
hundreds of squatters were induced not to re-attest in the hope that either
farming would be paralysed or District Councils' Resident Labour legislation jettisoned.'[41] In September, the Olenguruone Kikuyu helped organise a secret meeting on a Naivasha farm at which 700 squatters from 33
farms and the Kikuyu at the settlement were represented.[42] This was the
climax of the initial resistance to the new squatter orders. In 1947 militancy diminished, primarily because the district councils had started to
evict those who refused to accept the new contracts and loss of employment was too great a risk for most squatters, who had nowhere to go. By
February 1947, the Nakuru Labour Officer was already confidently
reporting that he had 'formed the opinion that the back of the Squatter
Resistance movement had been broken and there were indications of a
more general willingness to attest'.[43]

Kikuyu solidarity at Olenguruone, in contrast, remained unshaken.
Even Mbote wa Karamba, one of the four government-appointed headmen, organised a petition against evictions, which was sent to Kenyatta

who had recently returned from England and, when the settlement leaders were ordered to report to the District Commissioner at Nakuru, they set out instead to visit Kenyatta at Githunguri.[44] On 15 February 1947, a large crowd gathered outside the Settlement Office, shouting that the Settlement Officer must go and that Europeans should leave Kenya. The Chief Native Commissioner, Wyn Harris, was extremely alarmed by the protests, which he saw as 'a climax of disobedience, defiance and non-co-operation extending since 1942', and blamed the resistance on 'unscrupulous political agitators' who were using Olenguruone as a device to force the government to re-open the questions solved once and for all by the Kenya Land Commission. He complained:

> It is clear from the recent history of the Olenguruone Settlement, that the whole of the basis of the Settlement is now being used by certain Kikuyu as a political pawn against Government in the claim for the return of alienated land in the Kiambu area, and that neither improved conditions within the Settlement itself nor the generous concessions recently announced to the settlers at the *baraza* held by the District Commissioner, Nakuru, on 16 October, 1946, even when fully implemented, will in any way alter their claim now being put forward that they, the settlers, hold the land freehold and that Government has no right to interfere in any way or even to enforce rules of good farming.[45]

Finally on 22 March 1947, the Provincial Commissioner informed the non-co-operators that they must obey or leave Olenguruone within 14 days. At this threat, the crowd of 400 started to walk away. The Provincial Commissioner shouted at the retreating figures that, as they had failed to fulfil the conditions on their permits, he was now formally giving them notice to leave and any crops planted after 22 March would be destroyed.[46]

These threats merely strengthened Kikuyu solidarity and united legal and illegal residents against the government. When 25 leaders were summonsed, they refused to attend the magistrate's court and went into hiding among squatters on nearby farms. Tension grew. The Kikuyu *Karing'a* school committee, for example, decided that if they were forced out, they would burn down the school they had built rather than leave it for the government. After ten weeks, however, nothing had happened and the Kikuyu were still in residence. Each failure by the government to fulfil its threats convinced the residents that it would never carry out the evictions. Moreover, when the men who had fled the settlement in March began to return, they reported that they had been unenthusiastically received in Kiambu. The cool reception and the over-crowded conditions came as rather a shock to those who had never lived in the Kikuyu reserves. Until this visit, most had little idea of what conditions were like in Kikuyuland and were astonished to discover that many of the agricultural rules they were fighting against were rigorously applied in Kiambu. They returned to Olenguruone determined not to leave. Now they not only objected to the agricultural rules, but were also alarmed by their insecurity of tenure and feared that, even if they accepted the government's demands, they could still be evicted.[47]

In fact the 50 residents served with evictions were saved by the Attorney General, who advised the District Commissioner that the notices would not stand up in court. This was the first of several legal errors by the administration and relations between the Department of African Affairs and the Attorney General's chambers were soon extremely strained, because of what the administration considered the lawyers' over-cautious adherence to legal proprieties. Morgan, the Provincial Commissioner, was furious at this interference and started to blame the Attorney General and the cancellation of the eviction orders for 'all our present troubles'. This failure by the government to take any action bolstered confidence in the settlement that .the evictions would never take place. On 22 March 1947, they had been given two weeks to leave, but by mid-July virtually all the men had returned and the new season's planting was well under way.[48]

Meanwhile, the African Settlement and Land Utilization Board, the agricultural department, the administration and the legal department were all blaming each other for Olenguruone's failure.[49] No-one was willing to acknowledge that the whole scheme had been a catastrophe from the beginning. Not only had force had to be used to compel the residents to leave Maasailand, but it was now apparent that the area was totally unsuited to peasant cultivation. R.B. Malcolmson, acting as lawyer for the Kikuyu, delighted in exposing these deficiences and the bitter divisions within the government at hearings in the magistrate's court at Nakuru.[50]

The legal proceedings were long and involved, moving between the Kenyan Supreme Court and the East African Court of Appeal on intricate points of law over Kikuyu rights to appeal under Section 348(2) of the Criminal Procedure Code.[51] These legal arguments delayed further evictions for nearly a year until March 1948, when .22 cattle and 78 sheep, belonging to the first four appellants, were seized. After a brief period of shock, Kikuyu defiance quickly reasserted itself. Fox, the Settlement Officer, in fact warned: 'To date the defiant attitude remains unbroken and it cannot be said that we have made our point or any point. There are high hopes abroad that Government will once again step down from the first show of determined action.'[52] Morgan, the Provincial Commissioner, also considered that the prosecutions had simply increased Kikuyu morale and that the residents 'are quite convinced that we are not prepared to throw them out.' The government did however act and, between 30 July and 5 August 1948, after a 16-month delay, the huts and *dukas* of those who had been individually prosecuted were destroyed.[53]

Even this did not shake the confidence and resolve of the Olenguruone Kikuyu. Although most of the men in the settlement prudently vanished when the demolition parties arrived with 40 policemen, the women met them with shouts of derision. Gathungu Kunga's wives mocked the labourers and Gitebi's wife personally 'thanked' Inspector Potgieter for destroying the rats and bugs in her hut. Njoroge Waweru, even more defiant, hammered a note to the door of his abandoned house. His defiance provides an interesting insight into the residents' political understanding of government and demonstrates the willingness of some Kikuyu militants at Olenguruone to contemplate the use of force to overthrow colonial domination. Waweru warned:

> I want to inform you British, that you are not to spoil the boundaries of Olenguruone *shambas*. If you just think since you came to Kenya you have never seen an African with a gun. I am the one to inform you that the Kikuyu have more power than you have with guns. Just wait until the year 1949 you will have to be sorry for the rules which you are giving us now and when it will be my turn to order you in the same way.[54]

The administration had simply succeeded in transforming the Olenguruone Kikuyu into desperate militants and had got nowhere in its attempts to enforce what it considered to be sound agricultural practices.

Buttery, the new District Officer, maintained that the problems stemmed largely from the government's unwillingness to invest sufficient funds to develop the settlement. He told Wyn Harris, the Chief Native Commissioner, in May 1948, that Maher's plan could be implemented only if Olenguruone were allocated £250,000 over the next five years and given the necessary staff, equipment and enthusiastic residents. With its climate and isolated situation the settlement would succeed only if the government were willing to lavish considerable sums on ensuring that it worked.[55]

The expulsion of the Olenguruone Kikuyu

When the Court of Appeal for Eastern Africa gave its judgement against the Olenguruone residents on 20 February 1949, the Chief Native Commissioner introduced legislation empowering the administration to evict everyone without a valid residence permit, to impound all property and livestock and to destroy or sell huts and crops. The Kikuyu militants, however, warned the government that: 'our hardships have undoubtedly become noticeable to our fellow Africans elsewhere in the country. . . Today many of them very much fear and doubt the Government's real intention in the schemes for the settlement of Africans in selected areas under supervision'.[56] These were perceptive warnings. The Kamba, at Makueni, and the Teita, who were to be resettled in the Shimba Hills, were watching events at Olenguruone closely and might have reacted with alarm at any mass eviction. Paradoxically, this was the converse of the government's concern that other settlements might become contaminated unless an example were made at Olenguruone of those refusing to accept the settlement rules. Whichever way it turned, the government could not extricate itself from Olenguruone without severely damaging the African settlement programme.[57]

After further delays the government eventually acted. Early in the morning of 28 October 1949, shops in the centre of the settlement were destroyed and by the 30th, 900 cattle and 2,500 sheep had been seized. Two days later the first 18 houses were demolished and 100 acres of maize cut down. By 3 December all the original huts had been destroyed and burnt, but many Kikuyu had built temporary bivouacs and more than 2,200 people still refused to leave. Some had cunningly hidden maize, peas and potatoes from the police search parties and were living in hollows in the ground, protected by temporary bamboo roofs.[58]

As the evictions continued, the Special Branch intercepted a letter to Gitebi, the Olenguruone leader, from the leader of the Bataka Party in Uganda, Semakula Mulumba, who, to avoid detention following the riots in April 1949 had fled to London, where he had been welcomed by the Communist Party and by Mbiyu Koinange. In the letter, Mulumba urged Gitebi to continue the fight against the settlers who had confiscated their land.

Confidence among the Olenguruone Kikuyu was, however, crumbling. During the first few days of January 1950, another 100 families set out on foot for Elburgon to take refuge with squatter friends. The District Officer in Nakuru, it had been announced, was to be empowered to act as a magistrate and to hear cases at Olenguruone. When the first cases were heard in mid-January, the accused played into the government's hands by refusing to pay their 100-shilling fines. This enabled the administration to despatch them *en masse* to Bl Yatta – an inhospitable, arid area in northern Ukambani. On 1 February, 90 cases were heard and thereafter, until the middle of March, there were twice-weekly arrests of some 50 people who were sentenced to imprisonment at the Yatta Detention Camp. By 3 March, after a final major drive, Olenguruone was almost cleared. But as they left, the Kikuyu sought one last revenge; they spread arsenic over the pastures of the few residents who had co-operated and followed the agricultural rules. This parting blow eloquently testified to their bitterness and determination to fight for *githaka* land on *githaka* terms.[59]

The government optimistically believed the struggle was over and hoped that Olenguruone would quickly be forgotten, but in reality it was only the beginning of Kikuyu opposition to continued British rule and the privileged position of the European settlers. One incident in the last days of Olenguruone demonstrated the depth of popular feeling in Central

Province and the impact the struggle had made on the Kikuyu people. On 17 January 1950, the first batch of convicted Olenguruone residents had been despatched to the Yatta Detention Camp, via Karatina and Thika. When they arrived at Karatina, itself a centre of opposition to colonial rule in which the radicals were particularly influential, the prison cortège stopped to refuel and was immediately surrounded by crowds of inquisitive people who, on discovering they were the martyrs of Olenguruone, mobbed the prison vans and had to be driven back. All subsequent convoys to the Yatta followed a different route, carefully avoiding Kikuyuland in case there should be an attempt to release these heroes of the *wananchi* in transit.[60]

The depth of popular support for the residents is further demonstrated by the important role given to Olenguruone in several Mau Mau *nyimbo*. One of the most interesting of these was composed by former prisoners at the Yatta Detention Camp. It shows that a sophisticated political awareness developed in the settlement and that the Mau Mau radicals were committed to wider goals in their struggle for 'land and freedom'. The *nyimbo* declared that:

> There was great wailing in Olenguruone
> Even as we collected together belongings
> The enemy had scattered about.
> The enemy was telling us:
> Hurry up, quick.
> Are you forgetting you are criminals.

Chorus

> *We will greatly rejoice*
> *The day Kenyan people*
> *Get back their land.*

> We are being oppressed all over this land.
> Even our homes have been destroyed.
> And our bodies have been exploited.
> But do not be afraid.
> Because we are heading for a great victory.

> The British came from Europe
> In order to oppress our people
> Since then they have continued oppressing us.
> *Ngai*, when will they go back to Europe?

> We shall continue to suffer for our freedom;
> We shall continue struggling
> For the return of our stolen land.
> You British know that though you detain us
> For demanding our land and freedom,
> Kenya is ours for ever and ever.[61]

Whatever the administration had hoped, the struggle would go on.

Notes

1. C.G. Rosberg and J. Nottingham, *The Myth of Mau Mau*, pp. 243–4, 248–59. See also F. Furedi's unpublished paper, 'Olenguruone in Mau Mau Historiography', and his 'The Social Composition of the Mau Mau Movement in the White Highlands', p. 495; and T.M.J. Kanogo, 'Rift Valley Squatters and Mau Mau', p. 245.

2. For details of the climate and growing season at Olenguruone see KNA PC/RVP 6A/1/17/2, 'Olenguruone, 1948–50', J.F.D. Buttery, 'Report on Olenguruone Settlement', December 1948.

3. C.G. Rosberg and J. Nottingham, *The Myth of Mau Mau*, pp. 254–5; and F. Furedi's unpublished paper, 'Olenguruone in Mau Mau Historiography', pp. 3–5. For details of the Kikuyu Highlands Squatters Landowners' Association, see CO 533/543/38086/18 (1946–47), 'Petitions: Kikuyu Grievances', Samuel K. Gitebi to Creech Jones, 16 July 1947; and KNA Secretariat 1/12/8, 'Labour Unrest: Intelligence Reports, Central Province, 1947', report 20 February 1947.

4. KNA PC/RVP 6A/1/17/2, 'Olenguruone, 1948–50', Criminal Appeals Supreme Court, Nairobi, nos. 252, 253, 254 and 255 of 1948. *Decisions of the Court of Appeal for Eastern Africa*, vol. xv, 1948, pp. 118–120 (15, EACA, 118), criminal appeals, nos. 22, 23 and 24 of 1948; and *Decisions of the Court of Appeal for Eastern Africa*, vol. xvi, 1949, pp. 95–8 (16, EACA, 95), criminal appeals, nos. 178, 179, 180 and 181 of 1948; and I. Rosen and F. de F. Stratton, *A Digest of East African Criminal Case Law*, p. 229.

5. Maina wa Kinyatti, *Thunder from the Mountains*, pp. 53–6; and F. Furedi's unpublished paper, 'Olenguruone in Mau Mau Historiography', pp. 2–6.

6. KNA DC/NKU 6/2 'Olenguruone, 1947–50', Rennie to Creech Jones, 27 June 1947; and CO 533/577/38678/1 (1947–48), 'African Land Settlement: Olenguruone Settlement', I.D. Robertson', 11 July 1947; and A.B. Cohen, 14 July 1947.

7. KNA DC/NKU 4/1, 'Olenguruone Settlement', acting Native Courts Officer to Eric Davies, 8 March 1950; and memorandum for the Executive Council, 2 March 1950.

8. T.M.J. Kanogo's unpublished thesis, 'The History of Kikuyu Movement . . .', pp. 73–89.

9. See CO 533/641/38223, 'Kenya: Resident Native Labour Ordinance', minute dated 12 October 1936, for Whitehall's attitude to the 1937 Ordinance.

10. KNA DC/NKU 4/1, 'Olenguruone Settlement', Memorandum to the Executive Council, 2 March 1950. The decision to remove Kikuyu interpenetrators from Maasailand was promulgated in Government Notices, 832 and 1,030 of 1940, and 522, and 523 of 1941. See also DC/NRK 1/1/3, 'Narok Annual Reports', for 1939, pp. 4, 6, 20, 23; 1940 Report, pp. 3, 6; and 1941 Report, pp. 3, 10, for evidence of the Maasai administration's eagerness to remove the Kikuyu from Il Melili and Nairage Ngare. I am grateful to Richard Waller for many insights into the thinking of the field administration in Maasailand.

11. KNA PC/RVP 6A/1/3/1, 'Kikuyu in the Rift Valley Province', copy of letter from Elburgon farm manager to Officer-in-Charge, Maasai, 7 September 1936.

12. F. Furedi's unpublished article, 'Olenguruone in Mau Mau Historiography', pp. 1–2.

13. KNA DC/NRK 2/1/1, 'Handing Over Reports, Narok District, 1946–59', A.N. Bailward to R.A. Wilkinson, October 1946; and DC/NRK 1/1/3, 'Narok Annual Reports' for 1939, 1940 and 1941.

14. I am indebted for this information to Richard Waller.

15. KNA PC/RVP 6A/1/17/2, 'Olenguruone 1948–50', S.K. Gitebi to C.R. Attlee, 5 October 1949; and to HM King George VI, 19 December 1949.

16. For conflicting views on the Olenguruone rules, contrast KNA DC/NKU 4/1, 'Olenguruone Settlement', acting Native Courts' Officer to the Executive Council, 2 March 1950, and Gitebi's protests in PC/RVP 6A/1/17/2, 'Olenguruone, 1948–50', 5 October and 19 December 1949.

17. KNA PC/RVP 6A/1/17/2, 'Olenguruone, 1948–50', J.F.D. Buttery, 'Report on the Olenguruone Settlement', December 1948 for climatic and topographical details.
18. *ibid.*
19. *ibid*, S.K. Gitebi to C.R. Attlee, 5 October 1949; and to HM King George VI, 19 December 1949.
20. KNA DC/KBU 4/9, 'Olenguruone Settlement, 1940–44', C. Tomkinson, PC Central to DC Narok, 23 July 1940; and A.N. Bailward, Officer-in-Charge Maasai to DC Kiambu, 16 March and 17 April 1944.
21. KNA PC/RVP 6A/1/17/2, 'Olenguruone, 1948–50', S.K. Gitebi to HM King George VI, 19 December 1949.
22. *ibid.* This letter contained a detailed history of the settlement from the ex-squatters' perspective. See also the correspondence in DC/KBU 4/9, 'Olenguruone Settlement, 1940–44', to H.E. Lambert, DC Kiambu, in 1942.
23. KNA PC/RVP 6A/1/17/1, 'Olenguruone, 1946–48', notes on the Olenguruone *baraza*, 21 June 1943. Bailward's view is found in his letter to Rennie, 10 July 1946. For details of Lari and Kerita see M. Omosule's unpublished paper, 'An Assessment of the Role of the Kenya Land Commission Report', pp. 9–10, 17–28.
24. KNA PC/RVP 6A/1/17/1, 'Olenguruone, 1946–48', notes on the Olenguruone *baraza*, 21 June 1943.
25. F. Furedi's unpublished article, 'Olenguruone in Mau Mau Historiography', p. 2.
26. KNA DC/NKU 4/1, 'Olenguruone Settlement', acting Native Courts' Officer to Executive Council, 2 March 1950; and to Eric Davies, the Chief Native Commissioner, 8 March 1950. For the importance of the Olenguruone oath, see T.M.J. Kanogo, 'Rift Valley Squatters and Mau Mau', p. 245.
27. See comments in PC/RVP 6A/1/17/2, 'Olenguruone, 1948–50', J.F.D. Buttery, 'Report on Olenguruone', December 1948; and his extracts from the Agricultural Officer, C.D. Knight's 1943 report. See also R.D.F. Ryland's comments to the Secretary for Commerce and Industry, 2 July 1948, about the food situation in the settlement.
28. CO 533/557/38678/1 (1947–48) 'African Land Settlement: Olenguruone Settlement', I.D. Robertson, 11 July 1947; and A.B. Cohen, 14 July 1947.
29. *ibid*, I.D. Robertson, 11 July 1947.
30. *ibid*, A.B. Cohen, 14 July 1947.
31. The most influential reports included W. Allan, *Studies in African Land Usage in Northern Rhodesia*, and C.G. Trapnell and J.M. Clothier, *The Soils, Vegetation and Agricultural Systems of North–Western Rhodesia*, and Trapnell's article, 'Ecological Methods in the Study of Native Agriculture'.
32. KNA PC/RVP 6A/1/17/1, 'Olenguruone, 1946–48', Maher's report on Olenguruone, 22 January 1946; and the meeting of the Olenguruone sub-committee of the African Settlement Board, 19–20 February 1946. See also PC/RVP 6A/1/17/2, Olenguruone, 1948–50', for J.F.D. Buttery's comments on Maher.
33. PC/RVP 6A/1/17/1, 'Olenguruone, 1948–50', Maher's report, 22 January 1946.
34. *ibid.* Maher calculated that the residents would be able to generate the following income: 1.5 acres of wheat, or 12 bags, @ 20/- each, equals 240/-; half an acre of beans with maize interplanted, yields 2 bags @ 20/- each; and half an acre of potatoes, yields 20 bags @ 3/- each, equals 60/-. Total income of 340/-.
35. PC/RVP 6A/1/17/1, 'Olenguruone, 1946–48', minutes of F.W. Carpenter's *baraza* at Olenguruone on 16 October 1946.
36. *ibid.* For the background to these concessions see African Settlement Board to the Chief Native Commissioner, 5 July 1946; and A.N. Bailward to Rennie, 10 July 1946.
37. F. Furedi's unpublished paper, 'Olenguruone in Mau Mau Historiography', pp. 3–4; C.G. Rosberg and J. Nottingham, *The Myth of Mau Mau*, pp. 255–6.
38. C.G. Rosberg and J. Nottingham, *The Myth of Mau Mau*, p. 254.
39. In February 1946, Senior Chief Koinange, Chief Josiah Njonjo, Chief Waruhiu Kungu

and Eliud Mathu had presented a report on Olenguruone to the Kiambu Local Native Council. This severely criticised the government and declared that the Olenguruone Kikuyu held their land on *githaka* terms. See KNA PC/RVP 6A/1/17/1, 'Olenguruone, 1946–48', report of the committee chaired by Senior Chief Koinange, 14 February 1946. For the government's response, see E.L. Brooke Anderson, Chairman African Settlement and Land Utilisation Board, to PC Rift Valley, 10 October 1946.

40. KNA Lab 9/601, 'Resident Labour General, 1942–45', Hyde-Clarke to Mitchell, June 1946; and DC/NKU 1/5, 'Nakuru–Naivasha–Ravine Annual Report, 1946', p. 2.
41. KNA DC/NKU 1/5, 'Nakuru–Naivasha–Ravine Annual Report, 1946', p. 6.
42. KNA Lab 9/1071, 'Resident Labourers Ordinance: The Problem of the Squatter: *Ad Hoc* Committee, 1946–48', reports of Kenya African Union meeting at Naivasha, 17 November 1946, by M.S. Athumani and J. Kariuki.
43. Quoted by F. Furedi in his unpublished article, 'Olenguruone in Mau Mau Historiography', p. 4.
44. KNA PC/RVP 6A/1/17/1, 'Olenguruone, 1946–48', D.L. Morgan, acting PC Rift Valley, to Rennie the Chief Secretary, 3 February 1947.
45. *ibid.* Wyn Harris to D.L. Morgan, 17 March 1947.
46. KNA DC/NKU 6/2, 'Olenguruone, 1947–50', Wyn Harris to Olenguruone Kikuyu, 25 March 1947 and D.L. Morgan to P. Wyn Harris, 8 May 1948.
47. KNA PC/RVP 6A/1/17/1, 'Olenguruone, 1946–48', report by the District Commissioner R.D.F. Ryland, on the prosecution of four Olenguruone residents, 19 May 1947; and the Kikuyu Karing'a school committee to DO Olenguruone, 21 May 1947.
48. *ibid*, A. Crabb for acting Chief Native Commissioner to D.L. Morgan, 31 May 1947 and R.D.F. Ryland, DC Nakuru to D.L. Morgan, 11 July 1947. Morgan's comment was written in the margin.
49. *ibid*, C.O. Oates, Provincial Agricultural Officer, to S. Fox, District Officer, Olenguruone, 9 October 1947.
50. KNA PC/RVP 6A/1/17/2, 'Olenguruone, 1948–50', J.F.D. Buttery, 'Report on Olenguruone', December 1948; KNA DC/NKU 1/5, 'Nakuru–Naivasha–Ravine Annual Report, 1947', p. 15; and DC/NKU 6/2, 'Olenguruone, 1947–50', R. Black Malcolmson to Creech Jones, 2 May 1947.
51. The magistrate was entitled to hear the cases under the Minor Cases Procedure and Section 197 of the Criminal Procedure Code if the sentence imposed did not exceed one month's imprisonment or a £5fine. For details of the legal debate see KNA PC/RVP 6A/1/17/2, 'Olenguruone, 1948–50', Criminal Appeals Supreme Court, Nairobi, nos. 252, 253, 254 and 255 of 1948. *Decisions of the Court of Appeal for Eastern Africa*, vol. xv, 1948, pp. 118–20, (15, EACA, 118), criminal appeals, nos. 22, 23 and 24 of 1948; and *Decisions of the Court of Appeal for Eastern Africa*, vol. xvi, 1949, pp. 95–8 (16, EACA, 95), criminal appeals, nos. 178, 179, 180 and 181 of 1948.
52. KNA PC/RVP 6A/1/17/1, 'Olenguruone, 1946–48', S. Fox's report on action taken to remove four plot holders, and huts and crops, 18 March 1948.
53. *ibid*, D.L. Morgan to Wyn Harris, 8 May 1948. See also J.F.D. Buttery's first report to the African Settlement and Land Utilisation Board, 7 May 1948, in PC/RVP 6A/1/17/2, 'Olenguruone, 1948–50'.
54. KNA DC/NKU 6/2 'Olenguruone, 1947–50', R.D.F. Ryland, DC Nakuru to J.F.D. Buttery, DC Olenguruone, 14 July 1948; D.V. Kapila's protest to the Chief Native Commissioner, 3 August 1948; and J.F.D. Buttery to R.D.F. Ryland, 3 August 1948.
55. KNA PC/RVP 6A/1/17/2, 'Olenguruone, 1948–50*, J.F.D. Buttery, 'Report on Olenguruone', December 1948. One should perhaps consider that if the government took its claims seriously then the prototype African agricultural settlement should have been worth more than the miserly £10,000 which was spent during the ten years of its existence, especially when it was prepared to spend £80,000 on the new European primary school at Nakuru.
56. *ibid*, Olenguruone Kikuyu to Wyn Harris, the Chief Native Commissioner, 26 June

1949. For details of the new legislation see Wyn Harris, Chief Native Commissioner to D.L. Morgan, 7 June 1949.

57. KNA Lab 9/339, 'Labour Squatters: Olenguruone Settlement, 1945-51', P. Wyn Harris to D.L. Morgan, 17 March 1947.
58. KNA DC/NKU 6/2, 'Olenguruone, 1947-50', J.F.D. Buttery to D.L. Morgan, PC Rift Valley, 31 October 1949 and 7 November 1949. See also J.F.D. Buttery's situation report, 3 December 1949.
59. *ibid*, J.F.D. Buttery to R.D.F. Ryland, DC Nakuru, 16 November 1949, enclosing an intercepted letter from S. Mulumba to S.K. Gitebi, dated 11 November 1949. A.F. Sagar, District Officer, Olenguruone, to DC Nakuru, 16 January 1950 and P.H. Jones DO Nakuru, who had gone to Olenguruone as an assistant magistrate to hear the cases, to Provincial Commissioner, Rift Valley, 16 January 1950 and 21 January 1950.
60. *ibid*, A.F. Sagar, DO Olenguruone to DC Nakuru, 21 January 1950.
61. Maina wa Kinyatti, *Thunder from the Mountains*, pp. 55-6. It would appear that Maina wa Kinyatti has transposed these tape-recorded 'Mau Mau hymns' into Marxist idiom, distorting the complex ideology of Kikuyu peasant resistance.

Seven

The Peasant Revolt: Murang'a, 1947

The second colonial occupation severely disrupted Kikuyu society and undermined the position of colonial chiefs. This chapter places the peasant revolt in Murang'a during 1947 and 1948 within the wider context of the alienation of the Kikuyu and the origins of Mau Mau. We have seen how the government endeavoured to revive the traditional land authorities and to prevent the development of commercial farming and a local entrepreneurial élite which, it was feared, would produce greater social differentiation and undermine the fabric of Kikukyu culture and social order.[1] The competition for government patronage, however, continued to grow, and the commercial farmers and traders came increasingly to resent the privileged access of the chiefs to the rewards of the colonial state. Meanwhile, the administration and agricultural department's post-war policies, with their over-reliance on communal terracing, had alienated the peasantry and severely weakened the government-appointed chiefs. As the agricultural campaign gathered momentum, many of the older chiefs were replaced by a new clique of modernisers, who could be relied upon to support the new policies. But by dismissing the older chiefs, the administration weakened the ties of clientage between the chiefs and their people, just when the agricultural betterment campaign had increased popular opposition on the colonial régime. The administration's reliance on compulsory terracing created a latent constituency for the men of violence, who began to organise a campaign against the chiefs in the African press and to raise popular political consciousness. The effects of this political mobilisation upon the chiefs, the field administration and the Secretariat are briefly considered. The new Chief Native Commissioner, Wyn Harris, who had been Provincial Commissioner in Central Province until early in 1947, was unable to convince the legal department of the seriousness of the deteriorating situation in Kikuyuland.[2] The chapter concludes with a brief assessment of the factional divisions among the African political activists and their supporters.

The growth of popular discontent

It has become fashionable to suggest that increasing social differentiation in Kiambu, Murang'a and Nyeri was the crucial factor, if not indeed according to some historians the only factor, behind growing opposition by 'the poor peasants' to the chiefs and other collaborators with British rule. Such an interpretation is not wrong – poor peasants, *ahoi* and other members of junior lineages in Kikuyu sub-clans were squeezed and even 'proletarianised' as the cost of an acre of land rose from 100 goats in 1939 to 1,000 in 1952 – but it is only a partial explanation for the growth of popular discontent in the Kikuyu reserves between 1945 and 1952.[3]

The new generation of Kikuyu radical historians has correctly discerned that the process was not quite so simple as was once believed. *Ahoi* and the other Kikuyu 'tenants' were expropriated not only by the chiefs and their clients but also by the aspiring traders and cash-crop cultivators, who provided the backbone of support for the underground Kikuyu Central Association and the constitutionalist Kenya African Union under Kenyatta's leadership after June 1947.[4] Support for the political militants in the Kikuyu reserves was also a function of the effects of the post-war agricultural development programme and the massive influx of technical advisers, which amounted to a second colonial occupation almost as disruptive in its consequences for the ordinary African digging in his *shamba* as the first. While some chiefs attempted to insulate their people from the new demands of the agricultural and veterinary departments, others were more concerned with retaining the favour of the district administration and with safeguarding their privileged access to government patronage. Such chiefs zealously enforced the new soil-conservation regulations and communal terracing, and alienated their people. The following study of Murang'a in central Kikuyuland shows a close correlation between the locations in which the chiefs pushed terracing in the late 1940s and the centres of Mau Mau support in the early 1950s. As early as 1947, the government's agricultural policies had aroused such widespread opposition that they were undermining the foundations of the colonial state.[5]

'Mere events' ought not to be entirely subsumed within *la longue durée* of internal social differentiation among the Kikuyu, if we are to uncover the complexity of the past. This chapter charts the course of local events, 'the mere dust' of history, and it therefore places proportionately less weight than much recent work upon the underlying social processes.[6] The problems created by increasing differentiation, however, exemplified by the estates of over 150 acres acquired by chiefs such as Muhoya and Nderi in Nyeri, were obviously an important source of discontent. One index of this mounting frustration is the increase in court fees from land cases from £13,000 in 1949 to £24,000 only two years later.[7] But this alone does not adequately explain the dynamics of peasant opposition to the chiefs. The social strains were indeed there, but popular frustration needed a catalyst if it was to be transformed into violent resistance. In Murang'a and the other Kikuyu districts, the overt government intervention of the post-war terracing campaign and the host of new agricultural regulations focused resentment against the chiefs and enabled the rural radicals, with the help of the more politically-experienced urban militants, such as Mwangi Macharia in Murang'a or the Forty Group in Nyeri, to mobilise popular discontent and to organise a determined and protracted challenge to the chiefs and their allies in 1947 and 1948.[8]

The aims of the agricultural campaign

Norman Humphrey's reports on Nyeri and Machakos so alarmed the Nairobi Secretariat that it became convinced of the need for immediate action to avert an agricultural crisis in the Kikuyu reserves. It was feared that 'land-mining', continual cultivation and over-stocking had drastically impaired soil fertility. Various solutions were canvassed, most of which were based on the need for an intensive communal terracing campaign.[9] Only a few agricultural officers, such as Jack Benson in Meru, argued that a more effective approach would be to reward those Africans who adopted better farming techniques by allowing them to grow high-value cash crops. The encouragement given to these schemes, however, was dwarfed by the mobilisation of the peasantry in the terracing campaign.[10]

Chiefs competed to ensure that their location headed the district terracing figures and to retain official approval. Successful chiefs – that is, those who most rigorously enforced terracing and agricultural improvements upon their reluctant locations – were rewarded with wattle trading licences and schools to distribute among their supporters. Increasingly the administration came to assess a chief's performance in terms of how many miles of terracing had been dug.[11]

Colin Maher, the head of the Soil Conservation Unit, was responsible for this emphasis on terracing. He shared the fears of Humphrey and Lambert, and believed that remedial action was urgently required to prevent further destruction of the soil. Maher did, however, warn that terracing should be only one aspect of the land rehabilitation programme, which ought also to include strip cropping, paddocking of cattle and bracken clearing to open pastures. He insisted that terracing alone would prove inadequate to reverse agricultural decline and stressed the need for an integrated campaign to restructure the whole ethos of peasant cultivation.[12] As at Olenguruone, the administration knew what it wanted to do but, despite the Colonial Development and Welfare Act, it had neither the manpower, equipment nor finance to follow Maher's proposals. His perfectionist schemes were dangerous; both at Olenguruone and in Central Province, the best proved to be the enemy of the good. Theoretically, his integrated development plans followed the most recent theories about land use, crop rotations and anti-erosion measures, but, until the Swynnerton Plan of the 1950s, the over-stretched Kenyan agricultural department never had the capacity to implement them as a complete programme of reform. Instead, Assistant Agricultural Officers, pushed by the field administration, were forced to select one or two elements from the package and to stress these at the expense of balanced development, which Maher had insisted was essential. Usually this meant selecting the key feature of Maher's recommendations, which in Central Province was the construction of narrow-base terraces to catch the run-off on the upper slopes of the ridges. These required much hard, compulsory labour, which soon provoked popular opposition. Other elements of Maher's original plan, which had been designed to win support for the campaign, were ignored.[13] The administration and the Secretariat believed that such schemes would merely encourage 'excessive individualism' which was blamed for 'land-mining' and erosion. Humphrey, for example, had observed that in Nyeri: 'Individualism, indeed, is running riot and it is certain it is being carried so far that the future is fraught with danger if it continues uncontrolled.'[14] While the administration remained so resistant to any attempt to increase African production of remunerative crops, individual agricultural officers could make little headway, especially as the settlers were determined to destroy the peasant option, which they saw as a serious threat to their economic dominance. The settlers were determined that the cultivation of coffee, tea and pyrethrum should remain a European monopoly.[15]

Even within the agricultural department, this liberal, co-optive approach had many opponents, the most prominent of which were Hughes Rice, who served as Assistant Agricultural Officer in Nyeri, Murang'a and Machakos between 1944 and 1952, and J.T. Moon, the Provincial Agricultural Officer. Both refused to countenance any concessions to African opposition to terracing and contended that any signs of weakening resolve would endanger the progress already achieved and ensure that the communal campaign would disintegrate. Maher's perceptive warnings about excessive reliance on terracing were therefore ignored and compulsion came increasingly to dominate the agricultural campaign.[16]

To be effective, however, terraces had to be built on the contour, along a whole ridge. This meant that they had to cross several *shambas* belonging to different households. Popular opposition was soon aroused, for terracing not only required exhausting work, but also reduced the land available for cultivation. Philip Rimington, who became Assistant Agricultural Officer in Murang'a in 1949, recalled that terrace drains and run-offs were three feet wide and that when the excavated earth was piled up, either above or below them, no less than four to six feet of land was lost for every three-foot drop between the contour terraces. This provoked bitter resentment and, with the advantage of hindsight, he now considers that 'you've got to have some give and take, and you've got to adapt your terracing to the needs and lives and existence, I think. You just don't really bulldoze through the whole of a person's smallholding, which is in fact what we did do. And that is really where I think we sort of came unstuck'.[17] Leslie Brown was another convinced opponent of excessive terracing. In an interview just before his death in 1980, he recalled the resentment narrow-base terracing had created:

> They were undesirable in that they were relatively laborious to dig and required constant maintenance as natural erosion tended to fill them very quickly. They were, however, insisted upon by Colin Maher, senior soil conservation engineer, as policy – a profound error which could not be rectified until I became more senior and I and other officers fought the policy successfully.[18]

He also considered that the district administration was responsible for much of the opposition to terracing because:

> The Administration . . . liked to regard soil conservation as a punishment, and when some location was backward over tax paying and given to drunkeness and crime I was often required to go and lay on some soil conservation there. I usually made a token effort to do some but this was obviously an unsound point of view which should not have prevailed and I usually paid as little as possible attention to such requests as I could.[19]

Unfortunately, not all agricultural officers were so wise. While such attitudes prevailed among the field administration it was inevitable that terracing would eventually provoke resistance.

Although Maher's original programme had attempted to foster popular support for terracing by rewarding the co-operators with cheap manure and improved stock, once the campaign began, practical limitations on supervisory manpower, equipment and finance, distorted the aims, so that the reality experienced by Kikuyu and Kamba peasants was very different from the idealistic expectations of Maher and the Secretariat. Out in the maize *shambas*, compulsion dominated official thinking and attempts to win popular acceptance were at best half-hearted. By the time the campaign had percolated down to the ordinary African, it bore little resemblance not only to Maher's grandiose plan, but also to Lambert's or Wyn Harris's conception of a revitalised *Muhirig'a*.[20]

The rewards of chiefship

Throughout the 30 years between the outbreak of the First World War and the end of the Second, Kikuyu chiefs controlled the rewards of government patronage in the reserves through the Local Native Councils. Grants for ploughs or carts, new varieties of seed for cash crops, and preferential access to grade cattle were all used by the chiefs to enrich themselves and their supporters. Colonial chiefs could not afford to antagonise all their people, otherwise they would have ceased to command respect, so they all attempted to consolidate their position by the use of patronage to reward their immediate *mbari*.[21]

The chiefs' privileged access to the 'pork-barrel' of the colonial state, however, aroused resentment among aspiring cash-crop cultivators and traders who were excluded from government patronage. By the late 1920s, these ambitious outsiders had emerged as the leaders of the Kikuyu Central Association and challenged the chiefs' monopoly of power and rewards.[22] At the same time, many poor peasants were being forced to become migrant labourers or to sell their land to the emerging African élite to survive. Such people identified the chiefs as their exploiters. These processes were intensified during the war and the Mitchell era, when those who had surplus to extract profited as never before from the high prices offered on the black market. During these years social differentiation became increasingly apparent. While the chiefs and their allies prospered, poor peasants dependent on earnings from wage labour suffered from the high rate of inflation. Moreover, African traders who were known to oppose the chiefs found it virtually impossible to restock their shops or acquire spare parts to keep their lorries or *posho* mills functioning, for the district administration had left the distribution of rationed commodities largely to the chiefs.[23]

The chiefs also alienated the returning *askari*. In the political and economic rivalries of Kikuyuland, the ex-*askari* quickly discovered that a six-year absence, however socially prestigious, put them at a political disadvantage. Denied special representation on the Native Tribunals and the Local Native Councils, they saw the chiefs and the elders consolidating their control of government patronage. The *askari* were not given licences for trading or permits for shops; these went to the chiefs and their clients.[24]

In fact the administration was attempting to ensure that the new businesses were well run, viable concerns. The much-resented regulation limiting the number of shops to one for every 400 inhabitants, for example, was designed to protect the welfare of established traders and to ensure that newcomers did not waste their money competing with experienced businessmen. But to those who were refused licences – and they were in the majority – it simply provided further evidence of the domination of rural life and the suffocation of new business rivals by the established coterie around the chiefs. Aspiring African entrepreneurs were convinced that new financial opportunities were being restricted to acquiescent supporters of the chiefs and of the *status quo*. By 1947, when their savings had been dissipated or lost on ill-considered business ventures, the ex-*askari* were ready to add their voices to the growing chorus of peasant protest.[25]

The colonial régime in Central Province after 1945 was simply incapable of admitting all those who wanted to share in the rewards of state patronage. Unless the colony's whole political economy was fundamentally restructured and the privileged position of the European settlers abandoned, which Sir Philip Mitchell never comtemplated, the administration had no option but to restrict the number of Africans who could be incorporated on a first-come-first-served basis. Thus only the chiefs and their supporters were allowed to share in the pickings from Kenya's controlled economy, while requests from the emerging alternative élite had to be rejected. James Beauttah, for example, founder of the Kenya Automobile Association (a cartel of African bus owners), and Andrew Ng'ang'a, leader of the *Agikuyu na Worjoria Wao* (a co-operative of licensed egg exporters), who were in the vanguard of indigenous capitalism, became disgruntled and turned to political action. As Vice-President of the Kenya African Union in Central Province and secretary of the Murang'a district branch respectively, these men soon became noted opponents of the chiefs and, therefore, of the chiefs' allies in the district administration.[26]

The chiefs discovered after the war that it was increasingly difficult to satisfy both the administration and their people. Whereas in the inter-war years the position had provided many opportunities for capital accumulation through the manipulation of government and Local Native Council grants, after 1945 the administration made new demands on the chief, while the agricultural campaign aroused widespread opposition and considerably increased the risks of being a chief. Tenure of office became less secure and many chiefs were ignominiously dismissed for failing to enforce the new agricultural regulations.[27] This, of course, reduced the financial attractions of the post. In the 1920s and 1930s, a newly-appointed chief could confidently expect to have at least ten years in which to restructure the local trade networks to enrich himself and his supporters and to direct development funds into particular *mbari*, but after 1945 a new chief had virtually no time in which to exploit his position and to channel government money into his area. Instead he had immediately to begin to worry about defending his newly-gained authority as the political contest in the locations gathered momentum. The agricultural betterment campaign and soil terracing had to be enthusiastically supported, regardless of their divisive effects, if the chief was to retain official approval and to remain in office. As the men in the middle, the chiefs were under intense pressure from both the district administration, on the one hand, and their political opponents and increasing numbers of ordinary Africans, on the other.[28]

After the war, under Mitchell's drive to improve African agriculture, a chief was expected to instigate a social revolution in peasant life instead of being left to preside over his location and to ensure that the tax was paid and peace preserved, as had been the case during the inter-war years. For the first time the peasant quietly cultivating his *shamba* felt the full force of government intervention. At this critical juncture, however, the government decided to replace many of the pre-war generation of chiefs with younger, better-educated men, who would energetically support the agricultural campaign and 'modernise' their locations.[29] But these changes exacerbated the problems created by the campaign, for these new men often lacked popular support and had not yet established ties of clientage with which to withstand widespread opposition. They could only fall back on the government and the use of force to compel obedience.[30]

Until 1935 Murang'a was divided into two divisions; Maragua–Tana in the north and Chania–Maragua in the south, with 22 and 15 locations respectively. Between 1912, when the Political Record Books began, and 1935, Murang'a District had a total of 84 different chiefs; 54 in Maragua–Tana and 30 in Chania–Maragua, who served an average of nine years in the north and eleven in the south.[31] The post-war generation of chiefs, however, rarely survived this long, as can be seen from Table 7.1.[32]

Table 7.1: *Murang'a Chiefs 1944 to 1953*

Location	Chief	Dated appointed	Reasons for departure
1	Ndungu Kagori	1933	Served throughout
2	Njiri Karanja	1912	Retired old age; succeeded by son
	Kigo Njiri	1951	
3	Reuben Gachau	1927	Dismissed
	Mwangi Wambico	1949	Dismissed
	Samuel Githu	1953	
4	Kimani wa Thuo	1913	Dismissed for corruption
	Raphael Munyori	1946	Dismissed, but said to have resigned
	Paulo Mungai	1952	
5	Joseph Kangethe	1932	Dismissed
	Jibsam Mwaura	1945	Appointed African Administration

	Kuria Kinyanjui	1947	Dismissed
	Jibsam Mwaura	1951	
6	Karanja wa Kibarabara	1923	Dismissed for corruption
	Dishon Meri wa Wandia	1945	
7	Waweru Kehia	1932	Resigned old age
	Erastus Njeroge	1946	
8	Muriranja Mureithi	1908	Died alcoholism
	Ignatio Morai	1944	
9	Wakomo Muthenyi	1921	Resigned ill health
	Joshua Kogi	1945	
10	Sila Karimu	1936	Dismissed
	Aram Muhari Karema	1948	Dismissed
	Evan	1952	
11	Joseph Wanjie	1940	Retired honourably 1954, served throughout Mitchell era
12	Joel Michuki	1939	Succeeded his father who had been chief since 1908
13	Parmenas Mockerie Githendu	1936	Dismissed; became leader KISA
	Paulo Kiratu	1948	Dismissed
	Ben Jacob	1953	
14	Munyoroku Ndurwa	1941	Dismissed
	Pharis Kariuki	1943	Dismissed
	Wilson Morangi	1949	
15	Kigwaine Kamaru	1924	Resigned ill health
	Peterson Kariuki	1946	

The brief biographical studies in Table 7.1 point to some of the problems the post-war chiefs faced as they attempted to straddle the divide between the government and their people and to meet the demands imposed by the new interventionist policies. Only one of the earliest generation of chiefs, Njiri Karanja of Location 2, managed to survive in the Mitchell era. His former colleagues were dismissed or 'retired' and even Njiri was criticised for taking too little interest in terracing. Kimani wa Thuo of Location 4 and Karanja wa Kibarabara of Location 6 were replaced; they had taken to drink but were eventually dismissed when they were found to be trading the sugar ration and holding unauthorised land hearings. Corrupt old Muriranja Mureithi in Location 8 died of chronic alcoholism and was replaced by the dynamic Ignatio Morai.[33]

Even most of the first generation of Christian chiefs, who were appointed in the 1920s and early 1930s, failed to satisfy the stringent new requirements and were retired. Mwangi Wambico, for example, replaced

Reuben Gachau in Location 3 in 1949. The new chief was closely identified with the administration, having served as a clerk in the District Commissioner's office from 1945 until he was appointed chief. Wambico, however, failed to compel his people to dig terraces. Despite a warning from the District Commissioner early in 1951 that he must 'get round his location or else', he devoted most of his energies to developing his large wattle plantation rather than controlling his location. Finally he was replaced by his friend, Samuel Githu, an energetic young trader whom the administration hoped would prove a more forceful personality and control the location more effectively.[34]

In neighbouring Location 4, Raphael Munyori, who had replaced the disgraced Kimani wa Thuo, also failed and resigned on 16 October 1952, only four days before the declaration of the Emergency. On his appointment Munyori had been a popular choice, having recently secured a large majority in his election as vice-president of the Kandara Tribunal. Initially, he administered his location with great vigour and successfully put an end to illicit *tembu* brewing in Muruka, a notoriously bad spot where Nubian gin distilling was rampant, but by 1949 he had lost interest in soil conservation. Despite having been selected to attend one of the chiefs' courses at Kabete, Kimani's enthusiasm diminished as he gradually realised how deep rooted opposition was to the new interventionist government policies. By February 1952, the District Commissioner was complaining that Kimani did 'less than the minimum' and that 'the Administration could achieve nothing in Location 4'.[35]

In Location 5, Jibsam Mwaura, another former district clerk, resigned after only two years of service as a chief and his successor, Kuria Kinyanjui, was dismissed as ineffective in 1951. Aram Muhari Karema, who replaced Chief Sila Karimu in Location 10, also survived for only four years; while Paulo Kiratu, who succeeded the wily Parmenas Mockerie Githendu in Location 13 in 1948, was replaced in 1953. Location 14 was the worst in the district and between 1937 and 1952 had five different chiefs. Only Joseph Wanjie in Location 11, and Joel Michuki in Location 12, managed to cling to office throughout the Mitchell years.[36]

This rapid turnover of chiefs was a reflection of the more stringent criteria employed by the government during the second colonial occupation to measure progress. Chiefs who failed to produce impressive terracing statistics, for example, were condemned as inefficient and in the new interventionist atmosphere after the war, were dismissed. The field administration became much less sensitive to African opposition and pressed ahead with its agricultural theories about carrying capacity and crop rotations, ignoring signs of discontent. This arrogant attitude was not confined to Murang'a. Two cautious Nyeri chiefs, who had served with distinction for many years, were now criticised for obstructing the

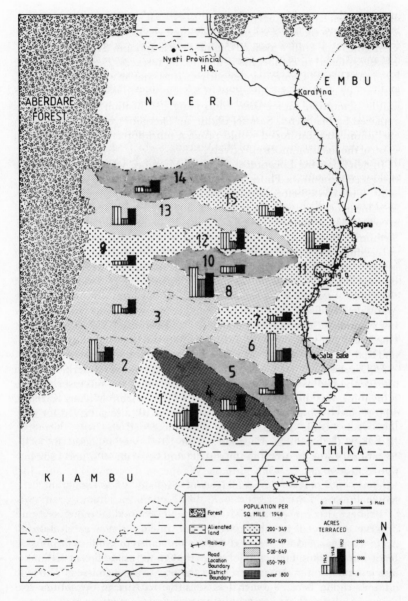

Map 7.1: *Population Density and Terracing in Murang'a*

Muhirig'a elders and for being too concerned with their own popularity.[37] Some Murang'a chiefs were also reluctant to push their people too far and realised that the new agricultural programme was generating bitter discontent. Chief Sila of Location 10 was one such sceptical old man of the pre-war generation of chiefs. Although he was regarded as the best farmer in the whole district, eager to adopt new techniques and crops, he ruled his location with great caution and did not push terracing too hard.[38]

Another chief who wished to remain on good terms with his people was Parmenas Mockerie Githendu, the best known and, in African political circles, the most influential of the Murang'a chiefs. Like Sila he was a member of the old school and refused to ruffle his location with over-zealous enforcement of terracing and soil conservation rules. As a longstanding member of the Kikuyu Central Association he was, unlike most chiefs, still close to the political activists and, as the administration was forced to admit, remained 'popular in his location since he makes little effort to enforce soil conservation measures'.[39] In 1931, the Kikuyu Central Association in Murang'a selected Parmenas to accompany Kenyatta to Britain to present evidence before the Joint Select Committee on Closer Union. He briefly attended Ruskin College, Oxford, before returning to Kenya in 1933 and was appointed chief three years later. Almost from the start he failed to fulfil the administration's expectations. The steep slopes of Mathioya in his location continued to be cultivated despite repeated orders to the contrary from the District Commissioner. Osborne, the District Commissioner in Murang'a throughout the war, however, astutely recognised that Parmenas was a popular chief and reported, 'I would only recommend his dismissal as a last resort. In spite of his deterioration he appears to command a large measure of general support.[40] This wise advice was ignored and, in 1948, Parmenas was dismissed, only to re-emerge as a prominent local politician and leader of the Kikuyu Independent Schools' Association throughout Murang'a. In his new position he soon became an even greater irritant to the district administration.

These chiefs realised that the terracing programme was alienating their people. Some of the older generation, like Kimani wa Thuo, Karanja wa Kibarabara and Wakomo Muthenyi, understood this opposition. However corrupt they might have been, unlike the new generation of chiefs who replaced them they did share the ambitions and suspicions of the ordinary Kikuyu peasant.[41] Even although they used their position to enrich themselves and exploited their people, over the course of 20 or 30 years as chiefs they established a complex network of obligations for favours rendered. Their long years in power had placed them at the centre of an intricate matrix of political antennae, penetrating deep into location life. They shared the thoughts of their peasant neighbours and quickly perceived the dangers involved in the post-war soil conservation drive.

Their obstinacy, tantamount to downright obstructionism, was an inarticulate condemnation of the agricultural campaign, which should have provided a potent warning to the field administration. The government, however, was not interested in warnings and pressed ahead regardless of the consequences. Mitchell himself insisted that the campaign must continue with 'a firm refusal to be rattled'.[42]

The growth of Kikuyu opposition

Discontent continued to lurk below the surface. The peasantry distrusted European intervention and failed to understand the need for the host of new regulations restricting cultivation near streams or on hillsides. Many suspected that, once the terraces had been completed, their land would be alienated to Europeans under the soldier settlement scheme. Garbled versions of Humphrey's reports spread through the reserves with the alarming news that thousands of families were to be dispossessed and thrown off their land. Since little attempt was made to explain the need for terracing, the arrival of agricultural department levellers to measure contour lines aroused further dismay.

The first resistance came from former soldiers who objected to communal labour and stopped their wives digging terraces.[43] Initially this was simply another step in their drive to secure special recognition from the chiefs and the administration, but the protest escalated into a wider anti-terracing campaign. Encouraged by local political activists, the former *askari* broadened their campaign early in 1946 by using the vernacular press to condemn female communal labour on the terraces. Popular disillusionment with terracing and the chiefs had not, however, become sufficiently pervasive to evoke a wide enough response and their campaign soon faltered. By the end of 1946, the District Commissioner, Desmond O'Hagan, was optimistic that the Kikuyu had finally realised the benefits of soil conservation.[44]

Between October and December 1946, more than 2,000 acres were protected each month in Murang'a and, over the year, approximately 7,000 miles of terraces were dug, more than double the figure for 1945. It was this sustained drive that destroyed Kikuyu acceptance of the colonial régime. Early in July 1947, Knight, the new Assistant Agricultural Officer, noted that 'only constant pressure keeps work going'. He failed, however, to draw the logical conclusion that the peasantry had been alienated and opposed these interventionist agricultural polices. The pressure to keep the campaign going, of course, was provided by the chiefs and the Native Tribunal elders. Both propaganda and force were used, and locational rivalry was encouraged to promote terracing. In an attempt to motivate the chiefs and their people, monthly lists of work completed in each location were sent round to be read out at *barazas*. So intense was the competition to do well among the new generation of chiefs, that some even published lists of the terracing done in each sub-location in order to stimulate their headmen and levellers on to greater efforts.[45]

The revolt when it came, only a fortnight after Knight's belated recognition that all was not well, completely destroyed Murang'a's famed system of *ngwatio* (communal labour). The year of disaster, 1947, had started extremely well. In January, 1,839 acres were terraced and this high level was sustained until July, but on Sunday 20 July, the Murang'a branch of the Kenya African Union held a meeting. This meeting, which was attended by over 10,000 people, was the first to be held in the district since Kenyatta had become President of the Kenya African Union on 1 June 1947, and he was the guest speaker. Kenyatta began by praising the soil-conservation campaign, emphasising to the crowd how important it was for erosion and declining fertility to be halted. The meeting, however, had become increasingly restless. They had come to hear him denounce, not praise, the terracing campaign. As the meeting progressed Kenyatta became aware that he was in danger of losing his audience and began to criticise certain aspects of the agricultural policy, particularly the reliance on female labour to dig terraces. The meeting finally resolved that no women should be compelled to join the *ngwatio* labour gangs. Until then the vast majority of the communal terracing workforce had been female. The resolution, therefore, was a direct challenge to the agricultural campaign and to the authority of the chiefs and the district administration.[46]

The following morning virtually no women turned out to work and only a few old men could be found digging terraces. By the middle of August even they had abandoned the slopes and all communal work had ceased. To prevent total collapse, the District Commissioner issued an order early in August that *shambas* would, in future, be individually measured and that prosecutions would follow unless terraces were dug by each cultivator within 15 days. It was hoped that this individualist approach and heavy fines would rekindle interest in *ngwatio* communal work, but by this time the chiefs' political opponents had mobilised peasant opposition to terracing and had proclaimed that 'the people were determined to have no more terracing at any price'.[47] In September, only 187 acres were protected and the agricultural campaign had totally collapsed. The greatest resistance had come from the north of the district, where the Kikuyu Central Association had always been strongest, around the Church Missionary Society stations at Kahuhia and Weithaga, and especially from the locations of Chiefs Ignatio, Joel and Joshua. Although the sharp steps taken by the government produced a small revival in October and November, when some 334 acres were terraced, the women still refused to return to work and the communal strategy had to be abandoned in favour of the allocation of specific tasks to each household.[48]

Compulsory female labour provided the government's critics with an easy target, for emotive appeals could be made to world opinion which was ignorant of the fact that, in Kenya, the main burden of cultivation and hard physical labour usually fell upon the women. The political activists were to prove adept at embarrassing the administration with appeals to the International Labour Organisation and the United Nations. The Secretariat quickly recognised that they had been outsmarted and warned the field administration that the use of compulsory female labour could not be defended by the British delegation to the International Labour Organisation. The administration, however, pointed out that there was simply no alternative but to use Kikuyu women to dig terraces.[49]

When the district administration attempted to enforce terracing, violence erupted. An Agricultural Instructor was assaulted in Location 12, terraces were destroyed in Locations 8 and 9 , and some Tribunals showed signs of refusing to convict 'malcontents'. Nevertheless, the chiefs prosecuted no less than 607 people in October alone for refusing to comply with agricultural orders. Meanwhile, Murang'a's share of Central Province's terracing fell in the first half of the year from 43 per cent to a mere 15 per cent and the work done by each cultivator was of a much lower quality than under the *ngwatio* method.[50]

Following the collapse, J.T. Moon, the Provincial Agricultural Officer, attempted to absolve his department of responsibility and blamed unscrupulous agitators for deceiving the peasantry with promises of less work. Similar excuses were made by the district administration, which blamed young militants from Nairobi and the local leaders of the Kenya African Union, such as Beauttah and Gideon Macharia. Coutts, the new District Commissioner who had taken over just before the disturbances did, however, recognise that popular discontent with the despotic rule of the chiefs might lie behind the trouble. Unfortunately he blamed the older generation of chiefs. He reported:

> . . . there can be no doubt that the people have a good deal on their side. The age of the old type of despot has definitely gone and no longer are the Kikuyu prepared to accept orders without questioning the right of the person to give them or the validity of the order itself. This is of course universal and merely a symptom of the birth of liberty.[51]

This may have been true, but the crucial factor was overlooked. The people were rebelling not against 'the old type of despot', but against the new generation of educated chiefs who were convinced supporters of the agricultural campaign. Resistance was concentrated in their locations and directed against them, not against the surviving representatives of the old style of chieftainship.

The previous District Commissioner, O'Hagan, had dimly perceived this before he was promoted to the Secretariat, in May 1947, because of his successes in Murang'a. He observed that 'land reclamation measures in a location depend entirely on the energy and powers of leadership of its chief. General support and encouragement are not enough, the chief as chairman of his location team must be the moving force directing operations and this can only be achieved by hard work, great energy and much enthusiasm'.[52] It was hardly surprising then that, when the storm broke, it was the newly-appointed zealous young chiefs who proved incapable of controlling the protest. The 'agitators' made least impression in Locations 1 and 2, where Ndungu Kagori and Njiri Karanja, of the older generation, had been chiefs since 1932 and 1912 respectively. In these locations in the extreme south of the district, the women were already beginning to resume terracing early in 1948, while in Chief Ignatio's former model Location 8, the soil conservation campaign was still badly disrupted.[53] Let us now look in greater detail at events in the locations controlled by the post-war generation of chiefs, such as Ignatio Morai.

Kikuyu chiefs and the peasant revolt

Chief Ignatio Morai was a former schoolmaster at the Mogoire Roman Catholic school and a devout Christian. He became chief in 1944 on the death of the notorious old Muriranja wa Mureithi. As an apostle of modernisation, who had improved his own smallholding – applying manure, enclosing his land, dipping his cattle and building terraces – Ignatio was not simply a 'collaborator', but firmly believed in the benefits that would result from the agricultural campaign. As a leading exponent of the new programme and a strict enforcer of the conservation regulations, he alienated many people in his location and was an easy target for the Kikuyu Central Association to single out for attack. As chairman of the Local Native Council's Agriculture Sub-committee, he was known to be the administration's most loyal supporter in Murang'a and had become a personal enemy of the local leaders of the Kenya African Union, especially James Beauttah, who led the opposition on the council to the chiefs. Ignatio was also politically exposed because the people in Location 8 had for many years endured the tyranny of his predecessor and had little sympathy for the colonial régime. Even Muriranja's old cronies failed to support Ignatio, for he had turned them out of their positions and denied their long-accustomed access to state patronage.[54]

During his first three years as chief, Ignatio was remarkably successful in mobilising his people to dig terraces. While old Chief Kigwaine in Location 15 managed to complete only 44,704 yards of terraces in 1946, Ignatio's produced 357,214 yards, almost eight times Kigwaine's figure and the second highest total in the district.[55] Before the revolt, the District Commissioner reported that Ignatio was:

. . . one of the most outstanding Kikuyu chiefs. He was in all respects the best Chief in the District. He is a great leader, is highly intelligent and is very popular with his people. His location has led the way in land reclamation measures . . . As Chairman of the Local Native Council Standing Committee for Agriculture, he played a leading part in persuading the people throughout the District to adopt better farming methods.[56]

With the revolt, however, this view rapidly changed. Early in 1948, when the agricultural officer went around Location 8 on safari, he discovered that Ignatio's own sub-location was more recalcitrant than the areas supervised by his headmen. Knight was surprised to find this and recorded: 'I hesitate to say that Chief Ignatio is losing his grip but this is the only location in which no communal work of any kind is being done and he cerainly does not 'go places' as he used to do nor does he seem to have much idea of what is, or is not, being done in his location.'[57] Ignatio's failure stemmed from his previous success. His remarkable terracing figures had been secured at the expense of growing popular discontent. The supposed revitalisation of the *Muhirig'a* and use of *ngwatio* labour, and the establishment of location and sub-location councils to advise the chiefs, had not concealed from the peasantry the fact that government demands had become far more onerous. The Kikuyu Central Association seized upon the dislike of terracing and consolidated its support before challenging the power of the new chiefs and the administration over the agricultural campaign.[58]

Chief Ignatio, who had been singled out for attack, initially fought back. One month after Kenyatta's visit to Murang'a, Ignatio accused Beauttah at the Local Native Council session on 21 August 1947, of 'nurturing evil counsels against him and further of stirring up trouble in his location'. Shortly afterwards he banned all political meetings in his location. The local Kenya African Union leaders responded by encouraging opposition to terracing and by calling a meeting in Location 8 for Sunday 24 August, where, supported by Councillor Isaak Gathanju, Beauttah demanded Ignatio's dismissal.[59]

Ignatio responded immediately by arresting Beauttah, Gathanju and two other political activists, Mwangi Macharia and Mwangi Thomas, for organising an illegal meeting. While on bail awaiting trial, Beauttah attempted to mobilise further opposition against Ignatio, issuing posters calling for a demonstration outside the courtroom on the grounds that he and his colleagues were being prosecuted for standing up for the people in their anti-terracing protests. On the day of the trial vast crowds gathered outside the District Commissioner's office. When the four heroes were sentenced to six weeks hard labour and each fined 100 shillings, the crowd became violent. Threats were made against Chief Ignatio, and an armed guard had to be placed on his village. On the evening of Sunday 28

September 1947, a riot occurred near the village and the guards shot into the crowd, killing one man and injuring another as they sought to protect the chief. After this incident, a levy-force of 24 Kenyan policemen, under the command of a European Inspector, were stationed at Kahuro to maintain order.[60]

Mwangi Macharia had also been active before his trial, stirring up opposition against terracing and the chiefs in the three most northerly locations of Chiefs Joel, Joshua and Parmenas. Even after his imprisonment these locations remained centres of resistance. When Macharia was released in November 1947, he had considerable success in arousing further opposition. He also improved contacts between his supporters in Murang'a, the Nairobi militants in the Forty Group and the trade unions, which, in the early 1950s, quickly spread the first Mau Mau oaths throughout the district. Macharia had emerged as a prominent figure in the African Workers' Federation during the general strike in Mombasa in January 1947. After being deported from Mombasa he was instrumental in forming the Federation's Nairobi branch before returning to his home district to organise opposition to the Murang'a chiefs.[61]

Ignatio was not the only new chief to encounter opposition. Chiefs Kimani, Waweru and Kigwoine had all retired in 1946. Their replacements were young, educated men, who were enthusiastic supporters of the second colonial occupation. Since replacing Chief Waweru in September 1946, Erastus Njeroge transformed Location 7 into a centre of terracing by producing the highest terracing figures in Murang'a, with 366,556 yards of communal work. Even before Kenyatta's meeting on 20 July 1947, however, there had been growing clandestine activity in his location by the Kikuyu Central Association. In June, for example, some Maragua residents had alleged that Njeroge had fined and imprisoned some women, and impounded their goats, for refusing to dig terraces. Subsequently the District Commissioner discovered that over-zealous *Muhirig'a* elders, probably with the chief's approval, had indeed been using force to ensure that their location headed the Murang'a soil-conservation league. Erastus, like most of the new chiefs, believed that the administration's main criteria for judging his success was the effectiveness of the terracing programme.[62] The chiefs and elders were convinced that their continuation in office depended upon the progress made with terracing and that the administration would turn a blind eye as to how exactly it was achieved. Ambitious headmen knew that if the chief failed they stood a good chance of succeeding to his position with its control over local patronage. The chiefs, headmen and *Muhirig'a* elders therefore became obsessed with terracing and failed to recognise that they were alienating the peasantry and driving them towards the political activists.[63]

The year 1948 was a quieter one in Murang'a, but the District Commissioner feared further trouble. He warned that: 'it appears as though there is a slow revival of political activity which unless directed into safer channels may result in about one year's time in another upheaval perhaps of greater magnitude than the last'.[64] Kikuyu acceptance of the colonial state and its most conspicuous representative, the chief, he recognised, would never be the same again in Murang'a. The situation had still not returned to normal. The women's revolt was not over. At the beginning of the year, for example, only Chief Ndungu in Location 1 had persuaded his women to return to work. When the Local Native Council tried to force a return in March 1948, serious resistance was provoked.

On 14 April 1948, more than 2,000 women from Location 15 appeared outside the District Commissioner's office chanting opposition to the new order. The following month they refused to participate in the grass-planting campaign, which had become an annual ritual for the whole community. These demonstrations forced Chief Peterson wa Kariuki, who had hitherto kept a low profile, to take firm action and to order specific women to plant grass. When they refused, he promptly had them arrested. When news of the arrests spread round the location, a large crowd of women assembled on 4 May and marched on the district headquarters, brandishing sticks and shouting abuse against the chief and the district administration. Tribal police had to be used to break up the demonstration and large numbers were arrested. When their cases were heard before the Native Tribunal on 8 May, another large crowd of angry women descended on the district headquarters and were only driven back by police truncheons. Murang'a gradually returned to normal, but discontent continued to simmer below the surface and suspicion of the chiefs and the agricultural department continued. The *wananchi* needed little provocation to erupt once more.[65]

The growth of resistance in Central Province and the reaction of the official mind

Although the problems created by the administration's obsession with narrow-base terracing were most severe in Murang'a, where the *ngwatio* system had originated and where the steep slopes made erosion particularly acute, the two other Kikuyu districts suffered similar disturbances. In Nyeri during 1946 there had been violent opposition to compulsory cattle dipping. Both the District Commissioner and Chief Nderi, who was an enthusiastic supporter of the policy, were attacked. The District Commissioner eventually had to advise the Executive Council that there would be serious trouble throughout the district unless the compulsory order was revoked.[66]

Kiambu was also disrupted by political protests in 1947.[67] As in Murang'a, it took two years for the peasantry to become thoroughly alienated by the government's interventionist polices. The worst affected areas, as in Murang'a, were the locations of those chiefs most closely identified with the new agricultural campaign. Chief Waruhiu's Githunguri division was badly disrupted. This had appeared to be the most progressive area. The Chura *Muhirig'a* had even rivalled Murang'a in using indigenous authorities to mobilise the peasantry for terracing.[68] As in Murang'a, the opposition was led by the area's Local Native Councillor. His election early in 1947 should have provided a warning that all was not well, but, as in Murang'a, this danger signal went unnoticed. Other signs of growing discontent were available. Wangige cultivators had refused to stop cultivating along the riverbanks. At the other end of Kikuyuland, at Karatina in Nyeri, cultivators destroyed the irrigation channels on the war-time dried-vegatable project when the government refused to turn it into an African co-operative. The administration, however, regarded these disturbances as individual incidents and failed to realise that they were the first signs of a general revolt against the second colonial occupation and the authority of the chiefs.[69] As a result, the provincial administration and the agricultural and veterinary departments had been ill prepared for the onslaught, which erupted in all three Kikyu districts in 1947.

In December 1946, the new Provincial Commissioner, Wyn Harris, had warned that 'the outward sign of unrest among Africans is a pernicious African press, increased activities of the known political agitators and opposition to many forms of Government activity in the Reserves, particularly if it is directed by Europeans or Chiefs'.[70] This, however, overlooked the crucial fact that it was the new development measures that were alienating the Kikuyu. Instead of attempting to reduce discontent, Wyn Harris adopted an intransigent attitude and insisted that all opposition must be defeated and agricultural reforms forced through. He proposed that the technical departments explain the need for the conservation campaign at *barazas* and ordered the field administration to gain the support of the leaders of African opinion, such as the officials of the traders' and farmers' associations. Unfortunately, instead of reducing fears of renewed land alienation, the agricultural campaign intensified African suspicions.

Wyn Harris attempted to bolster the chiefs by empowering them to ban political meetings, including gatherings of the Kenya African Union, under the Native Authority Ordinance of 1937.[71] In 1947, this Ordinance became the symbol of the chiefs' power and the focus of many attacks by the vernacular press and African politicians. The first critical article appeared in the Asian newspaper, the *Daily Chronicle*, which was sympathetic to the radical critics of British colonialism. It denounced the dictatorial powers of the chiefs, particularly Ignatio Morai, and alleged that 'the chief was gathering wool round the eyes of his immediate supervisors and the people could not do anything as long as he was in power'.[72] As the government's leading supporter in Murang'a, Ignatio had to endure sustained press criticism. The *Daily Chronicle* even alleged that Ignatio had deliberately ordered the shooting at Kahuro. Although the newspaper published an apology two months later, after a Commission of Enquiry, this did little to offset the harm that had been done to the chief's reputation.

The African newspaper, *Mumenyereri*, also denounced the chief for arresting Councillors Beauttah and Gathanju, who had merely been protecting their constituents from Ignatio's tyranny. Under the Native Authority Ordinance, the paper complained, the people had no redress against the arbitrary acts of the chiefs. One editorial protested:

> We, the public, demand the power to remove any Chief who becomes unpopular and power to say that a certain member of any Council cannot be ejected from any Council just because there is some difference between him and the President of the Council. If the public had power Mr James Beauttah and Isaak Gathanju would not leave the Fort Hall Local Native Council.[73]

This press campaign against prominent chiefs continued throughout 1947 and 1948.[74]

By July 1948, Wyn Harris, who had become the Chief Native Commissioner, was extremely alarmed. The newspaper attacks on Chief Ignatio were only the most scurrilous part of an organised campaign against everyone closely identified with the government. Four Kiambu chiefs, for example, were also denounced in the African press and, by mid-1948, a total of seven cases had been brought to court against prominent chiefs. While the campaign in Murang'a concentrated on Chief Ignatio and in Nyeri on Chief Muhoya, who had supported compulsory dipping at the height of its unpopularity in 1946, Chief Waruhiu endured the most attacks in Kiambu – both physical and verbal.[75] These three chiefs were the administration's most loyal supporters in their districts and were enthusiastic advocates of the post-war agricultural campaign. All three were devout Christians and noted opponents of the independent schools and churches. If they could be discredited then the other chiefs would have been seriously intimidated.

The first case against Waruhiu alleged he had destroyed a plantation of 400 wattle trees while imposing compulsory terracing. Despite strenuous attempts by Wyn Harris to ensure his acquittal, the judgement in the magistrate's court went against him. Even before his appeal was heard, a second case was brought against the chief for wrongful imprisonment. The administration feared the chief would again be found guilty, which would further undermine his authority and encourage complaints against other chiefs.

Protesting to the Attorney General about the impartial behaviour of the magistrate, Wyn Harris warned that 'from the Administrative point of view it is essential that Waruhiu's authority should be upheld as these cases are beginning to break the hearts of our better chiefs as they feel they have not got the support of government in keeping peace and good order in their districts'.[76] Despite such pressure, the Attorney General insisted on prosecuting Waruhiu and refused to invoke the Public Officer Protection Ordinance to safeguard the chief. The government's lawyers again refused to give way to the field administration's practical problems. The Solicitor General considered that Waruhiu was guilty and insisted that the law should proceed even if it meant discrediting the administration's main supporter in Kiambu. Chiefs, he argued, should no longer be allowed to behave like petty tyrants; a new era had dawned and responsible, educated Africans were entitled to be protected from wrongful arrest.

The split between the legal department (with its pristine notions of legal propriety more appropriate to the Inns of Court than to the African reserves) and the field administration forced Wyn Harris to warn the governor of the crisis in Kikuyuland and of the imminent collapse of the chiefs' authority. The Chief Native Commissioner informed the governor that 'the effects have been disastrous on our attempts to govern native areas'. The legal department, he complained, did not realise that the allegations against Waruhiu were part of a careful campaign to discredit the chiefs. Wyn Harris reminded Mitchell that two years before he had warned District Commissioners that, 'Individual attacks on chiefs alleging all sorts of malpractices are likely to be the next phase of those dissident elements who desire to make profit from indiscipline in the native areas.'[77] He informed the governor that the charges against Waruhiu were clearly designed to humiliate the chief and to destroy his colleagues' confidence in the government. 'I submit that before very long we will have no single chief, no tribal police or other authority running the risk of finding themselves held up to ridicule by the masses while Government feebly looks on.'[78] The colonial government, he declared, should not simply 'stand idly by while one of our most devoted servants is prosecuted on a criminal charge for doing what he conceived to be his duty'. Desirable though it might be in Britain, unquestioning adherence to legal propriety was impossible in Africa. Collaborators had to be protected from the African peasantry when the British increased their demands on Africa during the second colonial occupation. The Attorney General's refusal to withdraw the prosecution and to tarnish his department's legal integrity in order to help unpopular chiefs, marked an imporant step towards the disintegration in Kenya of Ronald Robinson's 'non-European foundations of European imperialism'.[79]

Although the charges against Chief Waruhiu were of most concern to the administration, there were several similar cases. For example, Chief Makimei, who helped the police break the strike at Uplands, had thereby 'incurred the odium of many dissident elements in his location' when several of the strikers had been shot. Wyn Harris admitted that Makimei was a very different character from the god-fearing Waruhiu and had been lucky, a few years earlier, to have escaped a manslaughter charge. Nevertheless, he insisted, 'the fact is that he has stood loyally by Government, at great personal risk to himself and incurred the dislike of many fellow Kikuyu'. Wyn Harris considered that the chief must be supported. When Makimei was finally convicted of 'grievous assault' the district administration was so concerned about the possible effect on other Kiambu chiefs that it paid Makimei's £50 fine and the further £40 awarded as compensation to his victim.[80]

These divisions between the field administration and the Attorney General did not, as Berman has argued, stem from the administration's frustration at its supremacy being challenged by the influx of specialist staff, or from any fear that the generalists were being supplanted by the technical departments. The District Commissioners remained 'king of the castle' and presided over district policy and politics. It was the District Commissioners who chaired the district committees established by Mitchell and who had the ear of the Secretariat, which was recruited from the same élite Colonial Service cadre. Indeed, many of the troubles caused by the second colonial occupation occurred because the Secretariat was only too willing to listen to the field administration, with its belief in the organic communalism of Kikuyu society, rather than to the more subtle agricultural department which, after the debacle of 1947, wanted to encourage African cash-crop production as a reward for those who adopted new agricultural methods. By 1950, the agricultural department was convinced that the new strategy provided the only way of transforming Kikuyu agriculture without provoking massive resistance, but the field administrators only became convinced by the outbreak of Mau Mau, which the agriculturalists had wanted to avoid.[81]

Even within the field administration there were profound disagreements about how to respond to the African politicians. Walter Coutts, who was the District Commissioner in Murang'a at the height of the peasant revolt, had only recently replaced O'Hagan when the troubles began. He was a liberal, anxious to establish good relations with the local Kenya African Union leadership and to relax the tight reins of control favoured by his predecessor. Paradoxically the strict conservative, Desmond O'Hagan, with his paternalist policies, was acknowledged to have been a popular District Commissioner. Even his greatest opponent, the wily James Beauttah, recalled 30 years later that O'Hagan had helped African traders and had tried to improve social welfare. With a conservative like O'Hagan, the Kenya African Union and the underground

Kikuyu Central Association knew where they stood and how far they could go.[82] If they stepped out of line, they were well aware that the full might of government would have immediately descended upon them. At the same time the chiefs were equally confident, under O'Hagan, that the District Commissioner would always back them up, in public at least. Coutts, however, thought that O'Hagan had been too strict and believed that constructive criticism from the educated Africans in the Kenya African Union should be encouraged. This encouraged the Kikuyu politicians to experiment to see what concessions they could extract from the new District Commissioner and undermined the confidence of the chiefs. Both O'Hagan and Coutts, however, failed to recognise that the agricultural campaign was destroying popular acquiescence in the colonial régime.[83]

The politicisation of the Kikuyu reserves

The terracing campaign highlighted the dependence of the colonial state in Kenya upon the chiefs and African collaborators. After 50 years of British rule the Kikuyu chief had become as securely established as his counterparts in Tanganyika. By the late 1940s, the distinction between direct and indirect rule was otiose. The disturbances in north Pare in 1945 and 1946, and in Sukumaland during the early 1950s, demonstrated that it was not simply the Kikuyu chiefs who were undermined by the second colonial occupation's disruptive impact on African societies.

Dr Iliffe has shown, in his discussion of the *Mbiru* crisis in Upare, that these post-war protests marked an important step forward in rural Africa in the evolution of political consciousness. Although the peasants in Kikuyuland and the Usambaras had identified a single grievance – compulsory terracing or graduated taxation – the techniques of opposition showed a new sophistication and marked the beginning of a new era of more militant opposition to British rule.[84] In Kikuyuland, the terracing campaign provided urban radicals, such as Mwangi Macharia and the Forty Group, with an issue around which to mobilise their popular constituency in the reserves, with whose support they could challenge their enemies, the chiefs. This politicisation of the Kikuyu peasantry also enabled the militants, with their close contacts with Nairobi, to undermine the authority of the more radical of the old-style activists of the illegal Kikuyu Central Association. The moderates in both organisations, in contrast, wanted to co-operate with the district administration and to be co-opted into the political nation so that they could get access to government patronage.[85]

Throughout Kikuyuland, the demands imposed on the peasantry by the agricultural campaign had eaten away the foundations of colonial control. The chiefs had been completely discredited. When the ordinary

Kikuyu finally protested, the political activists and the vernacular press turned on their rivals. Under this barrage of criticism, the chiefs became a more united political force and fought back, attacking the Kenya African Union, which they saw as the main centre of opposition to their domination of rural Africa. The chiefs sought every opportunity to bolster their own position by maligning the African politicians. This, of course, accorded well with the thinking of the field administration, which had little time for these upstart 'agitators' who were threatening the organic hierarchy of Kikuyu society. The District Commissioners then forwarded this distorted information to the Secretariat, where it was received as an accurate assessment of politics at the district level. In fact it was a political weapon in the chiefs' struggle to preserve their power and economic dominance. Neither the chiefs nor the administration were neutral observers of the political struggle in the reserves; both were interested parties in the growing conflict with the alternative élite which supported Kenyatta and the Kenya African Union.[86]

Thus, despite its arduous fight, the Kenya African Union could not shake the field administration's alliance with the chiefs. Indeed, as the chiefs came under attack they moved closer to the district administrators, who were equally determined to keep the terracing campaign functioning. Compulsory terracing was, therefore, both the major weakness and the greatest strength of the chiefs. Although the agricultural campaign had alienated the peasantry, the attacks of the Kenya African Union made it easy for the chiefs as a political class to strengthen their alliance with the administration and to discredit their political rivals who were seeking incorporation into the political nation. The protests failed because the chiefs tightened their control over the locations and launched a counter-attack on the political activists. For example, Chief Ignatio moved against James Beauttah, Murang'a's most prominent member of the Kenya African Union, who symbolised the alliance between the supposedly constitutionalist politicians and the 'subversive' Kikuyu Central Association.[87] To many chiefs, and increasingly to many government officials, the two organisations appeared to be virtually identical. After 1947, the Secretariat and Sir Philip Mitchell came to share this view and became suspicious of virtually all African politicians, including the moderates on the Legislative Council. The troubles in Murang'a during 1947 helped destroy Mitchell's hopes of a multiracial Kenya and drove him further into an alliance with the European settlers. This had disastrous consequences after 1950.

During the anti-terracing campaign, therefore, Macharia and the Forty Group successfully widened the divisions between the local politicians and their rivals, the chiefs, and prevented any compromise with the administration. Instead, they laid the foundations of a political alliance between the rural poor – disposed *ahoi* and poor peasants – who were being squeezed off their land and compelled to become wage labourers on the chiefs' and rich peasants' *shamba*, on the one hand, and the unskilled migrant workers and unemployed of 'outcast' Nairobi, on the other.[88] The struggle in Central Province during 1947 and 1948 marked the beginning of a new era in Kikuyu politics. The power of the constitutionalist élite diminished under the onslaught of the militants as the contradictions in their tenuous alliance with the Kikuyu poor became increasingly apparent. The aspiring traders and commercial farmers, from whom the local leadership for the Kenya African Union and earlier of the Kikuyu Central Association had been recruited, were in fact among the most conspicuous of the exploiters of the *ahoi* and poor peasant households. Only for a brief period in the late 1940s, when the chiefs had seemed about to topple from favour, had their mutual antipathy to the chiefs overcome their own internal divisions. With the failure of the anti-terracing campaign the alliance disintegrated and the militants became less active until the early 1950s, when they resurfaced as leaders of Mau Mau.[89]

Notes

1. CO 852/662/19936/2 (1945–46), 'Soil Erosion: Kenya', N. Humphrey, 'The Relationship of Population to the Land in South Nyeri', paragraphs 19–21; and H.E. Lambert and P. Wyn Harris, 'Policy in regard to Land Tenure in the Native Lands of Kenya', paragraph 62.

2. KNA MAA 8/68, 'Chief Waruhiu, 1948–52', P. Wyn Harris to Basil Hobson, 30 July 1948; and P. Wyn Harris to P.E. Mitchell, undated, but probably August 1948.

3. L. Cliffe, 'Nationalism and the Reaction to Enforced Agricultural Change in Tanganyika during the Colonial Period', pp. 17–23; J.M. Lonsdale, 'Some Origins of Nationalism in East Africa', pp. 131–6; and M.P.K. Sorrenson, *Land Reform in the Kikuyu Country*, pp. 105–9, provided many insights in the late 1960s which are in danger of being forgotten. Sorrenson, for instance, warned that there was no simple correlation between wealth and collaboration, or 'marginalisation' and rebellion. Too many recent studies have lost sight of the actual events and have forced Mau Mau into their favoured typology of peasant resistance. See Maina wa Kinyatti, 'Mau Mau', pp. 287–310; and his introduction to the collection of Mau Mau *nyimbo*, *Thunder from the Mountains*, pp. 1–8.

4. D. Mukaru-Ng'ang'a, 'Mau Mau,.Loyalists and Politics in Murang'a', pp. 365–83; and his thesis, 'Political History of Murang'a', pp. 69–73.

5. KNA DC/FH 1/26, 'Fort Hall Annual Report, 1947', pp. 1–6, 14–15.

6. The most vociferous representatives of this radical Kikuyu school are Maina wa Kinyatti, 'Mau Mau', pp. 287–310; and D. Mukaru-Ng'ang'a, in his thesis, 'Political History of Murang'a'. This interpretation has been popularised by Ngugi wa Thiong'o in his novels, and in the historical passages in *Detained*.

7. See A. Thurston's draft manuscript, 'The Intensification of Smallholder Agriculture in Kenya', p. 75.

8. KNA DC/FH 1/26, 'Fort Hall Annual Report, 1947', pp. 1–6; MAA 8/106, 'Intelligence Reports: Mumenyereri, 1947–50', C. Penfold, Director of Intelligence, to P. Wyn Harris, 10, 18, 20 and 21 October 1947. See also MAA 8/132, 'Law and Order: Legal Matters, 1947–51', P. Wyn Harris to Foster-Sutton, Attorney General, 25 November 1947, for attempts by the field administration to bolster the power of the chiefs.

9. CO 852/662/19936/2 (1945–46), 'Soil Erosion: Kenya', N. Humphrey, 'The Relationship of Population to the Land in South Nyeri', paragraphs 1–10 and 42–54.

10. A. Thurston's draft manuscript, 'The Intensification of Smallholder Agriculture in Kenya', pp. 24–30, 39–60; KNA Ag 4/419, 'Agricultural Development and the Maintenance of Soil Fertility: The Growing of High Priced Crops, 1933–51', J.T. Moon to Director of Agriculture, 5 February 1948; and L.H. Brown to DC Embu, 6 February 1948. See also Ag 4/125, 'Annual Agricultural Reports: Central Province, 1951', and contrast J.P. Benson's report for Meru with those from Murang'a and Nyeri.

11. KNA DC/FH 4/6, 'Chiefs and Headmen, 1937–54', *passim*; and Ag 4/451, 'Fort Hall Safari Diaries, 1948–51', especially the tours to Location 2, 17–21 February 1948; Location 8, 2–6 March 1948; Location 7, 9–13 March 1948; and Location 6, 5–8 April 1948.

12. KNA Ag 4/518, 'Reconditioning: Central Province, 1948–51', Colin Maher to Director of Agriculture, 30 November 1948; and the comments of J.T. Moon to the Director of Agriculture, 10 December 1948, in reply to Maher's criticisms.

13. *ibid.* See also KNA Ag 4/539, 'Reconditioning: Central Province, 1934–48', Colin Maher to the Senior Agricultural Officer, Nyanza, 28 January 1946.

14. CO 852/662/19936/2 (1945–46) 'Soil Erosion: Kenya', N. Humphrey, 'The Relationship of Population to the Land in South Nyeri', paragraph 21.

15. KNA Ag 4/419, 'Agricultural Development and the Maintenance of Soil Fertility: The Growing of High Priced Crops, 1933–51', J.T. Moon to Director of Agriculture, 5 February 1948; and Carolyn Barnes's thesis, 'An Experiment with African Coffee Growing in Kenya', pp. 161–4.

16. KNA Ag 4/539, 'Reconditioning: Central Province, 1934–48', T. Hughes Rice to J.T. Moon, 20 May 1946; and Ag 4/518, 'Reconditioning: Central Province, 1948–51', J.T. Moon, 3 February 1950.

17. A. Thurston's draft manuscript, 'The Intensification of Smallholder Agriculture in Kenya', pp. 46–7.

18. *ibid*, p. 48.

19. *ibid.*

20. For details of how the campaign impinged upon the peasant in his maize *shamba*, see KNA Ag 4/451, 'Fort Hall Safari Diaries, 1948–51', *passim*; and MAA 8/106, 'Intelligence Reports: Mumenyereri, 1948–51', Mrs M.W. Gathaku's letter in *Mumenyereri*, 29 September 1947; Johnson Maina Joshua's speech at Njumbii school, Location 13, Murang'a, reported in the same issue; and B.K. Ruhia's letter in *Mumenyereri*, 27 October 1947.

21. G. Kitching, *Class and Economic Change in Kenya*, pp. 188–99. For the rise of the *athomi* see unpublished papers by M.P. Cowen, 'Differentiation in a Kenya Location', *passim*; and G.C.M. Mutiso, 'The Creation of the Kitui Asomi'.

22. D.M. Feldman's thesis, 'Christians and Politics', pp. 160–224.

23. KNA MAA 7/49, 'chiefs and Headmen: Discipline, 1942–46'; and MAA 7/320, 'Chiefs Engaged in Commerce, 1948', for the problems this sometimes created. In Murang'a the clan elders supervised the rationing of sugar in each *itura*, see DC/FH 1/24, 'Fort Hall Annual Report, 1945', p. 9. For examples of chiefs who became successful businessmen, see G. Kitching, *Class and Economic Change in Kenya*, pp. 297–311, where nine of the fourteen case studies were chiefs; J.M. Lonsdale's

unpublished 'African Elites and Social Classes in Colonial Kenya', pp. 10-13; and B.E. Kipkorir, 'The Educated Elite and Local Society', pp. 255-68.

24. KNA Ag 4/77, 'Wattle Cooperative Societies, 1947-51', James Warnegi, Secretary, Central Province Wattle Growers' Association to G.J. Gollop, Agricultural Officer, Kiambu, 20 August 1948; C&I 6/782, 'Trading by Africans, 1946-50', especially Edward Karanja's complaint to the Secretariat, 27 May 1946; D. O'Hagan to A.C.M. Mullins, 17 October 1946; and A.C.M. Mullins to G.M. Rennie, 15 November 1946.

25. KNA DC/FH 1/25, 'Fort Hall Annual Report, 1946', pp. 9-10; and C&I 6/782, 'Trading by Africans, 1946-50', D. O'Hagan to A.C.M. Mullins, acting PC Central Province, 17 October 1946.

26. KNA DC/FH 1/24 'Fort Hall Annual Report, 1945', pp. 4-7; and John Spencer, *James Beauttah*, pp. 55-8, 64-76. See also E.S. Atieno Odhiambo, 'Seek Ye First the Economic Kingdom', pp. 223-51 for similar problems in Nyanza.

27. KNA DC/FH 4/6, 'Chiefs and Headmen, 1937-54', *passim*, contains detailed comments about every Murang'a chief; DC/FH 1/24 to 1/31, 'Fort Hall Annual Reports, 1945-52' all contain two or three pages about the behaviour of the chiefs.

28. KNA DC/FH 1/25, 'Fort Hall Annual Report, 1946', pp. 19-22; Ag 4/392, 'District Agricultural Annual Reports: Central Province, 1948', Fort Hall Agricultural Report, 1948, in which C.D. Knight observed: 'Terraces are extremely unpopular with African farmers, chiefs, Instructors, Officers and Native Tribunals, and at the present rate of digging, the end is not in sight and never will be. It behoves us to put on our thinking caps and try to design a method of completing the work rapidly so that other, more interesting avenues to Agricultural Progress may be explored. The word Agriculture is becoming associated in the public mind with nothing but digging terraces and the nauseating affluvium is bringing this Department into disrepute. The sooner we can stop terracing as our main effort and get moving in the direction of better farming the better.' See also Ag 4/118, 'Provincial Agricultural Handing Over Reports, 1942-51', especially the South Nyeri Handing Over Report, 3 March 1947.

29. See comments by P.S. Osborne in KNA DC/FH 1/23, 'Fort Hall Annual Report, 1944', p. 11; and by D. O'Hagan in DC/FH 1/24, 'Fort Hall Annual Report, 1945', p. 14. T. Hughes Rice, who served as agricultural officer in South Nyeri, Murang'a and Machakos during the Mitchell era, commented in 1944 that 'the location's best manure is the Chief's footsteps', see Ag 4/113, 'South Nyeri Monthly Agricultural Report, 1938-49', entry for July-September 1944.

30. KNA DC/FH 1/26, 'Fort Hall Annual Report, 1947', pp. 1-6, provides the official view. See also MAA 8/105, 'Intelligence Reports: Radio Posta, 1947-48', C. Penfold to P. Wyn Harris enclosing editorial, 16 October 1947, and Intelligence reports of the meetings in Nairobi of the Nyeri Reformed Kikuyu Society on 11 October and of the Forty Group on 12 October 1947. The Chief Native Commissioner's grave concern is evident in MAA 8/68, 'Chief Waruhiu, 1948-52', *passim*.

31. R.L. Tignor, *The Colonial Transformation of Kenya*, pp. 68-72.

32. Table 7.1 is based on material from KNA DC/FH 1/23 to 1/31, 'Fort Hall Annual Reports, 1944-52'; DC/FH 2/1(b), 'Fort Hall Handing Over Reports, 1929-60', J.H. Clive to P.S. Osborne, July 1944; P.S. Osborne to D. O'Hagan, April 1945; and F.A. Loyd to J. Pinney, August 1953; and DC/FH 4/6, 'Chiefs and Headmen, 1937-54', *passim*.

33. KNA DC/FH 4/6, 'Chiefs and Headmen, 1937-54', *passim*; and DC/FH 1/24, 'Fort Hall Annual Report, 1945', pp. 13-14, which presents the official view; while a more critical account can be found in MAA 8/108, 'Intelligence: Daily Chronicle, 1947-49', C. Penfold to P. Wyn Harris, 16 October 1947.

34. KNA DC/FH 4/6, 'Chiefs and Headmen, 1937-54', reports for Location 3.

35. *ibid*, reports for Location 4.

36. KNA DC/FH 2/1(b), 'Fort Hall Handing Over Reports, 1929–60', F.A. Loyd to J. Pinney, 20 August 1953, has some interesting comments on Michuki who was a rich man, who had many wives and much land. He tended to spend too much time on his own business interests and was never a strong chief. After the declaration of the Emergency, Location 12 was subdivided.

37. The two cautious old chiefs were Njaakio of Aguthi Location and Mutheithia of Mathira. KNA Ag 4/491, 'Nyeri Reconditioning Reports, 1944–46', entry for 8 August 1945, for comments on Aguthi; and Ag 4/518, 'Reconditioning: Central Province, 1948–51', J.A. Gardner's soil conservation report for July–December 1948.

38. KNA DC/FH 1/25, 'Fort Hall Annual Report, 1946', p. 21.

39. *ibid*, pp. 21–22; and KNA DC/FH 1/26, 'Fort Hall Annual Report, 1947', p. 6, where O'Hagan observed: 'The foibles of Clarence are, I regret to say, applicable to Parmenas – false, fleeting, perjured, but he out-does Clarence in one respect in that he is continuously (not once) drowning himself in a butt of Malmsey and coming up for more. Chief Parmenas Githendu is a super problem. He has the education, the ability and a hold on his people, but he continuously refuses to do the job. He is now a complete sponge and must soon be replaced.'

40. KNA DC/FH 4/6, 'Chiefs and Headmen, 1937–54', entry for Parmenas, 7 April 1945. For his early life see Parmenas Githendu's contribution to M. Perham (ed.), *Ten Africans*. KNA DC/FH 1/28, 'Fort Hall Annual Report, 1949', pp. 22–3 chronicles his subsequent career as a prominent figure in the Kikuyu Independent Schools' Association.

41. KNA DC/FH 4/6, 'Chiefs and Headmen, 1937–54', *passim*. The District Commissioners repeatedly expressed frustration at the backwardness of the older generation of chiefs.

42. P.E. Mitchell's despatch, 'Agricultural Policy in African Areas', p. 15. See also CO 537/4317/14322/10 (1949), 'Communism in the Colonies: East Africa', P.E. Mitchell to Creech Jones, November 1949.

43. KNA Ag 4/451, 'Fort Hall Safari Diaries, 1948–51', *passim*.

44. KNA DC/FH 1/25, 'Fort Hall Annual Report, 1946', pp. 6–7 and KNA MAA 2/5/223, 'Nairobi Advisory Council, 1946–49', meeting of the Advisory Council, 3 June 1946, for resolution condemning compulsory female labour on terracing.

45. KNA Ag 4/512, 'Fort Hall Monthly Agricultural Reports, 1940–49', C.D. Knight's report, April–June 1947.

46. KNA DC/FH 1/26, 'Fort Hall Annual Report, 1947', pp. 1–7; and Secretariat 1/12/8, 'Labour Unrest: Intelligence Reports, Central Province, 1947', C. Penfold, Director of Intelligence, to P. Wyn Harris, 22 July and 25 July 1947. These reports contain a detailed account of Kenyatta's speech and the resolutions passed at the meeting. See also KNA Ag 4/512, 'Fort Hall Monthly Agricultural Reports, 1940–49', report for January–June 1948 and DC/FH 3/1, 'Reports on the Kikuyu, 1950–52', paragraphs 181–262 for an assessment of the importance of female labour.

47. KNA DC/FH 1/26, 'Fort Hall Annual Report, 1947', p. 1.

48. KNA Ag 4/392, 'District Annual Agricultural Reports, 1948', Fort Hall Report.

49. KNA DC/FH 1/26, 'Fort Hall Annual Report, 1947', p. 1; and MAA 8/106, 'Intelligence Reports: Mumenyereri, 1947–50', C. Penfold to P. Wyn Harris, 16, 18, 20 and 21 October 1947.

50. KNA Ag 4/512, 'Fort Hall Monthly Agricultural Reports, 1940–49', July–September 1947 and KNA Ag 4/518, 'Reconditioning: Central Province, 1948–51', J.T. Moon's report on soil conservation, July–December 1947.

51. KNA DC/FH 1/26, 'Fort Hall Annual Report, 1947', pp. 2–3, 5–6.

52. KNA DC/FH 1/25, 'Fort Hall Annual Report, 1946', pp. 19–20.

53. KNA DC/FH 1/27, 'Fort Hall Annual Report, 1947', p. 1, and Ag 4/451, 'Fort Hall

Safari Diaries, 1948-51', contrast the report on Location 2, 17-21 February 1948, with the one for Location 8, 2-6 March 1948.

54. The administration's high regard for Ignatio is apparent throughout the Annual Reports. For a particularly effusive reference see KNA DC/FH 1/26, 'Fort Hall Annual Report, 1947', p. 6.

55. KNA Ag 4/512, 'Fort Hall Monthly Agricultural Reports, 1940-49', table in C.D. Knight's report for April-June 1947.

56. KNA DC/FH 1/25, 'Fort Hall Annual Report, 1946', p. 20.

57. KNA Ag 4/451, 'Fort Hall Safari Diaries, 1948-51', entry for 2-6 March 1948. For a more favourable view of Ignatio after the peasant revolt see the entry for 6-10 July 1948.

58. The Forty Group denounced terracing at a large meeting in Nairobi on 11 October 1947, see KNA MAA 8/105, 'Intelligence Reports: Radio Posta, 1947-48', extracts from Radio Posta for 16 October 1947, and the comments of C. Penfold to P. Wyn Harris.

59. KNA DC/FH 1/26, 'Fort Hall Annual Report, 1947', p. 2. See also KNA 8/106, 'Intelligence Reports: Mumenyereri, 1947-50', extract from *Mumenyereri*, 1 December 1947, for an African view of the conflict between Chief Ignatio and James Beauttah.

60. KNA DC/FH 1/26, 'Fort Hall Annual Report, 1947', pp. 2-3; MAA 8/105, 'Intelligence Reports: Radio Posta, 1947-48', C. Penfold to P. Wyn Harris, 31 October 1947; and MAA 8/108, 'Intelligence: Daily Chronicle', C. Penfold to P. Wyn Harris, 16 October 1947.

61. KNA Secretariat 1/12/8, 'Labour Unrest: Intelligence Reports, Central Province, 1947', C. Penfold to P. Wyn Harris, 25 August, and 3 September 1947. See also MAA 8/109, 'Intelligence and Security: African Workers' Federation, 1947-48', C. Penfold to P. Wyn Harris, 25 November 1947, for a report of Macharia's speech to the African Workers' Federation, Nairobi branch, on his release from gaol. For details of Macharia's career after his deportation from Mombasa, see KNA Secretariat 1/12/8, 'Labour Unrest: Intelligence Reports, Central Province, 1947', C. Penfold to P. Wyn Harris, and M. Singh, *History of Kenya's Trade Union Movement*, vol. 1, pp. 165, 270-1, 281, 293. Macharia was finally detained in May 1950 during the Nairobi general strike, of which he became the chief organiser following the arrest of Makhan Singh and Fred Kubai.

62. KNA Ag 4/512, 'Fort Hall Monthly Agricultural Reports, 1940-49', C.D. Knight's report for April-June 1947; Ag 4/392, 'District Agricultural Annual Reports, 1948', Fort Hall Report, especially the section on soil conservation; and Ag 4/518, 'Reconditioning Central Province 1948-51', Soil Conservation report for Fort Hall, January-June 1949. See also MAA 8/106, 'Intelligence Reports: Mumenyereri, 1947-50', extracts from *Mumenyereri*, 29 September 1947.

63. KNA DC/FH 1/25, 'Fort Hall Annual Report, 1946', pp. 6-7. See also the comments by several District Commissioners in DC/FH 4/6, 'Chiefs and Headmen, 1937-54', *passim*.

64. KNA DC/FH 1/27, 'Fort Hall Annual Report, 1948', pp. 1-2.

65. *ibid*, and J. Spencer, *James Beauttah*, pp. 82-3; and KNA DC/FH 1/30, 'Fort Hall Annual Report, 1951', p. 1.

66. KNA Ag 4/538, 'South Nyeri Agricultural and Veterinary Committee, 1946-48', Nyeri Local Native Council meeting, 29 September 1946; Ag 4/107, 'Veterinary Department: Central Province Annual Reports, 1940-53', Nyeri Annual Veterinary Report, 1946; and Secretariat 1/27/1, 'Animals: Diseases Control - Dipping, 1946', A.C.M. Mullins, acting PC Central, to G.M. Rennie, 26 September 1946; and report from the Superintendent of Police, Nyeri, 26 September 1946.

67. KNA DC/KBU 1/38, 'Kiambu Annual Report, 1947', pp. 1-5.

68. KNA Ag 4/539, 'Reconditioning: Central Province, 1934-48', V.A. Maddison, acting Provincial Commissioner, to F.W. Cavendish-Bentinck, June 1947.

69. KNA DC/FH 1/26, 'Fort Hall Annual Report, 1947', *passim*; and DC/KBU 1/38, 'Kiambu Annual Report, 1947', *passim* clearly show how the field administration continued to think in parochial terms.

70. KNA MAA 8/68, 'Chief Waruhiu, 1948-52', P. Wyn Harris to all District Commissioners, Central Province, 'Directive on the African Political Situation, Central Province', 11 December 1946.

71. *ibid.* See also KNA MAA 8/132, 'Law and Order: Legal Matters, 1947-51', Foster-Sutton to P. Wyn Harris, 29 October 1947; and P. Wyn Harris to all Provincial Commissioners, 28 November 1947.

72. KNA MAA 8/108, 'Intelligence and Security: Daily Chronicle', *Daily Chronicle*, 16 October 1947. A useful account of the African press at this time is F. Gadsden 'African Press in Kenya', pp. 515-35 which contains a detailed appendix of the African newspapers published between 1945 and 1952. The *Daily Chronicle* was, however, an Asian newspaper, published partly in English and, despite its title, partly in Gujerati.

73. KNA MAA 8/106, 'Intelligence Reports: Mumenyereri, 1947-50', C. Penfold to P. Wyn Harris, 10 December 1947, enclosing extracts from *Mumenyereri*, 1 December 1947.

74. KNA MAA 8/68, 'Chief Waruhiu, 1948-52', *passim*, for attacks on Kiambu chiefs; and DC/FH 1/26, 'Fort Hall Annual Report, 1947', pp. 2-6, for cases in Murang'a; and KNA MAA 8/68, 'Chief Waruhiu, 1948-52', P. Wyn Harris to Basil Hobson, 30 July 1948.

75. *ibid,* and P. Wyn Harris to H.E. Stacey, 22 November 1948; KNA DC/FH 1/26, 'Fort Hall Annual Report, 1947', pp. 2-6; and Secretariat 1/27/1, 'Animals: Diseases Control – Dipping, 1946', A.C.M. Mullins to G.M. Rennie, 26 September 1946. See also MAA 8/106, 'Intelligence Reports: Mumenyereri, 1947-50', *Mumenyereri*, 12 April 1948; and N.F. Kennaway, DC Kiambu, to P. Wyn Harris, 3 May 1948.

76. KNA MAA 8/68 'Chief Waruhiu, 1948-52', P. Wyn Harris to P.E. Mitchell, undated, but probably August 1948; and to Basil Hobson, 30 July 1948.

77. *ibid,* Basil Hobson to P. Wyn Harris, 12 August 1948; and to all District Commissioners, Central Province, 'Directive on the African Political Situation, Central Province', 11 December 1946.

78. *ibid,* P. Wyn Harris to P.E. Mitchell, undated, but probably August 1948.

79. R.E. Robinson, 'Non-European Foundations of European Imperialism', pp. 132-40.

80. KNA MAA 8/68, 'Chief Waruhiu, 1948-52', Shapley, Barnet, Archer and Co. (Solicitors) to N.F. Kennaway, DC Kiambu, 27 August 1948.

81. KNA MAA 6/13, 'Report of the Committee on Agricultural Credit for Africans, 1949-50', H.E. Lambert's memorandum submitted to the African Affairs' Committee, 8 November 1948; nd the various memoranda submitted by District Commissioners and agricultural officers. See also B.J. Berman's thesis, 'Adminstration and Politics in Colonial Kenya', pp. 303-36.

82. Interviews with D. O'Hagan in Nairobi, 24 April and 10-11 June 1981; and KNA DC/FH 1/25, 'Fort Hall Annual Report, 1946', *passim.*

83. KNA DC/FH 1/25, 'Fort Hall Annual Report, 1946', pp. 3 and 7; Ag 4/118, 'Provincial Agricultural Handing Over Reports, 1942-51', Fort Hall Handing Over Report, T. Hughes Rice to C.D. Wright, March 1947; and Ag 4/539, 'Reconditioning: Central Province, 1934-48', V.A. Maddison, acting PC Central to F.W. Cavendish-Bentinck.

84. J. Iliffe, *A Modern History of Tanganyika*, pp. 494-6, 503-7, 510-14; I.N. Kimambo, *Mbiru*, pp. 7-27; and A. Maguire, *Towards Uhuru in Tanzania*, pp. 107-41.

85. KNA MAA 8/109, 'Intelligence and Security: African Workers' Federation, 1947-48', C. Penfold to P. Wyn Harris, 16 December 1947, for early reports of discontent with

Kenyatta's leadership. For Kenyatta's increasing political isolation, see B. Kaggia, *Roots of Freedom*, pp. 81-2; and P. Abrahams, 'The Blacks', pp. 58-9. See also MAA 8/102, 'Intelligence and Security: Press Cuttings - Miscellaneous, 1948-50', C. Penfold to P. Wyn Harris, 16 June 1948, for reports of a meeting at James Gichuru's house of Kikuyu moderates, who were dissatisfied with Kenyatta's leadership of the Kenya African Union and Githunguri Teacher Training College.

86. B.J. Berman's thesis, 'Administration and Politics in Colonial Kenya', pp. 361-7, 372-98; and J.M. Lonsdale's unpublished 'African Elites and Social Classes in Colonial Kenya', pp. 10-13. The government's changing atitude to Mathu and the other African Legislative Councillors can be followed in CO 537/3588/38696 (1947-48), 'Activities of Mathu', *passim*; and CO 533/543/38086/38, 'Petitions by the Kikuyu Central Association: Kikuyu Grievances', P.E. Mitchell to Creech Jones, 28 February 1949. This new hostility is particularly apparent in KNA MAA 8/8, 'Intelligence Reports: Confidential Information, 1946-47', C.M. Johnston, DC Meru, to V.A. Maddison, 18 May 1947; and DC/FH 1/26, 'Fort Hall Annual Report, 1947', pp. 5-6.

87. KNA DC/FH 1/26, 'Fort Hall Annual Report, 1947', pp. 2-3.

88. KNA MAA 8/109, 'Intelligence and Security: African Workers' Federation, 1947-48', C. Penfold to P. Wyn Harris, 16 December 1947; MAA 8/105, 'Intelligence Reports: Radio Posta, 1947-48', C. Penfold to P. Wyn Harris, 24 October 1947, reporting meetings of the Nyeri Reformed Kikuyu Society in Nairobi on 11 October 1947, and of the Forty Group Friendly Union on 12 October 1947, which reveal the close ties between the Nairobi militants and political discontent inthe three Kikuyu districts. Mwangi Macharia's career in Mombasa, Nairobi and Murang'a between January 1947 and his detention in May 1950 provides one notable example.

89. The years 1948 and 1949 were comparatively quiet in Kikuyuland. See KNA DC/FH 1/27 and 1/28, 'Fort Hall Annual Reports, 1948 and 1949', *passim*; John Spencer, 'Kenya African Union and Mau Mau', pp. 203-18; and C.G. Rosberg and J. Nottingham, *The Myth of Mau Mau*, pp. 270-4.

Eight

Outcast Nairobi

Although African discontent was clearly growing in the Kikuyu reserves and the Rift Valley, it was in the towns, especially in the capital which had a population of over 100,000 by 1952, that it really threatened to erupt into violent conflict. During the war, for example, there were eight strikes in Mombasa and labour relations deteriorated drastically in Nairobi as the growth in population far outpaced the provision of new housing. Wages fell behind the high levels of inflation, which persisted throughout the 1940s, and competition for jobs increased as Nairobi's African population trebled between 1939 and 1952. As a result, there were growing numbers of unemployed and vagrants who depended on crime and the informal sector to eke out a meagre subsistence.[1] In Pumwani, the largest of Nairobi's locations, 14 men slept in a room, four to a bed, with the rest on the floor. They were the fortunate ones; many had to sleep in the open, or bed down in parked buses or under the verandas along River Road.[2]

The Secretariat decided to introduce a system of local consultation in the African locations under pressure from the African élite and agreed to build model estates. Unfortunately, these were too expensive for ordinary workers and placed a heavy burden of subsidised rents on the Municipal Council, much to the annoyance of European ratepayers. African Nairobi came low down on the Secretariat's list of priorities. As advocates of indirect rule, the Administration had little understanding of what it considered 'de-tribalised' urban Africans. Consequently, between 1947 and 1954, the presence of the administration and the police was extremely weak in the locations, which were abandoned to the control of the political-cal militants and their allies among the Kikuyu-dominated street gangs, who terrorised the Luo and Abaluhya inhabitants of the city.[3] This free-dom from government interference enabled the radicals to establish secure headquarters in Nairobi, from where they controlled the intro-duction of the Mau Mau oaths into the Kikuyu reserves and the

White Highlands, and organised concerted political action against the colonial state and moderate African politicians.[4]

The administration of African Nairobi

By 1947, the government's policies had provoked bitter resentment throughout Kikuyuland, the White Highlands and in the new settlement at Olenguruone, but perhaps the greatest failure of control had occurred in the back streets and hovels of the African locations of Nairobi. During the second half of 1947, it became increasingly apparent that the rule of law had collapsed in Pumwani and Shauri Moyo. The situation in African Nairobi was threatening to undermine the colonial régime at its heart, as violence and crime grew unchecked.

Just how complete the militants' control over the capital was, can be seen from a report to the CID by the Superintendant of African Locations, the moderate Kenya African Union leader, Tom Mbotela. It was, he warned:

> . . . common knowledge that armed gangs [move] around the African Locations and its outskirts at night . . . and the law abiding resident is afraid to go abroad at night. The number of assaults and threats to persons at night is on the increase . . . [while] the number of police patrols available in the locations are afraid to tackle these people, and they cannot be blamed.[5]

Askwith, the Municipal African Affairs Officer, agreed with the report and himself complained to the Nairobi Superintendant of Police that there was 'a definite tendency towards mob-rule in the Native Locations'. The small, easily-controlled African population of the inter-war years had burgeoned into an unruly mass of over 100,000, many of whom were scornful of British rule. Askwith warned that they were on the brink of a violent confrontation with the governnment. He told the police that 'Africans have now adopted an attitude of opposition to local and central Government which is very much more than a civil disobedience campaign. When the enforcement of laws or by-laws is attempted, physical and sometimes armed opposition is encountered. This will continue so long as the African knows that there is no real force behind the enforcement'.[6] When for example, the police had attempted to arrest illegal brewers at Marurani, they had been driven off by local Africans and their prisoners forcibly released. By the time the police had returned with rifles and bayonets, the culprits had vanished. At night armed gangs waylaid people with impunity and terrorised the locations. They were even beginning to infiltrate into the poorer Asian residential area of Eastleigh. Gangs of unemployed Kikuyu were roaming the streets in groups of 30, armed with pangas and knives. So effective was this reign of terror that incidents were rarely reported. Askwith informed the police that 'I have come to the conclusion that the lawlessness is part of a carefully conceived plan to bring the wheels of Government to a standstill by creating conditions of anarchy'.[7] In his opinion, 'the passing of laws which cannot be enforced is a waste of time'. The situation in Pumwani and most of the other locations had reached such a critical state that only large bodies of police, operating in military fashion, could be successful against such formidable opponents, and he called for 200 policemen to be transferred from the Northern Province to help re-establish control. Drastic action was essential before a crime wave hit the central business district and the European and Asian suburbs of the capital.

Both Askwith and Mbotela singled out Maina Heron, an unemployed Kikuyu from Ziwani, as the ringleader of the gangs and named him as the organiser of the infamous Forty Group. Originally from Murang'a, Heron was one of the main illegal traders in European beer and controlled prostitution in Ngara, where most of his gang lived and where he hired out African women to the local Asians. Each member of the group, Askwith alleged, received a salary of 30 shillings a month 'for the sole purpose of causing trouble and to do anything against law and order'.[8] The Forty Group was not simply a criminal gang but had close links with several African political organisations, such as the Nyeri Reformed Kikuyu Society, which the authorities believed was a front for the Group and for other advocates of violent confrontation.[9]

Following the detention in August 1947 of Chege Kibachia, the leader of the African Workers' Federation, and the shooting by the police in September of Kikuyu strikers at Uplands, the situation in the capital became extremely tense.[10] Police agents in the Forty Group warned the Special Branch that, at a meeting in Kariakor early in October 1947, it had been decided that all Europeans should be driven out of Kenya and that preparations were being made to attack prominent African supporters of the colonial government, such as Chief Johanna of Nyeri.[11] The government became increasingly concerned about its ability to retain control of Nairobi should a general strike break out. After the January 1947 strike in Mombasa, the Kenyan government carefully reconsidered its plans for resisting concerted strike action throughout the colony and established an emergency committee under the chairmanship of the member for law and order. Careful preparations were made to entrain police, troops and emergency labour from the northern frontier to likely trouble spots and to stockpile emergency supplies of food and essential materials. Throughout September and October 1947, discontent simmered and threatened to erupt into violent confrontation in Nairobi and the three Kikuyu districts, where the anti-terracing agitation was at its height. Tension increased when reports reached Nairobi of a general strike sweeping through Tanganyika, which had started among the dockers of Dar-es-Salaam.[12]

In Nairobi, preparations were made to introduce an emergency rationing system for meat, wood and petrol. The capital, however, consumed some 3,000 lbs of meat a day and even if the government had requisitioned all the available cold-storage space, it could only have maintained supplies for five days at the ordinary rate of consumption. Wood and fuel supplies were another serious problem. Householders were requested to increase their supplies, but the two leading bakeries each consumed one ton of wood a day and neither of them could store more than three tons. Three days supply of petrol were stored at Nairobi, Nakuru, Kisumu and Eldoret and, should the railway be disrupted, it was planned to restrict petrol supplies in the capital to three garages, where only doctors, transporters of essential supplies and those doing vital work were to be supplied. The Inland Revenue Department was to be responsible for all emergency distribution. Consumption of tinned milk, invalid and infant food, and canned foodstuffs in general were monitored and issue-permits printed in case the situation deteriorated rapidly.[13] Clearly the government viewed the threat of a general strike and civil disturbances in Nairobi with grave concern, but why had this crisis arisen, and why had it been allowed to escalate to such serious proportions? Let us consider these questions.

The presence of the field administration and of the police in African Nairobi was very weak. The capital, like the White Highlands, had largely been left to the control of the settler-dominated Municipal Council, which showed little interest in the appalling social problems of the African parts of the city. The Council and its European electorate only became interested in the locations when African discontent or crime threatened to spill over into the European business area or suburbs. With only one policeman to every 1,000 inhabitants, the authorities could do little to preserve control or to combat crime in the locations, even when the newly-constructed police station at Shauri Moyo was completed after the war. The Commanding Officer, James Juma, who was one of the few African Inspectors, and his force of five policemen, were overwhelmed by the scale of the organised crime and violence they discovered.[14]

The crux of the trouble in Nairobi was that the Municipal Council failed to decide how to deal with the African areas. Unable to decide whether the locations should be controlled by tribal associations with a hierarchy of chiefs and headmen, as in the reserves, or by a European-style system of local government, the Municipal Council wavered between the two options. Half believing in the myth of detribalised urban Africans while constantly being reminded of the authority of the tribal associations, the council and the government failed to evolve an effective system of control. The appointed African Advisory Council was not an effective democratic African local government with any independent authority, while proposals for government-appointed chiefs were rejected. Thus the authority of the colonial state was weakest at the very centre, among the poor of outcast Nairobi.[15]

As we have seen, the communalist prejudices of the administration had disastrous consequences in the Kikuyu reserves, but in Nairobi, amidst the complex ethnic *mélange* of the African locations, the tribal associations might have provided the most effective mechanism of social control. This had been recognised at the end of the war by Tom Askwith, the experienced Municipal African Affairs' Officer, who was on secondment to the council from the field administration. He had decided that government control over African Nairobi had already deteriorated so far during the war that the introduction of the full panoply of rural government, based on the various tribal associations, was essential. Impressed by the ability of the leaders of the associations to police the locations and to control fighting on VJ Day, and their enthusiasm for repatriating vagabonds and prostitutes, he concluded that the municipal authorities should acknowledge their corporate influence and foster their development into an effective system of tax collection and urban control.[16]

Although these proposals were initially accepted by the Provincial Commissioner of Central Province, they infuriated the African élite serving on the Nairobi Advisory Council, which had been established in 1939. This small but articulate section of the African population, led by Francis Khamisi, the General Secretary of the Kenya African Union, and the Abaluhya political activist, W.W.W. Awori, condemned the proposals as a retrograde measure designed to preserve ethnic suspicions in order to facilitate a 'divide and rule' policy. Instead of relying on tribal solidarities, as did most urban Africans, the élite representatives on the Advisory Council wished to secure their own incorporation into the colonial state and to be recognised as full participants in the political life of colonial Nairobi, with their own members on the Municipal Council. They would settle for nothing less than being themselves appointed to the posts of Assistant Municipal African Affairs Officer, Municipal Welfare Officer, and African Superintendents in each location to preside over the locational councils and control the allocation of accommodation. Their denunciation of Askwith's proposals was so vociferous that they forced the Chief Native Commissioner to reconsider and to devise a more democratic system of consultation, more in line with the Colonial Office's strategy of greater African political participation.

Only a few administrators, such as Askwith, recognised that most Nairobi Africans were still enmeshed in ethnic rivalries and were not yet ready to enter the democratic multi-tribal future espoused by the Kenya African Union and the African Advisory Council. The aspirations of the élite were completely unrealistic, given the tribal particularisms of the vast majority of the capital's African population, however 'progressive' they may have appeared to the liberal conscience. The Forty Group and

Mau Mau were to show that most urban Africans could only be mobilised by appeals to tribal solidarity and cultural specificities. Askwith had correctly perceived that control could only be achieved by appealing to the same forces. The élite, however, feared official recognition of the tribal associations' power, as this would mean that their own influence would be diminished and their incorporation blocked. Khamisi therefore protested that Nairobi Africans were not divided by tribalism and claimed that any attempt to establish 'Native Authorities' in the capital in a modified system of indirect rule would fail. When Mathu, Khamisi and Odede met Surridge and Askwith in November 1945 to discuss the future organisation of the locations, they successfully persuaded the officials to abandon the idea of reinforcing the power of the tribal associations and to introduce a ward structure, dividing the locations into three areas, Kaloleni–Shauri Moyo, Kariokor–Ziwani–Starehe, and Pumwani, rather than along ethnic divisions.[17]

After the war the power of the African élite grew considerably. Tom Mbotela was appointed Assistant Superintendent of Locations and authorised to collect rents and to allocate quarters on the advice of locational housing committees, which also selected the members of the African Advisory Council. This enjoyed considerable patronage, including deciding on who should be given resident or visitor passes. The Native Tribunals, which were composed of other prominent Africans, were empowered to hear cases under the municipal bylaws dealing with hawkers, vehicles for hire, public rickshaws, dead bodies, firearms and casual labour.[18] By 1946 certain members of the élite had become accepted by the government as valuable allies and co-opted on a personal basis into the political structure. Muchohi Gikonyo, for example, was nominated to the Central Commodity Distribution Board, where he used his position to benefit his friends and relations, successfully securing a license to run a tea stall for his brother on his demobilisation from the army. Gikonyo, a Murang'a Kikuyu, along with Khamisi was also appointed to the Municipal Council and occupied the important post of chairman of the Advisory Council's trade sub-committee. The following list of the active members of the Advisory Council reveals how strong the control of the moderates was and how successful they had been in forcing the government to incorporate them into the decision-making process.[19]

The list also reveals that the Kikuyu, who formed approximately 55 per cent of the capital's African population, were seriously under-represented among the influential officeholders on the Advisory Council, while the people from the Coast, who after the Second World War comprised only a small proportion of the total population, were extremely influential. Francis Khamisi, Tom Mbotela and Jimmy Jeremiah, who were possibly the three most influential members of the Advisory Council, all came from Coast Province, as did Maulidi Jasho. In contrast, only two of the

Table 8.1: *Senior Officials of the African Advisory Council, Nairobi, 1946*

African Members nominated by the Advisory Council to the Municipal Council	Francis Khamisi and Muchohi Gikonyo
Vice Chairman of the Advisory Council	Jimmy Jeremiah
Secretary of the Advisory Council	Tom Mbotela
Chairman Finance Sub-Committee	Francis Khamisi
Chairman of Trade Sub-Committee	Muchohi Gikonyo
Chairman of Welfare Sub-Committee	Tom Mbotela
Chairman New School Sub-Committee	Francis Khamisi
Chairman Native Affairs Sub-Committee	Jimmy Jeremiah
Sub-Committee on Unemployment and Crime	Tom Mbotela
	Muchohi Gikonyo
	Edward Mwangi
	Maulidi Jasho
	Jimmy Jeremiah
	Albert Awino
	Dedan Githegi *et al.*
Chairman Education Sub-committee	Dedan Githegi
Assistant Municipal African Affairs Officer	Dedan Githegi 16 votes
	Tom Mbotela 9 votes
Assistant African Welfare Officer	Justo Obwa

leaders, Muchohi Gikonyo and Dedan Githegi, were Kikuyu, while Justo Obwa, the Assistant African Welfare Officer was an Abaluhya. Thus the leaders of the African Advisory Council were isolated by class and ethnicity from the mass of illiterate unskilled Kikuyu, who formed by far the largest element in African Nairobi.[20]

The blocking by the élite of the Municipal Welfare Officer's attempts to establish an effective administrative presence in the African parts of the capital in alliance with the tribal associations, left the locations to the mercy of political gangs, which controlled organised crime and prostitution and intimidated the law-abiding African population. Gang warfare and crime were the most visible manifestations of African discontent with slum conditions, rampant inflation and growing unemployment. As early as January 1945, the rising crime wave was already causing such concern among the settlers that Mrs Olga Watkins moved an emergency debate in the Legislative Council. While Mrs Watkins and the other settler politicians emphasised the need for more effective policing and called for severer penalties, the two members representing African interests, Eliud Mathu and Archdeacon Beecher, stressed the social causes of crime. For them the crime wave 'is the outcome of social and economic disturbances . . . in so far as the African and crime is concerned we must look beyond the apparent circumstances and see that he is affected as a criminal by his social and economic circumstances'.[21] Whatever the causes of discontent and crime, the administration, its settler critics and the African moderates identified the crime wave as the most important problem to be tackled. In December 1948, Tom Mbotela, for example, considered that the rule of law had collapsed in 'outcast Nairobi' and drew an alarmist, but prescient, comparison with the anti-British revolt in Malaya which had just begun.[22] Let us examine the social and economic roots of African discontent in Nairobi.

Nairobi's housing crisis

Migrant labourers, separated from their families in the reserves and living in the towns for a few months at a time, provided a major barrier to increased efficiency in both industry and peasant agriculture. Returning home to the reserves at frequent intervals, the migrant labourer quickly forgot his newly-acquired skills and had to re-enter the urban world at the bottom, while his wife, alone on the family *shamba*, found it equally impossible to cultivate the new cash crops and became increasingly in debt to her richer neighbours and compelled either to sell some land or to become a hired labourer at crucial moments in the agricultural cycle. Trapped in this cycle of poverty, the migrant-labour question seemed, to the official mind, to provide a recipe for certain disaster unless a stabilised, efficient urban community could be created. Increased productivity would enable higher wages to be paid, which would allow the urban worker to bring his family to live in the city, which would, in turn, break the vicious circle of the migrant labourers' dependence on the reserves and periodic absences from the industrial economy.[23]

The Secretariat and field administration were even more concerned about Nairobi's housing shortage. Throughout the 1940s the number of new inhabitants grew rapidly, increasing by 17 per cent per annum.[24] In these circumstances the provision of new housing failed to keep pace. Although the government and the Municipal Council built new African locations near the industrial area, conditions deteriorated as dispossessed squatters and *ahoi* from the reserves flocked to Nairobi for employment, and sought refuge in the slums of Pumwani and in the shanty-towns, which had sprung up beyond the municipal boundaries at Dagoretti, Ngata Rongai and Quarry. It was not that the government and municipality failed to take any action, but rather that they were overwhelmed by the tidal wave of new urban immigrants. In the 20 years before the outbreak of the Second World War, the government and council had provided accomodation for nearly 4,500 Africans but had demolished Pangani, the shanty-town built by the capital's first African inhabitants at the beginning of the century. Between 1939 and 1947, state provision of housing for Africans in Nairobi nearly doubled. During the war a further 2,100 quarters were completed and in the first two years of Mitchell's governorship this was increased by another 2,219. New estates were built at Makongeni in 1940, Ziwani in 1943, Kaloleni in 1944, and at Marurani in 1946. Meanwhile accommodation was extended at Starehe, Shauri Moyo and Pumwani.[25]

Nevertheless, by 1947 the housing shortage in the capital was desperate. The government calculated that the African locations were grossly overcrowded, with at least 28 per cent more people than they were supposed to contain. Pumwani, the oldest, for example, had 375 people to the acre compared to the approved density of 225. Although it was the most overcrowded location, it was also by far the largest, containing over one-third of Nairobi's Africans. The labour department feared that the problem was even worse than the official figures had revealed, since many people had probably evaded the housing census through fear of being expelled as illegal residents or unemployed vagrants. The department estimated there might be another 13,000 people, who were being sheltered by friends in the area, who had not appeared on the official census which had recorded a total population of 15,000 for the location.[26] In the other locations, directly controlled by the municipality or Railway Administration, conditions were not quite so overcrowded. Many of these estates had been recently built and had higher public-health standards than the early locations, such as Kariokor, where the barrack-like conditions were grotesque. But even in the new locations conditions were cramped, especially as most accommodation housed at least 20 per cent more people than had been planned. Table 8.2 provides some index of the dreadful overcrowding which even those Africans who were sufficiently fortunate to have a roof over their heads had to endure.[27]

By 1947 it had become apparent that the government and municipality could not keep pace with the demand for housing. Each year the deficit of 26,000 beds was increased by another 10,000. To remove this shortage would have cost over £1,500,000, and would have required an expenditure of another £600,000 each year to house the continuing influx. Already the administration estimated that 82,000 Africans were living in housing designed to accommodate only 54,000. Two-thirds of them were staying in the African locations which were supposed to contain a maximum of 33,000, and Pumwani, the most decrepit area, contained somewhere between 15,000 and 28,000 people instead of the approved maximum of only 9,000. Another 4,000 people had nowhere to live, and were sleeping on verandas, in the streets, or in parked buses. Meanwhile a large shanty-town had developed in the swamp to the east of the commercial centre of the capital and unauthorised villages were springing up on farms to the east of the town. Somalis were renting shacks in Eastleigh and peri-urban settlements, like Kariobangi, which had been a thorn in the flesh of the administration for 20 years, were growing alarmingly.[28]

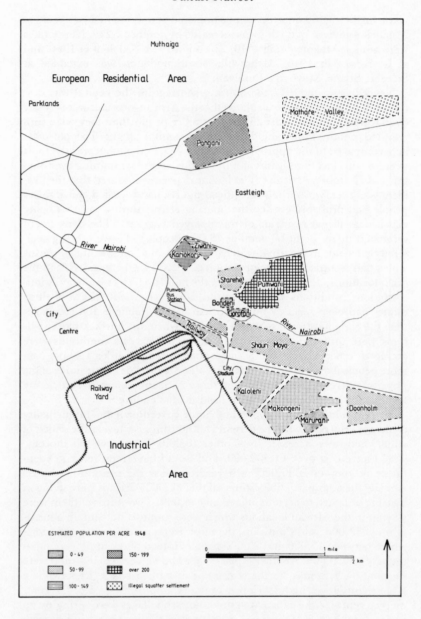

Map 8.1: *Population Densities of the African Locations of Nairobi*

Table 8.2: *Population Density Estimates for the African Locations of Nairobi in 1948*

Location	Date built	Quarters	Acreage	Theoretical Capacity	Theoretical Number per acre	Actual Number Accommodated	Actual Accommodated per acre	% Over-crowding
Government Built Accommodation:								
Railway Old Lhandies	Pre 1930	2,391	80	9,082	68	10,373	77	14
Government Starehe	Pre 1930	157	53	2,505	47	2,755	52	10
	1942	103						
	1944	82						
	1946	99						
Kariokor	1931	929	10	1,534	153	1,841	184	20
Shauri Moyo	1938	1,020	39	3,225	83	3,708	95	15
	1945	30						
Railway Makongeni	1940	1,200						
	1946	270	54	n.a.	n.a.	n.a.	n.a.	n.a.
	1947	336						
Ziwani Lodging Houses	1942	120	2	240	120	264	132	10
Ziwani	1943	163						
	1944	202	18	1,928	107	2,121	118	10
	1945	80						
Kaloleni	1944	102						
	1945	166	70	3,196	46	3,516	50	10
	1946	99						
	1947	245						
Marurani	1946	600	41	1,200	30	1,380	34	17
Pumwani Loan	1946	112	6	496	83	548	91	10
Public Works's Department	n.a.	n.a.	4	358	90	430	108	20
Non-Government Built Accommodation:								
Pumwani	Pre 1930	n.a.	40	9,000	225	15,000	375	66
Private Employers	n.a.	n.a.	5	228	46	228	46	nil
TOTAL		n.a.	422	32,992	78	42,164	100	28

181

The boom in government house building was unfortunately almost over. Once the 245 houses planned in Kaloleni had been completed, there were no plans to build any more. The only new accommodation for Africans authorised by the government after 1948 consisted of certain small self-help schemes, in which a few Africans were allowed to build their own houses on government land.[29] Despite evidence of urban discontent, the Kenyan government failed to appreciate the seriousness of the housing shortage and its effect on African opinion. Warnings from the field administration and the labour department failed to penetrate the Secretariat, which was preoccupied with the peasant revolt in Murang'a, squatter resistance in the White Highlands, the court cases over Olenguruone and the general strike in Mombasa.

One person who did understand the seriousness of the crisis in Nairobi was Askwith. In his 1948 report he complained that:

> It was disheartening for those concerned with the welfare of Africans in Nairobi . . . to see another year go by with no appreciable progress made in providing even a limited amount of housing for them. To see legitimately employed Africans sleeping under the verandas on River Road, in noisome and dangerous shacks in the Swamp, in buses parked by the roadside, and fourteen to a room in Pumwani, two to a bed and the rest on the floor. To see plans for new housing schemes hang fire month after month for some reason or another, while the number of Africans taking up employment grew and grew.[30]

Such conditions hindered the government's plans to increase industrial productivity and to create a permanent urban labour force, completely dependent on its industrial wages, which would help to reduce the pressure on the land in the over-populated reserves. Askwith became increasingly perturbed by the Municipal Council and Secretariat's complacency over the African housing shortage. The settler politicians were much more concerned about the high cost of improving African accommodation and overlooked the importance of the difficulties that remained. Complaints about excessive expenditure and the growing subsidisation of urban African accommodation were winning an increasingly favourable hearing in the Municipal Council. Askwith lamented what he saw as a complete failure to understand the need to provide cheap housing to improve African health and efficiency at work. Instead of being complacent about the number of new estates that had been built since the beginning of the war, he felt that greater vigour was required 'to retrieve the position at the eleventh hour', because the unprecedented post-war growth in population had created a dangerous shortage of accommodation.

Unfortunately, by 1947 the money available for housing under the Colonial Development and Welfare Act of 1945 was nearly exhausted, although the urban population was still soaring, growing by over 20 per cent from 53,000 in 1945, to 64,000 in 1946, and then to 77,000 in 1947. The government responded by attempting to control the inflow into Nairobi, refusing to sanction labour recruitment unless the employers provided housing. Askwith wanted to go even further and to make the provision of accommodation mandatory for the acquisition of an industrial licence. He also urged the Labour Controller to refuse to sanction permits for industrial expansion unless employers agreed to house their own workers, because the council could not begin to build sufficient accommodation.[31]

The Municipal Council could not carry the financial burden of providing even more African housing estates. It was not simply the problem of finding the initial capital outlay to construct new accommodation, but the accumulating burden of recurrent expenditure required to subsidise rents because of the low level of African wages. If Nairobi Africans were to afford to live in the municipality's new housing estates sub-economic rents had to be charged. Thus, while industry prospered the debt burden of the City Council grew from £587,566 in 1940 to £860,869 at the end of the war, before reaching £2,634,260 four years later; by 1957 municipal borrowing totalled £9,021,836.[32] The Nairobi Chamber of Commerce and many ratepayers viewed this escalating burden with alarm. Ernest Vasey, the mayor, warned the chief secretary that the housing estates would prove inadequate to satisfy rising African expectations long before the loans were repaid.[33] Until employers accepted that wages would have to be increased, the burden of housing the capital's African workforce would fall on the overstretched municipality. Employers joined forces with their staff in opposing the idea of increased rents, for this would have resulted in pressure for higher wages. Employers and Africans insisted that sub-economic housing was essential to Nairobi's industrial sector, but the burden of subsidisation limited the provision of accommodation and placed a severe strain on the financial resources of the council.

One of the reasons for this financial problem was that Nairobi had modelled its African housing on South Africa. Mitchell and several other influential officials and settler politicians had been greatly impressed by the example of the new African estates at Port Elizabeth. Carpenter, the Assistant Labour Commissioner, had been despatched to investigate African housing in South Africa.[34] These schemes, however, ignored the crucial problem that it was impossible to build similar accommodation in Kenya at a cost ordinary African workers could afford to pay. Not only were African wages in South Africa four times higher than in Kenya, but the unit cost of construction in Nairobi was much higher than in Port Elizabeth, since Kenya did not have the industrial base to provide cheap building materials. All the cement and concrete for the Nairobi estates, for example, had to be imported from South Africa because the Portland Cement Company had not yet been enticed to Kenya by the government's offers of protection and several local companies had all failed.[35] The attempts of the government-sponsored East African Industrial Research Board to manufacture tiles and glass in the colony had also proved to be expensive failures, since the high development costs meant that the poor quality finished product was often more expensive than high-quality imports. Another obstacle to cheap housing in Nairobi was that the building industry was dominated by Asian artisans; thus housing for low-income Africans was being built by comparatively well-paid Asians. As a result of these problems the unit cost of accommodation in Kenya was more than double that in South Africa, where the economic rent per room was only 61 shillings. The proportion of total average African incomes taken by rent in Port Elizabeth's new housing estates, therefore, was less than one-eighth that required for similar accommodation in Nairobi. Consequently, while South Africa could charge economic rents for the accommodation, the new Nairobi estates had to be heavily subsidised by the government and the council.[36]

Phillips and Booker, who investigated the causes of industrial discontent in Mombasa after the strikes of August 1945 and January 1947, recommended that rents should form no more than 17 per cent of total household incomes. If this rule had been applied to the new housing estates and there had been no subsidy, it would have meant that nobody earning less than 168 shillings per month could, theoretically, have afforded to live with their families in the new accommodation. The Phillips Report, however, discovered that out of the 13,000 Africans employed in Mombasa, 10,000 earned less than 40 shillings per month, the absolute minimum subsistence income for a single man, while only 300, just over 2 per cent of the workforce, earned over 100 shillings per month or more than 50 cents per hour. The wage structure of the Nairobi workforce was very similar.[37]

Industry, however, refused to increase wages or build housing for its employees while the productivity of the unskilled African labour force remained so low. This meant that the government could not enforce a law requiring employers to provide accommodation for their workers, since this would cripple Kenya's new industries and discourage others from investing in the colony. The Kenyan government's post-war industrialisation strategy depended on attracting multinational corporations to Kenya because of the low wages, which industry saw as a form of economic subsidy almost as important as the government's promises of protection from external competition. This low-wage economy, however, not only placed a heavy burden on the Municipal Council, but also hindered attempts to increase industrial productivity by creating a stable urban workforce, and undermined the government's schemes to reduce overcrowding in the reserves by creating new employment opportunities in the expanding industrial sector.[38]

Careful consideration was given to several ideas for solving these problems. The labour department suggested that the government should strictly enforce Section 31 of the 1937 Employment of Natives Ordinance which placed the burden of housing urban workers upon their employers. This, as we have just seen, was rejected because it would discourage investment and retard Kenya's industrial expansion. Many employers were already complaining about the department's interference and declared that the council's insistence on the construction of permanent structures to house workers would be prohibitively expensive. The most constructive suggestion for escaping this impasse was proposed by Vasey. He suggested the council raise the finances and build the accommodation, while industry subsidise the gap between the sub-economic rents paid by the workers and the full economic rent required by the council to cover its debt payments. The first of these joint estates, called 'Gorofani', was built between Bondeni and the Nairobi River. It consisted of 800 two-storey blocks with three men to a room. These were rented to Nairobi firms on long leases at economic rentals, which, it was hoped, would reduce the costs to both employers and the council.[39]

It was also believed that this solution would enable adjustments to be made when the Africans' incomes increased and their standard of living rose. Thus, as more families abandoned life in the reserves and settled in the towns, as better conditions were required and as wages increased, because of higher productivity, the number of individuals per room could be reduced. In the interim, the system ensured that the social burden of the rapid expansion of the city would not simply fall on the Council but would be shared with employers. This would not only reduce the municipality's debts and lessen the rate burden on the settler population, but would also enable new loans to be raised on the incipient Nairobi money market and in London to fund improved social services for the growing population. The first of these was the King George VI Hospital, completed in 1950 and designed to accommodate 650 African and 42 Asian patients, and the enlargement of the capital's water supply, achieved by constructing a second main from the Ruiru Dam and building the Chania Ssasumua Dam at a cost of £750,000. The council and the government also began to build more housing estates, first at Gorofani, and then at Bahati and Mbotela.[40]

This sharing of the burden of uneconomic housing between the council and industry, however, proved to be only a partial solution to the problems and in fact hindered the encouragement of stable African family life in the capital. The urban family remained a rare phenomenon. Only 7,600, or 13 per cent of the total African population in 1946 were women, while a mere 12 per cent were children. The average rent for a room at

Gorofani in the late 1940s was 28 shillings, or over 9 shillings per bed. These high charges meant that only a few, comparatively well-off Africans could afford to bring their wives and children to live in the new estates.[41] The picture the government painted of happy African families sitting on the lawns outside their homes was a propaganda myth to silence its critics in Britain. In reality, employers wanted to house as many workers as possible at the minimum cost and rarely considered what advantages might be gained from creating a contented, stable and more productive workforce.[42]

Few Kenyan industrialists were as far sighted as Lord Faringdon, a left-wing critic of colonial policy who warned in the *East African Standard* that:

> A certain number of Africans can, I believe, be absorbed in industry and commerce, but if they are to be so absorbed it must be on the condition that when they are removed from the Reserves they are accompanied by their wives and families who will be able to live with them in the urban areas . . . From this it clearly follows, in my view, that the wages paid to Africans must be adequate to enable them to support their wives and families as well as themselves, which is not at present the case. At the present time the Reserves are subsidising African wages.[43]

Social needs, it appeared, could not be reconciled with economic facts. The political and economic pressures that were driving African families into the urban centres after the war simply exacerbated the problems and ensured that wages remained at subsistence levels, precluding any improvement in labour productivity or in African living conditions.[44]

Another approach considered was an early example of the present-day site-and-service scheme. Since neither the council nor the government could afford to build enough housing in permanent materials to keep pace with the expansion of Nairobi, experiments were undertaken on cheaper semi-permanent materials. Many settlers suggested that the council was in financial difficulties because it wasted its money housing Africans in 'pokey replicas of a European home' instead of using traditional materials. Dressed stone, for example, could be replaced with pressed earth blocks. It was absurd, they argued, to provide every house with doors costing 50 shillings, when this added 50 cents a month to the rent.

The more moderate of these complaints were supported by Askwith, the Municipal Welfare Officer. He too was opposed to cramming Africans into poor European-style housing. Many, he declared, could not afford to furnish their homes and were forced to sleep on cement floors in badly-ventilated conditions, which were ideal for spreading tuberculosis and respiratory diseases. Mud and wattle, he argued, provided a more effective natural discouragement of mosquitoes and bugs. He recommended that only Africans who could afford to live in a European style should be housed in the new estates. The rest should be left to solve the housing shortage by building their own mud and wattle dwellings. This self-help approach would quickly end the artificial shortage of accommodation created by the British-based health regulations of the Municipal Council.[45]

The medical establishment, however, dismissed these proposals and insisted that only the strict enforcement of public-health regulations would prevent plague. Tuberculosis and relapsing fever, the experts argued, were associated with damp floors, inadequate ventilation and poor housing, and would spread rapidly in a shanty-town of mud huts. They pointed out that Kenya's housing regulations fell far below those deemed adequate by scientific opinion and needed to be made more stringent rather than relaxed. The ratepayers, they observed, would be the first to protest if cholera or plague spread to the European suburbs because the Medical Department had reduced its public-health standards in the African locations. Mud and wattle houses were perhaps adequate for the reserves, where homesteads were spread across the countryside, but they were completely unsuitable for the overcrowded African locations in Nairobi, where disease would rapidly spread throughout the population.[46]

Another solution was to encourage Africans to build their own houses provided they reached certain approved standards. Carpenter and the labour department, for example, suggested that the council should provide the land, roads and drains, but that the actual houses should be built by the more prosperous sections of the African community. This idea was enthusiastically supported by the *East African Standard*, which argued that provided the estates were carefully planned, it would be better to allow Africans to build their own houses from cheap materials to an approved standard than to leave them in the urban slums, which undermined every attempt to improve health and to create a contented working class.[47]

Prodded by these ideas, the government granted permission for 600 experimental self-help houses to be built north of the railway to Thika. The government supplied the materials at cost price and precise standards were specified. Supporters of the scheme hoped that it would provide family homes or social security for older Africans who had ceased to work, for they could rent out rooms and remain in the city on their retirement, instead of returning to the reserves. It was hoped that 6,000 beds would be provided by these self-help schemes. They were extremely popular among the wealthier sections of the African community. Within a short time more than 800 people had applied for the first 600 experimental plots. In Pumwani, where Africans had been building their own houses for many years, the government decided to legalise the situation and to grant 40-year leases. The Nairobi Chamber of Commerce and the labour department enthusiastically supported these new developments and urged Kenyans to follow the examples of Elizabethville, Leopoldville and

Bloemfontein, where self-built African housing on permanent foundations had been encouraged for many years. In the long term these had proved much better than the costly urban estates that had been built in Kenya. Many of the new estates were already extremely dilapidated. Marurani was in an appalling condition after less than six years' occupation. As costs continued to rise and the council could no longer afford to meet its self-imposed health standards, the self-help solution to the housing crisis became increasingly popular in official circles and among the ratepayers.[48]

The growth of African discontent

Rural Africans flocked to the capital during the 1940s only to discover that its streets were not paved with gold. Many were unable to find jobs and had to eke out a meagre subsistence in the informal sector as street hawkers or petty criminals for the men, or as illegal brewers or prostitutes for the women.[49] The appalling shortage of accommodation was not the only problem they had to overcome in the alien urban environment. Throughout the 1940s the general retail price index rose much faster than wages. Although the rate of inflation had briefly diminished at the end of the war, after June 1947 it increased dramatically until by June 1948 the retail price index was 20 points higher than it had been 12 months before. Food prices rose particularly sharply as the result of a combination of poor harvests and successful pressure from the European settlers for better producer prices. By March 1948, vegetable prices had risen by nearly 50 per cent, while milk now cost 1 shilling 75 cents instead of 1 shilling 10 cents per gallon. The cost of a bag of *posho* increased by almost 600 per cent between August 1939 and December 1948, rising from 5 to 29 shillings. During this period wages had barely doubled and had returned to their pre-depression levels. In real terms they were still far below wages in the late 1920s.[50]

The official retail price index and the cost of living allowances, which both the government and the railway awarded to their lower-paid workers, seriously underestimated the increase in the cost of living since the beginning of the war. These indices were based only on official prices and did not take account of black market prices. As we have noted, most urban Africans were heavily dependent on the black economy for many commodities, ranging from imported goods to vegetables and firewood from the neighbouring reserves.[51] Graph 8.1 vividly reveals the deteriorating economic situation faced by Africans in Nairobi during the 1940s. In particular, the upswing in inflation during 1947 coincided with a period of increasing political discontent, with growing popular support for the African Worker's Federation in Nairobi and increasing peasant opposition to the terracing campaign in the reserves. There was a close

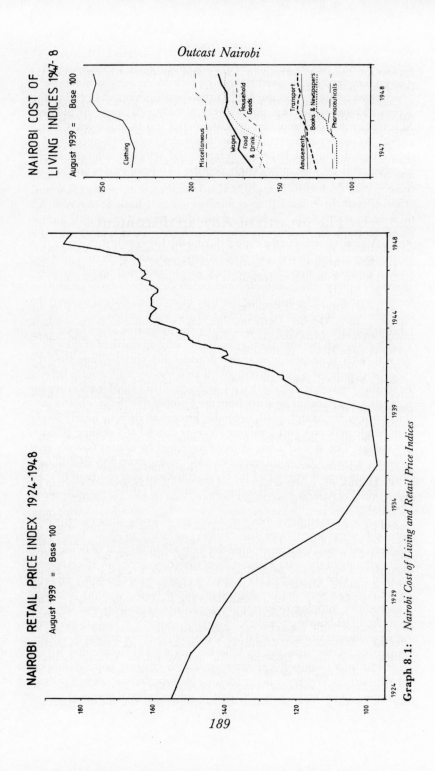

Outcast Nairobi

NAIROBI COST OF LIVING INDICES 1947-8

August 1939 = Base 100

Clothing

Miscellaneous

Wages

Food & Drink

Household Goods

Transport

Amusements

Books & Newspapers

Pharmaceuticals

1947   1948

NAIROBI RETAIL PRICE INDEX 1924-1948

August 1939 = Base 100

1924   1929   1934   1939   1944   1948

Graph 8.1: *Nairobi Cost of Living and Retail Price Indices*

189

correlation between African militancy and the deteriorating economic position of many Africans.[52]

Despite the government's attempts to improve urban housing, the majority of Africans in the capital experienced a marked deterioration in their standard of living. At the same time, *ahoi* and poor peasant families in Central Province, especially in Kiambu, were being squeezed off the land by the growing élite of commercial farmers. Many squatters were also being expelled from the White Highlands. Deprived of their land, these people flocked to Nairobi.[53] Hawking, brewing, prostitution and crime offered these new urban residents their only hope of survival. All these occupations were, however, deemed illegal by the colonial authorities. Thus, the desperately poor were involved in another battle with the state. Already antagonised by their recent loss of land, condemned to an alien urban existence, it was hardly surprising that the Kikuyu poor, who formed more than half of Nairobi's population, vented their dismay in political violence.

As these dispossessed squatters and poor peasants sought refuge in Nairobi, the African locations became even more overcrowded, unemployment increased and inflation mounted. More and more Africans were drawn to the metropolis and trapped within its web of despair. Pushed to the limits of human endurance, the Nairobi poor created their own alternative society in clandestine opposition to the forces of law and order and to the colonial state.[54] The colonial authorities were reduced to impotence and could merely bemoan the collapse of 'tribal values' and 'the sad demoralisation of a part of the indigenous population of the Colony leading to drunkenness, crimes of violence, idleness, dishonesty, theft and many other objectionable things'. They failed to appreciate that growing numbers of Africans had no alternative. In the White Highlands, in the reserves and, above all, in Nairobi, the plight of the majority of Africans had never been so desperate as it was after 1947.[55]

Nairobi Africans, however, were not a homogeneous community united by despair, but were bitterly divided by class and ethnic animosities. The world of the clerk earning 100 shillings per month was entirely different from that of the unskilled labourer, the illegal hawker, or the unemployed vagrant. The African élite demanded equal pay for equal work, a unified African and Asian civil service and the ending of the colour bar. In other words, it emulated the settler communities.[56] The urban poor were preoccupied with the struggle for survival. Condemned to a constant battle for existence, constitutional politics had nothing to offer them, it seemed, but deception.[57] Men like Tom Mbotela and Dedan Githegi, the Assistant Superintendent and Municipal Welfare Officer, were identified as their enemy; stooges of the Europeans.[58]

Class, however, was not the most important divide. Linguistic and cultural differences ensured that tribalism remained the most important influence upon daily life and political allegiances in the locations. Tribal associations not only provided the most effective mechanism of social control, but were also the only rudimentary welfare most Africans encountered. Life in the city intensified rather than diminished ethnic rivalries. Financial assistance, moral welfare, strike money and burial expenses were all provided within the confines of the tribe, or of even more parochial district associations. The 'detribalised' urban African was a myth.[59]

As conditions deteriorated in the face of growing unemployment and rampant inflation, tribal tension increased. In particular, the unemployed and low paid turned to crime to supplement their meagre resources. These criminal gangs were usually comprised of friends from the same area. The *mbari* was as potent a unit of organisation in the city as in the reserves, guaranteeing cohesion and support among the criminal fraternity as in every aspect of African life.[60] Consecrated by an oath, few dared to transgress group solidarity. Social pressure and superstition reinforced each other to ensure that the urban poor tacitly supported the men of violence. The authorities failed to perceive the extent to which the locations had become a distinct world in which law-abiding Africans faced such overwhelming pressures that they were forced to conform to the norms of outcast Nairobi. In consequence the administration and the police were forever complaining that 'it was astonishing to find how often criminals were arrested as unauthorised lodgers and how willingly many Africans offered them hospitality'.[61]

As early as January 1945, this problem had become so serious that Mortimer, who was then the Commissioner for Local Government, introduced an amendment to the Rent and Mortgage Bill to enable the Nairobi Council to expel tenants who broke the housing rules by subletting. Even those convicted of holding illegal liquor parties or tenants occupying family houses while their wives and children were in the reserves could be expelled. The Bill created widespread alarm. Many Africans feared that they would be thrown out of their homes for trivial offences once they were deprived of the protection of the original Ordinance. Archdeacon Beecher explained that many were apprehensive that 'they will be expelled from the municipal housing and will be condemned to that dog kennel existence that these fifteen thousand Africans in Nairobi have to undergo because there is no other housing available for them'.[62]

For these people, the casual labourers, hawkers and unemployed of Nairobi, crime provided the only way of surviving. Living in appalling conditions and in real deprivation, the outcasts of Nairobi resorted to crime. As the largest element in the population, the 30,000 Kikuyu and members of the related Embu and Meru people subjected the 12,000 Nyanza Africans and the 7,000 Kamba to an unending reign of terror. The returning *askari*, who spurned the training courses at Kabete and quickly dissipated their gratuities, the angry squatters expelled from the

European farms in the White Highlands, and the dispossessed *ahoi* of Kikuyuland, sought refuge in Pumwani with few illusions about the harshness of life. Crime paid; crime opened up new avenues for social advancement; it enabled the outcast to gain prestige provided the gangs did not prey upon their own kind and their own kind were defined in strictly tribal terms – kinsmen from the same *mbari* or migrant workers from the same rural location. For the Kikuyu criminal, this did not include the Luo or Abaluhya poor.[63]

Unable to control African Nairobi or to create a stable labour force, the Municipality resorted to pass laws, curfews and removal orders. Since reform and social improvement were too expensive, further legislation restricting the influx of Africans into the town in search of non-existent jobs offered an easy alternative. Municipal bylaws confined Africans to their locations or servants' quarters between ten at night and five in the morning, while visitors were not allowed to remain in the town for longer than 36 hours without employment unless they had a resident's or visitor's permit signed by the town clerk. When the Supreme Court declared these pass laws *ultra vires* in September 1945, new legislation, the Removal of Undesirable Natives Ordinance, had to be rushed through the Legislative Council to preserve the controls. These measures were, of course, bitterly resented by the African population and, in that they failed to tackle the problems responsible for the crime wave and for growing African discontent, were largely ineffective. They provided only another irritant to law-abiding Africans.[64]

Until Operation Anvil, which cleared all the disgruntled Kikuyu out of the capital in 1954, the government never seriously attempted to recover control of Nairobi's locations. The curfew bylaw, for example, did not extend to the locations, where African gangs were freely allowed to prowl the dark alleys, waylaying anyone sufficiently foolish to be about at night. Although 'reputable' Africans were issued with passes for one year, the stigma of these racial laws remained, generating further ill-will between the races. Social, economic and political divisions reinforced the racial barrier. G.R.B. Brown, who succeeded Askwith as Municipal Welfare Officer, warned that, 'to the natural envy felt by the poor for the rich is added the poison of racialism'.[65] Although it was in the workers' interests to reduce the number of unemployed and the mass of surplus labour, Africans resented pass laws and labour controls, such as the *kipande*, as an affront to their personal liberty. Europeans and Asians were not subjected to the humiliation of mass tax-collection checks on their way to work, or of being forced to work wherever the labour exchange directed them rather than being allowed to look for jobs they found congenial. So long as the police viewed all Africans as potential vagrants and criminals, instead of law-abiding members of the community, and while respectable African women continued to be arrested as prostitutes, then the image of government would remain tarnished and trust in the authorities undermined.[66]

In these circumstances, periodic eruptions of frustrated anger were inevitable. After several minor disturbances, the most protracted of which was a 16-day strike by members of the Transport and Allied Workers' Union against the Nairobi Council's taxi-cab bylaws, tension reached crisis point early in 1950 with the introduction of the Essential Services (Arbitration) Ordinance and the Voluntarily Unemployed Persons Ordinance.[67] These new laws reflected growing concern in the government and among the settlers at the inability of the authorities to control the flow of people into the capital. Unemployment had replaced shortages of labour and was blamed for the high crime rate in the capital. The campaign to rehouse the African community in new estates with improved social services, where the administration could keep more effective control than in Pumwani, had palpably failed. Alarmed by the financial cost, the colonial state had drawn back and resorted to its traditional policy of coercion. Reform and social improvement were too expensive; force seemed to be a cheaper option.[68]

The first Vagrancy Ordinance had been passed in 1902, but the new legislation introduced in 1949 was much more Draconian than any previous measure. The Vagrancy (Amendment) Bill of May 1949 empowered the authorities to repatriate anyone who failed to secure permanent employment after three months residence in Nairobi. This was followed by the Voluntarily Unemployed Persons (Provisions of Employment) Ordinance, finally approved in January 1950, which empowered the police to arrest anyone suspected of being a vagrant or unemployed. These powers of arrest were condemned at a mass meeting in the Desai Memorial Hall in Nairobi on Saturday 14 January as forced labour legislation. The following day when the Ordinance came into force, the shop workers section of the Labour Trade Union of East Africa held an even bigger meeting at the Kaloleni Social Hall in the centre of one of the African housing estates and, to the fury of the Kenyan government, sent petitions to the Secretary of State for the Colonies and the United Nations, protesting against the new restrictions.[69]

The Colonial Office also announced that Nairobi would become a city on 30 March 1950. The militant African politicians, led by two prominent trade unionists, Fred Kubai and Bildad Kaggia, decided that this would be an ideal opportunity to focus attention on the plight of urban Africans and called for a boycott of the celebrations. Kubai declared the celebrations 'a mere propaganda trick designed to make it appear to the outside world that democracy was on the march in this country'. Kikuyu opinion was further aroused by rumours that the civic celebrations were merely a plot to enlarge Nairobi at the expense of the Kikuyu reserves. It was reported that 32 square miles of Kiambu were to be added to the new city and that all the Africans were to be moved out to make way for another 12,000 European settlers.[70]

African resentment smouldered until 12 May 1950, when the Essential Services (Arbitration) Ordinance, empowering the government to prosecute workers who went on strike in essential industries, came into force. That morning Nairobi ground to a halt under the impact of the capital's first general strike. Makhan Singh and Fred Kubai, the two most prominent trade union leaders, were both arrested and charged with being officials of an unregistered organisation.[71] The following day another strike leader, Chege Kiburu, was arrested and the government declared the food, oil, power, lighting, posts, railways, roads and ports to be essential industries whose employees were not allowed to go on strike. The government then announced that Kubai had been arrested for the attempted murder of Councillor Muchohi Gikonyo. Gikonyo was the most prominent African to attend the civic celebrations six weeks earlier and narrowly escaped assassination a few days later when three shots were fired while he was closing his shop.[72]

Even before the news of Kubai's arrest on the attempted murder charge had become known, nearly 3,000 Africans were on strike in Nairobi and the police had had to use baton charges to break up crowds in Shauri Moyo. On 18 May, tear gas was used for the first time in Kenya in a pitched battle between demonstrators and the police in Shauri Moyo.[73] By the sixth day of the strike, 75 per cent of the Public Works Department's labour force had joined the strike and only 44 of the Municipal Cleansing Department's staff of 700 were at work, despite an offer of double pay for those who reported for work. The strikers' demands for a 25 per cent wage increase, regular annual increments, free accommodation or a housing allowance, sick leave, 14 days holiday per year and the establishment of a provident fund had been subsumed in a general protest against the deprivation and squalor most Africans had to endure in Nairobi and against government harrassment of the trades union. Kubai's arrest, to most Africans, simply showed the lengths to which the government would go in its unscrupulous campaign against the trade union, which seemed to be the only organisation capable of standing up to the colonial state and protecting the interests of the African masses.[74]

Police wireless cars toured the African locations, relaying information about crowd movements and clusters of demonstrators, and armoured cars were moved opposite the central police station. Demonstrations were concentrated in the Kaloleni Valley where large crowds of unemployed swelled the strikers' ranks. Police Bren-gun carriers and armoured cars patrolled the area, making regular circuits around the location, dispersing the crowds with more tear gas. Aften ten days, when Chege Kiburu was sentenced to eleven months hard labour, the strike remained unbroken. Intimidation of workers increased and some people had their heads shaved. More than 300 people had been arrested and the Public Works Department had dismissed over 100 strikers. Gangs of Kikuyu strikers roamed the streets, particularly the Asian residential areas, assaulting anyone found still at work, while others attempted to ensure total support for the strike in the locations. Most of their victims were Luo or Abaluhya, who flocked to enrol as special constables to deal with the Kikuyu.[75]

The strike revealed the divisions within the African community. This was the crucial flaw in the armour of the Kikuyu militants who dominated the trade unions. While in the cosmopolitan world of Mombasa social discontent had to mobilise the diverse elements in the population in a multi-tribal alliance, in the African locations of Nairobi dissatisfaction was often directed against other Africans. The Kikuyu domination of the locations, particularly Pumwani, meant that in the capital non-Kikuyu came to identify Kikuyu slum landlords as their exploiters. At the same time they were terrorised by the Kikuyu criminal gangs. Consequently the non-Kikuyu in the locations became profoundly sceptical, even hostile, to Kikuyu leadership.[76]

Conclusion

As early as 1947 the police and the administration had already been over-whelmed in Nairobi. Even after the geneal strike on May 1950, the government made little attempt to defeat the armed gangs which terro-rised the locations and used Nairobi as a secure base from which to politicise the discontented peasants in the reserves and the squatters in the White Highlands. Throughout the Mitchell era the administration had little control over events in Pumwani and Shauri Moyo, which provided a haven for the militants. Meanwhile the deplorable accommodation short-age, unemployment and rampant inflation alienated the capital's poor, driving the Kikuyu among them, who formed over half the city's popu-lation, into the arms of Mau Mau.[77]

Only a few months before the general stike, the Labour Commissioner, Hyde-Clarke, delivered a prescient warning to the Legislative Council. He declared that a new African township was urgently needed to house Nairobi's destitute, otherwise 'if we cannot answer this question quickly you can put paid to the question of better output, because relations will deteriorate . . . to such a degree that there will be no question of employ-ment and output. There will be riot and revolutions'.[78] His words went unheeded. Instead the Nairobi general strike confirmed the government in its diagnosis of the problems of the African locations and did not prompt it to reconsider its policy of repression. It failed to use the tribal associations, the only organised bodies in the locations capable of chal-lenging the power of the organised gangs, as a mechanism of social con-trol. The government instead chose to suppress African opposition.

Makhan Singh and the trade unions were condemned as subversive - as
front for agitators who had perverted the infant unions, swamped thei
responsible leaders and poisoned the minds of the masses.[79] The goverr
ment never paused to ponder whether its own actions could have led th
poor of Nairobi to emphasise the primacy of political action. After th
general strike, for example, over 2,000 Kikuyu were dismissed and force
to join the crowds of unemployed, who could only survive by crime.

Because the governor was aware of the need to promote economi
expansion and to improve housing and social services if, to use his ow:
words, they were going to stifle the 'communist' influence, he ovei
emphasised the importance of political stability as a prerequisite fo
Kenya attracting increased foreign investment.[80] All opposition, there
fore, would have to be crushed if Kenya was to develop the economic bas
from which the government could finance the increased provision of socia
benefits. Although the policy was destined to benefit Africans in the lon;
term, in the short term settler opinion and international capital had to b
assured of the colony's continuing stability. Once again, the power of th
settler community effectively foreclosed any possibility of the governmen
seriously attempting to solve the problems of the urban Africans, wh
were abandoned to the militants.

Notes

1. KNA Lab 9/1751, 'African Housing: General, 1946-51', memorandum by Josepl
   Mortimer, Mayor of Nairobi in 1930 and 1937, and father of C.E. Mortimer, Membe
   for Heath and Local Government, to Town Clerk, Nairobi, 23 February 1948; and CC
   533/558/38715 (1948), 'Municipal African Affairs Annual Report', 1947 Report
   pp. 6-7.
2. KNA Lab 9/1751, 'African Housing: General, 1946-51', T.G. Askwith's report or
   overcrowding in Pumwani, 30 July 1946.
3. KNA MAA 8/22, 'City African Affairs Officer: Correspondence, 1947-50', Torr
   Mbotela to Superintendent, CID, Nairobi, 28 October 1947; and T.G. Askwith tc
   Superintendent, CID, Nairobi, 29 October 1947; and CO 533/558/38715 (1948)
   'Municipal African Affairs Annual Report', 1947 Report, p. 4. See also *East Africar
   Standard*, 24 May 1950.
4. J. Spencer, *KAU*, pp. 208, 211-13, 221-4, 227-8; and C.G. Rosberg anc
   J. Nottingham, *The Myth of Mau Mau*, pp. 264-76.
5. KNA MAA 8/22, 'City African Affairs Officer: Correspondence, 1947-50', Torr
   Mbotela to Superintendent, CID, Nairobi, 28 October 1947.
6. *ibid*, T.G. Askwith to Superintendent, CID, Nairobi, 29 October 1947.
7. *ibid*. See also KNA Secretariat 1/12/6, 'Coast Province: Labour Unrest Correspondence, 1947', C.R.B. Brown, acting PC Coast to Foster-Sutton, 15 March 1947
   about the emergency preparations in Mombasa; and Secretariat 1/12/11, 'Laboui
   Unrest: Notes on Communications, Supplies and Transport, 1947', *passim*.
8. KNA MAA 8/22, 'City African Affairs Officer: Correspondence, 1947-50', Tom

Mbotela to Superintendent, CID, Nairobi, 28 October 1947. Mbotela had recently been appointed Superintendent of African Locations with responsibility for overseeing the administration of the capital's African housing estates.

9. KNA MAA 8/105, 'Intelligence Reports: Radio Posta, 1947–48', C. Penfold to P. Wyn Harris, 24 October 1947. See also *Radio Posta*, 16 October 1947, for reports of meetings of the Nyeri Reformed Kikuyu Society and the Forty Group in Nairobi; and F. Furedi, 'The African Crowd in Nairobi', pp. 282–5.

10. KNA MAA 8/109, 'Intelligence and Security: African Workers' Federation, 1947–48', for reports from C. Penfold to P. Wyn Harris of African Workers' Federation meetings in Nairobi on 25 October, 8 and 22 November, 14 and 15 December 1947, and 3 January 1948; MAA 8/105, 'Intelligence Reports: Radio Posta, 1947–48', *Radio Posta* editorial, 8 October 1947; and C. Penfold to P. Wyn Harris, 24 October 1947, See also Secretariat 1/12/8, 'Labour Unrest: Intelligence Reports, Central Province, 1947', C. Penfold to P. Wyn Harris, 29 August and 1 September 1947.

11. KNA Secretariat 1/12/8, 'Labour Unrest: Intelligence Reports, Central Province, 1947', C. Penfold to P. Wyn Harris, 9 October 1947.

12. KNA Secretariat 1/12/11, 'Labour Unrest: Notes on Communications, Supplies and Transport 1947', note to the Financial Secretary, J.F.G. Troughton, 2 February 1947 on the maintenance of essential supplies; and Secretariat 1/12/6, 'Coast Province: Labour Unrest Correspondence, 1947', G.R.B. Brown, acting PC Coast, to Foster-Sutton, 26 February and 15 March 1947; and J. Pinney, DC Isiolo, to Chief Native Commissioner, 24 March 1947. For the influence of the Tanganyika general strike, see KNA Secretariat 1/12/12, 'Labour Unrest: Inter-Territorial, 1947', Police Head Quarters, Dar-es-Salaam to Police Head Quarters, Nairobi, 30 September 1947. J. Iliffe, *A Modern History of Tanganyika*, pp. 402–4, provides a brief account of the events of September 1947 in Tanganyika.

13. KNA Secretariat 1/12/11, 'Labour Unrest: Notes on Communications, Supplies and Transport, 1947', note to J.F.G. Troughton, on maintenance of essential supplies, 2 April 1947.

14. KNA MAA 2/5/223, 'Nairobi Advisory Council, 1946–49', meetings of the Crime Committee, 19 and 26 June, and 15 August 1947; and MAA 7/491, 'Administration Policy: Urban Areas, Nairobi, 1945–47', T.G. Askwith to Marchant, Chief Native Commissioner, 9 November 1945, and to G.M. Rennie, 3 December 1945.

15. KNA MAA 7/491, 'Administration Policy: Urban Areas, Nairobi, 1945–47', T.G. Askwith to C. Tomkinson, 22 August 1945; C. Tomkinson to G.M. Rennie, 5 September 1945; T.G. Askwith's memoranda to Tomkinson, Marchant and Rennie, 14 September and 9 November 1945; and the counter-arguments of F. Khamisi, General Secretary of the Kenya African Study Union, to G.M. Rennie, 10 September 1945; and the meeting in the Secretariat between the officials and E.W. Mathu, Francis Khamisi, and F.W. Odede, 28 November 1945.

16. *ibid*, T.G. Askwith to C. Tomkinson, 22 August 1945.

17. KNA MAA 7/491 'Administration Policy: Urban Areas, Nairobi, 1945–47', note by Marchant, the Chief Native Commissioner, 19 September 1945; and by T.G. Askwith, 22 August, 27 October and 9 November 1945.

18. *ibid*. T.G. Askwith's memoranda, 9 November and 17 December 1945.

19. KNA MAA 2/5/223, 'Nairobi Advisory Council, 1946–49', Advisory Council meetings, 3–4 June and 2–3 September 1946.

20. Labour Department Annual Report, 1954, paragraph 30. In December 1953 the Kikuyu, Embu and Meru comprised 46.3 per cent of adult male African workers in Nairobi; the Luo and Abaluhya 27.6 per cent; and the Kamba 18.8 per cent. After Operation Anvil on 25 April 1954 these proportions became 26.7 per cent Kikuyu, Embu and Meru; 35.4 pe cent Luo and Abaluhya; and 25.6 per cent Kamba. The 1962 census figures were: 42.0 per cent Kikuyu; 16.9 per cent Abaluhya; 15.9 per cent Luo; 15.3 per cent Kamba; and others 9.9 per cent.

21. Legislative Council Debates, second series, vol. xx (1944–45), third session, 3 January 1945, cols. 612–649; and 10 January, cols. 651–675. Beecher had once been a student of the noted social pscychologist, Professor Sir Cyril Burt.

22. KNA MAA 2/5/223, 'Nairobi Advisory Council, 1946–49', Advisory Council meeting, 6–7 December 1948.

23. KNA Lab 9/57, 'East African Labour Conference, Entebbe, November 1949', memorandum prepared by the Kenya Labour Department on the stabilisation of labour; and Lab 9/99, 'Labour Efficiency Survey: Kenya and Uganda Railways and Harbours, Northcott Report, 1946–49', E.M. Hyde-Clarke to J.D. Rankine, 25 August and 16 September 1948; and Lab 9/2, 'Address on Labour Policy by Mr Hyde-Clarke, 1946', E.M. Hyde-Clarke, 6 November 1946.

24. CO 533/558/38715 (1948), 'Municipal African Affairs Annual Report', 1947 Report, pp. 6–7.

25. KNA Lab 9/1751, 'African Housing: General, 1946–51', T.G. Askwith to E.M. Hyde-Clarke, 20 November 1947. See also A. Hake, *African Metropolis*, pp. 48–50.

26. KNA MAA 8/22, 'City African Affairs Officer: Correspondence, 1947–50', T.G. Askwith to P.Wyn Harris, 20 November 1947; and Lab 9/1751, 'African Housing: General, 1946–51', T.G. Askwith, Annual Report on African Affairs in Nairobi, 1947, December 1947.

27. This information is taken from KNA Lab 9/1751, 'African Housing: General, 1946–51', T.G. Askwith to E.M. Hyde-Clarke, 20 November 1947.

28. *ibid*, F.W. Carpenter's memorandum on Nairobi housing, 9 March 1948; T.G. Askwith's comments on Joseph Mortimer's memorandum, 23 February 1948; and T.G. Askwith, Annual Report on African Affairs in Nairobi, 1947, December 1947.

29. *ibid*; and T.G. Askwith, Annual Report on African Affairs in Nairobi, 1948, December 1948.

30. *ibid*.

31. *ibid*, T.G. Askwith's comments on Joseph Mortimer's memorandum, 23 February 1948; and to the Town Clerk, Nairobi, 6 February 1947; F.W. Carpenter's memorandum on Nairobi housing, 9 March 1948; and E.M. Hyde-Clarke to Labour Officer, Nanyuki, 10 June 1948.

32. A. Hake, *African Metropolis*, p. 58. See also CO 533/546/38128/4 (1947–48), 'Loans: Requirements of Local Government Authorities', *passim*; and CO 533/547/38128/48 (1948–49), 'Loans: Requirements of Local Government Authorities – Nairobi Municipal Council', P.E. Mitchell to Creech Jones, 8 April 1948.

33. KNA Lab 9/1751, 'African Housing: General, 1946–51', E.A. Vasey to J.D. Rankine, 6 July 1949.

34. *ibid*, E.M. Hyde-Clarke to J.D. Rankine, 17 January 1950; and F.W. Carpenter, quoted in *East African Standard*, 15 September 1950.

35. KNA Lab 9/1751, 'African Housing: General, 1946–51', G.A. Atkinson, Colonial Liaison Officer, Building Research Station, to Colonial Labour Advisory Committee, 26 January 1950. See also H.L. Adams, Secretary for Commerce and Industry, to R.J.C. Howes, Secretary for Health and Local Government, 14 October 1949; and E.M. Hyde-Clarke to C.H. Thornley, Member for Labour, 2 February 1950; and 1949 Kenya Annual Housing Report: and F.W. Carpenter, quoted in *East African Standard*, 15 September 1950. See also KNA C&I 6/457, 'British Standard Portland Cement Co. Ltd.: Bamburi, 1951–56', *passim*; and C&I 6/390, 'Secondary Industry: Cement and Lime, 1943–49', H.L. Adams to East Africa Industrial Council, 11 May 1948; and to P. Wyn Harris, 17 July 1948; and minutes of the meeting of the East Africa Industrial Council, 10 June 1948; and the memorandum presented to the Council on proposals to manufacture cement, 22 September 1948.

36. KNA Lab 9/1751, 'African Housing: General, 1946–51', note by Miss N.M. Deverell, 28 March 1948. For the employers' response see C&I 6/445, 'Secondary Industries: East Africa Industries Ltd., 1949–53', H.W. Howell, of the Commonwealth Develop-

ment Corporation, to A. Hope-Jones, 11 September 1950; and C&I 6/243, 'East Africa Industries Ltd., 1950–57', General Manager's report, April–June 1950.

37. KNA Lab 9/60, 'Labour Conditions and Strikes, 1945–50', L. Silberman's comments on the Phillips Report, 1946, undated.

38. KNA Lab 9/1751, 'African Housing: General, 1946–51', E.M. Hyde-Clarke to J.D. Rankine, 17 January 1950; and to the Inter-African Labour Conference, Elizabethville, July 1950. See also N. Swainson, *The Development of Corporate Capitalism in Kenya*, pp. 116–18; and S.B. Stichter, *Migrant Labour in Kenya*, pp. 130–1.

39. KNA Lab 9/1751, 'African Housing: General, 1946–51', E.M. Hyde-Clarke to Labour Officer, Nanyuki, 10 June 1948. *East African Standard*, 17 August 1950, reported the rival view of the Nairobi Chamber of Commerce, which argued that 'there was definite evidence available that in a large number of cases, after a certain point had been reached, any further increases in wages resulted in a decrease in output or a reduction in working hours'; E.A. Vasey to J.D. Rankine, 6 July 1949; and T.G. Askwith, Report on African Affairs in Nairobi, 1948, December 1948.

40. A. Hake, *African Metropolis*, p. 57.

41. KNA Lab 9/1751, 'African Housing: General, 1946–51', T.G. Askwith to E.M. Hyde-Clarke, 20 November 1947; and E.M. Hyde-Clarke to C.H. Thornley, 2 February 1950; and MAA 8/22, 'City African Affairs Officer: Correspondence, 1947–50', T.G. Askwith to P. Wyn Harris, 20 November 1947.

42. CO 533/558/38715 (1948), 'Municipal African Affairs: Annual Report', contains some interesting propaganda photographs. See also KNA Lab 9/99, 'Labour Efficiency Survey: Kenya and Uganda Railways and Harbours, 1946–49', for the views of Dr C.H. Northcott, formerly Labour Manager of Rowntree and Co. Ltd, who surveyed 6,000 railwaymen in Nairobi; and the comments of E.M. Hyde-Clarke on his report, 25 August and 6 September 1949.

43. *East African Standard*, 10 April 1945.

44. KNA Lab 9/1841, 'Mombasa: Trade Disputes Tribunal, 1947', E.H. Robins's evidence, 17 February 1947; and evidence from Railways and Harbours' staff, 21, 26 and 27 February, and 4 March 1947; and Chege Kibachia of the African Workers' Federation, 29 April 1947, for the problems of surviving on subsistence wages in the urban arena. See also Lab 9/57, 'East African Labour Conference, Entebbe, November 1949', Kenya Labour Department's memorandum on stabilisation; Lab 9/30, 'Colonial Cooperation: African Labour Conference, Elizabethville, July 1950', for a discussion of African housing and sub-economic rents; Lab 9/1751, 'African Housing: General, 1946–51', E.M. Hyde-Clarke to J.D. Rankine, 17 January 1950; and Lab 9/789, 'African Affairs Committee, 1948–52', J.H. Lewis, from the African Settlement and Land Utilisation Board, memorandum on surplus population and the necessity of housing African workers outside the reserves, 14 July 1948; and T.G. Askwith's memorandum on urbanization in Kenya, 23 July 1948, for the government's view of these intractable problems.

45. KNA Lab 9/1751, 'African Housing: General, 1946–51', T.G. Askwith to E.M. Hyde-Clarke, 6 December 1950; and Dr D. Drury, Director of Medical Services, memorandum on African housing standards, 8 December 1947; and T.G. Askwith, recently promoted Commissioner for Community Development, to E.M. Hyde-Clarke, 6 December 1950. See also 'note D75', 'Space and Accommodation Standards for Low Cost Housing in Colonial Territories', May 1949, for the medical establishment's opinion.

46. *ibid*, Dr D. Drury to T.G. Askwith, 30 December 1950.

47. Editorial in *East African Standard*, 15 September 1950.

48. KNA Lab 9/1751 'African Housing: General, 1946–51', E.M. Hyde-Clarke to J.D. Rankine, 17 January 1950; and Lab 9/789, 'African Affairs Committee,

1948-52', meeting on 14 July 1948, to discuss the problem of surplus population and the need for housing African workers outside the reserves. See also F.W. Carpenter, quoted in *East African Standard*, 15 September 1950; and Lab 9/301, 'Problems of Old Age Security, 1943-45', *passim*.

49. S.B. Stichter, *Migrant Labour in Kenya*, pp. 130-1; Janet M. Bujra, 'Women entrepreneurs of Early Nairobi', pp. 213-34; S.B. Stichter, 'Workers, Trade Unions and the Mau Mau Rebellion', pp. 260-75; and N. Nelson, 'How Women and Men Get By', *passim*, for life in African Nairobi from the 1920s to the 1970s.

50. KNA CS 1/8/196, 'Cost of Living Commission: Incoming Correspondence, 1948-49', Director of Statistics, note about the General Retail Price Index, undated, but probably January 1949, and letter from the manager, Kaisugu Tea Estate, to the Commission, complaining about the price of *posho*.

51. KNA MAA 8/22, 'City African Affairs Officer: Correspondence, 1947-50', African Advisory Council to the Central Commodity Distribution Board, 22 June 1948; and Ag 4/381, 'Kiambu Monthly Agricultural Reports, 1940-49', G.J. Gollop, July–September 1947 report.

52. Graph 8.1 has been devised from information in KNA CS 1/8/196, 'Cost of Living Commission: Incoming Correspondence, 1948-49', *passim*. For a more extended treatment of these issues see S.B. Stichter, *Migrant Labour in Kenya*, pp. 130-1; and her 'Trade Unionism in Kenya', pp. 156-58; and KNA MAA 8/109, 'Intelligence and Security: African Workers' Federation, 1947-48'. See also S.B. Stichter, 'The Formation of a Working Class in Kenya', pp. 21-48.

53. G. Kitching, *Class and Economic Change in Kenya*, pp. 119-21, 129-30; and F. Furedi, 'The Social Composition of the Mau Mau Movement in the White Highlands', pp. 492-4. See also KNA DC/KBU 1/36, 'Kiambu Annual Report, 1945', p. 8.

54. KNA MAA 8/22, 'City African Affairs Officer: Correspondence, 1947-50', Tom Mbotela to Superintendent, CID, Nairobi, 28 October 1947; and T.G. Askwith to Superintendent, CID, Nairobi, 29 October 1947. This is equally true of Nairobi today, see Meja Mwangi's novels, *Kill Me Quick* and *Going Down River Road*.

55. KNA Ag 4/330, 'Provincial Agricultural Officers: Newsletters, 1939-51', T. Hughes Rice, February 1950.

56. KNA MAA 8/22, 'City African Affairs Officer: Correspondence, 1947-50', T.G. Askwith to P. Wyn Harris, 30 March 1948; and R. Frost, *Race against Time*, pp. 155-70. See also D. Goldsworthy, *Tom Mboya*, pp. 13-14, for its effect on one Nairobi African.

57. KNA Secretariat 1/12/8, 'Labour Unrest: Intelligence Reports, Central Province, 1947', C. Penfold to P. Wyn Harris, 25 September 1947; and MAA 8/109, 'Intelligence and Security: African Workers' Federation, 1947-48', C. Penfold to P. Wyn Harris, 4 November and 16 December 1947.

58. B. Kaggia, *Roots of Freedom*, pp. 78-82; and M. Singh, *History of Kenya's Trade Union Movement*, vol. 1, pp. 260-1. For Mbotela's view of the militants, see KNA MAA 8/22, 'City African Affairs Officer: Correspondence, 1947-50', Tom Mbotela to Superintendent, CID, Nairobi, 28 October 1947. See also his father's autobiography, J.E. Harris, *Recollections of James Juma Mbotela*, pp. 73-81.

59. KNA MAA 7/491, 'Administration Policy: Urban Areas, Nairobi, 1945-47', T.G. Askwith to C. Tomkinson, 22 August 1945; and CO 533/543/38086/5 (1945-47), 'Kikuyu Petitions and Memorials', Director of Intelligence and Security, Notes on African Unions, 6 November 1945, which lists the most prominent tribal and political associations. K. Little, *West African Urbanization*, pp. 24-65; and N.J. Westcott, 'Erica Fiah', pp. 88-92, provide useful summaries of their role in West Africa and in Dar-es-Salaam.

60. KNA MAA 8/105, 'Intelligence Reports: Radio Posta, 1947-48', C. Penfold to P. Wyn Harris, 24 October 1947, and *Radio Posta*, 16 October 1947. D. Parkin, *The Cultural Definition of Political Response*, pp. 36-44, details why the Luo in Nairobi have congregated in Kaloleni. It should, however, be remembered that this ethnic exclusive-

Outcast Nairobi

ness was fostered by the colonial government after Operation Anvil in April 1954, when Kaloleni became an almost exclusively Luo estate, and the Kikuyu, Embu and Meru were concentrated in Bahati. Tom Mboya was one of the few non-Kikuyu to live in Bahati at the height of the Emergency. See D. Goldsworthy, *Tom Mboya*, p. 28.

61. KNA Lab 9/1751, 'African Housing: General, 1946–51', T.G. Askwith, Annual Report on African Affairs in Nairobi, 1947, December 1947.
62. Legislative Council Debates, second series, vol. xx (1944–45), third session, 4 January 1945, Archadeacon L.J. Beecher, col. 505.
63. KNA MAA 7/491, 'Administration Policy: Urban Areas, Nairobi, 1945–47', T.G. Askwith to C. Tomkinson, 22 August 1945; MAA 8/22, 'City African Affairs Officer: Correspondence, 1947–50', T.G. Askwith to Superintendent, CID, Nairobi, 29 October 1947; and Lab 9/87, 'Labour Troubles: Nairobi, 1950', extract from *East African Standard*, 24 May 1950.
64. Legislative Council Debates, second series, vol. xx (1944–45), third session, 4 January 1945, Archdeacon L.J. Beecher, col. 505; KNA MAA 7/377, 'Legislation: Urban Pass Laws, 1946', *passim*; MAA 8/22, 'City African Affairs Officer: Correspondence, 1947–50', minutes of meetings to discuss vagrancy bylaws, 29 June, 9 August, 8 September and 12 October 1948, and 11 January 1949. See also MAA 2/5/223, 'Nairobi Advisory Council, 1946/49', Advisory Council meeting 21–22 January 1946, and the Crime Committee meetings on 19 and 26 June, and 15 August 1947. The meeting of the Advisory Council on 13–14 September 1948, however, expressed its 'thanks to Government for the way in which Bylaws (211 and 212) were being enforced, and congratulated the police on its efforts. It was recommended that the Spiv Squad should concentrate on Kariakor and Shauri Moyo, and the taxi ranks, and should work at night'.
65. KNA MAA 8/22, 'City African Affairs Officer: Correspondence, 1947–50', T.G. Askwith to Superintendent, CID, Nairobi, 29 October 1947; and MAA 2/5/223, 'Nairobi Advisory Council, 1946–49', Crime Committee, 19 and 26 June, and 15 August 1947; and the full Advisory Council meetings, 1–2 March and 13–14 September 1948. G.R.B. Brown's 'Observations on the Nairobi Strike', 23 May 1950, are interesting. When Askwith went on leave to Britain in 1949, before being appointed Commissioner for Community Development, Brown, who had been African Affairs Officer in Mombasa, was transferred to Nairobi to prevent a bid by the Municipal Council to appoint its own man to the post rather than to rely on the secondment of a member of the administration to the staff of the Municipal Council. This issue had caused concern both to the Secretariat and to the Nairobi African Advisory Council before Askwith's departure. See correspondence in MAA 8/22.
66. KNA MAA 7/491, 'Administration Policy: Urban Areas, Nairobi, 1945–47', T.G. Askwith's memorandum on African Grievances, 14 September 1945. See also CO 533/545/38091/10 (1944–47), 'Labour Registration and Identification, 1944–47', report of the sub-committee of the Labour Advisory Board, December 1946; and comments of G. Orde-Browne, 5 February 1947, for African opposition to the *kipande*.
67. M. Singh, *History of Kenya's Trade Union Movement*, vol. 1, pp. 240–50.
68. With the ending of the building campaign in 1948, the government relied increasingly on the vagrancy laws to resolve Nairobi's social problems. See MAA 8/22, 'City African Affairs Officer: Correspondence, 1947–50', meetings to discuss the relationship between crime, unemployment and vagrancy, 29 June, 9 August, 8 September, and 12 October 1948, and 11 January 1949. See also CO 533/556/38666 (1946–48), 'Removal of Undesirable Natives (Temporary) Legislation', P.E. Mitchell to George Hall, 4 May 1946; and Creech Jones's comments, 2 January 1948.
69. CO 533/566/6 (1950), 'Temporary Removal of Undesirable Natives Legislation', *passim*; and M. Singh, *History of Kenya's Trade Union Movement*, vol. 1, pp. 248–9.
70. *ibid*, pp. 252–3; and *Daily Chronicle*, 7 March 1950; and F.D. Corfield, 'Origins and Growth of Mau Mau', p. 83.

201

71. KNA Lab 9/87, 'Labour Troubles: Nairobi, 1950', cutting from *East African Standard*, 17 May 1950, giving details of the Essential Services (Arbitration) Ordinance; *Kenya Daily Mail*, 16 May 1950; and M. Singh, *History of Kenya's Trade Union Movement*, vol. 1, pp. 268–71. For details of the trials see M. Singh, pp. 277–86; and *East African Standard*, 24 May 1950, and 30 January, 1, 2, 3, 4, 7, 8, 14 and 17 February 1951.

72. M. Singh, *History of Kenya's Trade Union Movement*, vol. 1, p. 276; and F.D. Corfield, 'Origins and Growth of Mau Mau', p. 89.

73. *The Times*, 19 May 1950, and *East African Standard*, 19 May 1950.

74. M. Singh, *History of Kenya's Trade Union Movement*, vol. 1 pp. 272–7. Contrast with the comments of the Attorney General, K.K. O'Connor, reported in *Daily Herald*, 19 May 1950. When Eliud Mathu tried to speak to the strikers, he was shouted down and accused of being 'a traitor, bribed by Europeans'; see KNA Lab 9/87, report 20 May 1950; *The Times*, 20 May 1950; and *The Observer*, 21 May 1950.

75. *East African Standard*, 23 and 24 May 1950; and F.D. Corfield, 'Origins and Growth of Mau Mau', p. 89.

76. *East African Standard*, 24 May 1950. F. Furedi, 'The African Crowd in Nairobi', pp. 279–88; and S.B. Stichter, 'Trade Unionism in Kenya', pp. 167–72 and 'Workers, Trade Unions, and the Mau Mau Rebellion', *passim* (except p. 260) failed to recognise this fatal flaw in the campaign of the Nairobi militants, who were overwhelmingly Kikuyu.

77. F. Furedi, 'The African Crowd in Nairobi', pp. 285–8; and S.B. Stichter, 'Workers, Trade Unions, and the Mau Mau Rebellion', pp. 266–75; B. Kaggia, *Roots of Freedom*, pp. 79–82, 107–16; J. Spencer, 'Kenya African Union and Mau Mau', pp. 217–18; and C.G. Rosberg and J. Nottingham, *The Myth of Mau Mau*, pp. 269–76.

78. KNA Lab 9/1751, 'African Housing: General, 1946–51', E.M. Hyde-Clarke to J.D. Rankine, 17 January 1950, quoting his speech in the Legislative Council on 21 December 1949. See also MAA 8/22, 'City African Affairs Officer: Correspondence, 1947–50', G.R.B. Brown, 'Observations on the Nairobi Strike', 23 May 1950.

79. F.D. Corfield, 'Origins and Growth of Mau Mau', p. 89; and KNA Lab 9/87, 'Labour Troubles: Nairobi, 1950', *passim. The Times*, 26 May 1950, observed that 'the Kenya Government has tried to establish trade unionism on a sound basis among Africans, but has failed through the immaturity of the Africans who have been swayed by propaganda'.

80. KNA Lab 9/87, 'Labour Troubles: Nairobi, 1950', extracts from *Kenya Weekly News*, 26 May 1950; and *Tribune*, 26 May 1950. MAA 8/71, 'Communism, 1948–49', especially the meeting of the Secretariat sub-committee on communist subversion, 10 January 1949; and CO 537/4317/14322/10 (1949), 'Communism in the Colonies: East Africa', for a long report by P.E. Mitchell, November 1949.

Nine

A Change of Direction: the Agricultural Department's Abandonment of Communalism

With the breakdown of the conservation campaign following the peasant revolt, many agricultural officers recognised that many Kikuyu had been alienated by compulsory terracing and began to search for new ways of safeguarding the land. The field administration was sceptical of the new proposals and continued to rely upon the *Muhirig'a* elders and compulsion. Gradually the agricultural department won the argument, and, between 1950 and 1952, the Secretariat reluctantly accepted that progressive cultivators should be rewarded with the right to grow high-value cash crops, which had been restricted to settler farmers. This belated acceptance of African proto-capitalists, however, came too late to gain new support for the colonial state. If positive steps had been introduced in 1945, or even in 1948 after the collapse of the communal campaign, it might have been possible for the colonial régime to broaden its support, but the administration's opposition had delayed the adoption of the new strategy and by 1952 few benefits had filtered down to the Kikuyu peasantry.[1] In Meru and Embu, in contrast, where the district agricultural officers, Jack Benson and Leslie Brown, had experimented with peasant cash-crop production, many Africans by 1952 were already reaping the financial rewards. Consequently, these districts remained comparatively quiet during the Mau Mau Emergency.[2]

Field administration and agricultural department attitudes to the peasant option

In 1945 Tomkinson warned that African commercial cultivators would be forced to obey the *Muhirig'a* and to follow the agricultural regulations. He also reaffirmed that it was the government's policy to oppose the evolution of a class of large landowners, who would employ agricultural labourers.[3] These limitations inevitably slowed down the expansion of Kikuyu participation in the market economy. In addition, the opportunity was spurned to broaden the collaborative base of the colonial state and to incorporate the supporters of the Kenya African Union. Even the liberal minded Wyn Harris failed to realised that the administration's attempt to block the advance of the proto-capitalists and to shore up the authority of the chiefs, while increasing intervention in peasant agriculture, was alienating the people.[4] Until his departure for the Gambia, Wyn Harris remained one of the main supporters of the *Muhirig'a*'s attempt to supervise the agricultural campaign and a convinced opponent of any effort to reverse the communal strategy.

When Mathu and Kenyatta warned the Secretariat in August 1947, at the height of the disturbances in Murang'a, that unless the Settlement Board paid more attention to the criticism of the Machakos Local Native Council, Makueni would become another centre of confrontation between Africans and the government, their advice was ignored.[5] Cavendish-Bentinck had been informed that the African members of the Settlement Board were becoming restless and might resign because of pressure from Kenyatta over section 65 of the Native Lands' Trust Ordinance of 1938, which empowered the Board to oversee the agricultural campaign in the reserves.[6] Initially it seemed as if the protests in Murang'a and Olenguruone had merely strengthened the government's resolve to push ahead with terracing and to support the chiefs and the *Muhirig'a*. Sorrenson has suggested that 'the spirit of social reform which was abroad in Europe, and which in 1945 led to a Labour Government in Britain, was in Africa reinvigorating the ghosts of indirect rule'.[7] After 1947 this began slowly to change. The peasants' revolt destroyed Mitchell's agricultural strategy, not because compulsion was unable to produce a fundamental restructuring of African agriculture – although this was true – but because it had failed to incorporate the proto-capitalists in a wider political alliance, which could prop up the colonial state when the development campaign alienated the peasantry.

After 1947, the agricultural department, led by Leslie Brown, who had been transferred from Nigeria, belatedly attempted to appeal to this emerging élite and to broaden the colonial state's established clients with loans, individual land titles and high-value cash crops.[8] These rewards, they hoped, would provide a more powerful inducement to better farming than compulsion. Unfortunately these were at first minority views, even in the agricultural department. The communalists inside the agricultural department, led by Hughes Rice and the Provincial Agricultural Officer in Central Province, Trevor Moon, resisted Brown's new strategy, but by 1951 Brown had become the most influential agriculturalist in Kenya and Hughes Rice's ideas were discarded. He was then transferred from

Central Province to the backwaters of Nyanza where he could do less harm.[9]

From 1950 until the Emergency was declared in October 1952, the agricultural department and the field administration were locked in battle over the agriculturalists' new strategy.[10] Brown and his colleagues insisted that the peasant revolts in 1947 and 1948 were clear demonstrations of the depth of Kikuyu opposition to the compulsory agricultural betterment campaign, especially communal terracing. To press ahead and to ignore African protests was to ask for trouble; a new, more attractive approach was required, which would lessen suspicions about the second colonial occupation and persuade people voluntarily to adopt the new agricultural methods on their *shambas*. Compulsion had failed; African cultivators would have to be enticed to terrace their land and to reduce their dependence on maize and wattle.[11]

The evolution of a new consensus

Maher, the soil conservationist, had always advocated rewarding those who supported the agricultural betterment campaign.[12] He was now supported by Leslie Brown, who argued that 'progressive' African cultivators who followed the agricultural regulations should be given permission to grow high-value crops, such as coffee and tea, which had previously been restricted to settlers. Brown was determined to improve the tarnished image of the agricultural department among Africans, who had come to equate it with compulsory labour.[13] Brown and Maher were the two most able agriculturalists in Kenya and both were to acquire reputations far beyond the colony for their work and abrasiveness. Neither of them would tolerate opposition or interference from Nairobi. It was, therefore, almost inevitable that the collaboration would be marred by conflict.[14]

This began when Brown criticised the department for its obsession with narrow-base terracing. He advocated broad-base terracing, which although more difficult to construct would provide more permanent defences against erosion and, within a few years, would reduce the burden of communal terracing. Agricultural officers would cease being glorified policemen and would be able to devote their attentions to experiments with improved crops and techniques – tasks to which Brown was then able to devote less than 10 per cent of his time.[15]

At first Brown made little progress, even among his fellow agriculturalists. In February 1950, Trevor Moon, the Provincial Agricultural Officer, was still confident that compulsory narrow-base terracing would succeed. During 1949 the campaign had gathered momentum again and the acreage protected was now 47 per cent higher than in 1948.[16] Even in Machakos, the terracing figures for the last six months of 1949 were 200 per cent higher than they had been for the first half of the year, and

Hughes Rice had reported that in Nyeri nearly all the adult males were now digging terraces. Opposition also appeared to be declining in Murang'a where sub-location targets had been issued. November 1949, saw more than 1,000 acres terraced in a month for the first time since the 1947 disturbances.[17]

In 1950, however, the agricultural headquarters in Nairobi was dramatically reformed. Two assistant directors were appointed from outside Kenya: Roger Swynnerton, whose name was to become synonymous with the encouragement of peasant commodity production, was to supervise all fieldwork and Dr Tom Webster was to co-ordinate planning and research. This reorganisation freed G.M. Roddan, the deputy director, to liaise with the districts and to integrate local initiatives, such as Brown's in Embu, into central policy.[18] Swynnerton's appointment was particularly significant as it provided Brown and his supporters with a powerful defender in Nairobi. Swynnerton had been closely involved with encouraging African coffee and cotton cultivation in Tanganyika and had helped devise the Sukumaland development scheme, the most ambitious development project yet undertaken in East Africa which was designed to encourage African cash-crop cultivation.[19]

Under pressure from Brown and Swynnerton, by May 1951, even Moon was beginning to reconsider his position and to acknowledge that compulsory terracing had largely failed.[20] Swynnerton and Brown had already decided that African support for the conservation campaign would have to be 'bought'. Their new strategy rejected the communalist assumptions of the policy debates of 1944 and 1945 and encouraged individual enterprise. They sought to create a stratum of prosperous smallholders who practised mixed farming rotations and were allowed to grow high-value cash crops on permanent bench terraces, while domestic food crops were concentrated on the ridge tops. Brown confidently estimated that such families would be able to earn a cash income of at least £100 plus subsistence, compared to Humphrey's target figure of between £18 and £20.[21]

These advocates of change in the agricultural department also forced the administration to reconsider its opposition to individual land titles and loans for Africans.[22] Ever since the early 1920s, these issues had provided a rallying cry for all shades of African political opinion, ranging from the chiefs to the Kikuyu Central Association.[23] Until the late 1940s, their demands had been ignored but, as the reassessment of agricultural policy gathered momentum, the administration began to consider the issues more carefully. Any move towards individual titles in Kenya's African reserves should fulfil four aims. It should ensure sound agricultural practices were followed by those who gained individual titles; prevent fragmentation and the emergence of sub-economic holdings; provide security for Africans who wished to buy more land or improve their *shambas by* removing the fear that the land could be redeemed under Kikuyu law without any compensation for improvements; and provide security on which long-term agricultural credit could be based.[24]

When this question was considered in Whitehall in December 1944, the Colonial Office's Committee on African Land Tenure insisted that it was essential 'to ensure that the community retains the power to guard against the growth of individual rights in land, while at the same time not impeding the development of such rights, under the proper control of the community, to the extent that they are an essential concomitant of economic growth or social progress'.[25] Humphrey's investigations in Nyeri in 1944 had convinced many administrators that individualism was already rampant among the Kikuyu and needed to be curtailed if land degradation was to be reversed.[26] The Committee's declaration seemed to justify a strident reassertion of communal authority after the uncontrolled war years. Three years later in a very different climate it could equally be used to justify the new policies of Brown and his colleagues, which recognised the changes in Kikuyu society and, in a reversal of Tomkinson's and Mitchell's policies, attempted to construct a new network of collaborators, who would be dependent upon government loans and technical advice.[27]

Under pressure from the agricultural department and the Kenya African Union a committee was eventually appointed under J.H. Ingham to consider introducing agricultural credit for Africans. Its ponderous interim report of October 1949 highlighted the conflict between the paternalism of the administration and the commitment of certain agriculturalists to a more *laissez-faire* approach. The committee admitted that African agricultural productivity could be increased only by borrowing capital to introduce improved farming techniques, but it also declared: 'At the outset, however, we must state emphatically the dangers inherent in any attempt to make credit available in an agricultural community at that stage of development which the African had reached today.'[28] The difference between Kenya and the various colonies in which government loans had been introduced was that those schemes had been designed to mitigate the evil effects of existing debts to private money lenders who did not exist in Kenya. The committee, therefore, considered that: 'We would be doing the country a permanent disservice were we to advocate the introduction of a widespread scheme of agricultural credit which would result in agriculturalists living permanently in advance of their income and under the continual fear of foreclosure.'[29] The field administration was also concerned about the political dangers associated with loans guaranteed by land – the only property of sufficient value most Africans could offer as security. Foreclosure would involve a political confrontation, as the peasantry would consider it a direct attack on their land rights by the settler-controlled government.[30]

The main problem was that, although the granting of a lease would provide security, Africans could still be evicted if they did not obey the agricultural regulations. Their security was thus far from absolute, especially if the banks were to be allowed to foreclose on defaulters. Most Africans were unwilling to accept a scheme that declared the land they considered their property was only held on a 21 year lease. Mathu, the only African on the Ingham Committee, refused to sign the report since he considered it exaggerated the danger of large-scale defaulting and set interest rates so high that most potential borrowers would be discouraged from applying.[31] Although most agricultural officers favoured the changes, the administration remained apprehensive. Despite the Provincial Commissioners' decision in April 1948 to experiment with special titles in Kiambu, the district where the pressure for individual titles was strongest, no action was taken.[32]

It should be noted, however, that greater acceptance of individualism could be a double-edged weapon. Although it could be used, as Brown and Benson wished, to co-opt the proto-capitalists into the government's alliance and to strengthen the peasant option, it could also be used by the settlers and their supporters in the Secretariat to enforce agricultural reform in an even more draconian manner, completely overriding any African opposition by the threat of mass evictions for those who disobeyed the conservation regulations. The attack on African communalism did not only come from the Kenya African Union and the new co-optive strategy, which was being devised by some local agricultural officers. The settlers and some 'hard men' in the Secretariat, notably R.P. Armitage, the Assistant Secretary for Agriculture, were also beginning to question whether African customs were hindering the progress of the second colonial occupation. They did not want to incorporate the African alternative élite, which supported Kenyatta and the Kenya African Union, but to override opposition to essential conservation measures. The destruction of the land, they argued, would be stopped only when those who refused to accept agricultural orders were evicted. Such an approach, of course, necessitated a fundamental change in attitudes towards African land tenure and a move to individualism.[33]

In a secret report, Armitage reminded his colleagues in the Secretariat and other policy makers that the Kenya Land Commission had proposed that the government should guide tenure from native custom towards individual titles. This attack from the hardliners on African communal land tenure provides a timely reminder that the post-war development campaign had stemmed from an altruistic desire to serve African interests, despite the fact that it had been based upon the paternalist preconceptions of a few key individuals, most notably Mitchell, Wyn Harris, Lambert and Humphrey, rather than upon a premeditated attempt to allow the settlers to destroy the peasant option. These paternalist defenders of African communalism, therefore, by the early 1950s were bring criticised by both the advocates of peasant commodity production – the economic manifestation of Cohen's co-optive strategy – and the pro-settler lobby which feared the emergence of a new group of collaborators who might use the peasant option to undermine the settlers' economic hegemony. Under this combined onslaught, the resistance of the administration to individual titles and consolidation slowly began to diminish.[34]

Eventually, in 1951, the Ingham Committee tentatively proposed establishing a few co-operative credit societies and offering some carefully-monitored loans, issued by the Government Land Bank on the recommendation of district committees composed of the District Commissioner, the local agricultural and veterinary officers and two Africans. Preference, it was suggested, should be given to co-operative societies or to individuals organised in group farms or co-operative credit societies. A few individuals of proven farming ability were also to be eligible, provided their applications were approved by the location council. Should a location earn a bad name for defaulting, then loans would be curtailed and additional funds allocated to areas that repaid promptly. It was hoped that this measure would inculcate a sense of financial responsibility into the location councils and associate them with the scheme. Communal land tenure, however, remained inviolate. Personal character, either individual or collective, had to provide the main proof of security, since both Mitchell and H.E. Lambert refused to countenance any tampering with African communal tenure.[35] This debate over individualism and loans was not confined to Kenya. These challenges to pre-war ideas of 'organic' development had been discussed at the Cambridge Summer School in 1947, and at Jos in Nigeria two years later, but the problems of intellectual adjustment were especially difficult in pioneering colonies like Kenya. Gradually, however, the agriculturalists undermined the confidence of the administration and forced it to consider new options.[36]

Too little, too late: the failure of co-option

The agricultural department's new strategy, however, could only be introduced once most arable land had been terraced. Only then could the positive elements designed to raise African living standards come to the fore, such as mixed farming, crop rotations, enclosure, individual titles and land consolidation. Unfortunately compulsory terracing had destroyed any chance there might have been of gaining new collaborators. After 1945 the administration opposed the peasant option and refused to abandon either its communalist ideology or its alliance with the Kikuyu chiefs.[37] When the agricultural department belatedly began once again to encourage peasant production and to seek an alliance with the entrepreneurial élite of Kikuyuland, it was four years too late. Four years of compulsory terracing had alienated the peasantry and discredited the moderate African politicians who had sought incorporation. The peasant revolt of 1947, which had precipitated the agricultural department's new strategy of greater sensitivity to African opinion, had itself demonstrated the depth of peasant discontent which would have to be overcome in Kikuyuland. By 1947 the Kikuyu reserves were irredeemably alienated from the colonial régime. The changes in agricultural policy were insufficiently dramatic to regain lost ground. The new policy of promoting smallholder production advanced very slowly and by 1952 few Kikuyu had gained any benefits.[38]

The strategy was based upon careful analysis of local vegetation, soils and rainfall patterns to discover which cash and subsistence crops were best suited to a particular area. Brown, who was a trained zoologist as well as an agriculturalist, devised precise zonal agricultural plans during 1951 and 1952.[39] The first priority of these plans was to ensure that each zone was self-sufficient in food, since it was feared that North Nyanza and the Trans Nzoia might soon be unable to meet rising demand.[40] The other feature of the plans was the introduction of high-value cash crops, which would raise average household cash earnings to £100 per annum and also act as an incentive to the adoption of an integrated and sound farming system, since only those cultivators who obeyed the agricultural regulations were to be allowed to grow the new crops.[41]

Essentially Brown was proposing that the Kikuyu proto-capitalists be rewarded with loans, technical advice and new remunerative crops. This, of course, was completely the reverse of the administration's shibboleths. The individualists were now to be courted and rewarded on condition they supported the agricultural betterment campaign. A few 'progressive' farmers were already leading the way. The agricultural department hoped that, as they became increasingly numerous and prosperous, others would be encouraged to co-operate. In Kiambu, for example, one farmer was earning £400 per annum from his ten-acre plot; another received £100 a year from selling carnations to the Nairobi market and £400 from pyrethrum.[42] Brown estimated that it was theoretically possible to earn 5,700 shillings per annum from a six and a half acre plot, with two acres of arable land, three acres grazing, and half an acre of fodder crops, poultry or fruit and, most important, half an acre of coffee.[43] In practice, he set his sights rather lower and aimed to generate £100 surplus income per household per annum.[44] In theory, this appeared to be an ideal solution to 'the roots of rural poverty', which, according to Humphrey's calculations, would admirably suit the average-sized Kikuyu holding. The abandonment of the settlers' monopoly on high-value cash crops, which Humphrey had failed to tackle, appeared to have transformed the economic potential and rewards of the peasant option.

A Change of Direction

Although estimates of the profitability per acre of various crops can be misleading, varying considerably according to the fertility of the soil and climatic conditions, they do demonstrate the dramatic difference between the prices offered for the new cash crops with which the agricultural department could reward collaborators, and the staple crops of the Kikuyu *shamba*. It should, of course, be remembered that the acreages of the new high-price crops were carefully restricted by agricultural officers.

Table 9.1: *Comparative Profitability per acre of Selected Crops in Central Province in 1952*

Tobacco (prepared as snuff)	9,000 shillings
Coffee (maximum)	7,310 shillings
Pineapple	6,230 shillings
Coffee (minimum)	2,150 shillings
Potatoes	1,485 shillings
Pyrethrum (mature)	1,290 shillings
Sisal	784 shillings
Castor Oil Seed	450 shillings
Tobacco (finely cured)	187 shillings
Pyrethrum (immature)	180 shillings and 60 cents
Green Gram	139 shillings and 13 cents
Maize	131 shillings and 35 cents
Beans	121 shillings and 16 cents
Other Pulses	90 shillings and 75 cents
Wattle Bark	87 shillings
Millets	57 shillings and 13 cents

The new strategy was implemented most quickly in Meru and in Embu, where Brown himself had been agricultural officer. In Embu he had ensured that the new approach was introduced earlier and encouraged more assiduously than in other parts of Central Province where the agricultural department was still recovering from the 1947 revolt and had not yet had time to reconsider its policies.[45] The quick adoption of the scheme in Meru sprang from the fact that the district had been the scene of experiments with African coffee growing since 1937. It was, therefore, not a question of starting from scratch, preparing the district for new cash crops, but of expanding the existing plots.[46] Moreover, in Meru the *Njuri Ncheke* had been encouraged to direct agricultural programmes since the 1920s. It was not, therefore, regarded as an alien resuscitation but was acknowledged by the people to have a legitimate right to intervene. Meru Africans, therefore, enjoyed the rewards of the new tactics much earlier than the Kikuyu. By 1952, for example, there were more than 6,473 coffee growers with 1,822 acres of coffee trees compared to less than 1,000 growers in 1948.[47] Jack Benson, the local agricultural officer, triumphantly observed that:

> My contention that the development of the coffee industry would eventually lead to improved systems of agriculture in those areas where it was started are I believe now being justified. The rapid progress towards a better system of agriculture which is being developed in Chogoria . . . can be attributed largely to the fact that growers, having followed our advice on coffee with remarkable success have become so confident that they will now follow it in other directions.[48]

Only those cultivators who had built cattle bomas, terraced their land, and manured their crops had been allowed to plant coffee. The rest had seen the advantages of co-operation and had begun to adopt some of the recommended farming techniques in the hope that they too would eventually be rewarded with the privilege of coffee growing. Benson explained his tactics: 'Those people who are most progressive individually are assisted to the fullest extent for it is through them that we have been able, to a slow and increasing extent, to modify useful customs and to weaken and dispense with the bad ones.'[49] This meant that the Meru peasantry had quickly perceived that there was a close relationship between acceptance of agricultural regulations and wealth from coffee.

Meru, however, was a large, fertile district, covering 3,740 square miles. Land was not a scarce resource as among the Kikuyu. Kiambu, for example, had 20 per cent more people than Meru on less than one-sixth the area. The struggle for land and possible ecological collapse were much less acute, therefore, than in Kikuyuland. Of the three Kikuyu districts, Nyeri was the one where the agricultural officers found it easiest to persuade the district administration to adopt the new strategy. The Nyeri betterment scheme had originated from the plans of the local agricultural committee in 1948, and was in many respects the most carefully integrated of the various development plans. It was based upon encouraging mixed farming throughout the area. Progress, however, varied considerably. While fragmented holdings had largely been consolidated in Chief Muhoya's location in North Tetu, there were few progressive farmers in Othaya.[50]

Much of the success of the Nyeri scheme was due to Osborne, who became District Commissioner after his successful tour in Murang'a. As early as 1948, he had endorsed plans to introduce coffee, pyrethrum and tea, and, with the enthusiastic support of his agriculturalists, had organised marketing and the processing of African co-operative societies.[51] The district was later divided by Brown into three agricultural zones based on rainfall and altitude. In the highest zone, which in 1948 was largely uninhabited and covered with bracken, dairy farming and wattle plantations were encouraged. It was hoped that once this land, which was over 6,000 feet, had been cleared and opened to pasture following a communal grass-planting campaign, it would relieve the population pressure on the overcrowded middle zone, between 4,500 and 6,000 feet, and demonstrate the economic potential of a few well-nourished cows. It was hoped that this would encourage others to introduce paddocking, rotational grazing, stock dipping and controlled breeding. Grass, it was predicted, would prove to be a highly remunerative cash crop, once it had 'metamorphosed' into milk.[52]

The middle zone was the most densely populated part of all three Kikuyu districts, with population densities in some locations of over 600 to the square mile. It was, therefore, the area most urgently in need of a high-value cash crop to relieve pressure on the land. Coffee and commercial fruit growing were to provide the financial incentive to agricultural improvements in these areas. Permission to cultivate these new crops, of course, was initially restricted to those who had already accepted the agricultural department's advice, which usually meant the chiefs and their supporters. Thus, malcontents were still excluded from sharing the district's new prosperity. The new strategy had not yet broadened the base of collaboration in the middle zone. In the lowest, more arid areas, mixed farming, tobacco and rice were to be introduced to stimulate similar farming improvements, but these also had not yet filtered down to the mass of the people.[53]

In theory, the new agricultural campaign coincided for the first time with the ambitions of ordinary Africans and offered them a higher standard of living in return for supporting the colonial order. In practice, however, the campaign was still dominated by terracing, since all these who wished to be considered to grow the new crops had to protect their slopes. Little seemed to have changed. Schools were used to demonstrate better farming methods and to propagate bench terracing. Dotted around the district, existing in all agricultural and climatic zones, they provided a far more extensive system of demonstration centres in which the rewards of co-operation could be clearly shown. The agricultural officer in Murang'a enthusiastically declared that 'all this adds up to the finest form of propaganda imaginable – the impetus from within'. Many parents, however, objected to having to help build the schools' terraces or to provide stock. It seemed to be yet one more infringement of African freedom by the second colonial occupation.[54]

Agricultural progress and the emergence of new collaborators was still very slow. Brown, for example, complained that although in certain locations the proportion of land under sound use was considerably above the general mean, particularly in the Iriaini and North Tetu locations of Nyeri, Chief Magugu's locations in Kiambu and the bracken zone of Murang'a, in most parts of Central Province improvements remained 'pitifully inadequate'. The vast majority of the Province, he reported, was:

> still covered with fragmented holdings run on a primitive shifting culti-vation system, which, in less fertile soil, would have brought ruin long ago. There are large areas where, as far as the eye can see, the land is still one hundred per cent unsoundly used, though various rot stopping measures such as narrow base terraces have been put in . . . Progress in improved farming is still nowhere near keeping pace with increasing population, fragmentation and degeneration.[55]

If the agricultural department could as yet see little return from the new approach this was even more true of the Africans.

The second colonial occupation had enabled the state bureaucracy to penetrate to new depths and had profoundly disrupted Kikuyu life. The following extract from the safari diaries of the agricultural officer in Murang'a show just how demanding the new agricultural rules were on the ordinary Kikuyu when the might of the government descended upon them as never before. In February 1948, he inspected work in headman Ngure's part of Location 2 near Kirera. He noted:

Kirera: Shocking demonstration of terraces. Mere scratches in the ground neither wide nor deep enough. Assistant Agricul-tural Instructor Pithon Kamau. Another lot of terraces dug by the same group rather worse. Kaptein told to redig all immediately and Agricultural Instructor Geoffrey to ensure correct size.

Gathanjo: Eight men digging. Work quite fair. Found a young man sitting at home so his *shamba* was terraced on the spot (Nganga Kareja).

Irati: Nothing doing at all. Told Agricultural Instructor to start individual measuring . . . A woman name Wambui Gikonyo, a widow, found digging up a good runway near the Irati bridge. To be run (i.e. prosecuted) at once and all to be grassed in the rains. Njeha Warugi of Gathanje mak-ing *tembo*. Headman Ngure says he has permission but very much doubt it. The drinking in this sub-location is very bad – led by Headman?[56]

Such in-depth pressure continued throughout Mitchell's governorship and European inspection became increasingly regular. On reading these agricultural reports of the late 1940s one is struck by how often the Kikuyu had to redig all the terraces they had so laboriously constructed because of a mistake by the Assistant Agricultural Instructor. Almost invariably in the early years of the agricultural betterment campaign the terraces were incorrectly marked out at the contour and were virtually useless. Until 1950, the expansion in the number of barely trained agricultural staff far exceeded the ability of the small experienced staff to inspect their work on a regular basis. This meant that when the agricultural officer eventually did manage to get round the locations, he found much of the work had been so badly supervised that it had to be done again.[57] This, of course, further antagonised the peasantry and destroyed their support for the agricultural betterment campaign. By the time there were enough European supervisory staff to keep a close eye on development schemes throughout the district, most of the population had been completely alienated from agricultural development schemes by their previous experiences and were extremely suspicious of anything the government proposed.[58] In 1945 there had usually been only one European agricultural officer per district, who relied on a handful of African assistants, but by 1952 European staff were thick on the ground, interfering in virtually every facet of Kikuyu life.[59]

In Nyeri, for example, there were nine European officers, including the provincial headquarters' staff, by the time the Emergency was declared. In 1952, Embu had ten European agriculturalists, Machakos eleven, Murang'a five, Kiambu four, Meru three, and Kitui only two. The total African staff employed on agricultural work in Central Province had also expanded dramatically since the war. In 1952, the agricultural department employed 373 Africans, the African district councils had 1,199 (with the Development and Reconstruction Authority employing another 429 in the province), the African Settlement and Land Utilization Board 1,053, and the agricultural development programme a mere twelve. By the Emergency, therefore, there were 44 European agriculturalists in Central Province to supervise 3,066 Africans. Meanwhile the staff of the veterinary department had expanded equally dramatically and by 1952 numbered nearly 1,000 in Central Province.[60] This tremendous expansion meant that even the most recalcitrant African could not escape the two technical departments. The agricultural officer in Murang'a, for example, received reports on the smallholding of the Kikuyu Central Association activist, Job Muchuchu, which was condemned for its 'filthy compound and revolting pig styes'.[61] Muchuchu, it is interesting to note, was generally regarded as a successful fruit farmer with carefully cultivated crops of oranges, lemons and custard apples. The agricultural department's increased manpower enabled it to concentrate upon known recalcitrants and to force them to adopt new techniques and to terrace their land, while the veterinary department harassed them until they began to innoculate and cull their cattle.[62]

As Table 9.2 shows, by the early 1950s the demands of the second colonial occupation were far above the levels of 1947, when communal terracing had provoked such virulent opposition:[63]

Table 9.2: *Terraces Constructed in South Nyeri, 1945 to 1954*

	Narrow-base Terraces	Bench Terraces
1945	637 miles	nil
1946	654 miles	nil
1947	1,865 miles	nil
1948	c.2,500 miles	nil
1949	c.2,500 miles	nil
1950	3,155 miles	21 miles
1951	3,833 miles	61 miles
1952	3,832 miles	228 miles
1953	1,382 miles	250 miles
1954	1,079 miles	1,452 miles

Brown's strategy of building the more durable bench terraces only really gathered momentum after the declaration of the Emergency. In 1951 and 1952, as far as the Kikuyu peasants were concerned, the agricultural campaign was indistinguishable from the earlier communal approach. So far only known supporters of the colonial régime had been rewarded with the lucrative new cash crops. According to official calculations, the average family income in the middle zone of Murang'a was still only 918 shillings per annum, and 735 shillings in the bracken zone.[64] Although earnings were estimated to have increased fourfold since 1947, in real terms little improvement had occurred and production had ceased to grow. The explanation for this failure to translate the new policy into positive results was that Brown's plans to promote peasant production and to reward collaborators with high-price cash crops had been undermined by the field administration, which had delayed action until it was too late.

Many Local Native Councils had also diverted revenue raised by the agricultural cess to non-agricultural purposes, with less than 25 per cent being ploughed back into agricultural improvements. This obstructionist attitude on the part of District Commissioners and Local Native Councils inevitably meant that development was much slower than it might have been. In Murang'a, for example, in 1952 there were only 383 households allowed to grow coffee, while in Kiambu the first seedlings were not even planted until April 1953. The same was true for tea and pyrethrum. By 1952, only 779 acres of pyrethrum had been planted in Central Province and the African tea crop was even smaller – a mere 35 acres in Nyeri, expected to increase to 500 acres by 1958 when it would still amount to less than 3 per cent of the district's total agricultural area.[65] Thus, although the agricultural department theoretically abandoned compulsory communal terracing and adopted the strategy of encouraging peasant cultivation of high-priced cash crops in an attempt to encourage individualism rather than vainly attempting to preserve Africa's mythical communalism, this remained effectively hidden from the Kikuyu. This time, when their anger boiled over again, their reaction proved far more violent than in 1947. Whatever Mitchell may have reported to Whitehall, in reality the situation in the Kikuyu reserves was still deteriorating and the peasantry had become thoroughly disillusioned with the second colonial occupation, which seemed to be entrenching the economic domination of the chiefs and their cronies. The Kikuyu masses remained obdurately opposed to agricultural change. Coercion had merely increased the influence of the political activists and produced violent attacks upon the chiefs, headmen and agricultural instructors, who were the most exposed representatives of the colonial state.[66]

Notes

1. KNA Ag 4/125, 'Annual Agricultural Reports: Central Province Districts, 1951', C.D. Knight's Fort Hall report; T.B. Spence's Kiambu report; and T. Hughes Rice's Machakos report; Ag 4/328, 'Annual Agricultural Report; Central Province, 1951', *passim*; and Ag 4/410, 'Central Province and Districts: Annual Agricultural Reports, 1952', especially L.H. Brown's Provincial report; and G. Gamble's Nyeri report.
2. KNA Ag 4/125, 'Annual Agricultural Reports: Central Province Districts, 1951', J.P. Benson's Meru report; Ag 4/118, 'Provincial Agricultural Handing Over Reports, 1942-51', H.B. Ambrose's Embu handing over notes, 15 October 1951; and Ag 4/410, 'Central Province and Districts: Annual Agricultural Reports, 1952', L.H. Brown's Provincial report; T.R. Golding's Embu reports; and V.E.M. Burke's Meru report. See also A. Thurston's draft manuscript, 'The Intensification of Smallholder Agriculture in Kenya', pp. 26-8, 52-60; and the African Land Development Board's Report on African Land Development in Kenya 1946-55, pp. 93-104. For details of discontent in Meru see J.T.S. Kamunchuluh, 'The Meru Participation in Mau Mau', pp. 196-206.
3. KNA DC/NYI 2/1/20, 'Mr Humphrey's Report on South Nyeri, 1944-47', C. Tomkinson's interim report on development to G.M. Rennie, 14 May 1945.
4. CO 852/662/19936/2 (1945-46), 'Soil Erosion: Kenya', H.E. Lambert and P. Wyn Harris, 'Policy in Regard to Land Tenure in the Native Lands of Kenya', *passim*; and KNA MAA 8/68, 'Chief Waruhiu, 1948-52', P. Wyn Harris to all District Commissioners, Central Province, 'Directive on the African Political Situation, Central Province', 11 December 1946.
5. KNA MAA 8/20, 'African Settlement: Teita Hills, Makueni, Ukamba Land Unit and Lambwe Valley, 1947-51', minutes of the meeting of the African Settlement and Land Utilisation Board, 13 June 1947; the second quarterly report of the African Settlement and Land Utilisation Board on Makueni, 20 June 1947; the resolution of the Machakos Local Native Council on Makueni, 13 August 1947; and R.J.C. Howes to A.C.M. Mullins, Provincial Commissioner, Central, 13 August 1947. See also CO 533/556/38668 (1946-47), 'African Resettlement', F.W. Cavendish-Bentinck to A.B. Cohen, 25 January 1947.
6. CO 533/538/38005/20 (1947), 'Land Commission: Native Lands Trust Board', minutes of the meeting of the Executive Council, Kenya, 25 August 1947; and

F.W. Cavendish-Bentinck to R.P. Armitage, Secretary for Agriculture, 26 August 1947.

7. M.P.K. Sorrenson, *Land Reform in the Kikuyu Country*, p. 58.

8. KNA MAA 6/13, 'Report of the Committee on Agricultural Credit for Africans, 1949–50', interim report of J.H. Ingham's committee, 29 October 1949; MAA 6/14, 'Committee to Make Recommendations on Agricultural Credit for African Farmers, 1949', report of the Colonial Economic Advisory Committee, forwarded by Creech Jones, 6 March 1947; minutes of preliminary meetings of the Ingham Committee, 2 May, 11 July, 8 August and 1 September 1949. Ag 4/80, 'Agricultural Conferences and Meetings, 1933–51', minutes of the meeting of Central Province Agricultural Officers, 18–19 October 1948; Ag 4–419, 'Agricultural Development and the Maintenance of Soil Fertility: The Growing of High Priced Cash Crops, 1933–51', J.T. Moon to D.L. Blunt, Director of Agriculture, 5 February 1948; and L.H. Brown to R.E. Wainwright, 6 February 1948; and Ag 4/125, 'Annual Agricultural Reports: Central Province Districts 1951', J.P. Benson's Meru report.

9. For Hughes Rice's approach see KNA Ag 1/1079, 'Soil Erosion Native Areas, 1946–54', T. Hughes Rice's memorandum, 'Soil Conservation Organisation in Fort Hall as Adapted from the Indigenous *Ngwatio* System', February 1947; and Ag 4/330, 'Provincial Agricultural Officer: News Letters, 1939–51', T. Hughes Rice's report in the February 1950 issue of the youth conference in Nyeri on 1–2 September 1949.

10. KNA DC/FH 1/29, 'Fort Hall Annual Report, 1950', pp. 1, 11–12; MAA 7/842, 'Provincial Commissioner's Meetings, 1945–51', minutes of meeting with D. Rees-Williams, Under Secretary of State for the Colonies, 29 April 1948; and MAA 6/13, 'Report of the Committee on Agricultural Credit for Africans, 1949–50', H.E. Lambert's memorandum on land titles, 8 November 1948. See also M.P.K. Sorrenson, *Land Reform in the Kikuyu Country*, pp. 60–71.

11. KNA Ag 4/80, 'Agricultural Conferences and Meetings, 1933–51', District Agricultural Officers Conference at Kisumu, 29–30 August 1949; and Central Province Agricultural Officers Conference, 11–12 October 1949.

12. KNA Ag 4/539, 'Reconditioning: Central Province, 1934–48', C. Maher to Senior Agricultural Officer, Nyanza, 28 January 1946; Ag 1/1065, 'Soil Erosion: Native Areas, 1943–46', A.C. Maher to G.M. Rennie, 'Agricultural Changes as Alternatives to Disaster in the Native Areas', undated; A.C. Maher's memorandum on the aims of soil conservation planning, 6 March 1945; and A.C. Maher to D.L. Blunt, 'Notes on Estimates for the Development of the Native Reserves', 1 June 1945. See also Maher's dispute with the Nyanza administration over discontent in Kitosh, North Nyanza, with the demands imposed on the peasantry by the terracing campaign, in Ag 1/1074, 'Soil Erosion: Nyanza Province, 1946–52', A.C. Maher to D.L. Blunt, 3 February 1947; D.L. Blunt to F.W. Cavendish-Bentinck, 14 February 1947.

13. KNA Ag 4/518, 'Reconditioning: Central Province, 1948–51', L.H. Brown to J.T. Moon, 15 December 1949; Ag 4/358, 'Monthly Agricultural Reports: Embu District, 1945–49', L.H. Brown's Half-Yearly report, January–June 1949; AG 4/392, 'Central Province Districts Agricultural Annual Reports, 1948', L.H. Brown's Embu report; and Ag 4/80, 'Agricultural Conferences and Meetings, 1933–51', minutes of the meeting of Agricultural Officers, Central Province, 18–19 October 1948.

14. For details of Maher's career, and especially his difficult relations with his superiors, see his personal file, KNA Ag 2/274, 'A.C. Maher: Agricultural Officer, 1929–52', *passim*. Maher resigned from the Kenya Agricultural Service at the earliest possible opportunity, on 30 June 1950, when he was 45, and retired to his farm on the Kinangop. Brown, in contrast, rose to become Chief Agriculturalist in Kenya.

15. KNA Ag 4/80, 'Agricultural Conferences and Meetings, 1933–51', L.H. Brown to J.T. Moon, 21 August, 1948, and 26 October 1948. Brown estimated that he spent 74 hours per month on routine administration and only three hours on experimental work.

A Change of Direction

See also Ag 4/518, 'Reconditioning: Central Province, 1948-51', L.H. Brown to J.T. Moon, 15 December 1949; and Ag 4/392, 'Central Province Districts Agricultural Annual Reports, 1948', L.H. Brown's Embu report. Maher never became reconciled to bench terracing, see Ag 1/1079, 'Soil Erosion Native Areas, 1946-54', A.C. Maher to S. Gillett, 30 November 1948; J.T. Moon to S. Gillett, 10 December 1948; and memorandum on bench terracing by Mr Hill, Assistant Agricultural Officer, Fort Hall, December 1948; and Ag 4/518, 'Reconditioning: Central Province, 1948-51', A.C. Maher to J.T. Moon, 12 January 1950.

The alternative methods of terracing propounded by Maher and Brown are illustrated below.

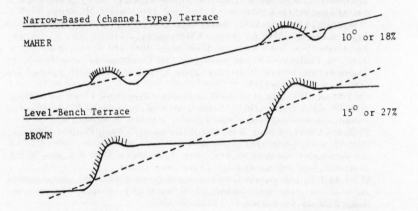

Source: D.B. Thomas, 'Some Observations on Soil Conservation in Machakos District, with special reference to terracing', Institute of Development Studies, Occasional Paper No. 27, 1978.

16. KNA Ag 4/518, 'Reconditioning: Central Province, 1948-51', J.T. Moon to S. Gillett 3 February 1950; and E.H. Windley to F.W. Cavendish-Bentinck, 'Central Province Soil Conservation Report, July–December 1949'.
17. *ibid.* E.H. Windley to F.W. Cavendish-Bentinck, 'Central Province Soil Conservation Report, July–December 1949'.
18. KNA Ag 4/80, 'Agricultural Conferences and Meetings, 1933-51', minutes of the Provincial Agricultural Officers' meeting, 9 June 1950.
19. A. Thurston, 'The Intensification of Smallholder Agriculture in Kenya', pp. 87-9, G.A. Maguire, *Towards Uhuru in Tanzania, passim*, provides a detailed history of the political consequences of agricultural development in Sukumaland.
20. KNA Ag 4/518, 'Reconditioning: Central Province, 1948-51', J.T. Moon to S. Gillett, 8 May 1951; and Ag 4/328, 'Annual Agricultural Report: Central Province, 1951', especially J.T. Moon's subsection on soil and water conservation.
21. KNA Ag 4/502, 'Annual Agricultural Reports: Central Province 1942-55', Agricultural Education Report, Fort Hall, 29 December 1952, for details of L.H. Brown's speech to the conference of primary school teachers, 1-6 December 1952.
22. KNA MAA 6/13, 'Report of the Committee on Agricultural Credit for Africans, 1949-50', *passim*; and MAA 6/14, 'Committee to Make Recommendations on Agricultural Credit for African Farmers, 1949', minutes of committee meetings, 2 May, 11

A Change of Direction

July, 8 August and 1 September 1949; and D. O'Hagan, 11 October 1949; and M.P.K. Sorrenson, *Land Reform in the Kikuyu Country*, pp. 60-71.

23. C.G. Rosberg and J. Nottingham, *The Myth of Mau Mau*, pp. 43, 93-4. See also D.M. Feldman's thesis, 'Christians and Politics', pp. 219-24, for details of the business activities of the early political activists.

24. KNA MAA 6/13, 'Report of the Committee on Agricultural Credit for Africans, 1949-50', H.E. Lambert's memorandum on African Land Titles to the African Affairs Committee, 8 November 1948.

25. CO 852/557/16708 (1945), 'Land Tenure Panel', Minutes of the meeting of the Colonial Social Science Research Council to discuss African land tenure, forwarded to Kenya, 28 December 1944. See also KNA MAA 6/14, 'Committee to Make Recommendations on Agricultural Credit for African Farmers, 1949', Creech Jones to P.E. Mitchell, 6 March 1947.

26. CO 852/662/19936/2 (1945-46), 'Soil Erosion: Kenya', N. Humphrey, 'The Relationship of Population to the Land in South Nyeri', paragraphs 19-24; and KNA DC/NYI 2/1/20, 'Mr Humphrey's Report on South Nyeri, 1944-47', N. Humphrey to D.L. Blunt, 'A Preliminary Report on Agricultural Conditions in South Nyeri', 22 September 1944; W. Lyne Watt to D.L. Blunt, 27 October 1944; and C. Tomkinson to G.M. Rennie, 14 May 1945.

27. KNA MAA 6/13, 'Report of the Committee on Agricultural Credit for Africans, 1949-50', *passim*; and Ag 1/1079, 'Soil Erosion: Native Areas, 1946-54', G.S. Cowley, Provincial Agricultural Officer, Rift Valley, to S. Gillett, 20 August 1951.

28. KNA MAA 6/13, 'Report of the Committee on Agricultural Credit for Africans, 1949-50', paragraph 3, 29 October 1949.

29. *ibid*, paragraph 4. See also KNA MAA 6/14, 'Committee to Make Recommendations on Agricultural Credit for African Farmers, 1949', Creech Jones to P.E. Mitchell, 6 March 1947, enclosing report by the Colonial Economic Advisory Committee on short and long-term credit; and memorandum by Sir Malcolm Darling, formerly of the Indian Civil Service, undated.

30. KNA MAA 6/13, 'Report of the Committee on Agricultural Credit for Africans, 1949-50', H.E. Lambert's memorandum to the African Affairs' Committee on African Land Titles, 8 November 1949.

31. *ibid*. Lambert observed: 'Although in actual fact the method of setting apart and lease would give an absolute security to the individual, as long as he behaved himself, it is not surprising that he feels some doubt about it, and fears a snag somewhere, when he is told that the land, which in his eyes (and those of all his tribe) belongs to him entirely for his lifetime and thereafter to his sons is now (by way of giving him a better title to it) offered to him on a lease of twenty-one or thirty-three years only.' See also E.W. Mathu's minority report and his memorandum on land titles in the African Land Units, 1 July 1949.

32. M.P.K. Sorrenson, *Land Reform in the Kikuyu Country*, pp. 61-71.

33. CO 533/538/38005/20 (1947), 'Land Commission: Native Lands Trust Board', R.P. Armitage's report, 'Land Management and Utilisation in Kenya', August 1947. For an outright attack on Armitage's proposals, see P. Wyn Harris to F.W. Cavendish-Bentinck, 9 August 1947.

34. M.P.K. Sorrenson, *Land Reform in the Kikuyu Country*, pp. 61-71; and KNA MAA 8/25, 'African Affairs' Committee: Minutes, 1948-52', meetings 3 November; and 4 November 1948; 13 April 1949; 4 August 1949; 5 October 1950; and 15 March 1951.

35. KNA MAA 6/13, 'Report of the Committee on Agricultural Credit for Africans, 1949-50', paragraphs 12-21; and H.E. Lambert's memorandum on land titles to the African Affairs' Committee, 8 November 1949; and CO 533/553/38557/8, 'Colonial Development and Welfare Schemes' (1947-48), P.E. Mitchell to George Hall, 17 April 1946, later published as 'General Aspects of the Agricultural Situation in Kenya'. See also M.P.K. Sorrenson, *Land Reform in the Kikuyu Country*, p. 60.

36. R.O. Hennings, Secretary for Agriculture, 'Some Trends and Problems of African Land Tenure in Kenya', pp. 122–34; Lord Hailey, 'The Land Tenure Problem in Africa', pp. 3–7; and his revised edition of *An African Survey*, pp. 775–811. See G.B. Masefield, 'Farming Systems and Land Tenure', pp. 8–14; C.K. Meek, 'Some Social Aspects of Land Tenure in Africa', pp. 15–21; C.W. Rowling, Adviser on Land, Nigeria, 'An Analysis of Factors Affecting Changes in Land Tenure in Africa', pp. 21–8; and H.H. Fosbrooke, Senior Government Sociologist, Tanganyika, 'Public Opinion and Changes in Land Tenure', pp. 28–36. See also C.K. Meek, 'The Amsterdam Land Tenure Symposium', pp. 113–14; KNA Ag 4/330, 'Provincial Agricultural Officer: News Letters, 1939–51', G.F. Clay, the Agricultural Adviser to the Secretary of State, address to the Cambridge Summer School, 11 September 1948, reprinted in the monthly newsletter, April 1949.

37. CO 852/557/16707/2 (1946), 'Land Tenure Policy: Kenya', H.E. Lambert's report on 'Central Kavirondo Land Tenure', 29 August 1946; CO 852/662/19936/2 (1945–46), 'Soil Erosion: Kenya', N. Humphrey, 'Relationship of Population to the Land in South Nyeri', and H.E. Lambert and P. Wyn Harris, 'Policy in Regard to Land Tenure in the Native Lands of Kenya'. See also KNA DC/FH 4/6, 'Chief and Headmen, 1937–54'.

38. KNA DC/FH 1/26, 'Fort Hall Annual Report, 1947', pp. 1–6, 15; MAA 8/106, 'Intelligence Reports: Mumenyereri, 1947–50', C. Penfold to P. Wyn Harris, 16 October, 18 October and 20 October, 10 and 19 November, and 10 December 1947.

39. KNA Ag 4/118, 'Provincial Agricultural Handing Over Reports, 1942–51', L.H. Brown to J.T. Moon, Central Province Handing Over Report, 5 December 1950; and L.H. Brown's Handing Over Notes, Embu, 8 February 1951. For the subsequent implementation of the zonal plan in Nyeri, see Ag 4/387, 'A Review of the Cash Crop Situation, 1960–66', *passim.*

40. Humphrey had first pointed to this alarming possibility in CO 852/662/19936/2 (1945–46), 'Soil Erosion: Kenya', N. Humphrey, 'The Relationship of Population to the Land in South Nyeri', paragraphs 6 and 54. See also CO 533/553/38557/8 (1947–48), 'Colonial Development and Welfare Schemes', P.E. Mitchell to George Hall, 17 April 1946, 'General Aspects of the Agricultural Situation in Kenya'.

41. KNA Ag 4/518, 'Reconditioning: Central Province, 1948–51', J.T. Moon to S. Gillett, 8 May 1951; Ag 4/502, 'Annual Agricultural Reports: Central Province, 1942–55', L.H. Brown, Department of Agriculture Report, 1952, p. 2; DC/NYI 7/1, 'Nyeri District Programme of Work, 1951', *passim*; and Ag 4/125, 'Annual Agricultural Reports: Central Province and Districts, 1951', J.P. Benson's Meru report. For attempts to stimulate peasant production, see Ag. 4/118, 'Provincial Agricultural Handing Over Reports, 1942–51', Major G.O. Hughes to C.A.B. Thurburn, Handing Over Report, Marketing Officer, Nyeri, 15 January 1951.

42. KNA Ag 4/410, 'Central Province and Districts: Annual Agricultural Reports, 1952', T.B. Spence's Kiambu District report; and L.H. Brown's Central Province report, for details of the earnings of various African progressive farmers.

43. KNA Ag 4/502, 'Annual Agricultural Reports: Central Province, 1942–55', L.H. Brown quoted in the Agricultural Education Report, Fort Hall, 29 December 1952.

44. These estimates of comparative profitability per acre have been adapted from KNA Ag 4/410, 'Central Province and Districts: Annual Agricultural Reports, 1952', L.H. Brown's Central Province Report, Appendix D. Ag 4/330, 'Provincial Agricultural Officer: News Letters, 1939–51', November–December 1950 issue contains similar estimates from North Nyanza.

45. KNA Ag 4/80, 'Agricultural Conferences and Meetings, 1933–51', L.H. Brown to J.T. Moon, 21 and 26 August 1948; and minutes of the meetings of Central Province Agricultural Officers, 18–19 October 1948; 3–4 February 1949; and 19–21 October 1949; Ag 4/118, 'Provincial Agricultural Handing Over Reports, 1942–51', L.H. Brown's Embu Handing Over Notes, 8 February 1951; and Ag 4/392, 'Central

Province Districts' Annual Agricultural Reports, 1948', L.H. Brown's Embu Report. Brown did, however, continue with the terracing campaign, see Ag 4/358, 'Monthly Agricultural Reports: Embu District, 1945–49', reports for July–September 1947; January–June 1948; and January–June 1949.

46. KNA Ag 4/392, 'Central Province Districts' Annual Agricultural Reports, 1948', J.P. Benson's Meru report: Ag 4/125, 'Annual Agricultural Reports: Central Province Districts, 1951', J.P. Benson's Meru report; and Ag 4/410, 'Central Province and Districts: Annual Agricultural Reports, 1952', V.E.M. Burke's Meru report.

47. KNA Ag 4/410, 'Central Province and Districts: Annual Agricultural Reports, 1952', V.E.M. Burke's Meru report, Appendix ii, Annual Report of the Coffee Officer, Embu. These 6,473 growers represented 9 per cent of the total male population of the district or approximately 30 per cent of the family heads living within the approved coffee-growing areas. Coffee exports from Meru totalled £40,000, the largest single item in the district's external earnings. It was intended to double the coffee area over the next two years. See also Ag 4/125, 'Annual Agricultural Reports: Central Province Districts, 1951', J.P. Benson's Meru report for information on the high quality of Meru coffee. For a detailed study of agricultural change in Meru, see F.E. Bernard, *East of Mount Kenya*.

48. KNA Ag 4/392, 'Central Province Districts' Annual Agricultural Reports, 1948', J.P. Benson's Meru report.

49. *ibid.*

50. KNA Ag 4/410, 'Central Province and Districts: Annual Agricultural Reports, 1952', L.H. Brown's Central Province report; and G. Gamble's Nyeri District report; and RH Mss.Afr.s. 596, 'European Elected Members' Organisation', 38(A)/1 'Mau Mau, 1947–55', file 55, 'Kikuyu and Mau Mau: The Land'; and a letter from L.H. Brown, published in *East African Standard*, 17 April 1953.

51. KNA Ag 4/419, 'Agricultural Development and Maintenance of Soil Fertility: The Growing of High Priced Crops, 1933–51'; DC/NYI 7/1, 'Nyeri District Programme of Work, 1951', *passim*; and Ag 4/392, 'Central Province Districts' Annual Agricultural Reports, 1948', T. Hughes Rice's Nyeri report.

52. KNA Ag 4/410, 'Central Province and Districts: Annual Agricultural Reports, 1952', L.H. Brown's Central Province report; and G. Gamble's Nyeri District report; and Ag 4/419, 'Agricultural Development and Maintenance of Soil Fertility: The Growing of High Priced Crops, 1933–51', L.H. Brown's memorandum, 6 February 1948.

53. KNA Ag 4/419, 'Agricultural Development and Maintenance of Soil Fertility: The Growing of High Priced Crops, 1933–51', L.H. Brown, 6 February 1948. See also Ag 4/387, 'A Review of the Cash Crop Situation 1960–66', undated memorandum on the cash crop zones of Nyeri; Ag 4/518, 'Reconditioning: Central Province 1948–51', E.H. Windley to F.W. Cavendish-Bentinck, 13 January 1950; and Ag 4/410, 'Central Province and Districts: Annual Agricultural Reports, 1952', G. Gamble's Nyeri District report.

54. KNA Ag 4/80, 'Agricultural Conferences and Meetings, 1933–51', C.D. Knight's memorandum on 'The Development of Smallholdings', undated, but probably June 1950; and Ag 4/330, 'Provincial Agricultural Officer: News Letters, 1939–51', T. Hughes Rice's report on the Nyeri Youth Conference in the February 1950 issue.

55. KNA Ag 4/410, 'Central Province and Districts: Annual Agricultural Reports, 1952', L.H. Brown's Central Province report.

56. KNA Ag 4/451, 'Fort Hall Safari Diaries, 1948–51', C.D. Knight's report of his tour around Location 2, 17–21 February 1948.

57. KNA Ag 4/451, 'Fort Hall Safari Diaries, 1948–51' *passim*, especially Knight's comments on Assistant Agricultural Instructor Gacheru and Kapitein Kahega Kimani of Location 2, in his report of 17–21 February 1948; and on Assistant Agricultural Instructors Ngunjiri Kibugu, Macharia and Grishon of Location 8, in his report dated 2–6 March 1948.

58. KNA MAA 8/106, 'Intelligence and Security: Mumenyereri, 1947–50', C. Penfold to P. Wyn Harris, 16 and 27 October 1947; and Secretariat 1/12/8, 'Labour Unrest: Intelligence Reports, Central Province, 1947', Provincial Intelligence Report no. 2, 1947, 18 March 1947.
59. KNA Ag 4/410, 'Central Province and Districts: Annual Agricultural Reports, 1952', L.H. Brown's Central Province report. By 1952 the number of European agricultural staff consisted of one Provincial Agricultural Officer, two Assistants, nine District Agricultural Officers, and 32 Assistant Agricultural Officers. There were also four African Assistant Agricultural Officers, 734 Agricultural Instructors, 484 Assistant Agricultural Instructors and 121 Produce Inspectors.
60. KNA DC/NYI 2/1/16, 'Development and Welfare Planning, 1944–48', R. Daubney, Director of Veterinary Services, 'Post-War Development for the Veterinary Department', 22 August 1944; and Ag 4/107, 'Veterinary Department: Annual Reports, 1940–53', *passim*.
61. KNA Ag 4/451, 'Fort Hall Safari Diaries, 1948–51', C.D. Knight's report of his tour through Location 5, 20–23 January 1948 and his report on Location 2 for comments on the extensive farming activities of the Kikuyu Central Association activist, Petro Njuguna, who grew mulberries, raspberries, figs, avocado pears, mangos, custard apples, Cape tomatoes, plums, peaches and apples for the Nairobi market.
62. KNA Ag 4/102, 'Veterinary Monthly Reports: Central Province, 1943–50', A.E. Dorman to F.W. Ashton, 'Veterinary Handing Over Report, Nyeri', 11 November 1946; and F.W. Ashton's report, March 1947; and Ag 4/107, 'Veterinary Department: Annual Reports, 1940–53', F.W. Ashton's 'Nyeri Annual Report, 1946'; R.A. Hammond's 'Central Province Annual Report, 1945', N. King's 'Nyeri Annual Report 1949' and A.E. Dorman's 'Nyeri Annual Report, 1951'.
63. KNA Ag 4/113, 'South Nyeri: Monthly Agricultural Reports, 1938–49', *passim*; and African Land Development in Kenya 1946–55: Report by the African Land Development Board, pp. 81–2.
64. KNA Ag 4/502, 'Annual Agricultural Reports: Central Province, 1942–55', C.D. Knight's estimates of agricultural income per taxpayer, 15 April 1953. Contrast the estimates from Embu, Machakos, Nyeri and Kiambu with L.H. Brown's target of £100 in 'Agricultural Education Report, Fort Hall', 29 December 1952; and Ag 4/410, 'Central Province and Districts: Annual Agricultural Reports, 1952', L.H. Brown's Central Province report.
65. KNA Ag 4/410, 'Central Province and Districts: Annual Agricultural Reports, 1952', L.H. Brown's Central Province report, especially the section on Agricultural Betterment Funds.
66. KNA DC/FH 1/26, 'Fort Hall Annual Report, 1947', pp. 1–6, 15; DC/FH 1/27, 'Fort Hall Annual Report, 1948', pp. 4–5, 11, 12, MAA 8/68, 'Chief Waruhiu, 1948–52', *passim*; and Ag 4/410, 'Central Province and Districts: Annual Agricultural Reports, 1952', G. Gamble's Nyeri District report.

Ten

The Drift to Mau Mau

By 1950 rumours of a subversive organisation called 'Mau Mau' and reports of secret oathing ceremonies had begun to disturb the field administration in the Kikuyu reserves and the White Highlands. The millenarian sects became more and more vociferous and anti-European, while attacks on chiefs and agricultural instructors, which had declined since the peasant revolt, increased in frequency until the Othaya Division of Nyeri was virtually abandoned. Settler cattle were maimed and crops set on fire. In January and February 1952, for example, there were numerous cases of arson in Nyeri, both in the reserve and on the neighbouring European farms, until a collective fine of £2,500 was imposed on the local Kikuyu.[1] Settler farms in Timau were attacked and barns destroyed. Indeed, during the royal visit to Nanyuki on 7 February 1952, five grass fires could be seen. During the next five weeks another 58 fires were started around Nanyuki and thousands of acres of grazing were destroyed. A Turkana herdsman, who had worked in the area for 25 years, reported that 'I have never before seen fires like this year. I am getting very frightened, as I know these fires are the work of Mau Mau who have come here to destroy the white man'.[2] Meanwhile, in Murang'a James Beauttah resumed his campaign against the chiefs and disrupted the anti-rinderpest campaign, while hundreds of women from seven locations destroyed eleven cattle crushes in November 1951. Eventually 500 of them were arrested and many were sent to prison. In February 1952, Beauttah, Andrew Ng'ang'a and the Rev. Petro Kigondo, the leader of the independent churches in Murang'a, were all sentenced to two years hard labour for their part in the troubles. Order was only restored in Locations 6 and 7, the centre of the demonstrations, with the arrival of a large police levy.[3]

Mitchell and the myth of multiracialism

Despite this mounting violence. Mitchell remained confident until the end of his governorship on 21 June 1952 that his policies would succeed. He was not alone in this view. Although he was soon to be bitterly criticised for his failure to take action against Mau Mau, on the day of his retirement the *East African Standard* praised him for having been an able governor who had resolutely tackled the problems of African agriculture created by the 'ignorant man and his wife with a hoe' and for having reduced the threat of land degradation. The editorial concluded by saying that Mitchell 'has left not all the answers, but the wisdom and the thought and the high example which will give him his well-earned place in the historian's record as the most able public servant and personal influence in the remarkable story of East African progress'.[4]

This high praise did not, however, survive for long the deteriorating situation in the reserves and on European farms. On 10 July, Michael Blundell, the new leader of the European Elected Members demanded that the government arrest Kenyatta and declare a state of Emergency. There was, he warned, a 'subversive organization which is like a disease, spreading through the Colony, and the leaders have a target, and that target is the overthrowing of the Government, and my information leads me to believe that target may well be within nine months'.[5] Four days later the Commissioner of Police forwarded a long memorandum to the Secretariat on 'Kikuyu Political Activity'. It was the second attempt by the police to warn that the reserves were getting out of control. Violence had reached such a level, Police Commissioner O'Rorke observed, that it could not be dismissed as:

> . . . one of their periodical manifestations of discontent . . . (but) something far more dangerous to the peace and good order of the Colony. I am forced to the conclusion . . . that something in the nature of a general revolt among the Kikuyu people against European settlement and the policy of Government has been planned and that the plan has already begun to be put into effect.[6]

The Commissioner also reported that there had been a mass oathing ceremony in Nairobi, which had been attended by over 800 people. He suggested that the Mau Mau oath had become a killing oath, directed against Europeans and loyalists. Within three weeks of Mitchell's departure, therefore, a mass of evidence was presented to the Secretariat warning it of the serious situation among the Kikuyu and of the prospect of an imminent revolt. Why had Mitchell failed to take resolute action; was it from ignorance or from a willfull refusal to accept the evidence presented to him by the field administration?

Most informed opinion had been unhappy about the deteriorating situation for some time. The *Kenya Weekly News*, which reflected opinion among the settler farmers in the White Highlands, categorically refuted the governor's optimistic assessment. His statement, it observed, 'must have surprised many who read it. In truth, the political situation is now more disturbing and the prospect more anxious than it has been since 1936'.[7] Many settlers shared the paper's view. At an election meeting at Londiani, Hubert Buxton, a retired District Commissioner, warned that virtually the whole Kikuyu tribe had been 'contaminated' with Mau Mau. Wilfred Havelock, the Legislative Councillor for Kiambu, shortly afterwards led a delegation of Thika settlers to see O'Rorke, the Commissioner of Police, and the member for Law and Order, Whyatt, They left extremely dissatisfied with Whyatt's refusal to detain suspected Mau Mau leaders and with O'Rorke's assertion that they were being alarmist since at the most, only 10 per cent of Kikuyu had taken any Mau Mau oaths.[8]

The settlers and many members of the administration, by early 1952, were already seriously dissatisfied with the attitude of the member for Law and Order. Whyatt's legal duties as Attorney General hampered his effectiveness as the enforcer of public order. He not only was responsible for drafting the law but also acted as the Director of Public Prosecutions, deciding which cases should be brought to court. As such, his primary function was as guardian of the law rather than as defender of public order and security.[9]

Until the declaration of Emergency on 20 October 1952, Mitchell continued to insist that Kenya was more peaceful than ever before and that the policy of multiracialism was beginning to work.[10] An African élite was emerging, which could one day play a prominent role in the political and economic life of the colony in collaboration with the settlers. Although exhausted, Mitchell clung to office until after the royal visit to Kenya in February 1952, which was to be his great moment. He could ill afford to have this cancelled because of rumours of Kikuyu unrest. To the end Mitchell hoodwinked the Colonial Office with his optimistic declarations into thinking that his government had tackled the problems of land degradation in the reserves, squatters in the White Highlands and the urban housing shortage. Mitchell, of course, astutely informed Whitehall that many problems remained unsolved, but definitely indicated that Kenya was now on course to become a contented multiracial society. Constitutional African politicians, for example, were being incorporated at the centre, where there were now four African Legislative Councillors, and into the reorganised African district councils, which had been granted new powers, in the localities. These men, Mitchell hoped, would soon replace the discredited Kenyatta and the self-serving agitators in the Kikuyu Central Association, who, he thought, were behind the discontent. He sincerely believed they had little popular support.[11]

Why did Mitchell reach these conclusions and inform the Colonial Office that all was well in Kenya? Was he shielded from the truth by his admirers in the Secretariat failing to forward unpalatable district reports which contradicted his hopes of a contented multiracial Kenya, or was the mentally-exhausted governor simply refusing to accept reports of increasing Mau Mau activity? The reason probably lay somewhere in between these two explanations. Isolated in Nairobi, the senior officers in the Secretariat (who after Wyn Harris's departure were not Kikuyu exprts) failed to recognise the seriousness of the threat to colonial rule which was developing in the Kikuyu reserves, in the White Highlands and in the African locations of Nairobi. They therefore suppressed or played down the field administration's reports of trouble to avoid offending Mitchell and to shield him from his critics, Clarence Buxton and S.V. Cooke.[12] Whatever the case, the conspiracy of silence in the Secretariat strengthened the governor's reluctance to heed advice. Mitchell was an opinionated man and refused to recognise that a Kikuyu rebellion was imminent. Determined to end his career on a triumphal note, he subconsciously refused to accept that his eight years in Nairobi were ending in the collapse of the colonial state.[13]

The Secretariat, however, was equally responsible for the failure to move against Mau Mau. Rankine, Davies and Whyatt lacked the courage to go behind Mitchell's back and to warn the Colonial Office of the seriousness of the situation. All three were cautious time-servers unwilling to risk their careers. Mitchell had got rid of the only man in the Secretariat who had consistently stood up to him, Wyn Harris. First as Labour Commissioner, then as Provincial Commissioner in Central Province, and finally as Chief Native Commissioner, Wyn Harris had refused to be intimidated or to conceal unpleasant truths. He was, therefore, promoted out of the way to the governorship of the Gambia in 1949. His successor, Eric Davies, was an unimaginative colonial administrator, unable to adapt to the Colonial Office's strategy of incorporating African politicians into the policy-making process. Thus, whereas Wyn Harris had liked Kenyatta, whom he recognised as a political pragmatist trying to control the various political factions inside the Kenya African Union and to unite the constitutionalists and the militants, Davies only saw him as an extremist agitator and failed to appreciate that Kenyatta was a subtle political operator. Unlike Wyn Harris, he failed to realise that Kenyatta should not be judged too harshly as he needed room to manoeuvre politically to reconcile the rival factions inside the Kenya African Union, not to mention the trades unions and the Mau Mau Central Committee, the *Muhimu*.[14]

Shortly after Wyn Harris's departure, the liberal wing in the Secretariat suffered a second blow when Cecil Penfold was promoted from the post of Director of Intelligence and Security in 1950. The new director, who came from the Gold Coast, lacked his predecessor's understanding of the complexities of Kenya African politics, which was based upon twenty years of work in the colony and five years as Director of Intelligence. Penfold had acquired a sophisticated knowledge of the rivalries in the Kenya African Union and in the trades unions.[15] Unlike the field administration, which received most of its information from chiefs wanting to discredit African politicians who threatened their authority, the Special Branch had its own independent network of informers and received hundreds of detailed reports from its agents, who had penetrated into the inner councils of the Kenya African Union. There was, for example, a police informer inside the *Muhimu* until his cover was blown by an unsuccessful police raid on Senior Chief Koinange's home at Banana Hill, where they had expected to discover members of the *Muhimu* assembled for one of the early oathing ceremonies.[16] The new director lacked Penfold's ability and was unable to stand up to the field administration's simplistic interpretation of African politics. Unlike the Special Branch, most District Commissioners had little understanding of Kenyatta's moderating influence upon the Kikuyu militants. Instead they stigmatised the Kenya African Union as a subterfuge behind which Mau Mau operated.[17]

Windley, the Provincial Commissioner in Central Province, for example, denounced the Kenya African Union during his opening speech to an agricultural conference organised for primary-school teachers. 'The Kenya African Union and Mau Mau', he declared, 'were synonymous terms for the evil influence which was undermining the social structure and initiating a rule of force by gangs of thugs'. Coutts's reaction was symptomatic of the inability of the field administration and the Secretariat to adjust to the abrasive criticism of the post-war generation of African politicians. Most District Commissioners regarded all political activity as subversive and dismissed African politicians as agitators, whom they saw as undermining the government's authority and outside the accepted limits of political life in colonial Kenya. Coutts, for example, who had been a liberal himself when first appointed District Commissioner in Murang'a just before the peasant revolt in 1947, had never forgiven Kenyatta for his speech against compulsory female labour, which had destroyed the *ngwatio* terracing campaign in the district.[18]

When Eliud Mathu, Thuku and Senior Chief Waruhiu organised an anti-Mau Mau campaign in Kiambu, which culminated in a meeting at Kiambu township attended by 30,000 people, Kenyatta, ex-Senior Chief Koinange and James Gichuru, the former President of the Kenya African Union who had recently been appointed a chief in the area, had all been present. Yet, despite Kenyatta's denunciation of violence and warning that it would prejudice the newly-appointed Royal Commission, the field administration refused to believe in his sincerity. It complained that speeches by Kenyatta, as well as those of Chiefs Koinange and Gichuru, had been politically ambiguous and cleverly constructed to avoid any outright denunciation of Mau Mau. This was probably true, but their caution stemmed as much from fear of assassination by Mau Mau as from passive support for the movement. For any of them to condemn Mau Mau would have dealt it a major blow. They were therefore under intense pressure to moderate their attacks, Kenyatta having been warned that an outright condemnation would bring a swift response from the militants and would not be tolerated. In fact Kenyatta went as far as he dared to satisfy the authorities; if he was to retain any influence over the militants he could not go as far in his denunciations of Mau Mau as the administration wanted. In private he informed Kennaway, the District Commissioner in Kiambu, that he had little influence over the radicals and warned him that if the government banned Kenya African Union meetings following the great rally in Nyeri in July, it would play into the hands of the extremists and weaken the restraining influence of the moderates. The administration, however, ignored these warnings.[19]

The Government's response

Faced with mounting criticisms from the press and settler politicians and by even more disturbing reports from the field administration, the Secretariat began to take Mau Mau seriously in July 1952. Following Blundell's warning in the Legislative Council and O'Rorke's report, the acting Chief Secretary convened a meeting to consider the situation as outlined in the Police Commissioner's report of 29 July. The Member for Law and Order, the Chief Native Comissioner, all the Provincial Commissioners and several other senior officials were present, but neither O'Rorke nor the Director of Intelligence and Security were invited to attend, since 'matters of higher policy, which would be discussed, were not the concern of the police'. Thus the administration's prejudice against the police prevented the Secretariat from consulting the Special Branch about the political divisions inside the Kenya African Union.[20]

Berman has rightly criticised the field administration for 'a preoccupation with technique over the substance of policy and by an absorption in the exigencies of short-run control'.[21] This meeting clearly revealed that even the Kenyan Secretariat had failed to recognise that the collaborative base of the state would have to be broadened to include the proto-capitalists, who supported Kenyatta's faction in the Kenya African Union, if the colonial régime was to withstand the strains of the post-war era, and its increasing demands upon the African peasantry. Eric Davies's attitude typified the limited understanding of the political situation on the part of even the higher echelons of the Secretariat. The Chief Native Commissioner did not recognise that Kenyatta was a moderate: a constitutionalist, albeit of an unorthodox variety, who was waiting to be recruited as a new collaborator in the colonial order. Davies never got beyond denouncing him as the evil genius behind Mau Mau. He declared that:

> Although there was as yet no concrete evidence to prove that Jomo Kenyatta was behind the Mau Mau movement, there was every reason to believe that he was one of the leaders of this society. This conviction was strengthened by the fact that Mau Mau activities increased sharply in areas which he visited, and also by the display of Mau Mau emblems on the platform from which he addressed a crowd of 20,000 at Nyeri on 26 July. Moreover, all efforts to persuade him to publicly denounce the society had failed and there could therefore be no doubt that he intended to pursue his hundred per cent programme, which was designed to secure the eviction of the European Government and Settlement from Kenya.[22]

But apart from such assertions, the Chief Native Commissioner could not provide any evidence to link Kenyatta with Mau Mau. The member for Law and Order insisted that there was insufficient evidence to convict Kenyatta and refused to detain him and his lieutenants under the Deportation (Immigrant British Subjects) Ordinance. When they met again to discuss the question four weeks later on 17 August, Davies and Whyatt still could not agree. While the Chief Native Commissioner insisted that 'the utmost should be done to have Jomo Kenyatta put away by some means or other under the present law', the member for Law and Order remained adamant that this was impossible. He resisted any suggestion that the Emergency Powers Ordinance should be invoked since 'there was, in fact, no Emergency, and the measure at this time was unncessary'.[23]

While these discussions were under way Potter, the acting governor who had only recently arrived from Uganda where he had been Chief Secretary, received two delegations from the European members of the Legislative Council on 8 and 18 August. They urged that emergency powers should be taken in Kikuyuland and that the leaders of the Kenya African Union should be arrested. They also demanded that the British government should make it quite clear that Kenya could not follow the Gold Coast's path to African majority internal self-government. Potter rejected these demands and observed that although the situation in Central Province was grave, it did not yet warrant declaring a state of Emergency. The Kenyan government would not stifle the emergence of African nationalism, but would seek to divert it towards accepting multi-racialism. Both the British and Kenyan governments would, he promised, ensure that the European community retained an important role in the Kenya of the future.

John Whyatt, the Attorney General, who came in for much criticism at these meetings, forwarded a dramatic account of the proceedings to the Colonial Office. He observed:

> I have been present on one or two occasions in other Colonies when the Governor has received a deputation but I have never seen the like of this one before. All the European Elected Members (with two exceptions) rolled up at Government House in their cars and seated themselves at the long table in the Executive Council room facing Potter, the Commissioner of Police and myself. They then proceeded to state their views, Blundell acting for the most part as spokesman though the others joined in from time to time. When I say that they put forward their views, that is an understatement; it would be more correct to describe them as being in the nature of 'demands'; and as I sat there listening to them the thought flashed through my mind, 'This must be what it is like to be present at a coup d'etat'.[24]

The settlers demanded the immediate proclamation of a state of Emergency in the Kikuyu areas, the detention without trial of all 'political agitators', the appointment of a Commander-in-Chief (like General Briggs in Malaya) to supervise the destruction of Mau Mau, and the appointment of a European Elected Member as member for Law and Order forthwith. They also demanded that the Kenyan government issue a statement 'to the effect that African nationalism would not be tolerated' and anyone who remained politically troublesome should automatically be prosecuted for sedition.

The settler associations were restless at the government's inaction. Humphrey Slade, the Legislative Councillor for the Aberdares, and the Provincial Commissioner for the Rift Valley both attended a meeting of the executive committee of the Thomson's Falls Association, where the level of violence had escalated alarmingly. The local District Commissioner had already recommended imposing a collective fine in the Laikipia area to stop cattle maiming and the firing of crops, stopping bus traffic between Laikipia and Kikuyuland, closing the independent schools, which were seen as centres of subversion, and giving the District Commissioner summary powers to hear Mau Mau cases. Following this tense meeting the Provincial Commissioner reported that emergency powers should be taken to arrest all the local malcontents; and on 27 August he imposed a curfew on the Narok Marmanet and Ol Joro Orok wards and on the African locations at Thomson's Falls and Rumuruti.[25]

Meanwhile, Potter had informed the Colonial Office about the deteriorating situation. He warned that the Kenya African Union was simply a front for the subversive activities of Mau Mau. Potter reported:

> The main overt Kikuyu political organization is the Kenya African Union which, while purporting to represent all Africans, does not do so, but is in fact Kikuyu controlled, under the leadership of Jomo Kenyatta . . . The covert organization is the proscribed Mau Mau

secret society, the terms of whose illegal oath include the killing of Europeans when the war horn blows and the rescue of Kenyatta should he ever be arrested, and there need be little doubt, though there is no proof, that he controls this revolutionary organisation in so far as it is still susceptible to control.[26]

Unlike Mitchell and Rankine, Potter was prepared to heed the warnings of the field administration and had taken immediate action to warn the Colonial Office and to regain control in Kikuyuland and the White Highlands. Warnings from the police and the district administration were no longer ignored and even before the new governor, Sir Evelyn Baring, arrived in September, Whitehall had been fully apprised of the situation. Whether Potter and his advisers identified the real leaders of Mau Mau is, however, a different question.[27]

On 9 September, the Commissioner of Prisons was appointed to investigate subversion and the role of the Kikuyu independent schools. He prepared dossiers on leading African politicians suspected of being Mau Mau leaders. By that time the member for Law and Order had finally been persuaded to prepare legislation to restrict movement at night and to license printing presses to reduce the flow of subversive literature. Plans were also prepared to restrict the movement of suspected Mau Mau members. This legislation was forwarded to the Colonial Office and, on 16 September, the member for Law and Order and the Chief Native Commissioner went to London to explain the crisis. On their return, these Ordinances were rushed through a special meeting of the Legislative Council on 23 September and approved by the new governor on 3 October.[28]

When Baring finally arrived on 29 September, he was faced with reports of escalating violence. On 25 September, attacks on European farms in the Timau area, north of Mount Kenya, had reached new heights when four gangs had disembowelled 146 cattle and 380 sheep and set fire to five maize cribs. Baring was immediately given a detailed report on Mau Mau by Eric Davies and within a week of arriving in the colony, began a tour of the trouble areas in Central Province. Shortly after his return to Nairobi, the government's staunchest Kikuyu supporter, Senior Chief Waruhiu of Kiambu, was murdered on his way home from an interview with Baring at Government House.[29] After attending the funeral, Baring informed the Colonial Office that the Kenyan government was facing a planned revolutionary movement, controlled from Nairobi, and that a state of Emergency would have to be declared. The Kenyan government carefully considered the consequences of arresting Kenyatta and other African politicians. It was, they decided, essential to preserve international confidence in the colony's stability and Kenyatta's detention as the leader of Mau Mau would provide the most effective means of reasserting control. They anticipated that there would be violent opposition to his detention, but that this would be a short-term reaction and that, deprived of direction, the Mau Mau movement would quickly disintegrate.[30] In fact, exactly the reverse happened. There was little immediate response to the declaration of the Emergency, but the panic expulsion of thousands of Kikuyu squatters from the White High-lands by the settler-controlled district councils brought thousands of dis-possessed young males with nothing to lose into Central Province, where they joined the landless Kikuyu in the reserves and entered the forests of Mount Kenya and the Aberdares to fight for *Uhuru* and land in the Land and Freedom Army. Once again the administration's advice proved to be dangerously wrong.[31]

Oliver Lyttelton, the Conservative Secretary of State, approved the declaration of the Emergency and the detention of the Kenya African Union's leaders on 14 October 1952. During the next six days careful preparations were made; 'Jock Scott Operation', the code name for the swoop, was timed for midnight on 20 October, by which time a battalion of the Lancashire Fusiliers would have arrived in Nairobi to support the King's African Rifles should there be widespread resistance or an uprising. In the event there was little opposition and by eight o'clock on the morning of 21 October 1952, 186 African politicians and trade unionists, including Kenyatta, Kubai and Kaggia, had been detained. The Mitchell government had failed. Metropolitan resources would now be increasingly needed, not merely to repair the fabric of the Kenyan state but to reconstruct it more radically than ever Mitchell had dared.[32]

Notes

1. KNA DC/FH 1/31, 'Fort Hall Annual Report, 1952', pp. 1–6, 11–18; DC/FH 2/1/4, 'False Prophets: *Watu wa Mungu*, 1934–60', report from the Presbyterian Church of East Africa, Tumutumu, 2 May 1952; Ag 4/410, 'Central Province and Districts: Annual Agricultural Reports, 1952', G. Gamble's Nyeri District report; and *East African Standard*, 26 February 1952.
2. F.D. Corfield, 'Origins and Growth of Mau Mau', pp. 125–6.
3. KNA DC/FH 1/30, 'Fort Hall Annual Report, 1951', pp. 1, 4: Ag 4/107, 'Veterinary Department: Annual Reports, 1940–53' R.D.G. Wachira's Fort Hall Veterinary report, 1951; and MAA 2/5/146, 'Kenya African Union, 1948–52', acting Native Courts Officer to P.E. Mitchell, 16 November 1951; and P.E. Mitchell to O. Lyttelton, 19 November 1951, for evidence of the Kenyan government's exasperation with Beauttah's activities. J. Spencer's *James Beauttah*, pp. 73–6 records Beauttah's account of the events of July 1947 in Murang'a; p. 102–3 suggests that the first oathing cere-mony in Nyeri had been held in February 1947, (Kenyatta, Mbiyu Koinange and Beauttah had been present). The first ceremony in Murang'a was held at Rev. Petro Kigondo's house in July 1947. Kigondo had earlier administered the KCA oath to the

youthful Kenyatta at CMS Pumwani in December 1928. See also D.M. Feldman's thesis, 'Christians and Politicians', pp. 219-20 for details of Kigondo's involvement with the Kikuyu Central Association in the early 1920s when he was the District Commissioner's clerk and a leading businessman in the district. In 1928 Kigondo had been one of the Kikuyu Central Association candidates elected to the Local Native Council before the controversy over female circumcision.

4. Editorial, *East African Standard*, 21 June 1952.
5. Legislative Council Debates, second series, vol. xlviii, 1952, first session, second sitting, 10 July 1952, cols. 172-98; and 11 July 1952, cols. 281-349.
6. M.S. O'Rorke to J. Whyatt, 'Kikuyu Political Activity', 14 July 1952, quoted by F.D. Corfield, 'Origins and Growth of Mau Mau', p. 141.
7. *Kenya Weekly News*, 14 March 1952.
8. RH Mss. Afr. s. 596, Box 38 (A) File 1, 'European Elected Members Association', ff. 53, Kendall Ward's memorandum, 'The Rise of Mau Mau: European Warnings', 17 March 1953; and KNA MAC/KEN 33/1, 'Kenya State of Emergency: Church Missionary Society, Weithaga, Fort Hall, 1947-50', Canon M.G. Capon's reports, and MAC/KEN 33/2, 'Kenya State of Emergency: The Electors Union', Kendall Ward's memorandum, 7 August 1952; and Kendall Ward to M. Blundell, 7 August 1952.
9. F.D. Corfield, 'Origins and Growth of Mau Mau', pp. 32-7.
10. P.E. Mitchell, *The Sunday Times*, 19 October 1952.
11. CO 533/566/8 (1951), 'The Kenya African Union', P.E. Mitchell to J. Griffiths, 3 May 1951; CO 533/543/38086/38 (1949), 'Kikuyu Central Association', P.E. Mitchell to Creech Jones, 28 February 1949; and KNA MAA 2/5/146, 'Kenya African Union, 1948-52', P.E. Mitchell to O. Lyttelton, 19 November 1951.
12. RH Mss. Britt. Emp. s. 390, 'C.E.M. Buxton', Box 3, File 4, ff.1-4, C.E.V. Buxton to P.E. Mitchell, 15 August 1948; and ff. 32-9, C.E.V. Buxton's memoranda about the Emergency, undated, but probably February 1953; RH Afr.s. 596, 'European Elected Members Organisation', Box 38(A), File 1, 'Mau Mau 1947-53', C.E.V. Buxton's memorandum on 'The Kikuyu Association', February 1947; C.E.V. Buxton to Kendall Ward, 22 September 1947; C.E.V. Buxton to P.E. Mitchell, 15 August 1948; Kendall Ward's memorandum, 'The Rise of Mau Mau: European Warnings', 17 March 1953; and KNA MAC/KEN 33/2, 'Kenya State of Emergency: The Electors Union', *passim*: MAA 8/102, 'Intelligence and Security: Miscellaneous Press Cuttings, 1948-50', *East African News Review*, 22 January 1948, for report of S.V. Cooke's speech on African discontent and MAA 8/108, 'Intelligence and Security: Daily Chronicle, 1947-49', 14 January 1948 for Cooke's criticism of the chaos in the Secretariat, See also CO 537/3588/38696 (1947-48), 'Activities of Mathu', S.V. Cooke's speech in the Legislative Council, 9 January 1948.
13. RH Mss. Afr. r. 101, P.E. Mitchell's diaries, *passim*, especially 1 January 1952. Any qualms he felt about the future were blamed upon the poor quality of the European Elected Members and their opposition to multiracialism: see the entry for 31 December 1951. See also *The Sunday Times*, 19 October 1952, and his press statement while in London for King George VI's funeral, 20 February 1952.
14. KNA CS 1/14/14, 'Chief Native Commissioner: Speeches, 1949-52', Notes for collective Punishment Debate, 7 December 1951; CO 537/3646/47272/1 (1948), 'Political Intelligence Reports: East Africa', Kenya Political Summary, September – October 1948, dated 6 December 1948. Contrast Wyn Harris' observations on Kenyatta in CO 537/3591/38733 (1948), 'Petitions to the United Nations', minutes of meeting with Kenyatta, 15 October 1948, with Mitchell's fears in CO 537/4317/14332/10, 'Communism in the Colonies: East Africa', *passim*. For the opinion of an African conservative see KNA MAA 2/5/146, 'Kenya African Union, 1948-52', T. Mbotela to E.R. St. A. Davies, 28 April 1951; and E.H. Windley to E.R. St. A. Davies, 1 September 1951.

15. KNA MAA 8/106, 'Intelligence and Security: Mumenyereri, 1947–50'; MAA 8/102, 'Intelligence and Security: Miscellaneous Press Cuttings, 1948–50'; MAA 8/109, 'Intelligence and Security: African Workers Federation, 1947–48; MAA 8/108, 'Intelligence and Security: Daily Chronicle, 1947–49'; MAA 8/8, 'Intelligence Reports: Confidential Information, 1946–47'; MAA 8/105, 'Intelligence and Security: Radio Posta, 1947–48'; MAA 8/71, 'Communism, 1948–49'; MAA 2/5/146, 'Kenya African Union, 1948–52'; Secretariat 1/12/6, 'Coast Province Labour Unrest: Correspondence, 1947'; and Secretariat 1/12/8, 'Labour Unrest: Intelligence Reports, Central Province, 1947', are the most important Intelligence files which have been consulted and contain many reports by Penfold and his agents. See also CO 537/4336/14335/6 Part ii (1949), 'Colonial Intelligence Summary'; and CO 537/4715/47272/A, 'Political Intelligence Summaries: Kenya'.
16. B. Kaggia, *Roots of Freedom*, p. 10.
17. B.J. Berman, 'Bureaucracy and Incumbent Violence', pp. 147–52, and N.S. Carey Jones, *The Anatomy of Uhuru*, footnote p. 84.
18. KNA Ag 4/410, 'Central Province and Districts: Annual Agricultural Reports, 1952', report of teachers' agricultural training conference, Fort Hall, 1–6 September 1952, and interview with D. O'Hagan, Coutts's predeccessor as District Commissioner in Murang'a, in Nairobi, June 1981. For detailed reports of Kenyatta's speech see KNA Secretariat 1/12/8, 'Labour Unrest: Intelligence Reports, Central Province, 1947', C. Penfold to P. Wyn Harris, 22 and 25 July 1947.
19. F.D. Corfield, 'Origins and Growth of Mau Mau', pp. 152–3; and interview with N.F. Kennaway, the District Commissioner in Kiambu, February 1948 to November 1950, and July 1951 to February 1953, in Nairobi, September 1979. Corfield on pp. 301–8 reprints the report by the Assistant Superintendent of Police, Nyeri, of Kenyatta's mass meeting on 26 July 1952, as a damning indictment of his involvement in Mau Mau. In fact, the report can be read as a valiant attempt by Kenyatta to undermine the power of the militants despite considerable opposition from militants in the audience. This was not the speech of a radical, but of a Kikuyu moderate who wished to avoid a violent confrontation with the authorities. J. Murray-Brown, *Kenyatta*, pp. 290–2, analyses Kenyatta's speech at Kiambu on 24 August 1952. See also Mahtu's warnings in CO 537/3588/38696 (1947–48), 'Activities of Mathu', E.W. Mathu's memorandum, 'The Freedom of Assembly', July 1947.
20. F.D. Corfield, 'Origins and Growth of Mau Mau', p. 143.
21. B.J. Berman, 'Bureaucracy and Incumbent Violence', p. 147.
22. Quoted in F.D. Corfield, 'Origins and Growth of Mau Mau', pp. 142–3.
23. *ibid*, p. 144–5.
24. CO 852/437, 'Proposals to Deal with Disturbances Arising from the Activities of the Mau Mau Secret Society: Kenya', J. Whyatt to P. Rogers, 2 September 1952.
25. *ibid*, pp. 149–50. For details of the subversive activities of the independent schools and churches, see KNA DC/FH 1/31, 'Fort Hall Annual Report, 1952', pp. 11–18; MAA 6/634, 'Intelligence Reports: Central Province, 1948–53; W.H. Cantrell to D. O'Hagan, 'Report on the Position of African Anglican Church Schools and Churches in the Fort Hall District', 15 July 1953; and MAC/KEN 33/1, 'Kenya State of Emergency: Church Missionary Society, Weithaga, Fort Hall, 1947–50', Canon M.G. Capon's reports to the Church Missionary Society headquarters, London, September 1949 – August 1950, and September 1950 – August 1951; and the report of the Fact Finding Committee on Independent Schools and Churches of the Standing Committee of Synod, March 1950; and Rev. N. Langford-Smith to Synod, June 1950.
26. H.S. Potter to P. Rogers, Colonial Office, 17 August 1952, quoted in F.D. Corfield, 'Origins and Growth of Mau Mau', pp. 150–1. For similar warnings see KNA MAC/KEN/33/1, 'Kenya State of Emergency: Church Missionary Society, Weithaga, Fort Hall, 1947–50', *passim*; and RH Mss. Afr.s. 596, 'European Members Organi-

sation', Box 38(A), File 1, ff. 18, Canon M.G. Capon's interview with the African Affairs' Commitee of the Electors' Union, 5 March 1948; Major C.E.V. Buxton to P.E. Mitchell, 15 August 1948; and Kendall Ward's memorandum on 'The Rise of Mau Mau: European Warnings', 17 March 1953.

27. H.S. Potter to P. Rogers, 17 August 1952, quoted in F.D. Corfield, 'Origins and Growth of Mau Mau', pp. 150–1, 153–4.

28. F.D. Corfield, 'Origins and Growth of Mau Mau', p. 154. The independent schools in Murang'a were particularly associated with the political militants, see KNA DC/FH 1/31, 'Fort Hall Annual Report, 1952', pp. 11–18; and MAA 7/634, 'Intelligence Reports: Central Province, 1948–53', W.H. Cantrell to D. O'Hagan, 15 July 1953. DC/FH 1/29, 'Fort Hall Annual Report, 1950', pp. 15–21; and DC/FH 1/30, 'Fort Hall Annual Report, 1951', pp. 14–16, provide insights into the estrangement between the field administration and the independent schools in the district, and report the victory of the militants, led by Ndegwa Metho, over the more moderate Paulo Mungai, who was eventually appointed chief of location 4 in 1951. See also F.D. Corfield, 'Origins and Growth of Mau Mau', p. 154.

29. J. Murray-Brown, *Kenyatta*, pp. 294–5; F.D. Corfield, 'Origins and Growth of Mau Mau', pp. 157–8; and KNA DC/KBU 1/43, 'Kiambu District Annual Report, 1952', p. 2.

30. C.G. Rosberg and J. Nottingham, *The Myth of Mau Mau*, pp. 276–9; and R. Buijtenhuijs, *Essays on Mau Mau*, pp. 35–45. For the opinion of one militant see M. Mathu, *The Urban Guerrilla*, p. 17. See also L.S.B. Leakey, *Defeating Mau Mau*, p. 108; and B.J. Berman, 'Bureaucracy and Incumbent Violence', p. 170. Berman concluded that 'while small numbers of Kikuyu began to move into the forests on the fringes of the reserves as early as July and August 1952 in response to the demands being made by Europeans for a state of emergency, the underground movement posessed neither coherent plans, organization or training for guerilla combat nor a significant stockpile of modern arms. Moreover, the arrest of the Emergency largely decapitated the movement, depriving it of virtually all of its educated top leaders, and left the situation in the hands of local leaders and the rank and file. It was not until the early months of 1953 that the bands in the forests were sufficiently organized to resist the colonial security forces which had invested the Kikuyu reserves . . . The Emergency, in reality, was a pre-emptive attack, carried out by the incumbent colonial authorities against a significant segment of the African political leadership of Kenya and its supporters'.

31. A. Thurston's draft manuscript, 'Intensification of Smallholder Agriculture in Kenya', pp. 105–7. See also R. Buijtenhuijs, *Essays on Mau Mau*, p. 41, for interesting observations on the role of squatters from Nyeri in Laikipia, and the introduction of oathing in these areas.

32. F.D. Corfield, 'Origins and Growth of Mau Mau', pp. 159–61; and B. Kaggia, *Roots of Freedom*, pp. 116–19, for an account of what happened on 20 October by one of the Mau Mau *Muhimu*.

Eleven

Conclusion

At the end of the war the Kenyan government faced three crucial problems: agricultural reform in Kikuyuland, the squatters, and the urban problems of African Nairobi. As we have seen, the government quickly abandoned Whitehall's strategic goals for mere tactical survival. Survivors from the era of indirect rule could not adjust intellectually to the subversive ideas emanating from Whitehall. Ronald Robinson's 'moral disarmament of African Empire' had not diminished their belief that African self-government was centuries rather than decades away.[1] Whereas Whitehall wanted to incorporate and secure the collaboration of educated Africans through training in local government and then to devolve power at the centre, the field administration remained committed to its allies, the chiefs, even although indirect rule had always been applied half-heartedly in Kenya. It was the field administration and the chiefs, however, who had to implement Whitehall's plans. This was the fundamental flaw in the Colonial Office's grand design; it could command but it could never guarantee that its orders would be obeyed. With Mitchell's support, these men on the spot effectively determined the pace of change and controlled the flow of information to London.[2]

Mitchell's 40 years as a colonial administrator in East Africa proved a handicap rather than the asset Whitehall had expected. His earlier career had never exposed him to the problems of African nationalism he had to face in Kenya. Some exposure to the more radical politics of West Africa would have provided him with a more useful experience for post-war Kenya than having dealt with the supine Tanganyika African Association.[3] The Colonial Office, in contrast, had perforce to deal with this assertive populist nationalism and to incorporate its leaders. After the war, Britain's African collaborators were under attack from their people. In East and Central Africa, however, the search for new allies was not as imperative as in the West, since the colonial state could depend upon settler support. But in the new international climate settler political ambitions were an embarrassment and, in East Africa, Uganda had demonstrated that peasant producers could serve Britain's purposes more cost effectively than European farmers if a reliable group of African collaborators could be found.[4]

Such subversive thoughts had already begun to cross the official mind in Whitehall during the Attlee government. Although Creech Jones's beliefs became somewhat tarnished after he became Secretary of State in October 1946, this was perhaps more because of pressure from senior Cabinet colleagues, who simply wanted to use the colonies to finance Britain's trade deficit with the United States and to use colonial resources to rebuild the British economy, than because he was captured by the Colonial Office. It could equally be argued that Hinden's Fabian strategy swept through the Colonial Office between 1945 and 1950 and captured the official mind. Certainly Andrew Cohen shared most of Creech Jones's and Hinden's ideals.[5]

Mitchell and the field administration in Kenya, in contrast, failed to adapt to post-war circumstances and to the growth of African politics. Kenyatta was quite unlike any other African they had met; he was an educated, devious, professional politician, whom Creech Jones and Hinden knew better than most administrators. Kenyatta was also a spellbinding orator with complete control over his Kikuyu audiences. Mitchell, the paternalist indirect ruler, was completely unqualified to deal with such a rousing nationalist leader, who proved to be a much more subtle politician than the settlers.[6]

The Kenyan administration's ultimate failure, therefore, should be set against the transformed political scene in Kenya and in Whitehall. By 1947, the government's paternalist policies had virtually collapsed amidst widspread African opposition. For the last five years of Mitchell's governorship, the Kenyan state drifted aimlessly while the field administration and agricultural department fought over what direction the second colonial occupation should take in the reserves, and the settler district councils and the labour department were locked in conflict over the squatters' fate. Moreover, little attempt was made to reassert control over African Nairobi or to tackle the capital's acute housing shortage. Kenya's industrial policy discriminated against local Asian entrepreneurs, who might have created jobs, and vainly concentrated upon attracting international capital to invest in the new industrial area near the railway station. These international corporations, however, were only interested in investing in Kenya because of the colony's low wages. Low wages, however, prevented the stabilisation of the labour-force and the creation of a pool of skilled manpower. This economic strategy failed to produce any industrial 'take-off' or to ease the plight of 'outcast Nairobi'. Between 1945 and 1952 the city nevertheless attracted peasants from the reserves and dispossessed squatters, who joined the growing number of unemployed and destitute, depressing wages further and exacerbating Nairobi's social problems.[7]

Agricultural policy in Kikuyuland and the failure of incorporation

The government, encouraged by Humphrey and Lambert, moved against the proto-capitalists in 1945. It discovered that although it had been relatively easy to encourage African production during the depression and the war, it was impossible to staunch the flow. In post-war Kenya, the administration's paternalist policies and opposition to the peasant option quickly alienated the Kikuyu and drove them into the arms of the African politicians. By attempting to restrain and, indeed, to reverse the process of African accumulation, which had been let loose in the 1930s, the administration spurned the advances of the aspiring traders and commercial farmers, who in the first years of Mitchell's governorship had tried extremely hard to break into the magic circle, with its access to government patronage. Just when incorporation had seemed about to be attained, they were blocked by an alliance between the district administration, the settlers and the chiefs.

The administration saw these proto-capitalists as a threat to its continued control of rural Africa. It also feared that economic individualism would have disastrous ecological consequences and result in the dispossession of *ahoi* and other junior lineages from the *mbari*, which would shatter the social fabric of Kikuyuland. Humphrey's alarmist report on the situation in Nyeri had provided the administration with justification for its atavistic attack on the Kikuyu proto-capitalists.[8]

The settlers and chiefs had less altruistic motives. They saw the large-scale wattle and maize cultivators as a threat not to the social equilibrium of the reserves, but to their own privileged position. The settlers recognised that Kikuyu cultivators in the reserves and squatters in the White Highlands posed a serious challenge to their economic hegemony and that Africans could produce high-standard cash crops with less state support than many settlers. Moreover, if the settlers' economic primacy were questioned, their wartime political advances would disappear. The Kikuyu chiefs were equally hard-headed about the challenge to their power from the Kenya African Union. Their economic advantages over the alternative élite depended on the continued domination of the Local Native Councils by the chiefs and their clients. If this were broken and members of the alternative élite, like Beauttah and Ng'ang'a, were allowed some government patronage, then they would soon be able to mount a challenge to the established economic power of the chiefs. Thus, while the settlers were using their strong economic position to defend their wartime political gains, the chiefs, even more successfully, used their privileged political access to the district administration to bolster their economic dominance and to exclude the challengers, who attempted to use the Kenya African Union as a battering ram to gain incorporation into the colonial state.[9]

While the colonial state in West Africa was, therefore, at Whitehall's insistence, being weaned from its dependence on the chiefs and, in the Gold Coast and Southern Nigeria, induced to allow greater participation by the educated alternative élite and, in the last analysis, was even willing to incorporate the radicals of the Convention People's Party once they had demonstrated they had popular support, in Kenya the government responded to the 1947 crises by rushing to prop up the faltering authority of the chiefs. Indeed, when the struggle was at its fiercest, in the Kikuyu reserves during the peasant revolt, the Kenya African Union irreparably damaged its chances of incorporation because of its confrontation with the chiefs over terracing and was discredited in the eyes of the government.[10] Without the ability to mobilise sustained support even in Kikuyuland, the Kenya African Union was unable to force the authorities to abandon the chiefs, or more importantly the settlers, who controlled the political 'levers' the African politicians were denied. Unlike Nkrumah or the Kenyan settlers, Kenyatta could not translate political discontent into seats on the Legislative Council. Thus, instead of destroying the chiefs, the agricultural disturbances of 1947 cemented their alliance with the government.[11]

By 1947, the government's agricultural strategy had disintegrated. District Commissioners and agricultural officers could no longer take solace from the governor's persistent declarations that all was well and that Kenya was gradually becoming a multiracial society in which educated Africans could participate in the economic, political and social life of the colony. These men in the districts knew that this was palpably untrue and that frustration, especially amongst the Kikuyu, was threatening to erupt into violence.[12] The agricultural campaign, with its compulsory communal terracing two mornings per week, had provided the Nairobi militants with a ready-made constituency with which to challenge the African moderates' rural power base. Even by 1952, the benefits of the agricultural department's new strategy of encouraging peasant cash-crop production had not yet filtered down, while terracing continued unabated and the various agricultural regulations were enforced with even greater intensity as the number of European specialists in the technical departments grew to supervise this second colonial occupation. In his discussion of the origins of decolonisation, Ronald Robinson perceptively noted that the 'nationalists had to contrive a situation in which their rulers ran out of collaborators'.[13] The agricultural campaign in Kikuyuland had made this task easy by undermining the authority of the chiefs. But the moderates had lost control of the campaign to the militants who were not afraid of provoking the colonial régime, while the proto-capitalists had begun to draw back from a violent confrontation. Equally many poor peasants recognised that their interests were not the same as those of the alternative élite, who merely wanted to gain recognition from the district administration and a share in local patronage. Indeed, many of the proto-capitalists in the Kenya African Union were themselves seizing the land of the poor or former *ahoi* and were asserting private land rights over the commonage.[14]

The struggle in the reserves, therefore, was not simply a two-way contest between the loyalists and the alternative élite, but also included the mass of Kikuyu peasants, who, after the failure of the anti-terracing campaign in 1947, began to desert the proto-capitalists and to turn to the militants who had close ties with Nairobi. It was therefore extremely difficult for Kenyatta and his associates to translate the anti-colonial nationalism of the small modern élite 'into broader terms of indigenous, neo-traditional politics . . . [so that] it could challenge and overthrow the imperial collaborative system and set up a rival system of non-collaboration', as Ronald Robinson postulated. Instead, the rural radicals formed an alliance with the urban activists who wanted not to be incorporated into the colonial state but to destroy it. Increasingly the African moderates were squeezed between the chiefly establishment and the urban *nihilists* and could exercise little influence over the course of events, which escalated into violent conflict.[15]

The fate of the Kikuyu squatters

By 1952 the government's policies had also collapsed in the Rift Valley, where the settler-controlled district councils were allowed to rush ahead with their anti-squatter policies and to reduce squatter cultivation and stock rights, regardless of the effects upon the food supplies and incomes of squatter families. Despite warnings from the labour department and the administration in the surrounding reserves that the district councils were going too far too fast, the Secretariat refused to intervene and allowed the settlers to obstruct the labour department's attempts to devise a policy that would gradually, over the course of a generation, transform squatters into wage labourers. Yet, despite the provocative behaviour of the district councils, the mass expulsion of squatters from the White Highlands and Olenguruone was, in itself, insufficient to precipitate a major revolt. Squatter discontent was only one of several ingredients in Mau Mau.

Ranger has pointed out that 300,000 Ndebele squatters were moved from European estates in Matabeleland under the Land Apportionment Act in the late 1940s and early 1950s, which was far more than the number of Kikuyu affected by district council orders in Kenya.[16] In Kikuyuland, however, land was a scarce resource and when the dispossessed squatters returned to the reserves they discovered that their *githaka* land rights had been reapportioned among the senior lineage of the *mbari*. It was, therefore, impossible for the squatters to be reabsorbed into the Kikuyu reserves, where social divisions, based primarily on restricted access to land, were already causing conflict. The former squatters, therefore, could not be co-opted by the chiefs and the *mbari* leadership as a new group of dependents. Instead, they clashed with the rural landowners, intensified social tensions, and became a rural 'proletariat', denied access to land except as wage labourers for the African accumulators of the established élite around the chiefs and their rivals in the Kenya African Union.[17]

In contrast, Kalenjin squatters were able to fit back into life in the reserves. As Tabitha Kanogo shows, most squatters in western Kenya had not irreparably cut themselves off from their relations in the African Land Units.[18] They regarded squatting more as a form of migrant labour than as an opportunity to continue the peasant option on settler farms, away from the overcrowded reserves. The Kikuyu risked much more with the squatter option and, when their comparatively prosperous existence was curtailed after the war, their resentment was much greater than among the Kalenjin and Abaluhya.[19]

The response of the squatters in the Nyanza, Trans Nzoia and Uasin Gishu districts was also less militant because the settler alliance of anti-squatter forces had dissolved. The settler maize and wheat farmers and the plantation interests had delayed moves against the squatters until 1947 or 1948, by which time squatter resistance in Naivasha and the Aberdares had already been defeated. The western Kenyan district councils, disturbed by the conflict in the Kikuyu squatter areas, had therefore moved with great caution. Another crucial factor was that in the west, where the Kikuyu comprised only a small proportion of the squatter population, most of whom were Abaluhya, Nandi or Elgeyo, the majority of squatters still had aceess to land in the reserves.[20] These squatters, therefore, were able to challenge a divided settler community, and could shatter the tenuous agreement between the anti-squatter dairy and stock farmers and the apprehensive cereal farmers and the plantation sector by threatening to return to the reserves and thus exacerbate the existing labour shortages. This would have had serious repercussions as the squatters provided over 50 per cent of the local farm labour force and were indispensable during the harvests.[21] Thus, by 1951 the squatters in the three western district council areas had so alarmed the cereal farmers that they had compelled the settler cattle interest to back down and to accept a much more limited and slower reduction of squatter stock and cultivation in exchange for higher wages as the labour department had consistently advocated.

The squatters' access to land in western Kenya had also ensured that, despite the fears of the field administration, for a short time it had been possible to absorb large numbers of squatters and their cattle into the North Nyanza, Nandi and Elgeyo reserves without provoking an ecological crisis. This sojourn in the reserves, however, turned out to be a temporary move and, before the resulting tensions had time to surface, the pressure on the reserves was eased. Following the declaration of the Emergency, the panic-stricken district councils bordering on Central Province quickly expelled their remaining Kikuyu squatters, who were forced to return to Kikuyuland where they joined the Land and Freedom Army in the forests.[22] Western Kenya, however, benefited from the Kikuyu's plight, because this mass expulsion of the Kikuyu enabled Abaluhya, Nandi and Elgeyo squatters to flood back into the White Highlands to fill the deficiencies in farm labour created by the Kikuyus' enforced departure. Mau Mau therefore eased the pressure in the non-Kikuyu reserves and, paradoxically, forestalled the development of potentially militant protest movements, such as Elijah Masinde's *Dini ya Msambwa* among the southern Abaluhya of Bukusu, and helped to ensure that the revolt would remain a purely Kikuyu fight against the British.[23]

Outcast Nairobi

In Nairobi, the militants' control over the locations and shanty towns was virtually absolute; the police seldom ventured into the area after dark. Thousands continued to sleep in the open and to scrounge a meagre living in the informal sector or from crime. The destitute, with nothing to lose, posed the most serious challenge to the government. They looked first to Chege Kibachia and the African Workers' Federation and, after his arrest in August 1947, to Fred Kubai, Bildad Kaggia and Mwangi Macharia for leadership. The Kikuyu, who formed over half the city's total population, were particularly resentful. Many of them had only recently been squeezed off their land by the proto-capitalists or been forced to leave the White Highlands because of the new restrictions on squatters. Nairobi offered them their only refuge. Full of thousands of unemployed vagrants, Nairobi was the centre of militant opposition and provided the required anonymity for the militants to co-ordinate protests in the reserves and the White Highlands and to control the introduction of the Mau Mau oath to unite the Kikuyu against the colonial régime.[24]

The militants suffered a heavy blow with the collapse of the Nairobi general strike in May 1950 and the arrests of Makhan Singh, Fred Kubai and Mwangi Macharia, but they quickly recouped their position because of the intransigence of the City Council and other employers, who dismissed thousands of Kikuyu strikers when they returned to work. This peremptory behaviour bolstered support for the militants when they were at their weakest.[25] During the next few months they reassessed their strategy and, within a year of their defeat by the government, Kubai and Kaggia captured control of the Nairobi branch of the Kenya African Union from Mbotela and the educated élite and began to use it as a power base from which to challenge Kenyatta's control over the nationalist movement and to usurp the position of the aspiring alternative élite, who were Kenyatta's main supporters. Trades union activity, centred around Kubai's semi-skilled followers in the Transport and Allied Workers' Union, became less important as the militants switched to nationalist politics, behind the facade of which they continued their mass oathing campaign, which they expanded beyond Nairobi into the Kikuyu reserves and the White Highlands.[26]

African politics

The Indianists have taught us that the British had little to fear from the politics of the locality.[27] Peasant revolts provided little threat to the stability of the empire provided they were restricted to one region. This was equally true in Africa. The Second World War and the second colonial occupation, however, transformed the scale of African political activity. Local disturbances, such as those in Murang'a during 1947, threatened to engulf neighbouring Kiambu and Nyeri as the effects of peasant protest rippled from one ridge to another. But even more important, as was clearly shown during the general strike of September 1947 in Tanganyika, the roads and the railway provided a trail along which the flame of resistance could travel between the centre and the locality.[28] Once the second colonial occupation had disturbed rural Africa, linkages were quickly established between the reserves and Nairobi as the reverberations of trouble in the districts were registered throughout the colony. Indeed local action was increasingly directed from Nairobi. The capital's taxis and country buses, as well as the railway, provided the arteries along which African politics flowed as urban militants began to organise rural resistance.[29]

Gallagher has described this process in India and West Africa, but the same holds true for Kenya, particularly after the Second World War when African politics began to take over from settler politics as the main cause of government apprehension. He observed:

> In Africa, as in India, much of the impetus behind the mass parties came from the policies of the government itself. It was the government which pushed ahead with economic development; consequently it had to intervene more continuously, more forcefully, inside African society than it had done before . . . The government . . . furnished the structure for mass parties. It produced the grievances; it also provided the way in which these grievances could find a vehicle for their expression. As it busied itself more in the affairs of its subjects, so it had to seek support (or at least acquiescence) from larger numbers of them.

Perforce it had dragged them out of the politics of localities and districts into wider arenas, into the politics of provinces and finally of the nation.[30]

In particular, he pointed out that the weakness in Whitehall's local government strategy, whether as designed by Lord Hailey or later in Cohen's famous despatch of 1947, was that concentration on local institutions did not 'divert attention from the centre . . . Instead it allowed the feared African politician to turn his locality into his bailiwick, and then to bond together one bailiwick with another in wider arenas of political action'.[31]

The Murang'a disturbances of 1947 mark the beginnings of this process in Kenya. The colonial régime could no longer isolate one district from its neighbours. The politically conscious élite seized on local problems to browbeat the field administration by complaining to the Secretariat or Whitehall. Even the Colonial Office did not escape unscathed, for the Russians could be relied upon to give publicity to any attack on British imperialism in the United Nations.[32] Under Kenyatta's leadership, the Kenya African Union mastered these political devices, but, by arousing peasant opposition, played into the arms of the chiefs and militants, for the peasant revolt had simply alienated the government and foreclosed any possibility of co-opting the moderates. Mitchell and the field administration reacted to the peasant revolt by concluding that Kenyatta and the Kenya African Union had shown themselves to be unscrupulous demagogues who refused to work within the limitations of the colonial system and were, therefore, unworthy of patronage. This refusal to incorporate the African proto-capitalists, of course, simply strengthened the influence of the militants who could argue that moderation and constitutional politics had failed to produce any reforms.[33]

This saga was repeated at the district level where the new politicians sought acceptance by the chiefs and district officials. The administration's alliance with the chiefs and traditional elders, however, precluded it from reaching any agreement with these rival elements. Moreover, its commitment to the communalist ideology of organic development and the preservation of 'traditional Africa' hindered it from recognising that the Kenya African Union, rather than the chiefs, now represented African opinion. As the effects of the second colonial occupation penetrated into the maize *shambas*, the stalwart faithfuls of the Kikuyu Central Association and the returned *askari* of a younger generation coalesced to challenge the political and economic power of the chiefs and their clients, whom they denounced as government stooges.[34]

Even in the localities the dimensions of political activity were transformed. Whereas in the 1920s, opposition to the chiefs was manifested through *mbari* solidarity, the second colonial occupation provided the African politicians with an issue around which to mobilise pan-*mbari* opposition and to organise resistance throughout the location and, indeed, the district and province.[35] The second colonial occupation in fact enabled the Kenya African Union to emerge as a nationalist movement, with support throughout the colony, not simply among the Kikuyu in Central Province. Although they remained the most politically conscious group in the movement, Kenyatta ensured that all the main tribes were represented in its leadership. Compared to the Kikuyu Central Association, or Thuku's unsuccessful East African Association, the Kenya African Union was able to tap popular discontent outside Kikuyuland to a much greater degree than any of its predecessors.[36] The confines of tribe were turned into a political resource by men like Beauttah, Awori and Ngei during the Kenya African Union's internal political bargaining. Indeed, tribalism became a tool for the new movement and ceased to be an insurmountable obstacle to nationalist solidarity. But, as Anil Seal has pointed out for India, 'what seems to have decided political choices in the localities was the race for influence, status and resources. In the pursuit of these aims, patrons regimented their clients into factions which jockeyed for position . . . However persuasive the slogans from the top, they can have made little impact upon the unabashed scramblers for advantage at the bottom'. This was equally true in Kenya. The aims of the African élite were never the same as those of the peasantry or urban unemployed.[37]

Some thoughts on Mau Mau

This book is Kikuyu-centric because the Kikuyu bore the brunt of the post-war social engineering, dominated African politics and provided most of Kenya's African traders and commercial farmers. The process of internal social differentiation was more advanced among the Kikuyu than elsewhere in Kenya because of their close ties with the international economy, both as wage labourers and cash-crop cultivators. Moreover, the second colonial occupation progressed most rapidly in Central Province. Thus, whereas the Kikuyu peasantry had already been antagonised by the demands of the terracing campaign in 1947, the agricultural development programme was still only beginning in Nyanza and did not really get under way in Machakos, despite Mitchell's 'D Day', until 1950.

However, once the agricultural campaign gatherered momentum in Machakos after 1950, it quickly aroused widespread resistance and, by 1954, the field administration had almost lost control of the district as it had in Kikuyuland. For six months in 1954, Machakos Kamba tottered on the brink of joining the Mau Mau revolt. By then, however, the

Kikuyu forest fighters had already been driven out of the reserve and forced to seek refuge in the forests. The Kamba, therefore, wisely waited for the outcome of the conflict and did not join forces with their Kikuyu neighbours.[38]

Settler distrust of all Kikuyu during the rebellion benefited other Africans, especially in the Rift Valley and Nyanza. We have seen how Kikuyu squatters were replaced by Nandi and Abaluhya resident labourers on settler farms, thereby averting conflict over access to land in the reserves, but the mass screening exercise of 'Operation Anvil' in April 1954 equally drastically reduced the number of Kikuya in Nairobi and provided new employment opportunities for other Africans. In the short term, Mau Mau enabled the Kenyan government to harass its Kikuyu opponents, to strengthen its alliance with the Kikuyu loyalists and to reduce the tensions created in western Kenya by the second colonial occupation and by the anti-squatter measures of the settler district councils, at the expense of suspect Kikuyu.[39] At the same time, fundamental Kikuyu land-tenure reforms were pushed through, creating consolidated smallholdings and entrenching the land rights of collaborators in Kiambu, Murang'a and Nyeri. Without the Emergency, the government would have been unable to press these reforms upon a reluctant peasantry. Mau Mau provided a useful excuse behind which the field administration and agriculturalists were able to institute the social reconstruction they had earlier contemplated but had been powerless to achieve.[40]

The different effects of the second colonial occupation and of the Emergency on particular districts therefore ensured, along with the government's ban on pan-tribal political associations, that nationalist solidarity was not yet achieved. The Emergency seemed to provide an opportunity for the non-Kikuyu to catch up and to gain greater access to hitherto Kikuyu dominated education, skilled employment and commercial opportunities. But in fact it laid the foundations for the subsequent success of Kikuyu businessmen and commercial farmers by sweeping away traditional obstacles to private tenure and bank loans, which ensured Kikuyu domination of Kenyatta's neo-colonial state and allowed the Kikuyu proto-capitalists to become Kenya's first indigenous bourgeoisie. The tribal division of power in the Kenyan state had to be reworked when the Kikuyu were readmitted to political activity and was ultimately resolved in the five-year struggle for power and access to state patronage between 1961 and 1966 – first, before independence, with the Kalenjin and the Coast Africans who supported the Kenya African Democratic Union and then, after 12 December 1963 and the attainment of *Uhuru*, in the more difficult contest with Kenya's second most powerful tribe, the Luo.[41]

Most interpretations of the origins of Mau Mau date the government's

Conclusion

loss of control in Nairobi and Kikuyuland from 1950, but this is three years too late; 1947 was the key year. The administration never really reasserted its authority after the disturbances of September 1947. In Nairobi, Makhan Singh, the Indian communist, helped Kaggia and Kubai to create a stronger, more politically conscious trades union movement from the remnants of the African Workers' Federation. In alliance with the Kikuyu street gangs, the urban political militants quickly established a firm grip over 'outcast' Nairobi, although they alienated the non-Kikuyu inhabitants of the locations.[42]

The prestige of the chiefs, the agricultural department and the field administration never recovered from the blows they suffered in 1947 during the peasant revolt. Politics in the reserves came to be dominated by a new group of rural radicals, such as Beauttah, Gathanju and Mwangi Macharia, who had close contacts with the Nairobi militants. They continued to criticise the chiefs and the soil conservation campaign. During 1950 and 1951, oathing spread rapidly throughout Kikuyuland, cementing peasant resistance by binding the peasants not only by particularist appeals to tradition, but also by making them break their psychological acceptance of British authority in a specific act of illegality and declaration of support for the militants. Thus, the individual was subsumed within the Kikuyu community. Oathing signified the psychological acceptance of resistance and marked the first step along the path to armed rebellion. By October 1952, this step had already been taken by many Kikuyu. The divisions had been drawn.[43]

Mau Mau's uniqueness, however, should not be unduly exaggerated. Throughout British Africa, the consequences of the second colonial occupation on peasant life were a key factor in the growth of mass support for African nationalism. The Tanganyika African National Union's strength in Sukumaland during the 1950s, the 1953 disturbances in Nyasaland and the support for the Convention People's Party in the southern Gold Coast, like Mau Mau in Kikuyuland, all mobilised peasant support for the nationalist élite in the capitals because of the demands the post-war agricultural development campaign made upon rural Africans. The second colonial occupation enlarged their vision and brought many Africans, for the first time since the conquest, into sustained opposition to the colonial order. Whether the immediate focus of discontent was destocking as in Sukumaland, the uprooting of the cocoa crop because of swollen shoot disease as in the Gold Coast, or terracing and soil conservation regulations as in Kenya and Nyasaland, once the peasantry were aroused the days were numbered for colonial rule.[44]

Just as the various provinces of Kenya were disturbed by the second colonial occupation at various times, equally different British colonies in Africa experienced its impact at different moments and with different consequences. In the Gold Coast, the agricultural department's attempt

Conclusion

to eradicate swollen shoot disease during the late 1940s generated support in the south-east of the colony for Nkrumah's Convention People's Party and discredited the chiefs. This enabled Nkrumah to gain support beyond his original urban base and to sweep the cocoa-growing areas in the 1951 election. In Nyasaland, however, the soil conservation campaign gathered momentum more slowly and only began to arouse peasant opposition after 1950, culminating in the 1953 disturbances, which were associated with the establishment of the Central African Federation.[45]

The effects of the occupation also differed profoundly in the settler-dominated colonies of Kenya and the Rhodesias. In the Rhodesias, especially in the south, the hold of the settler farmers over the state and the economy was much stronger than in Kenya. Northern Rhodesia had nearly twice as many Europeans as Kenya, and Southern Rhodesia had more than five times as many. Moreover, during the rule of the British South Africa Company before 1923, the settlers had effectively restricted African peasant production. Even the mining interests in Northern Rhodesia had been tied into the settler economy and had accepted the higher cost of settler-grown food supplies from Southern Rhodesia and South Africa in return for a guaranteed supply of cheap migrant labour. In Kenya such a bargain between metropolitan and settler capital could not be struck. The interests of the settler food producers, who had formed the Kenya Farmers' Association to gain control over the maize market and who wanted to secure the maximum return for their crops, and the large-scale employers, who wanted to minimise their labour costs, always conflicted. African peasant producers were therefore able successfully to undercut the settler farmers and to continue to supply the domestic market; they had established their independent position in the Kenyan economy.[46]

These economic differences, of course, stemmed from the fact that after 1923 the Rhodesian settlers became their own masters with complete control over their colonial state. They continued the British South Africa Company's policy of suppressing peasant production with even greater zeal. In Kenya, by contrast, 1923 saw the Devonshire Declaration of the paramountcy of African interests. Although it has long been fashionable among historians to deride this vague pledge, and although it is true that the British and Kenyan governments failed to live up to their promise, the fact that Kenya was subordinate to the metropolitan control of the Colonial Office did ensure that African interests were considered and sometimes nurtured. Thus, while African proto-capitalists were strangled in Southern Rhodesia, in Kenya the Kikuyu were allowed to become a serious economic threat to the settlers' dominant position in the colonial state during the depression and the Second World War.[47]

The settlers, however, were largely able to exclude their Kikuyu challengers from the White Highlands. This ensured that the process of capital accumulation was turned inward upon the Kikuyu reserves, which further exacerbated the growing social pressures over access to land and the problems of internal differentiation. Mau Mau, therefore, was not only a collision between settler and Kikuyu proto-capitalists, struggling to become an indigenous capitalist élite, but was also an eruption by the landless and those who had lost out in the scramble for resources in the reserves against Kikuyu accumulators. These tensions were apparent inside the Kenya African Union. The Kikuyu proto-capitalists, who were not allied with the chiefs, supported Kenyatta and the moderates who provided the leadership of the movement until 20 October 1952, but it was the dispossessed have-nots who provided the recruits for the forest fight which developed once the British had detained virtually all the leading political activists – moderate and militant alike.[48]

The reason why Mau Mau was so bloody and by far the most dramatic example of post-war African opposition to the demands of the second colonial occupation and of disillusionment with British colonialism, was that several streams of discontent coincided among the Kikuyu and precipitated the revolt. The Kikuyu were not simply deeply disrupted by the agricultural campaign and the second colonial occupation, but were also bitterly divided among themselves. In many respects Mau Mau was a Kikuyu civil war between the rich and the poor; the Christian missions versus the adherents of the independent churches; the old against the young. The Kikuyu reserves had been more fully integrated into the international economy than any other African Land Unit in Kenya and were already experiencing a three-way conflict – between the chiefs and the established traders; the aspiring commercial farmers and traders who supported Kenyatta and the Kenya African Union; and the mass of Kikuyu, who were being squeezed in the fight for land and commercial control by the two rival élites.[49]

These problems of internal differentiation were further exacerbated by the wider conflict between the Kikuyu and the European settlers, which was most blatant in the White Highlands whre they stood face to face. Outcast Nairobi, which was the militants' power-base against the settlers and chiefs (and after 1951 also against Kenyatta and the moderates in the Kenya African Union) provided a refuge for those disgruntled Kikuyu who had either been defeated in the struggle in the reserves and the White Highlands or were simply innocent victims.

The government's failure to create its vision of a multiracial Kenya and the outbreak of the Mau Mau rebellion shortly after Mitchell's retirement, were almost inevitable outcomes of this unique combination of intractable problems. Until the British government could select and support a Kenyan governor with the courage to sacrifice the settlers and to incorporate the alternative African élite around Kenyatta and the Kikuyu Central Association faction inside the Kenya African Union, long-term

Conclusion

political stability was impossible. Despite his vast experience of East Africa, Philip Mitchell was not that man. He had never even begun to understand the problem. In the 1940s only the subtle political minds of Harold Macmillan and Jomo Kenyatta had really grasped what needed to be done. The Mau Mau rebellion, however, foreclosed the settler option once and for all and, in the early 1960s, enabled Macmillan and Kenyatta, with the help of Macleod, Mboya, Blundell and MacDonald, to reach an arrangement which satisfied the Kikuyu élites (both loyalist and Kenyatta-ite) and the British.[50] But that is another story.

Notes

1. CO 533/549/38232 (1946–47), 'European Settlement', P.E. Mitchell's speech to the Nairobi Caledonian Society, 30 November 1946; CO 533/549/38232/15 (1946–47), 'European Settlement Squatters', P.E. Mitchell to Creech Jones, 14 April 1947. RH Mss. Brit.Emp.s. 365, 'Fabian Colonial Bureau', Box 5, File 3, ff. 70, contains Rita Hinden's hostile reaction to Mitchell's paternalism. She observed to H. Beer, a Kenyan settler, in a letter dated 27 February 1948, 'I am afraid I do not admire the speech as much as you do. He is so insistent that what we have to do is to establish British values and standards in Kenya, and hardly mentions the fact that Africans may perhaps have some values and standards which they desire to keep. I agree that British imperialism may – to some people – be an expression of faith and purpose, and it is stupid to use it just as a term of abuse. But I do not like imperialism even when it is a faith, and I shall continue to work for its ending as soon as possible. That does not mean to say that we have to walk out of Kenya tomorrow – but it does mean that all our efforts are strained to achieve the day when we can walk out and leave a democracy – independent of race – behind us.' Mitchell was never able to understand such views. Africans, he considered, would for many years, perhaps centuries, be unready to receive independence.

2. CO 533/561/12 (1950), 'Petitions and Memorials: Kikuyu People'; CO 533/561/14 (1950), 'Petitions: East African Trades Union Congress'; CO 533/566/7 (1950), 'The Kenya African Union'; and CO 533/566/8 (1951), 'The Kenya African Union', *passim*, all clearly show how the Colonial Office simply reiterated the views of the Kenyan government in replies to African petitioners. Whitehall had no alternative but to accept Mitchell's advice, since it lacked any alternative sources of information. As the situation became increasingly tense in Kenya it became futile to send petitions to the Colonial Office in order to circumvent the Kenyan government. Invariably the reply simply repeated verbatim the counter-submission of the Kenyan authorities.

3. Until the last years of his Kenyan governorship Mitchell had never encountered the kind of sustained African opposition or populist politics West Africa governors had endured in the 1920s and 1930s. See J. Miles, 'Rural Protest in the Gold Coast', pp. 152–70; and M. Crowder, *West Africa under Colonial Rule*, pp. 454–78.

4. C. Ehrlich, 'The Uganda Economy', pp. 397–475.

5. CO 533/547/38132/465 (1947), 'Visit of Mbiyu Koinange to the United Kingdom', P.M. Koinange to Creech Jones, 24 June 1947, records the concern of one political activist at the failure of Creech Jones and the Labour Government to fulfil their promises. See also R.E. Robinson, 'Sir Andrew Cohen', pp. 353–63, and 'Andrew

Conclusion

Cohen and the Transfer of Power in Tropical Africa', pp. 50–68. For an account of American economic pressure upon the Attlee government, see E.A. Brett, S. Gilliatt and A. Pople, 'Planned Trade, Labour Party Policy and US Intervention', pp. 130–42.

6. Negley Farson, Mitchell's journalist friend, provided an unusually sympathetic account of Kenyatta in his book on Kenya, *Last Chance in Africa* pp. 113–31, as did Wyn Harris in CO 537/3591/38733 (1948), 'Petitions to the United Nations', minutes of meeting with Kenyatta, 15 October 1948. Mitchell, in contrast, came to believe that Kenyatta was the organiser of opposition to the government and an avowed communist. This view was encouraged by reports such as CO 537/3646/47272/1 (1948), 'Political Intelligence Reports: East Africa',· Kenya report, September–October 1948. J. Murray-Brown's semi-official biography, *Kenyatta*, pp. 264–96, avoids controversy and fails to provide an adequate account of Kenyatta's political activities between his return in Kenya in September 1946 and his arrest in October 1952.

7. A. Hake, *African Metropolis*, pp. 53–63; S.D. Stichter, 'The Formation of a Working Class in Kenya', pp. 34–44; and her 'Workers, Trade Unions, and Mau Mau Rebellion' pp. 259–75. See KNA Lab 9/30, 'Colonial Cooperation: African Labour Conference, Elizabethville, July 1950', E.M. Hyde-Clarke, 'Notes on Efficiency of Labour', undated; Lab 9/452, 'Minimum Wage Ordinance, 1947–51', T.G. Askwith, 28 December 1946 Lab 9/644, 'Labour Exchange: General Policy, 1944–56', P. Wyn Harris to the Executive Council, 15 February 1944; and Lab 9/1090, 'Report of the Central Minimum Wages Advisory Board, 1947', E.M. Hyde-Clarke, 10 April 1947; and A. Hope-Jones, 16 April 1947, for various attempts by the Kenyan government to overcome the problems of Kenya's inefficient, low-wage economy.

8. CO 852/662/19936/2 (1945–46), 'Soil Erosion: Kenya', N. Humphrey, 'The Relationship of Population to the Land in South Nyeri', *passim*; KNA DC/NYI 2/1/20, 'Mr Humphrey's Report on South Nyeri, 1944–47', N. Humphrey to D.L. Blunt, 'A Preliminary Report on Agricultural Conditions in South Nyeri', 22 Sepember 1944; and DC/NYI 2/2/4, 'Mr Humphrey's Report on Agriculture in South Nyeri, 1945', *passim*, but especially D.L. Morgan to C. Tomkinson, 28 March 1945.

9. KNA Secretariat 1/1/12, 'Report of the Joint Agricultural and Veterinary Services Sub-Committee of the Development Committee', *passim*, for settler attitudes to the peasant option; and J.M. Lonsdale's unpublished paper, 'African Elites and Social Classes in Colonial Kenya', pp. 10–14, for one account of the struggle between the chiefs and the alternative élite around Kenyatta and the Kikuyu Central Association for political and economic power. See also B.E. Kipkorir, 'The Educated Elite and Local Society', pp. 254–68.

10. Creech Jones, 'The Place of African Local Administration in Colonial Policy', pp. 3–6; R.E. Robinson, 'The Relationship of Major and Minor Local Government Authorities', pp. 30–3, and his article, 'The Progress of Provincial Councils in the British African Territories', pp. 59–68; R.A. Stevens, 'The Application of English Local Government Principles in Africa', pp. 68–73; Earl of Listowel, 'The Modern Conception of Government in British Africa', pp. 99–105; and the African Studies Branch of the Colonial Office, 'A Survey of the Development of Local Government in The African Territories since 1947', pp. 1–83. For developments in Kenya see D. O'Hagan, 'African's Part in Nairobi Local Government', pp. 156–8; the African Studies Branch of the Colonial Office, 'Local Government Reorganisation in the Eastern Provinces of Nigeria and Kenya', pp. 18–19, 25–9; and KNA DC/FH 1/26, 'Fort Hall Annual Report, 1947', pp. 1–6, 15; and DC/FH 1/27, 'Fort Hall Annual Report, 1948', pp. 1–2, 4–5, 11. See also S.D. Mueller's thesis, 'Political Parties in Kenya', pp. 1–7, 22–40.

11. KNA DC/FH 1/26, 'Fort Hall Annual Report, 1947', pp. 1–6; and MAA 8/68, 'Chief Waruhiu, 1948–52', *passim*.

12. *ibid.* Wyn Harris was particularly concerned about the government's loss of control over the Kikuyu reserves, see P. Wyn Harris to P.E. Mitchell, August 1948.

Conclusion

13. R.E. Robinson, 'Non-European Foundations of European Imperialism', p. 138.
14. J.M. Lonsdale's unpublished paper, 'Explanations of the Mau Mau Revolt', pp. 4-6, 8-10; and KNA Secretariat 1/12/8, 'Labour Unrest: Intelligence Reports, Central Province, 1947', C. Penfold to P. Wyn Harris, 25 September 1947 and 10 October 1947.
15. R.E. Robinson, 'Non-European Foundations of European Imperialism', p. 138; F. Furedi, 'The African Crowd in Nairobi', pp. 282-9; and S.B. Stichter, 'Workers, Trade Unions and the Mau Mau Rebellion', pp. 260-75.
16. T.O. Ranger, *Peasant Consciousness and Guerilla War in Zimbabwe* pp. 99-132.
17. G. Kitching, *Class and Economic Change in Kenya*, pp. 128-30, 144-6, 288-97.
18. T.M.J. Kanogo's unpublished paper, 'Comparative Analysis of the Aspirations of the Kikuyu, Luo and Luhya Workers in the White Highlands', pp. 10-17, and CO 533/549/38232/15 (1946-47), 'European Settlement: Squatters', J.H. Martin, 'The Problem of the Squatter: Economic Survey of Resident Labour in Kenya', 24 February 1947. Martin discovered that 72% of squatters surveyed in the Uasin Gishu, 51 per cent in Trans Nzoia and 52 per cent in Naivasha claimed to have land in the reserves, but while the claims of Kikuyu squatters were probably based only on a vague claim to *githaka* land rights, those of Nandi, Luo and Abaluhya squatters in the Uasin Gishu and Trans Nzoia were based on hard fact and frequent periods of residence in the reserves.
19. T.M.J. Kanogo's thesis, 'The History of Kikuyu Movement . . .', pp. 245-379; and F. Furedi, 'The Social Composition of the Mau Mau Movement in the White Highlands', pp. 492-504. See also T.M.J. Kanogo, 'Rift Valley Squatters and Mau Mau', pp. 243-51 and M. Tamarkin, 'Mau Mau in Nakuru' pp. 228-37. B.A. Ogot, 'Politics, Culture and Music in Central Kenya', pp. 277-86, which remains one of the few serious studies of Mau Mau's ideological aims, has emphasised the centrality of the land issue to the rebellion. See also J.M. Lonsdale's unpublished essay, 'Kenya's Civil War and Glorious Revolution'.
20. CO 533/549/38232/15 (1946-47), 'European Settlement: Squatters', J.H. Martin, 'The Problem of the Squatter; Economic Survey of Resident Labour in Kenya', 24 February 1947.
21. KNA Lab 9/326, 'Resident Labour: Trans Nzoia, 1945-57', F.R. Bancroft to T.C. Colchester, 7 November 1946; and Lab 9/598, 'Resident Labour: Trans Nzoia, 1943-56', A.C. Hoey to F.W. Cavendish-Bentinck, 12 February 1946. See also Lab 9/247, 'Labour for Pyrethrum, 1953', *passim*; and Lab 9/351, 'Supply: Labour Shortage, 1946-49', A.T. Wise to E.M. Hyde-Clarke, 5 February 1947, 'Special Labour (Native) Census, 1946'.
22. C.G. Rosberg and J.Nottingham, *The Myth of Mau Mau*, pp. 285-6.
23. KNA Secretariat 1/2/2, 'Nyanza Province, 1949-50', P. Wyn Harris to the Executive Council, 13 July 1949; and minutes of meeting to discuss the *Dini ya Msambwa*, Kakamega, 6 September 1949; and C.M. Deverell to K.K. O'Connor, 12 October 1949. See also C.G. Rosberg and J. Nottingham, *The Myth of Mau Mau*, pp. 328-30; G.S. Were, 'Politics, Religion and Nationalism in Western Kenya', pp. 92-103; and A. Wipper, 'Elijah Masinde - a folk hero', pp. 157-81.
24. J. Spencer, *KAU*, pp. 208, 211-13, 221-4, 227-8.
25. KNA MAA 8/22, 'City African Affairs Officer: Correspondence, 1947-50', G.R.B. Brown to E.R. St. A. Davies, 23 May 1950.
26. J. Spencer, *KAU*, pp. 202-32; and B. Kaggia, *Roots of Freedom*, pp. 79-83, 108-9. R. Buijtenhuijs, *Essays on Mau Mau*, pp. 12-35; and R.M. Githige's thesis, 'The Religious Factor in Mau Mau', pp. 149-244, discuss the origins and significance of Mau Mau oaths.
27. J. Gallagher, *The Decline, Revival and Fall of the British Empire*, pp. 145-9; J. Gallagher, G. Johnson and A. Seal, *Locality, Province and Nation*; and especially A. Seal, 'Imperialism and Nationalism in India', pp. 3-6, 15-27. See also A. Seal, *The Emergence of Indian Nationalism*, pp. 341-51.

Conclusion

28. J. Iliffe, *A Modern History of Tanganyika*, pp. 402-4, and his article, 'The Creation of Group Consciousness among the Dockworkers of Dar-es-Salaam, 1929-50', pp. 63-4.
29. J. Spencer, 'Kenya African Union and Mau Mau', p. 205; and *KAU*, pp. 202-32, 239-40; M. Singh, *History of Kenya's Trade Union Movement*, vol.1, pp. 240-5, 268-9 for information about the long struggle between the Nairobi City Council and the Transport and Allied Workers' Union over the taxi-cab bylaws, which may partly explain the militancy of Nairobi's taxi drivers and their prominent role in Mau Mau oathing.
30. J. Gallagher, *The Decline, Revival and Fall of the British Empire*, p. 148.
31. *ibid*, p. 147.
32. CO 537/3591/38733 (1948), 'Petitions to the United Nations', A.B. Cohen to J. Galsworthy, 12 October 1948; J. Galsworthy to J. Fletcher-Cooke, 14 October 1948 and A.B. Cohen to P.E. Mitchell, 14 October 1948. See also CO 537/4661/38733 (1949), 'Petitions to the United Nations', P. Wyn Harris to A.B. Cohen, 23 February 1948; and CO 537/2545/96038/1 (1947), 'Soviet Propaganda in Colonial Newspapers', *passim*.
33. CO 537/3588/38696 (1947-48), 'Activities of Mathu', *passim*; CO 533/543/38086/38 (1949), 'Petitions: Kikuyu Central Association', P.E. Mitchell to Creech Jones, 28 February 1949; and CO 533/540/38032 (1949), 'Legislative Council', P.E. Mitchell to Creech Jones, 11 December 1948; CO 533/566/7 (1950), 'Kenya African Union', P.E. Mitchell to Creech Jones, 31 January 1950; and CO 533/566/8 (1951), 'Kenya African Union', T. Mbotela to P. Rogers, 28 April 1951; and P.E. Mitchell to J. Griffiths, 3 May 1951.
34. KNA DC/FH 1/25, 'Fort Hall Annual Report, 1946', pp. 7, 9-10; MAA 7/2, 'Nyeri Ex-Soldiers Association, 1945-47', D. O'Hagan to W.S. Marchant, 6 July 1946; and Secretariat 1/12/1, 'Manpower and Civil Reabsorption, 1946', A.L.B. Perkin to G.M. Rennie, 'Manpower, Demobilisation and Reabsorption', pp. 18-57, 28 February 1946.
35. KNA DC/KBU 1/38, 'Kiambu Annual Report, 1947', pp. 1-6; DC/KBU 1/43, 'Kiambu Annual Report, 1952', pp. 1-4; DC/FH 1/26, 'Fort Hall Annual Report, 1947', pp. 1-6, 15; DC/FH 1/27, 'Fort Hall Annual Report, 1948', pp. 1-2, 4-6, 11; DC/FH 1/31, 'Fort Hall Annual Report, 1952', pp. 1-5, 11-18. See also MAA 8/68, 'Chief Waruhiu, 1948-52', P. Wyn Harris to K.K. O'Connor, 30 July 1948; and to P.E. Mitchell, August 1948; and Secretariat 1/12/8, 'Labour Unrest: Intelligence Reports, Central Province, 1947', *passim*.
36. J. Spencer, *KAU*, pp. 224-5. In November 1951 the Central Committee of the Kenya African Union consisted of:

President	Jomo Kenyatta	Kikuyu
General Secretary	J.K. Otiende	Abaluhya
Assistant General Secretary	Paul Ngei	Kamba
Treasurer	Harry L. Nangurai	Maasai
Assistant Treasurer	William Kioko	Kamba
Trustees	R. Achieng Oneko	Luo
	Mbiyu Koinange	Kikuyu
	Gideon Nzaka Rimba	Giriama
Auditor	Peter Okondo	Abaluhya
Committee Members	Fred Kubai	Kikuyu
	Bildad Kaggia	Kikuyu
	James Beauttah	Kikuyu
	Senior Chief Koinange	Kikuyu
	Charles Wambaa	Kikuyu
	Jonathan Njoroge	Kikuyu

Conclusion

Jessie Kariuki	Kikuyu
James Njoroge	Kikuyu
Isaac Kitabi	Kamba

Thus while the main offices were distributed among the main tribes, the Kikuyu still dominated the committee. Overall there were ten Kikuyu members, three Kamba, two Abaluhya, and one member each from the Luo, Maasai and Giriama.

37. J. Gallagher, *The Decline, Revival and Fall of the British Empire*, p. 148. Many obstacles to nationalist solidarity, of course, remained. The moderate Coast African, Tom Mbotela, who served as Superintendent of African Locations in Nairobi, and who was ousted by the militants from the Vice Presidency of the Kenya African Union at the elections in November 1951, had earlier complained that: 'As regards the Kikuyu, the time has also come when they should abolish this deplorable idea of thinking that everything good in the city should be for the Kikuyu and nobody else'. This view was shared by many other non-Kikuyu inhabitants of the city, and partly explains why Mau Mau was unable togain the support of Africans from Nyanza and the Coast, and remained a Kikuyu dominated movement. See CO 533/562/7 (1950), 'Information on Trade Unionism in Kenya by Tom Mbotela', Tom Mbotela, 'Memorandum on African Interests in Nairobi', 20 July 1950. Mbotela was assassinated by Mau Mau on 27 November 1952. A. Seal, 'Imperialism and Nationalism in India', p. 3, examines the same process in India.

38. KNA DC/MKS 1/1/33, 'Machakos Annual Reports, 1955–56' and MAA 7/112 'Policy: Kamba in Nairobi and Mombasa, 1954–56'.

39. D. Mukaru-Ng'ang'a, 'Mau Mau, Loyalists and Politics in Murang'a', pp. 366–83; M. Omosule, 'Kiama Kia Muingi', *passim*; and C.G. Rosberg and J. Nottingham, *The Myth of Mau Mau*, pp. 303–8.

40. A. Thurston's draft manuscript, 'The Intensification of Smallholder Agriculture in Kenya' pp. 123–204; M.P.K. Sorrenson, *Land Reform in the Kikuyu Country*, pp. 97–252; and M. McWilliam, 'The Managed Economy', pp. 257–69.

41. G. Wasserman, *Politics of Decolonization*, *passim*; D. Goldsworthy, *Tom Mboya*, pp. 131–46, 166–93, 232–46; and C. Gertzel, *The Politics of Independent Kenya*, *passim*.

42. C.G. Rosberg and J. Nottingham, *The Myth of Mau Mau*, pp. 262–76; R. Buijtenhuijs, *Essays on Mau Mau*, pp. 17–35; B.J. Berman, 'Bureaucracy and Incumbent Violence', pp. 165–72; S.B. Stichter, 'Workers, Trade Unions and the Mau Mau Rebellion', pp. 269–70; M. Singh, *History of Kenya's Trade Union Movement*, vol. 1, pp. 161–287; and S.B. Sticher, 'Trade Unionism in Kenya', pp. 155–72. See also CO 533/561/14 (1950), 'Petitions: East African Trades Union Congress', East African Trades Union Congress to E. Parry, Assistant Labour Advisor to the Secretary of State, 23 November 1949; and J.D. Rankine's note, 20 October 1950; CO 533/562/7 'Information on Trade Unionism in Kenya by Tom Mbotela', *passim*; and CO 533/566/6 (1950), 'Temporary Removal of Undesirable Natives Legislation', J.D. Rankine to Creech Jones, 18 January 1950.

43. J. Spencer, *KAU*, pp. 204–10, 239–40, and his article, 'Kenya African Union and Mau Mau', pp. 207–12, 214–18. R.M. Githige's thesis, 'The Religious Factor in Mau Mau', pp. 76–116 analyses Kikuyu traditional oaths; pp. 117–59, Kikuyu Central Association oaths. Mau Mau oaths and the 'Oath of Unity' are discussed on pp. 160–210; and the Batuni oath on pp. 211–38.

44. G.A. Maguire, *Towards Uhuru in Tanzania*, pp. 27–31, 59–78, and his article, 'The Emergence of the Tanganyika African National Union in the Lake Province', pp. 639–66; Wendy Sykes's draft manuscript on 'Sukumaland', *passim*; D. Austin, *Politics in Ghana*, pp. 58–66, 159–61. For information on opposition to soil conservation measures in colonial Nyasaland, I am grateful to William Beinart, Richard Grove and Megan Vaughan.

Conclusion

45. D. Austin, *Politics in Ghana*, pp. 58–66, 159–61. Oral information from William Beinart and Richard Grove. See also R.I. Rotberg. *The Rise of Nationalism in Central Africa*, pp. 257–62.

46. The following essays from R. Palmer and N. Parsons (eds), *The Roots of Rural Poverty in Central and Southern Africa*, reflect the influence of under-development theory on African historiography in the late 1970s: M. Muntemba, 'Thwarted Development', pp. 345–61; R. Palmer, 'The Agricultural History of Rhodesia', pp. 227–45; I. Phimister, 'Peasant Production and Underdevelopment in Southern Rhodesia', pp. 255–64; and B. Kosmin, 'The Inyoka Tobacco Industry of the Shangwe People', pp. 279–85. See also C. Van Onselen, *Chibaro* pp. 74–127. It should, however, be noted that recent work by Wolfgang Dopfke and T.O. Ranger has cast some doubt on the destruction of the peasantry thesis so fashionable in the 1970s.

For the Kenyan peasantry see P. Mosley, *The Settler Economies*, pp. 71–143; D. Mukaru-Ng'ang'a, 'What is Happening to the Kenyan Peasantry?', pp. 10–13; and M.P. Cowen's unpublished papers, 'Patterns of Cattle Ownership and Dairy Production', pp. 23–43 and 'Differentiation in a Kenya Location', *passim*. For an assessment of what has happened to the Kenyan peasantry since independence see P. Anyang'-Nyong'o, 'What the Friends of the Peasant are', pp. 17–26 and 'The Development of a Middle Peasantry in Nyanza', pp. 108–20; A.L.N. Njonjo 'The Kenya Peasantry', pp. 27–40; and M.P. Cowen, 'The Agrarian Problem', pp. 57–73.

47. R.E. Robinson, 'The Moral Disarmament of African Empire', pp. 92–93; and R.E. Gregory, *Sidney Web and East Africa passim*, for the Colonial Office's agonising over African interests.

48. R. Buijtenhuijs, *Esays on Mau Mau*, pp. 49–51 and H.K. Wachanga, *The Swords of Kirinyaga*, pp. xv–xvi; until he entered the forest Wachanga was the General Secretary of the Mau Mau Central Committee, the *Muhimu*.

49. B.A. Ogot, 'Revolt of the Elders', pp. 136–145; and MAA 7/634, 'Intelligence Reports: Central Province, 1948–53', W.H. Cantrell to D. O'Hagan, 15 July 1953, 'Report on the Position of African Anglican Church Schools and Churches in the Fort Hall District.' J.M. Lonsdale's unpublished paper, 'Explanations of the Mau Mau Revolt', pp. 5–6, 8–10, considers these questions. For the socio-economic background to Kikuyu differentiation and political conflict , see G. Kitching, *Class and Economic Change in Kenya*, pp. 117–21, 128–130; and M.P. Cowen's unpublished paper, 'Differentiation in A Kenya Location' *passim*. Maina wa Kinyatti, 'Mau Mau', pp. 292–3 provides a radical perspective on the struggle between the moderates, led by Kenyatta, and the Mau Mau militants for control over the Kenya African Union in 1951 and 1952.

50. For Macmillan see CO 967/57/46709 (1942), 'Sir Arthur Dawe's Memorandum on a Federal Solution for East Africa and Mr Harold Macmillan's Counter-Proposals', H. Macmillan to Sir George Gater, 15 August 1942. The fullest account of Kenyatta's activities during this period is J. Murray-Brown, *Kenyatta*, pp. 261–96, but it lacks a theoretical framework to organise 'mere events' and ignores important questions. One suspects that he deliberately chose to avoid controversy. D. Goldsworthy, *Tom Mboya*, pp. 93–146, 166–93; G. Wasserman, *Politics of Decolonization*, *passim*; Sir Michael Blundell, *So Rough a Wind*, pp. 261–318; D.F Gordon, 'Mau Mau and Decolonization', pp. 329–45; B.E. Kipkorir, 'Mau Mau and the Politics of the Transfer of Power in Kenya', pp. 314–26, provide some useful insights. See also D.W. Throup, 'The Origins of Mau Mau', pp. 399–433. R.F. Holland, 'The Imperial Factor in British Strategies' and J. Darwin, 'British Decolonization since 1945', pp. 165–86, 187–209, provide interesting assessments of Britain's imperial decline. For a brief discussion Mau Mau's role in the ending of empire see R.F. Holland, *European Decolonization*, pp. 144–9, 236–48.

Biographical Appendix

Official Members of the Executive Council

The Governor

Sir Henry Moore	1940–1944
Sir Philip Mitchell	1944–1952
Sir Evelyn Baring	1952–1959

The Chief Secretary and Member for Development

Sir Gilbert Rennie	1939–1948
Hon. J.D. Rankine	1948–1952
Hon. H.S. Potter	1952–1954

The Attorney-General and Member for Law and Order

Hon. S.W.P. Foster-Sutton	1945–1949
Hon. K.K. O'Connor	1945–1952
Hon. J. Whyatt	1952–

Financial Secretary and Member for Finance

Hon. J.F.G. Troughton	1944–1950
Hon. V.G. Matthews	1950–1952
Hon. E.A. Vasey	1952–1959

Chief Native Commissioner and Member for African Affairs

Hon. W.S. Marchant	1944–1947
Hon. P. Wyn Harris	1947–1949
Hon. E.R. St. A. Davies	1949–1953

The Member for Agriculture and Natural Resources

Hon. F.W. Cavendish-Bentinck	1945–1955

The Member for Education and Labour and Deputy Chief Secretary

Hon. C.H. Thornley	1948–1952

The Member for Health and Local Government
Sir Charles Mortimer   1946–1952

The Member for Commerce and Industry
Hon. A. Hope-Jones   1950–1960

Heads of Technical Departments

Director of Agriculture
D.L. Blunt   1945–1948
S. Gillett   1948–1951
G.M. Roddan   1951–1956

Director of Education
C.E. Donovan   1945–1947
R. Patrick   1947–1952
W.J.D. Wadley   1952–

Director of Medical Services
Dr N.M. MacLennan   1945–1950
Dr T.F. Anderson   1950–

Director of Veterinary Services
R. Daubney   1944–1947
E. Beaumont   1947–1951
R.A. Hammond   1951–

Labour Commissioner
P. Wyn Harris   1944–1946
E.M. Hyde-Clarke   1946–1951
F.W. Carpenter   1951–

Field Administration Central Province

Provincial Commissioners
C. Tomkinson   1943–1946
P. Wyn Harris   1946–January 1947
A.C.M. Mullins   February1947–April 1948
E.H. Windley   April1948–December 1948
A.C.M. Mullins   January1949–May 1949
E.H. Windley   May1949–March 1950
C.M. Johnston   April1950–November 1950
E.H. Windley   November1950–January 1953
D. O'Hagan   January1953–September 1953

District Commissioners Embu
I.R. Gillespie   1943–1946

R.E. Wainwright	1946–February 1950
J.H. Chandler	February1950–October 1950
R.E. Wainwright	October1950–September 1951
R.A. Wilkinson	September1951–1954

District Commissioners Kiambu

A.C.M. Mullins	May1944–January 1945
W.F. Coutts	January1945–March 1945
A.C.M. Mullins	March1945–February 1947
E.H. Windley	April1947–February 1948
N.F. Kennaway	February1948–November 1950
M.E.W. North	November1950–July 1951
N.F. Kennaway	July1951–February 1953

District Commissioners Kitui

R.D.F. Ryland	July1944–August 1947
F.R. Wilson	4 August1947–24 August 1947
K.W. Simmonds	August1947–January 1948
W.F.P. Kelly	January1948–March 1949
J. Pinney	April1949–October 1949
W.F.P. Kelly	October1949–July 1952
P.J. Browning	July1952–September 1952
R.A.M. Birkett	September1952–1953

District Commissioners Machakos

G.R.B. Brown	May1944–1946
R.J.C. Howes	1946–June 1948
J.W. Howard	June1948–December 1949
J. Pinney	December1949–August 1950
J.W. Howard	August1950–May 1951
J. Pinney	May1951–July 1951
J.K.R. Thorp	July1951–November 1952
D.J. Penwill	November1952–1953

District Commissioners Meru

V.M. McKeag	1943–July 1945
C.M. Johnston	July1945–June 1947
N.F. Kennaway	June1947–February 1948
C.M. Johnston	February1948–April 1950
R.G. Brayne-Nicholls	April1950–October 1953
F.D. Homan	October1950–April 1953

District Commissioners Murang'a

P.S. Osborne	July1944–April 1945
D. O'Hagan	April1945–May 1947
W.F. Coutts	May1947–January 1949

F.A. Loyd	January1949–February 1950
F.D. Homan	February1950–October 1950
F.A. Loyd	October1950–August 1953

District Commissioners Nairobi

D. O'Hagan	November1944–April 1945
E.G. St C. Tisdall	April1945–December 1945
J.D. McKean	December1945–December 1948
P.J. de Bromhead	December1948–January 1949
J.D. McKean	January1949–October 1949
C.F. Atkins	October1949–1953

District Commissioners Nanyuki

J.B.S. Lockhart	1947–June 1951
A.D. Galton-Fenzi	June1951–January 1952
J.B.S. Lockhart	January1952–March 1952
A.D. Galton-Fenzi	March1952–July 1953

District Commissioners Nyeri

D.L. Morgan	1943–September 1945
P.S. Osborne	September1945–June 1948
F.A. Loyd	June1948–January 1949
P.S. Osborne	January1949–September 1950
A.C.C. Swann	September1950–March 1952
O.E.B. Hughes	March1952–September 1953

District Commissioners Thika

E.D. Emley	1943–1946
H.A. Carr	1946–June 1948
G.E. Noad	November1948–June 1950
C.J. Denton	June1950–September 1950
R.S. Winser	September1950–March 1951
D.G. Christie-Miller	March1951–July 1951
M.E.W. North	July1951–September 1952
R.S. Winser	September1952–1954

Biographical Appendix of Administrators and Politicians

Askwith, Thomas, G.
b. 1911; ed. Haileybury and Cambridge University; District Officer, Kenya 1936; Municipal African Affairs Officer, Nairobi, 1945–49; Principal the Jeanes School, Kabete, and Commissioner for Communal Relations, 1950–54; served in the Secretariat 1954. Askwith was a former Olympic oarsman and Diamond Sculls champion. At Kabete he proved

to be too paternalistic and did not get on with the 18 year-old Tom Mboya, who was president of the students' council.

Awori, Wyclife Work Waswa
b. 1925 in Nambale, Western Kenya; ed. Kakamega High School and Mulago Hospital, Kampala, to train as a health inspector with the Nairobi Municipal Council; resigned 1945; journalist and editor of *Radio Posta*, *Habari za Dunia*, *Tribune*, which were kept afloat by Ernest Vasey, the settler politician; a close associate of Henry Gathigira, Pio Gama Pinto and E.K. Shaldah; Treasurer of the Kenya African Union, 1946; Vice President, 1946–47, but could not co-operate with Kenyatta, who forced him to resign; in 1947 was closely associated with the African Workers' Federation and nearly succeeded Chege Kibachia as its General Secretary; retired from politics and became a successful businessman and large farmer in co-operation with his father Canon Jeremiah Awori; appointed as Legislative Councillor for North Nyanza, 1952–56; died Nairobi, 5 May 1978.

Baring, Evelyn
1st Baron Howick of Glendale; GCMG (1955), KCMG (1942), KCVO (1947). b. 1903; younger son of 1st Earl Cromer, Consul-General in Egypt; ed. Winchester and New College, Oxford; 1st Class Hons in Modern History; entered Indian Civil Service, 1926; Secretary to the Agent of the Government of India in South Africa, 1929; retired 1934; Merchant Banker, 1934–42; Governor of Southern Rhodesia, 1942–44; High Commissioner in South Africa and to Basutoland, Bechuanaland and Swaziland, 1944–51; Governor of Kenya, 1952–59; Director Swan, Hunter and Wigham Richardson 1960; Chairman Commonwealth Development Corporation 1960–72; Chairman Nature Conservancy, 1962. He was a devout Anglo-Catholic and an authority on Swahili literature; and a boyhood friend of many senior Conservative politicians such as the Earl of Home, the Secretary of State for Commonwealth Relations, 1955–60. An aristocrat, he was the complete antithesis of Mitchell. His appointment appealed to the snobbish prejudices of many Kenyan settlers.

Battershill, William Denis
KCMG (1941), CMG (1938); b. 1896; ed. King's School, Worcester. War service in India and Iraq, 1914–19; Cadet Ceylon 1920; clerk to the Legislative Council, Ceylon 1928; Assistant Colonial Secretary, Jamaica, 1929–35; Colonial Secretary, Cyprus, 1935–37; Chief Secretary, Palestine, 1937–39; Governor of Cyprus, 1939–41; Assistant Under-Secretary of State, Colonial Office, 1941–42; Deputy Under-Secretary of State, Colonial Office, 1942–45; Governor of Tanganyika, 1945–49.

Battershill was the Colonial Office's 'spy' among the East African governors, but he was much less successful than Mitchell in Kenya and Hathorn Hall in Uganda at implementing the second colonial occupation. His behaviour became increasingly erratic and he retired to Cyprus, aged 53, in 1949.

Beauttah, James

b. c. 1888; originally called Mbutu wa Ruhara; raised at Lower Muhito in Mukuruwe-ini Division of Nyeri District; his parents died while he was still a child; houseboy in 1900 to a Mnyamwezi policeman in Fort Hall town; moved to Nairobi in 1903. ed. Rabai mission school, Mombasa, and Buxton High School. Trainee telegraphist, Rabai, 1910. In 1911 posted to Bombo in Uganda; resigned from the Post Office in 1932; helped form the Kikuyu Central Association in Nairobi in 1924; settled Maragua, Murang'a in 1936; elected to the Murang'a Local Native Council with Job Muchuchu in 1937; founded the Murang'a Land Board Association to fight for the alienated Kikuyu lands, and the Kenya African Traders Association; 1945 joined the executive committee of the Kenya African Union; Vice President of the Kenya African Union in Central Province, 1947–51; a member of the Labour Trade Union of East Africa 1946. Sentenced to two years imprisonment 12 February 1952 for organising anti-inoculation protests in Murang'a; detained 1952–58; defeated in 1963 general election.

Beecher, Leonard James

CMG b. 1906; ed. St. Olaves School, Southwark, and Imperial College, London, and Institute of Education, London. Physics and mathematics master with Church Missionary Society at Alliance High School, Kikuyu, 1927; headmaster Kahuhia Teacher Training College; married 1929, Gladys Leakey, second daughter of Canon Leakey, the first Anglican missionary at Kabete; ordained 1930; Archdeacon 1945; Member for African interests on the Legislative Council 1943–47; and on the Executive Council, 1947–52; Bishop of Mombasa, 1953–64; Archbishop of East Africa, 1960–70; retired to Karen, a Nairobi suburb.

Blundell, Michael

KBE (1962). b. 1907; ed. Wellington College, where he was a friend of Patrick Gordon Walker, later Secretary of State for Commonwealth Relations, 1950–51. Became a farmer in Kenya in 1925, starting as a farm manager; Second Lieutenant, Major, Lieutenant Colonel, and Colonel with the Royal Engineers, 1940–45, in Ethiopia and South East Asia; Chairman of the Board for European Settlement 1946–47; European Legislative Councillor for the Rift Valley constituency, 1948–63; Leader of the European Legislative Councillors 1952–54; Member of the Executive Council, 1952; Minister on the War Council, 1954–55; Minister of Agriculture, 1955–59 and 1961; Leader of the New Kenya Group, 1959; Director of Barclays Bank, Kenya and sixteen other companies; retired to Muthaiga, Nairobi. Blundell left Kenya for two years in the early 1930s to train as an opera singer in Vienna. He became politically more liberal as he grew older; an astute political operator. Publications: *So Rough a Wind* (London 1973).

Blunt, Denzil Layton

CMG (1945). b. 1891; ed. Shrewsbury and King's College Cambridge. Indian Education Department, 1912–14; European War, Royal Army Signals Corp, 1915–19; farming in England 1919–22; agricultural research at Cambridge, 1922–26; Senior Agricultural Officer, Kenya, 1926–33; Director of Agriculture, Cyprus, 1933–37; Director of Agriculture, Nyasaland, 1937–39; Director of Agriculture, Kenya, 1939–49. Retired to his Limuru farm.

Brown, Leslie H.

b. 1917; ed. St. Andrews University and the Imperial College of Tropical Agriculture, Trinidad. Nigerian Agricultural Service, 1940–46; transferred to Kenya, November 1946; Assistant Agricultural Officer; Embu, 1947–51; Provincial Agricultural Officer, Central Province, 1951–56; Deputy Director of Agriculture, June 1956. Brown was a dynamic and far-sighted character, but was abrasive and could not get on with his colleagues. Fortunately his superiors recognised his abilities. He had a searing tongue which he frequently employed on the field administration. Became a noted authority on African ornithology.

Buxton, Clarence E.V.

Served European war, wounded, became a Major and won the Military Cross. Assistant District Officer, East African Protectorate, October 1919; District Officer, Kenya, 1922; acting District Commissioner, Narok, January–June 1923; District Officer, Murang'a, 1925; District Commissioner Kajiado, October 1928–April 1931; District Commissioner, Kisii, 1933; District Commissioner, Narok, March 1935–April 1937; Officer-in-Charge, Maasai, May 1937–May 1938; seconded· to Palestine, September 1938; retired to his coffee farm in Kiambu, 1939. Buxton was the exact opposite of Mitchell; as a District Commissioner he was loyal to his subordinates and critical of his superiors. A former war hero, he cut a dashing figure with the ladies. From 1947 Buxton was extremely critical of Mitchell for ignoring the subversive threat posed by the African political ogranisations in Kikuyuland and persistently warned him that Kenyatta should be arrested.

Biographical Appendix

Caine, Sydney
KCMG (1947), CMG (1945); b. 1902; ed. Harrow County School and the London School of Economics. Assistant Inspector of Taxes, 1923–26; transferred to the Colonial Office, 1926; Secretary of the West Indies Sugar Commission, 1929; Financial Secretary Hong Kong, 1937; Assistant Secretary, Colonial Office 1940; Member of the Anglo-American Caribbean Commission, 1942; Financial Adviser to the Secretary of State, 1942; Assistant Under-Secretary, 1944; Deputy Under-Secretary, 1947–48; Third Secretary, the Treasury, 1948; head of the UK Treasury Delegation to Washington, 1949–51; Chief World Bank Mission to Ceylon, 1951; Vice-Chancellor of the University of Malaya, 1952–56; Director of the London School of Economics, 1957–67; Member of the Independent Television Authority, 1960–67; published *The Foundation of the LSE* and *British Universities: Purpose and Prospects*. Caine was a fierce exponent of *laissez-faire* policies and was highly critical of Mitchell's attempts to secure guaranteed prices for tropical cash crops; he consistently attempted to minimise government participation in colonial development.

Cavendish-Bentinck, Ferdinand William
Eighth Duke of Portland 1977–80; KBE (1956), CMG (1941), MC; b. 1889; ed. Eton, and RMC Sandhurst. Served in Malta and India, severely wounded in European war 1914–18; Staff Officer, War Office; Assistant Adjutant, RMC Sandhurst; Liberal candidate South Kensington, 1922; worked for Vickers Ltd 1923–24; private secretary to the governor of Uganda, 1925–27; Hon. Sec. Kenya Convention of Associations, 1930; Legislative Councillor for Nairobi North, 1934–45; Legislative Councillor, 1934–60; Member of the Executive Council, 1938–60; Member for Agriculture, 1945–55; Speaker of the Legislative Council, 1955–60; leader of the Kenya Coalition, a right-wing settler party opposed to Blundell's New Kenya Group, 1960; retired in Muthaiga; died aged 91 in December 1980. Cavendish-Bentinck was the Eamon de Valera of Kenyan politics; a tall, gaunt figure with a will of iron, totally dedicated to Kenya as a 'White Man's Country'; a die-hard imperialist, but personally charming. As a minister he was, however, indecisive, often agonising over minor decisions. He epitomised the settlers' capture of the colonial state during the war when he served as chairman of the Agricultural Production and Settlement Board, 1939–45; as Timber Controller for East Africa, 1940–45; and as a member of the East African Civil Defence and Supply Council, 1940–45.

Cohen, Andrew Benjamin
KCMG (1952), CMG (1948), KCVO (1954), OBE (1942); b. 1909; ed. Malvern and Trinity College, Cambridge; double first in Classics. Inland

Revenue 1932; transferred to the Colonial Office, 1933; seconded to control food supplies in embattled Malta, 1940–43; Assistant Secretary, Colonial Office, responsible for East Africa, 1943–47; Assistant Under-Secretary for Africa (the 'King of Africa') 1947–51; Governor of Uganda, 1952–57; Permanent British representative on United Nations' Trusteeship committee, 1957–61; Director General of the new Department of Technical Co-operation, 1961–64; Permanent Secretary of the Ministry of Overseas Development, 1964–68. On his father's side, Cohen was descended from the *haute juiverie* of business, and on his mother's, from a radical Unitarian family. Cohen was a large, exuberant man, with an enormous appetite for food and work. He was intellectually aggressive, extremely untidy, physically unattractive, and a brilliant and far-sighted colonial administrator. Cohen married in 1949. During the 1950s he tried to become a Labour Member of Parliament. Had been expected to become Permanent Secretary for the Colonies; published *British Policy in Changing Africa* (1959).

Cooke, Shirley Victor
Assistant District Officer, East African Protectorate, January 1917; Somalia patrol against the 'Mad Mullah', 1917–18; Political Officer, Turkana, 1921; District Officer, Kajiado, January–April 1923; District Commissioner, Kenya, 1928; Assistant District Commissioner, Kisumu, 1930; transferred to Tanganyika, 1931–38; resigned from the Colonial Service, 1938; elected settler Legislative Councillor for the Coast, 1938–63; settler Member of the Executive Council 1952, but unseated by his colleagues. Cooke was a vituperative Irishman; his tongue often got him into trouble as an administrator and he was often out of step with his settler colleagues; resigned from the African Settlement Board with Mathu in 1947 because of the government's failure to reopen the White Highlands' question. Mitchell considered appointing him as Member for Education in 1950, but gave the job to Ernest Vasey instead.

Coutts, Walter Fleming
KCMG (1961), CMG (1953), Kt. (1961), MBE (1949); b. 1912; ed. Glasgow Academy, St Andrews University and St John's College, Cambridge. District Officer, Kenya, 1936; Secretariat, 1946; District Commissioner Murang'a 1947–49; Administrator St Vincent, 1949; Minister for Education, Labour and Lands, Kenya, 1958–61; Special Commissioner for African elections, 1955; Chief Secretary, Kenya, 1958–61; Governor of Uganda, 1961–62.

Daubney, Robert
CMG (1939), OBE (1937), M.Sc., MRCVS. b. 1891, ed. Manchester Grammar School, Liverpool University, George

Washington University, Cambridge University, and Royal Veterinary College, London. Served European war, 1914–18; Helminthologist, Ministry of Agriculture 1920; joined Colonial Veterinary Service 1925; Director Veterinary Services, Kenya, 1937–46; Director of East African Central Veterinary Research Institute, 1939–46; Veterinary Adviser to the Egyptian Government, 1946–53. Daubney was a brilliant scientific researcher, but not a very practical supervisor of his staff. The veterinary department was more concerned with safeguarding settler-owned stock and with devising new serums for exotic stock than with devising a veterinary policy for the African reserves.

Davies, Eric Reginald St. Aubrey
OBE (1945); b. 1905; ed. Felsted School and Corpus Christi College, Cambridge. Cadet, Kenya, 1928; District Commissioner Nairobi, 1940; Information Officer, 1943–45; deputy Provincial Commissioner 1946; Provincial Commissioner, Coast Province, 1947–49; Chief Native Commissioner, September 1949–1953. Later served as Lieutenant-Governor of the Isle of Man where he retired. When Davies visited the Colonial Office in 1953 to discover where he was to be transferred, he was initially told that he should visit the labour exchange around the corner; eventually the Colonial Office relented and he was 'sentenced' to the Isle of Man.

Dawe, Arthur James
KCMG (1942), CMG (1938), OBE (1932); b. 1891; ed. Berkhamstead School and Brasenose College, Oxford. War service, 1914–18; joined the Colonial Office, 1918; Assistant Principal, 1920; private secretary to Leo Amery, 1920; and to E.F.L. Wood, 1921; Principal, 1921; secretary of the Commission of Enquiry into the affairs of the Freetown Municipality, 1926; Secretary to the Malta Royal Commission, 1931; Assistant Secretary, 1936; Assistant Under-Secretary for Africa, 1938–45; Deputy Under-Secretary for Palestine, 1945–47, when he retired.

Deverell, Colville Montgomery
KCMG (1957), CMG (1955), CVO (1953), OBE (1946); b. 1907; ed. Portora School, Enniskillen and Trinity College, Dublin, where he read law, and Trinity College, Cambridge. District Officer, Kenya, 1931; clerk to the Executive and Legislative Councils, 1938–39; Civil Affairs Branch, East African Command, served in Somaliland and Ethiopia, 1941–46; Secretary of the Development and Reconstruction Authority, Kenya, 1946–49; acting Financial Secretary 1949 and acting Chief Native Commissioner, 1949; Administrative Secretary, Kenya, 1949–52; Colonial Secretary, Jamaica, 1952–55; Governor of the Windward Islands, 1955–59; Governor of Mauritius, 1959–62.

Francis, Edward Carey
b. 1897; ed. William Ellis School, London, and Peterhouse, Cambridge;
Senior Wrangler. Lieutenant, Royal Artillery, 1916–19; Fellow of Peterhouse and University Lecturer in Mathematics, 1922–28, and as Bursar of Peterhouse, 1924–28; served with the Church Missionary Society in Kenya, 1928–62; Principal of Maseno School, 1928–40; Headmaster of Alliance High School (the Eton of Kenyan schools for Africans), 1940–62; assistant master at Pumwani Secondary School, 1962–66. Carey Francis was a brilliant maths master, a devout Evangelist and an unrelenting paternalist. At Maseno he quarrelled with the young Oginga Odinga, and as the new headmaster of Alliance High School soon drove his three senior African masters, E.W. Mathu, J.S. Gichuru and J.D. Otiende, from the staff.

Gater, George Henry
GCMG (1944), KCB (1941), Kt. (1936); b. 1886; ed. Winchester and New College, Oxford; 2nd class in Modern History; Diploma in Education. Oxfordshire Education Committee, 1911–12; Assistant Director of Education, Nottinghamshire, 1912–14; served in the war in Gallipoli, Egypt and France, was twice wounded; awarded DSO and bar, Commander Legion of Honour, and *Croix de Guerre*. Director of Education, Lancashire, 1919–24; Education Officer, London County Council, 1924–33; Clerk of the London County Council, 1933–39; Permanent Under-Secretary for the Colonies, 1939; Joint Permanent Secretary at the Home Office, 1939–40; Permanent Secretary at the Ministry of Supply, 1940; Permanent Secretary, Ministry of Home Security, 1940–42; Permanent Under-Secretary for the Colonies, 1942–47; Chairman School Broadcasting Council, 1948; Member of the Advisory Council of the BBC, 1952; Warden of Winchester, 1951–59.

Gichuru, James Samuel
b. 1914 at Thogoto in Kiambu; ed. CSM Kikuyu, Alliance High School, and Makerere College, 1933–34. Master at Alliance High School, 1935–40, but quarrelled with Carey Francis; Headmaster of CMS Junior Secondary School, Kikuyu, 1940–50; secretary of the Kenya Union of Teachers throughout the 1940s; President of the Kenya African Union, 1944–47; Vice-Chairman of Kiambu Local Native Council, 1948–50; Chief of Dagoretti location, Kiambu 1950–December 1952; restricted 1955–60, but allowed to continue teaching; acting President of the Kenya African National Union, 1960–61; MP Kiambu 1961–63; and Limuru 1963–82; Minister of Finance, 1962–69; Minister of Defence, 1969–79; and Minister of State, Office of the President, 1979–82.

Biographical Appendix

Gillett, Stuart
b. 1903; ed. Faversham Grammar School, Bedford School and the South Eastern Agricultural College, Wye, 1928. Assistant Agricultural Officer, Kenya, 1928; Agricultural Officer and Experimentalist, 1932; senior coffee officer, 1946; Commissioner for European Settlement, 1947; Director of Agriculture, 1949–51; Chairman of the Overseas Food Corporation, 1951.

Griffiths, Rt. Hon. James
PC (1945). b. 1890; ed. Bettws Council School, Ammanford, and Labour College, London. Coalminer; secretary of the Ammanford Trade Council, 1916–19; Agent Llanelly Labour Party, 1922–25; Miners' Agent for the Anthracite Mines Association, 1925–36; President South Wales Miners' Federation, 1934–36; executive committee of the Miners' Federation of Great Britain, 1934–36; Labour MP Llanelly, 1936–70; Minister of National Insurance, 1945–50; Secretary of State for the Colonies, 1950–51; Chairman of the Labour Party, 1948–49; Member of the National Executive, 1939–59; Deputy Leader of the Labour Party, 1955–59; Secretary of State for Wales, 1964–66.

Hall, George Henry
PC (1945), 1st Viscount Hall, 1946. b. 1881; ed. Penrhiwceiber Elementary School, Glamorganshire. Coalminer from the age of twelve at Penrhiwceiber colliery; check-weighter, local agent of the South Wales Miners' Federation, 1911–22; Labour MP Aberdare, 1922–46; Civil Lord of the Admiralty, 1929–31; Parliamentary Under-Secretary, Colonial Office 1940–42; Financial Secretary to the Admiralty, 1942–43; Parliamentary Under-Secretary at the Foreign Office, 1943–45; Secretary of State for the Colonies, 1945–46; First Lord of the Admiralty, 1946–51; Deputy Leader of the House of Lords, 1947–52.

Hall, John Hathorn
GCMG (1950), KCMG (1941), DSO, OBE, MC, *Croix de Guerre*. b. 1894; ed. St Paul's, and Lincoln College, Oxford. Military Service, 1915–18; Egyptian civil service, Ministry of Finance, 1919; Assistant Principal, Colonial Office, 1921; Principal, 1927; British representative to the Permanent Mandates Committee of the League of Nations, 1926–37; seconded to the Foreign Office, 1932; Chief Secretary, Palestine, 1933–37; British Resident, Zanzibar, 1937–40; Governor of Aden, 1940–44, Governor of Uganda, 1944–51.

Hammond, Robert Alston
OBE (1950), MRCVS, b. 1906; ed. Plumtree School, Southern Rhodesia, University of Liverpool, and the Royal Dick Veterinary

College, Edinburgh. Veterinary Officer, Kenya, 1930; Deputy Director of Veterinary Services, Kenya, 1947-52; Director of Veterinary Services, 1952.

Harris, Percy Wyn
KCMG (1952), CMG (1949), MBE (1941). b. 1903; ed. Gresham's School, Holt, and Gonville and Caius College, Cambridge; 2nd class Hons in Natural Sciences. District Officer, Kenya, 1926; Settlement Officer, Kikuyu Land Claims, 1939-40; District Commissioner, Nyeri, 1941-43; Labour Liaison officer, 1943-44; Labour Commissioner, 1944-46; Provincial Commissioner, Central Province, 1946-47; Chief Native Commissioner, 1947-49; Governor of the Gambia, 1949-58. 1929 made second ascent of Mt Kenya; first visit to North Island, Lake Turkana, 1931; member of the Mt Everest expeditions of 1933 and 1936. In 1933 took part in first assault with L.R. Wager and reached 28,000 feet. In retirement sailed a yacht around the world.

Hobson, (John) Basil
Q.C. (1950), b. 1905; ed. Sherborne; solicitor, 1929; Deputy Registrar, Supreme Court, Trinidad, 1936; Middle Temple, 1938; Crown Counsel, Uganda, 1939; served in the King's African Rifles, 1939-41; Deputy Judge Advocate, East African Command, 1941-44; Solicitor General and Legislative Councillor, Kenya, 1947-51; Chairman Labour Advisory Board, 1948-49; Attorney General, Nyasaland, 1951.

Hope-Jones, Arthur
KBE (1964), CMG (1956), b. 1911; ed. Kirkby Lonsdale and Christ's College, Cambridge; 1st class Hons in History; Columbia University (Commonwealth Fund Fellow), Brookings Institute, Washington DC. Fellow of Christ's College, Cambridge, 1937-46; war service 1939-46; economic adviser to the Anglo-Iranian Oil Company in Iran, 1944-46; economic adviser to the Kenyan government, 1946-48; Member of Commerce and Industry, 1948-60; Director and adviser to various companies since 1960; Chairman, London Sumatra Plantations Ltd since 1978. Publications: *Income Tax and the Napoleonic Wars* (1939).

Howes, Richard John Clyde
MBE; b. 1906; ed. King Edward VII School, Lytham, and Jesus College, Cambridge. Military service, King's African Rifles, 1941-42; Cadet, Kenya, 1929; District Officer, 1930; private secretary to Sir Joseph Byrne; Assistant Secretary, East African Governor's Conference, 1942; Secretary to the High Commissioner, Kenya and Uganda Railway and Harbours, 1944-45; Secretary, Development and Reconstruction Authority, 1945-46; Secretary to the Member for Health and Local

Government, 1946; District Commissioner Machakos, 1946–48; acting Commissioner for Local Government, 1949.

Hughes Rice, Thomas
b. 1907, Assistant Agricultural Officer Nyanza, 1939; served King's African Rifles, 1941–44, became Lieutenant Colonel; Assistant Agricultural Officer, Nyeri, 1944–45; Murang'a, 1945–47; 1947–51; Machakos, 1951–53; Provincial Agricultural Officer, Nyanza, 1953–56; Assistant Director of Agriculture, 1956.

Humphrey, Norman
b. 1897; ed. Haberdashers' Hampstead School; Military service, 1915–16; Agricultural Officer, Kenya, 1930: agricultural course at Cambridge, 1933; Senior Agricultural Officer, Kenya, 1940; sociological research in Kenya, 1944.

Hyde-Clarke, (Ernest) Meredyth
MBE. b. 1905; ed. St George's School, Harpenden; the London School of Economics and Wadham College, Oxford. Coffee farmer in Kenya, 1926; Cadet, Kenya, 1927; Assistant Secretary in the Secretariat, 1939; Personal assistant to the Chairman Agricultural Production and Settlement Board (Cavendish-Bentinck) 1944; Civil Reabsorption Officer, 1945; Deputy Labour Commissioner, 1945–46; Labour Commissioner and Legislative Councillor, 1946–51; chairman of the sub-committee of the Labour Advisory Board on African Registration, 1948.

Johnston, Carruthers Melvill
b. 1909; ed. Shrewsbury and Brasenose College, Oxford. Cadet, Kenya, 1933; District Commissioner, Meru, July 1945–June 1947 and February 1948–April 1950; Provincial Commissioner, Rift Valley, February 1951–July 1951 and March 1952–August 1953; Provincial Commissioner, Central Province, April–November 1950 and September 1953. Nicknamed 'Monkey'.

Jones, Arthur Creech
b. 1891; ed. Whitehall Boys' School. Civil servant in the War Office and the Crown Agents' Office, 1907–16; secretary of Camberwell Trades Council and Borough Labour Party, 1913–22; member of the No-Conscription Fellowship, 1915; imprisoned, September 1916–April 1919; Secretary to the National Union of Docks, Wharves and Shipping Staffs, 1919–22; national secretary of the administrative, clerical and supervisory section of the Transport and General Workers' Union, 1922–29; Executive Committee of the London Labour Party, 1921–28;

organising secretary of the Workers' Travel Association, 1929-39; defeated Labour candidate, Heywood and Radcliffe, 1929; Labour MP Shipley, 1935-50 and Wakefield, 1954-64; Chairman of the Labour Party's Advisory Committee on Imperial Affairs, 1943; Member of the Colonial Office's Advisory Committee on Education, 1936-45; Chairman Fabian Colonial Bureau, 1940-45; Vice Chairman of the Commission on Higher Education in West Africa, 1943-44; Parliamentary Private Secretary to Ernest Bevin, 1940-44; Under-Secretary for the Colonies, 1945-46; Secretary of State for the Colonies, 1946-50. Published *Trade Unionism Today, The Ruhr*, and ed. *Fabian Colonial Essays*.

In 1926 he instructed Clements Kadalie, general secretary of the South African Industrial and Commercial Workers' Union on trade union organization and this marked the beginning of his interest in colonial affairs. Creech Jones, however, did not visit Africa until 1944 when he went to West Africa; as Under-Secretary he toured East Africa with Andrew Cohen in August-September 1946. Creech was an ineffective performer in both Cabinet and the House of Commons and his relations with Attlee were distinctly cool. He would probably have been dropped from the Cabinet had he not lost his seat at Shipley in the 1950 general election. He was a protégé of Ernest Bevin. Creech Jones was a civil libertarian and less interested in colonial development.

Kaggia, Bildad Mwanganu

b. 1922 at Dagoretti; ed. Kahuhia School, Murang'a, where he was a classmate of B.M. Gecaga. Clerk District Commissioner's Office, Murang'a 1939-42; joined the army, and served in Egypt, Libya, Syria and Britain, 1942-45; rose to become staff sergeant. Refused to join the Kenya African Union as it was too élitist and conservative. Formed his own independent Anglican Church, the *Dini ya Kaggia*, 1945. Joined the Kenya African Union when Kenyatta became President in 1947; President of the Clerks' and Commercial Workers' Union, 1948; President of the Labour Trade Union of East Africa, 1950; General Secretary of the Nairobi branch of the Kenya African Union, 1951-52; arrested 20 October 1952; detained 1952-61; Assistant Minister of Education, 1963-June 1964; Deputy Leader of the Kenya People's Union, 1966-69; Chairman of the Cotton, Lint and Seed Marketing Board, 1970-71; Chairman of the Maize and Produce Board, 1971; published *The Roots of Freedom* (1975). MP for Kandara, 1963-66.

Kennaway, Noel Frederick

b. 1908; ed. Oundle and Clare College, Cambridge. Cadet, Kenya, 1931; District Commissioner, Kwale, 1945-46; Meru, June 1947-February 1948; Kiambu, February 1948-November 1950 and July

1951–February 1953; Provincial Commissioner, Coast Province, February 1953. Retired to Karen, Nairobi.

Kenyatta, Jomo
b. 1889; ed. CSM Kikuyu, London School of Oriental and African Studies, and London School of Economics. Carpenter;· interpreter in the Kenya Supreme Court; worked for the Nairobi Water Board, 1921–26; joined Young Kikuyu Association, 1922; General Secretary of the Kikuyu Central Association, 1928; editor of *Muigwithania*, the Association's newspaper, 1928–29; left for Britain, February 1929; visited Moscow; visit to Britain to submit evidence to the British government, 1931, remained until 1946; attended Quaker College, Woodbrooke, Birmingham, visited Moscow again and attended the Negro Workers' Congress in Hamburg; 1933–36 assistant in phonetics, London School of African and Oriental Studies; at the London School of Economics with Malinowski; published *Facing Mount Kenya* in 1938; organiser fifth Pan-African Congress in Manchester, 1945; married Edna Clarke, 1942; returned to Kenya, September 1946; elected President of the Kenya African Union, June 1947; detained 20 October 1952 until 1961; elected to the Legislative Council in January 1962; Prime Minister 1963–64; President 1964–78.

By 1952 Kenyatta had lost his influence over the political militants, he was becoming depressed at their reckless behaviour and had begun to drink heavily. He found it difficult to adjust to Kenya's racist society after 15 years in Britain; few Africans shared his intellectual interests, while the Europeans regarded him with profound suspicion as a dangerous communist agitator. Detention made him a political martyr and restored his reputation among the Kenyan masses as the leader of the nationalist movement, which had become tarnished between 1946 and his detention in 1952.

Khamisi, Francis Joseph
b. 1913 at Rabai near Mombasa; ed. Catholic High School, Kabaa. Employed by the East African Meteorological Service, 1937–39; editor of *Baraza*, 1939–45; General Secretary of the Kenya African Union, 1944–47; chief clerk with African Mercantile, Mombasa 1948–58; member of the Nairobi African Advisory Council, 1939–48; appointed member of the East African Central Assembly, 1957–61; elected Legislative Councillor, Kenya, for Mombasa, 1958–61; member of the Nairobi Municipal Council, 1946–47; member of the Mombasa Municipal Board, 1950–60; editor of *Baraza*, 1961–79.

Kibachia, Chege
b. 1920 in Kiambu; ed. Alliance High School, 1939–42, where he was taught by Eliud Mathu and James Gichuru. Worked with the Kiambu Chicken and Egg Sellers Co. 1943–45; then with the East African Clothing factory in Mombasa, 1945–47; emerged as President of the African Workers' Federation during the general strike in Mombasa in January 1947; detained because of his trade union activities, August 1947; detained Baringo 1947–57; 1964 appointed Industrial Relations Officer in the Labour Department in Mombasa; Senior Labour Officer, Mombasa, 1964; member of the Industrial Court of Kenya since 1979. Even after his detention the Kenyan government contemplated sending Kibachia on a course of trade union affairs at Ruskin College, Oxford; he was far from regarded as a hopeless militant, but they chose Meshak Ndisi instead.

Koinange, Peter Mbiyu
b. 1907 at Njunu in Kiambu; ed. CMS Kiamba, Kabete Primary School, Buxton High School Mombasa, and Alliance High School; Hampton Institute, Virginia, 1927–31; Ohio Wesleyan University, 1931–35; Teachers' College, Columbia University, 1935–36; St John's College, Cambridge, 1936–37; and Institute of Education, London University, 1937–38. He refused to serve on non-European terms in the Kenya Education Department; founded and was Principal of the Kenya Teachers' College at Githunguri, 1939–48; failed to be selected as the first African Member of the Legislative Council in 1944 despite campaigning for the job; a founder of the Kenya African Union in 1944, but became more closely involved after Kenyatta's return in 1946; delivered Kenya Land Petition to London with Achieng Oneko in 1951 and was still in London when the Emergency was declared; worked with the London Co-operative Society, 1951–59; the Kenya African Union's representative in London, 1951–59; Director of the Bureau of African Affairs in Ghana, 1959–60; Secretary General of the Pan African Freedom Movement for East, Central and South Africa in Dar-es-Salaam, 1961–62; MP for Kiambu, 1963–79, Minister for Pan African Affairs, 1963–64; Minister of Education, 1964–66; Minister of State, Office of the President, 1966–78; Minister for Water Development, 1978–79. Kenyatta married Koinange's sister in 1947; she died in childbirth in 1948. Koinange was Kenyatta's closest political associate from 1936 when they met in London until 1978.

Koinange wa Mbiyu
b. 1870s to 1881; a member of the *mbari ya Njunu*, which owned large tracts of land in southern Kiambu; appointed headman under his father Mbiyu, who was a government chief, in 1905; succeeded as chief in 1908;

Senior Chief of Kiambu, but without locational responsibilities in 1938; retired as Senior Chief in 1949; President of the Kikuyu Association in 1919; dominated the Kiambu Local Native Council from the mid-1920s until the 1940s; one of three witnesses appointed by the government to give evidence to the Joint Select Committee on Closer Union in London; active in raising funds for the Kenya Teachers' College at Githunguri; a member of the Executive Committee of the Kenya African Union, 1947–52; detained 1952–60. Koinange became increasingly radical after the Kenya Land Commission report, which was published in May 1934; by 1940 the government no longer trusted him because of his close relations with the Kikuyu Central Association. Became close friend and father-in-law of Kenyatta after 1946. Father of Mbiyu Koinange.

Kubai, Fred
b. of a Kikuyu father and a Giriama mother in Mombasa in 1915. Worked as telegraphist and became active in trades unionism; organizing secretary of the Kenya African Road Transport and Mechanics' Union, which became the Transport and Allied Workers' Union, in 1947; acting General Secretary in 1948; formed the East African Trades Union Congress in 1949, of which he was the President; organised boycott of the Nairobi Royal Charter celebrations in 1950; arrested but acquitted for attempting to assassinate Muchohi Gikonyo; Chairman of the Nairobi Branch of the Kenya African Union, 1951–52; editor of *Sauti ya Mwafrika*, 1951–52; arrested 20 October 1952; detained 1952–61; Member of the Mau Mau Central Committee, the *Muhimu*, 1948–52; failed to oust Tom Mboya from the leadership of the Trade Union movement after his release; MP Nakuru East 1963–74 and since 1983; Assistant Minister of Labour, 1963–74; since July 1985 has been Assistant Minister in the Office of the President. Between 1948 and 1952 Kubai was perhaps the most feared man in Kenya because of his close contacts with the Nairobi Kikuyu criminal gangs, such as the Forty Group, the *Anake a Forty*, and Mau Mau; Kubai controlled oathing in Nairobi from 1949–52; and was the leader of the militants.

Lloyd, Thomas Ingram Kynaston
GCMG (1951), KCMG (1947), CMG (1943), KCB (1949). b. 1896; ed. Rossall, RMA Woolwich, and Gonville and Caius College, Cambridge. Served in the Royal Engineers on the Middle Eastern front, 1916–19; Assistant Principal, Ministry of Health, 1920; transferred to the Colonial Office, 1921; Principal, 1929; Secretary of the Palestine Commission, 1929–30; Secretary of the Royal Commission to the West Indies, 1938–39; Assistant Secretary, 1939; Assistant Under-Secretary, 1943; Permanent Under-Secretary, 1947–56. Lloyd was a keen gardner, and *Country Life* referred to his garden at Radlett as 'probably the most

beautiful in Hertfordshire'. In his memoirs, Lyttelton observed that 'Tom Lloyd was an example of the best in the Civil Service, wise and salty in his judgements, never in a panic or a hurry, enlightened and broad-minded on colonial policy, a good judge of men . . . Some said that he did not allow his imagination to walk abroad but only took it on a lead for a short time. If this were true I should be far from saying that it was a fault in the permanent head of a department . . . With all this, he had perhaps too much loyalty for some of his particular swans who had 'turned, in the stress of colonial affairs or under the erosive influence of Government Houses, into geese.'

Lyttelton, 1st Viscount, (Oliver)

PC (1940), DSO, MC. b. 1893; ed. Eton and Trinity College, Cambridge. Grenadier Guards, 1915–18; Managing Director, Metal Box Co. Ltd; Conservative MP Aldershot, 1940–54; President of the Board of Trade, 1940–41; Minister Resident in the Middle East, 1941–42; Minister of Production, 1942–45; President of the Board of Trade, 1945; Chairman Associated Electrical Industries, 1945–51; Secretary of State for the Colonies, 1951–54; Chairman Associated Electrical Industries, 1954; Chairman of the N. Ireland Development Council, 1955; Chairman of the National Theatre, 1962; President of the Institute of Directors, 1954. Published *Memoirs of Lord Chandos* (1962). Lyttelton was an unreconstructed right-wing Conservative imperialist, and had had little previous experience of the colonies when he was appointed Secretary of State; he had hoped to be Chancellor of the Exchequer.

Maher, Alfred Colin

b. 1905; ed. Cambridge University and the College of Tropical Agriculture, Trinidad. Assistant Agricultural Officer, Kenya, 1929; Agricultural Officer, 1931; Secretary of the Board of Agriculture and the Maize Enquiry Committee, 1932; agricultural experimentalist on coffee and cereals in Trans Nzoia, 1933; Head of the Soil Conservation Unit, 1938–50. Resigned and farmed on the Kinangop. Maher was an intellectual, uninterested in sport or heavy drinking, and did not get on with his colleagues. After his appointment as experimentalist in 1933, he worked alone and kept his relations with other agricultural officers to the minimum. He did not suffer 'fools' gladly; a theoretician who was not interested in *ad hoc* reforms. Maher resigned in 1950 when he was passed over in the reconstruction of the agricultural department. Three weeks later his wife committed suicide, leaving him with four young children to raise. He failed to get a job with the Overseas Food Corporation in Tanganyika, or as a professor at the College of Tropical Agriculture in Trinidad. Maher was a frequent contributor to the Kenyan press on agricultural subjects; his wife was, for many years, the Trans Nzoia correspondent of the *East African Standard*.

Marchant, William Sydney
CMG (1942), OBE (1937), b. 1894. Served European war, 1915–18; Cadet, Kenya, 1919; Deputy Provincial Commissioner, Zanzibar, 1935–37; Deputy Provincial Commissioner, British Solomon Islands, 1939–43; Chief Native Commissioner, Kenya, 1943–47; Labour Adviser to the Overseas Food Corporation, 1947–50.

Masinde, Elijah
b. 1910; ed. Church of God Mission School, Kima, in Western Kenya; a keen footballer; became a physical instructor; Native Tribunal Court Process Server, N. Nyanza, 1937–42; formed the *Dini ya Msambwa* in 1942, an anti-European cult; sentenced to prison, 1945–46; detained at Lamu, 1948–61. Masinde has been imprisoned several times since independence for preaching defiance of authority.

Mathu, Eliud Wambu
b. Riruta in Kiambu in 1910; ed. Riruta Primary School, CSM Kikuyu, Alliance High School, Fort Hare University in South Africa, Exeter University, and Balliol College, Oxford. History master at Alliance High School 1940–43; Principal of Dagoretti High School, 1943; President Kenya Union of Teachers in the 1940s; nominated to the Legislative Council, 1944–57; nominated to the Executive Council, 1952; member of the East African Central Assembly, 1948–60; served with the United Nations Economic Commission for Africa, 1960–64; Chairman of the Council of the University of East Africa, 1963–69; Private Secretary to the President of Kenya, and Comptroller of State House, 1964–77; Chairman of Kenya Airways, 1977–80.

Mathu was Kenya's leading African politician from 1944–57. His relations with Kenyatta and Koinange were strained, but during the late 1940s Mathu became increasingly critical of the government. Despite his abilities, the British ceased to trust him and in 1954 appointed Ohanga instead of him as the first African minister. Three years later they engineered his defeat in the first African elections for the Legislative Council by the Meru politician, Bernard Mate. Mathu, however, was too moderate a figure, tainted by his colonialist past, to emerge as a powerful politician in independent Kenya, although he probably exercised considerable influence behind the scenes as Kenyatta's private secretary.

Mitchell, Philip Euen
GCMG (1947), KCMG (1937), CMG (1933), MC. b. 1890, fifth son of Capt. Hugh Mitchell of the Royal Engineers, who was working as a railway engineer in Spain; ed. St. Paul's School, and Trinity College, Oxford; 2nd class in Classics. Assistant Resident, Nyasaland, 1912–15;

Lieutenant, King's African Rifles, 1915–18; ADC and private secretary
to the Governor of Nyasaland 1918–19; Assistant Political Officer,
Tanganyika, 1919; Assistant Secretary for Native Affairs, Tanganyika,
1926–28; Provincial Commissioner, Northern Province, 1928; Secretary
for Native Affairs, 1928–34; Chief Secretary, Tanganyika, 1934–35;
Governor of Uganda, 1935–40; deputy Chairman of the East African
Governors' Conference, 1940–41; political adviser to General Wavell,
1941–42; British Plenipotentiary in Ethiopia and Chief Political Officer to
East Africa High Command, with the rank of Major-General 1942;
Governor of Fiji and High Commissioner in the Western Pacific,
1942–44; Governor of Kenya, 1944–52. Retired to his farm at Subukia,
1952–63; and to Gibraltar, 1963–64. Published *African Afterthoughts*
(1954).

Mitchell refused to remain in Kenya when Kenyatta came to power
since he still believed him to have been the leader of Mau Mau. Mitchell's
personal ideology reflected his inter-war experiences in Tanganyika and
Uganda, where the chiefs had been the cornerstone of the colonial state
and African politicians had hardly existed or could easily be dismissed as
agitators – half educated men in trousers misleading the noble men in
blankets. Although Fiji had provided Mitchell with a vision of a multiracial society, which he hoped could be created in Kenya as well, he was
unwilling to co-opt Mathu, let alone Kenyatta. The Colonial Office, as we
have seen, had selected him to reassert metropolitan authority in Kenya,
because not only was the he their most experienced East Africanist, but he
also had a reputation for being anti-settler. This was probably true – he
never got on socially with the settler politicians or businessmen in
Nairobi, who ostensibly came from a similar background. While he was
willing to accept that the settlers had captured certain key positions within
the state during the war and had quickly recognised that it was politically
inadvisable to dislodge Cavendish-Bentinck from his position as a 'virtual
Minister of Agriculture', he refused to make any major concessions to the
Kenya African Union, even when the moderate constitutionalists were
firmly in command during 1945 and 1946. Throughout his years in
Kenya, Mitchell remained conceptually stuck in the mud of indirect rule
and his successes in Tanganyika and Uganda in the 1920s and 1930s. To
him (and many other senior administrators) African politicians were by
definition 'agitators', against whom the *waranchi* had to be protected. As
their demands became increasingly strident, paternalism and 'a firm
refusal to be rattled' were even more essential. For this kind of blinkered
mind, the rumours of discontent among the squatters in 1946, the violent
disturbances in Murang'a in 1947, or the continual troubles in Olenguruone, simply provided further proof of the irresponsibility and short-
term, selfish aims of these troublecausers. Now was the time for the
colonial government to stand firm and to push ahead with its agricultural

development programme in Central Province and to prevent further land degradation. The men in blankets had to be protected from their unscrupulous leaders. Indeed to Mitchell's paternalist mind, the demonstrations against terracing and dipping stiffened his resolve. He was convinced that the agitators knew, like himself, that the agricultural campaign would eventually succeed, raise African living standards and create a contented peasantry. These politically inspired protests were their last desperate throw, before the benefits became evident to the *wananchi*. If only the government stood firm and the agricultural department pressed ahead, Kenya would soon emerge out of the tunnel of despair into a future of organic development and political tranquility, well on the way to a stable, multiracial future. The late 1940s might be a difficult time, but if only he could hold on, the alarmists would be discredited, African opposition would subside, and Philip Mitchell in the early 1950s would be justified, and confirmed as a great colonial governor.

Mitchell therefore refused to lose his nerve and clung to office, despite his increasing exhaustion and ill health. Next year, if not this, he was firmly convinced, would prove him right. The governor obstinately refused to heed warnings about Mau Mau or the deteriorating position in the reserves or the White Highlands and convinced himself, in his lonely isolation, that they would wither away. The ship of state would sail through the present storm into a peaceful, sunny anchorage, with the governor at the helm. As his views became known in the administration, District Commissioners who after 1950 were already having to fight to keep control of their districts, found that their warnings were watered down in the Secretariat, who knew what the governor wanted to hear, and Mitchell refused to warn Whitehall of the impending doom. As African resistance grew in the 1950s, during the last two years of Mitchell's governorship, there was a loss of political will and self-confidence in the field administration.

Moore, Henry Monck-Mason
GCMG (1943), KCMG (1935), CMG (1930). b 1887; ed. King's College School, Cambridge and Jesus College, Cambridge. Cadet, Ceylon, 1911; Assistant Colonial Secretary, 1914–16 and 1919–20; Salonika campaign, 1916; Private Secretary to the Governor of Ceylon, 1919–20; Colonial Secretary, Bermuda, 1922–24; Principal Assistant Secretary, Nigeria, 1924–27; Deputy Chief Secretary, Nigeria, 1927–29; Colonial Secretary, Kenya, 1929–34, Governor of Sierra Leone, 1934–37; Assistant Under-Secretary, Colonial Office, 1937–40; Governor of Kenya, 1940–44; Governor of Ceylon, 1944–48; Governor-General of Ceylon, 1948–49; retired to Cape Town, 1949–64. Moore never got over the experience of serving as Byrne's Colonial Secretary when he bore the front of settler criticism during the depression. When he

returned as governor he wanted a quiet life, and allowed the settlers to make considerable political gains during the war.

Morgan, David Loftus
CMG (1952), MBE (1943). b. 1904; ed. Harrow and Trinity College, Cambridge; gained upper second in History. Cadet, Kenya, 1926; District Officer, 1928; District Commissioner Nyeri, 1943–45; Provincial Commissioner, Rift Valley, 1946 to February 1951; Resident Commissioner, Swaziland, 1951–56. Morgan had little time for African opposition and had no understanding of the complex problems which faced the field administration in post-war Kenya.

Mortimer, Charles Edward
Kt. (1950), CBE (1943). b. 1886; ed. Hartley College, Manchester. Son of Joseph Mortimer, Mayor of Nairobi in 1930 and 1937; Methodist Minister, 1910–16 in Britain; clerk Land Department, Kenya 1917; Land Assistant, 1920–27; Lands Secretary, 1928–38; Commissioner for Lands and Settlement, 1938–39; Commissioner for Local Government, Lands and Settlement, 1939–46; Member for Health and Local Government, 1946–50 and 1952–54.

Mullins, Aubrey Charles Madgewick
b. 1903; ed. St Andrew's College, Grahamstown, South Africa, and Keble College, Oxford. Cadet, Kenya, 1926; Assistant District Commissioner, 1926; District Commissioner, Kiambu, May 1944–January 1945 and March 1945–February 1947; Deputy Provincial Commissioner, 1946; Provincial Commissioner, Central Province, February 1947–April 1948 and January–May 1949; and Provincial Commissioner, Coast Province, 1949–52.

Odede, Fanuel Walter
b. 1912 at Uyoma, Central Nyanza; ed. Maseno Secondary School, Alliance High School, Veterinary Training Centre at Maseno, and Makerere College. Assistant Veterinary Officer at Maseno, 1941; appointed temporary member of the Legislative Council during Beecher's absence in 1945; advanced study in Britain; appointed lecturer in Veterinary Science at Makerere; Director of the Associated Press of East Africa Ltd, 1952; acting President of the Kenya African Union following Kenyatta's detention, October 1952–March 1953; detained 1953–October 1960; MP 1961–63 and October–December 1974.

O'Hagan, Desmond
CMG (1952). b. 1909 at Nyeri, where his father was a coffee planter; ed. Wellington College and Clare College, Cambridge. Cadet, Kenya, 1931;

Inner Temple, 1935; private secretary to the British Resident in Zanzibar, 1937; District Commissioner, Kenya, 1940; District Commissioner, Nairobi, November 1944–April 1945; District Commissioner, Murang'a, April 1945–May 1947; Native Courts' Adviser, 1948–52; Provincial Commissioner, Coast Province, 1952–January 1953 and September 1953–1959; Provincial Commissioner, Central Province, January–September 1953; head of the Passenger Transport Board in Tanganyika, 1959–62, Retired to his wife's family's coffee farm at Kiambu. O'Hagan was a firm paternalist who encouraged African entrepreneurs, but would not tolerate opposition; he was a popular District Commissioner with the Kikuyu in Murang'a between 1945–47, and was very successful at encouraging terracing.

Ohanga, Benaiah Apolo
b. 1913 at Gem, Central Nyanza; ed. Maseno School and Alliance High School. Teacher, 1933–45; in 1949 went on courses in primary education and local government in Britain; member Central Nyanza District Education Board, 1943–48; secretary of the Luo Language Committee and a member of th Kenya Language Board, 1945; nominated Legislative Councillor, 1947–57; 1954 appointed first African Minister, served as Minister of Community Development and Rehabilitation, 1954–57; Nairobi City Education Officer, 1958–63; Secretary and Executive Officer, Kenya Overseas Scholarship Committee, 1963; Member Nairobi City Council, 1961–63; Inspector of Children in the Ministry of Home Affairs, 1963–66; Vice President of the Central Organisation of Trade Unions, 1966.

Osborne, Paul Stanley
b. 1908; ed. Christ's Hospital, and Sidney Sussex College, Cambridge. Cadet, Kenya, 1931; District Commissioner, Murang'a, July 1944–April 1945; District Commissioner, Nyeri, September 1945–June 1948, and January 1949–September 1950; and District Commissioner North Nyanza, September 1950–1952.

Penfold, Cecil
b. 1906; ed. Lancing and Oxford University. Police Constable, Kenya, 1930; Assistant Superintendent, 1933; Superintendent and Director of Intelligence and Security, 1946–50; Assistant Commissioner of Police, 1950.

Potter, Henry Steven
KCMG (1955), CMG (1948). b. 1904; ed. Shrewsbury and Queen's College, Cambridge; 3rd in Law. Cadet, Kenya, 1926; District Officer, Kenya, 1928; Deputy Financial Secretary, 1944–45; Financial Secretary,

Uganda, 1945–48; Chief Secretary, Uganda, 1948–52; Chief Secretary, Kenya, 1952–54; British Resident, Zanzibar, 1954–60. Potter acted as governor from Mitchell's departure in June until Baring arrived in September. Unlike Mitchell, he immediately informed Whitehall that the situation in the Kikuyu areas was getting out of control.

Rankine, John Dalzell
KCMG (1954), CMG (1947), KCVO (1956). b. 1907, son of Sir Richard Rankine, Chief Secretary, Nyasaland, 1920–27, Chief Secretary Uganda 1927–30, and British Resident, Zanzibar, 1930–37; ed. Christ's College, Christchurch, New Zealand, and Exeter College, Oxford; 2nd in History. Cadet, Uganda, 1931; District Officer, Uganda, 1933; Assistant Secretary of the East African Governors' Conference, 1939–42; Assistant Colonial Secretary, Fiji, 1942–45; Colonial Secretary, Barbados, 1945–47; Chief Secretary, Kenya, 1947–52; Resident Zanzibar, 1952–54; Governor of Western Nigeria, 1954–60. Rankine was Mitchell's protégé from 1935–52 and went in awe of him.

Rennie, Gilbert McCall
KCMG (1949), CMG (1941), Kt. (1946), GBE (1954), MC. b. 1895; ed. Stirling High School, and Glasgow University. Military service, 1915–19, acting brigade major. Cadet, Ceylon, 1920; police magistrate, 1923; District judge, 1925; Controller Finance and Supply, 1932; Secretary to the Governor, 1934; Financial Secretary, Gold Coast, 1937–39; Chief Secretary, Kenya, 1939–48; Chairman of the Development and Reconstruction Authority, 1945–48; Governor of Northern Rhodesia, 1948–54; High Commissioner in London for the Federation of Rhodesia and Nyasaland, 1954–61; Chairman UK Freedom from Hunger Campaign, 1965.

Ryland, Richard Desmond Fetherston-Haugh
b. 1904; ed. Sedbergh and Lincoln College, Oxford. Cadet, Kenya, 1928; District Commissioner, Kitui, July 1944–August 1947; District Commissioner, Nyeri, April 1948–December 1950 and March 1952–January 1953; Provincial Commissioner, Rift Valley, November 1948–January 1949 and July 1951–March 1952.

Scott, Lord Francis Montagu-Douglas
b. 1879, sixth son of the sixth Duke of Buccleuch; ed. Eton and Oxford. Served in the army, 1899–1919, ADC to the Viceroy of India, 1905; settled in Kenya, 1919; Member of the Legislative and Executive Councils in the 1920s and 1930s; following Lord Delamere's death was the leading settler politician throughout the 1930s; severely injured in the leg during the First World War; his leg was amputated just before his

Biographical Appendix

death in 1952. Mitchell hated him, because Scott viewed the governor as a middle-class upstart and treated him as such.

Singh, Makhan
b. 1913 in India; came to Kenya in 1927; ed. Government Indian High School, Nairobi. Formed Labour Trade Union of East Africa, 1934; led two month strike in Nairobi in 1937; formed Labour Trade Union of East Africa, 1939; interned in India, 1940–45; returned to Kenya on 22 August 1947; worked for the East African Indian National Congress, 1947–49; took over the African Workers' Federation in 1949; formed East African Trade Union Congress, 1949, with Fred Kubai as President, and Makhan Singh as Secretary; organised boycott of the Nairobi Charter celebrations, 1950; arrested during the Nairobi general strike on 15 May 1950; detained May 1950–October 1961; tried unsuccessfully to re-enter the trade union movement; retired to write a history of the Kenyan trade unions. Published *History of Kenya's Trade Union Movement to 1952* (1976), and *History of Kenya's Trade Union Movement, 1952–56* (1980). Singh was a member of the Indian Communist Party and embarrassed Kenyatta and Mathu by calling for immediate independence for Kenya at a joint meeting of the Kenya African Union and the East African Indian National Congress in April 1950.

Tempany, Harold Augustin
Kt. (1946), CMG (1941), CBE (1933), D.Sc., FRIC, FCS. b. 1881; ed. privately and University College, London. Assistant government chemist, Leeward Islands, 1903; JP Antigua, 1910; Legislative Councillor, Antigua, 1912; Director of Agriculture, Mauritius, 1917–29; Director of Agriculture, Malaya, 1929–36; Assistant Agricultural Adviser to the Secretary of State, 1936–40; Agricultural Adviser to the Secretary of State, 1940–46. Published *Principles of Tropical Agriculture*.

Thornley, Colin Hardwick
KCMG (1957), CMG (1953), CVO (1954). b. 1907; ed. Uppingham and Brasenose College, Oxford; read Jurisprudence. Cadet, Tanganyika, 1930; seconded to Colonial Office, 1939–45; Private Secretary to the Secretary of State, 1941–45; Administrative Secretary, Kenya, 1945–47; Deputy Chief Secretary, Kenya, 1947–52; Member for Education and Labour, 1947–52; Chief Secretary, Uganda, 1952–55; Governor of British Honduras, 1955–61; Member of the Regional Boundaries Commission, Kenya, 1962; Director of Save the Children Fund, 1965–74.

Thuku, Harry
b. 1895 at Kambui; ed. Gospel Missionary School, Kambui. Compositor, *Leader of British East Africa*, a settler newspaper, 1911–17; telephone operator at the Treasury, 1917–21; founded East African Association, 1921; detained February 1922–December 1930; President of the Kikuyu Central Association, August 1932; disagreements with Jesse Kariuki and Joseph Kangethe; formed Kikuyu Provincial Association, 1935; President Kenya African Union, 1944–45. By 1945 Thuku had become a loyalist; he was a strong opponent of Mau Mau and in 1952 organised meetings with Chief Waruhiu against the movement.

Troughton, John Frederick George
MBE (1936), b. 1902; ed. St Andrew's College, Dublin and Trinity College, Dublin; gold medal in mental and moral philosophy. Cadet, Kenya, 1926; District Officer, 1928; Secretary to the Kenya Land Commission, 1933; clerk to the Legislative and Executive Councils, 1933; seconded to the Colonial Office, 1936; and to BBC News, 1936; Deputy Financial Secretary, Kenya, 1939–44; Economic and Development Secretary, Kenya, 1944–46; Financial Secretary, 1946–49; Member of the Kenya Legislative Council, 1943–49; Controller of Finance, Overseas Food Corporation in East Africa, 1949–50; Member East African Central Assembly, 1949–50; Director Uganda Development Corporation, 1950. Troughton quarralled with Mitchell when he was Deputy Chairman of the East African Governor's Conference, 1940–41 and their relations between 1944 and 1949 were always strained.

Vasey, Ernest Albert
KBE (1959), CMG (1945). b. 1901; left school aged twelve at Bromley. Served on the Executive Committee of the National Conservative Association, the West Midlands Unionist Association and the Junior Imperial League; active in West Midlands' Conservative politics, 1929–37; migrated to Kenya in 1937; elected for Westland to the Nairobi Municipal Council, 1938–50; Mayor of Nairobi, 1941–42 and 1944–46; succeeded Cavendish-Bentinck as Legislative Councillor for Nairobi N. 1945–50; Member for Education, Health and Local Government, 1950–52; Minister of Finance and Development, 1952–59; Tanganyika Minister of Finance, 1959–62; economic adviser to the World Bank, 1962–66; Resident representative of the International Bank for Reconstruction and Development, Pakistan, 1963–66. Vasey was a liberal in settler politics; indeed he financed W.W.W. Awori's newspaper, *Radio Posta*, in the late 1940s.

Vincent, Alfred
b. 1891; ed. Russell Hill, Purley. Vincent was a prominent Nairobi businessman, Managing Director of Motor Mart and Exchange; Chairman, International Airadio (EA) Ltd.; Chairman, Greenham (EA) Ltd and of the Savings and Loan Society Ltd; Member of the Legislative Council, 1942–48; Member of the Executive Council, 1944–48; Member of the East African Central Assembly, 1948–53; Member of the inter-territorial Supply and Production Council; Chairman of the East African Airways Corporation. Vincent was the leader of the settler elected members from 1944–48. Mitchell was disappointed with him when he failed to support multiracialism during the Closer Union controversy and merely followed the diehards. He was a weak and ineffective politician and retired in 1948 to concentrate on his business activities, which were based on his position as East African representative for General Motors and the Ford Motor Co.

Windley, Edward Henry
b. 1909; ed. Repton and Cambridge University where he read anthoropology. Cadet, Kenya, 1931; District Commissioner, Kiambu, April 1947–February 1948; Provincial Commissioner, Central Province, April 1948–December 1948, May 1949–March 1950, and November 1950–January 1953. A man of considerable private means.

Bibliography

Archival sources

1. Kenya National Archives, Nairobi
A large number of files from central government ministries were consulted as well as a selection of District and Provincial correspondence. These included:
Government House Deposit Four
Secretariat
Chief Secretary Deposit One
Chief Secretary Deposit Two
Labour Deposit Two
Labour Deposit Nine
Labour Deposit Eleven
Agriculture Deposit One
Agriculture Deposit Two
Agriculture Deposit Four
Member for African Affairs Deposit One
Member for African Affairs Deposit Six
Member for African Affairs Deposit Seven
Member for African Affairs Deposit Eight
Member for African Affairs Deposit Nine
Member for African Affairs Deposit Ten
Member for African Affairs Unclassified, i.e. files from the old catalogue which had not been
    reclassified when I left Nairobi in September 1981.
Commerce and Industry Deposit Six
Commerce and Industry Deposit Seven
Defence Deposit Nine
Defence Deposit Ten
Defence Deposit Fifteen
Education Deposit One
Attorney General Deposit One
Central Christian Educational Association
The Murumbi Archive
Provincial Commissioner Central Province
Provincial Commissioner Nakuru
Provincial Commissioner Rift Valley Province
Provincial Commissioner Nyanza Province
District Commissioner Nakuru
District Commissioner Kiambu
District Commissioner Fort Hall (Murang'a)
District Commissioner Nyeri
District Commissioner Machakos
District Commissioner Kajiado
District Commissioner Narok

Bibliography

District Commissioner Teita–Taveta
  Some Annual Reports, Political Record Books, Handing Over Reports and Intelligence Reports concerning Central Province, Kiambu, Fort Hall and Nyeri were consulted on microfilm at the Seeley History Library, Cambridge.

2. Public Record Office, London
Series C.O. 533 Kenya Original Correspondence
Series C.O. 537 Colnial General Supplementary Original Correspondence.
Series C.O. 543 Kenya Miscellanea, 1901–1946
Series C.O. 544 Kenya Sessional Papers
Series C.O. 822 East Africa Original Correspondence
Series C.O. 852 Economic Original Correspondence
Series C.O. 967 Private Office Papers
Series C.O. 968 Defence Original Correspondence
Series W.O. 276 East Africa Command, 1936–1954
Series Cab. 134 Cabinet Committees: General Series, 1945 onwards.

3. Rhodes House Library, Oxford
Collections of private papers:
Records of the Fabian Colonial Bureau (RH Mss.Brit.Emp.s. 365)
Records of the Electors' Union and the European Elected Members' Organisation (RH Mss.Afr.s. 596)
Thomas G. Askwith (Rh Mss.Afr.s. 1170)
Clarence Edward Victor Buxton (RH Mss.Afr.s. 1103)
Arthur Creech Jones (RH Mss.Brit.Emp.s. 332)
Colin Maher (RH Mss.Afr.s. 1741)
Philip Euen Mitchell (RH Mss.Afr.r. 101)
Stephen Howard Powles (RH Mss.Afr.s. 1121)

4. Private Collections
The Standard Newspaper Group, Nairobi, allowed access to their press-cuttings library which contains many extracts not only from the *East African Standard*, but from a wide range of other Kenyan and British newspaers and includes many original documents such as official reports and election manifestos.

Unpublished theses

Anderson, D.M., 'Herder, Settler and Colonial Rule: A History of the Peoples of the Baringo Plains, Kenya, circa 1890 to 1940', (Ph.D., Cambridge, 1982).
Barnes, C., 'An Experiment with African Coffee Growing in Kenya: the Gusii, 1933–1950' (Ph.D., Michigan State, 1976).
Behrmann, C.F., 'The Mythology of British Imperialism', (Ph.D., Boston, 1965).
Berman, B.J., 'Administration and Politics in Colonial Kenya', (Ph.D., Yale, 1973).
Breen, R.M., 'The Politics of Land: the Kenya Land Commission 1932–33 and its Effects on Land Policy in Kenya', (Ph.D., Michigan State, 1976).
Cowen, M.P., 'Capital and Household Production: the Case of Wattle in Kenya's Central Province, 1903–64', (Ph.D., Cambridge, 1978).
Feldman, D.M., 'Christians and Politics: the Origins of the Kikuyu Central Association in Northern Murang'a, 1890–1930', (Ph.D., Cambridge, 1979).
Githige, R.M., 'The Religious Factor in Mau Mau', (M.A., Nairobi, 1978).
Hay, M.J. 'Economic change in Luoland: Kowe, 1890–1945',(Ph.D., Wisconsin, 1972).
Horowitz, D., 'Attitudes of British Conservatives towards Decolonization in Africa during the Period of the Macmillan Government, 1957–63', (D.Phil., Oxford, 1967).
Kanogo, T.M.J., 'The History of Kikuyu Movement into the Nakuru District of the Kenya White Highlands, 1900–1963', (Ph.D., Nairobi, 1980).
Kennedy, D.K., 'A Tale of Two Colonies; the Social Origins and Cultural Consequences of White Settlement in Kenya and Rhodesia, 1890–1939', (Ph.D., University of California, Berkeley, 1981).

Bibliography

Mosley, P., 'The Settler Economies: Studies in the Economic History of Kenya and Southern Rhodesia, 1900-1963', (Ph.D., Cambridge, 1980).

Mueller, S.D., 'Political Parties in Kenya: Patterns of Opposition and Dissent, 1919-1969', (Ph.D., Princeton, 1972).

Mukaru-Ng'ang'a, D., 'Political History of Murang'a', (M.A., Nairobi, 1978).

Redley, M.G., 'The Politics of a Predicament; the White Community in Kenya, 1918-1932', (Ph.D., Cambridge, 1976).

Westcott, N.J., 'The Impact of the War on Tanganyika, 1939-49', (Ph.D., Cambridge, 1982).

Unpublished papers and reports

Berman, B.J., 'Provincial Administration and the Contradictions of Colonialism: "Development" Policy and Conflict in Kenya, 1945-52', Cambridge Conference on the Political Economy of Kenya, 1975.

Cowen, M.P., 'Concentration of Sales and Assets: Dairy Cattle and Tea in Magutu, 1964-1971', Institute of Development Studies, Nairobi, Working Paper No. 146.

—— 'Differentiation in a Kenya Location', Paper No. 16, Eighth Annual Conference of the East African Universities Social Science Council, December 1972.

—— 'Patterns of Cattle Ownership and Dairy Production, 1900-1965', mimeo, 1979.

—— and K. Kinyanjui, 'Some Problems of Class Formation in Kenya', mimeo, Institute of Development Studies, Nairobi, March 1977.

—— and F.Murage, 'Wattle Production in the Central Province: Capital and Household Commodity Production, 1903-1964', mimeo, Nairobi, July 1975.

—— 'Notes on Agricultural Wage Labour in a Kenya Location'.

Furedi, F., 'Olenguruone in Mau Mau Historiography', Paper presented to the Conference on the Mau Mau Rebellion, Institute of Commonwealth Studies, London, 29 March 1974.

Kanogo, T.M.J., 'Comparative Analysis of the Aspirations of the Kikuyu, Luo and Luhya Workers in the White Highlands, 1900-1930', History Department, Nairobi, Seminar Paper.

—— 'The Kikuyu Squatter Phenomenon in the Nakuru District of the Rift Valley: An Interpretation', History Department, Nairobi, Seminar Paper No. 21, May 1977.

Lonsdale, J.M., 'The Growth and Transformation of the Colonial State in Kenya, 1929-52' History Department, Nairobi, Seminar Paper No. 17, August 1980.

—— 'African Elites and Social Classes in Colonial Kenya', for the Round Table, Elites anciennes et nouvelles et colonisation, Maison des Sciences de l'Homme, Paris, July 1982.

—— 'Explanations of the Mau Mau Revolt, Kenya 1952-56', University of Cape Town African Studies Seminar, 27 July 1983.

—— 'Kenya's Civil War and Glorious Revolution: Notes Towards a Peasant Ideology', unpublished essay.

Maher, A.C., 'Soil Erosion and Land Utilisation in the Kamasia, Njemps and East Suk Reserves', Agricultural Department, Nairobi, mimeo, 1937.

Mutiso, G.C.M., 'The Creation of the Kitui Asomi', mimeo, Institute of Development Studies, Nairobi, Working Paper No. 304, October 1977.

Omosule, M., 'An Assessment of the Role of the Kenya Land Commission Report in the Mau Mau Outbreak', Historical Association of Kenya Annual Conference, August 1981.

Sykes, W., 'Sukumaland', report for the Oxford Development Record Project, 1983.

Thurston, A., 'The Intensification of Smallholder Agriculture in Kenya: the Genesis and Implementation of the Swynnerton Plan', report for the Oxford Development Record Project, 1983.

Westcott, N.J., 'The Politics of Planning and the Planning of Politics: Colonialism and Development in British Africa, 1930-1960', Development Studies Association Conference, 1981.

Bibliography

Official publications

1. United Kingdom Government: Parliamentary Papers and Colonial Reports

1934 Cmd. 4556 *Report of the Kenya Land Commission* (Chairman Sir Morris Carter)
1934 Cmd. 4580 *Kenya Land Commission: Summary of Conclusions Reached by His Majesty's Government*
1936 Col. 116 *Report of the Commission Appointed to Enquire into and Report on the Financial Position and System of Taxation in Kenya* (Sir A. Pim)
1946 Col. 191 *Inter-Territorial Organization in East Africa*
1946 Col. 193 *Labour Conditions in East Africa* (G. St. J. Orde-Browne)
1947 Col. 210 *Inter-Territorial Organization in East Africa: Revised Proposals*
1950 Cmd. 7987 *The British Territories in East and Central Africa, 1945–1950*
1952 Col. 290 *Land and Population in East Africa: exchange of correspondence between the Secretary of State for the Colonies and the Governor of Kenya on the appointment of the Royal Commission*
1955 Cmd. 9475 *East Africa Royal Commission, 1953–55: Report* (Chairman Sir Hugh Dow)
1960 Cmd. 1030 *Historical Survey of the Origins and Growth of Mau Mau* (F.D. Corfield)

2. Kenya Government Publications

1941 *Report on the Housing of Africans in Nairobi*
1941 *Interim Report of a Committee Appointed to Advise as to the Steps to be taken to deal with the Problem of Overstocking in order to Preserve the Future Welfare of the Native Pastoral Areas* (East Africa Pamphlet No. 293)
1943 *Report of the Food Shortage Commission*
1943 *Report of the Sub-Committee on Post-War Employment of Africans*
1945 *The Kikuyu Lands: the Relation of Population to the Land in South Nyeri* (N. Humphrey); and *Memorandum on Land Tenure in the Native Lands* (H.E. Lambert and P. Wyn Harris)
1945 *Post-War Settlement in Kenya: proposed schemes*
1945 *Report on Native Tribunals* (A. Phillips)
1945 *Report of the Committee of Inquiry into Labour Unrest in Mombasa* (Chairman A. Phillips)
1945 *Proposals for the Reorganization of the Administration in Kenya* (S.P. No. 3)
1946 *Report of the Development Committee*, 2 vols. (Chairman J.F.G. Troughton)
1946 *General Aspects of the Agrarian Situation in Kenya*, Despatch No.44 (17 April 1946) from Sir Philip Mitchell
1947 *The Agrarian Problem in Kenya* (Note by Sir Philip Mitchell)
1947 *Report of the Taxation Enquiry Committee, Kenya, 1947* (Chairman R.P. Plewman)
1947 *The Liguru and the Land: Sociological Aspects of some Agricultural Problems of North Kavirondo* (N. Humphrey)
1948 *Nairobi, Master Plan for a Colonial Capital* (L.W.T. White, L. Silberman, and P.R. Anderson) (London, 1948)
1948 *An Inquiry into Indian Education in East Africa* (A.A. Kazimi); and *Report of Committee on Educational Expenditure*
1948 *A Ten Year Plan for the Development of African Education*
1949 *Report of the Select Committee on Indian Education*
1949 *African Education in Kenya: Report of a Committee Appointed to Enquire into the Scope, Content, and Methods of African Education, its Administration and Finance, and to Make Recommendations* (Chairman Rev. L.J. Beecher)
1950 *Report of Committee on Agricultural Credit for Africans* (Chairman J.H. Ingham)
1950 *Report of a Commission of Inquiry Appointed to Review the Registration of Persons Ordinance 1947* (Chairman B.J. Glancy)
1951 *Agricultural Policy in African Areas* (P.E. Mitchell)
1951 *African Education: a Statement of Policy*
1953 *Report of the Inquiry into the General Economy of Farming in the Highlands* (L.G. Troup)
1954 *The Psychology of Mau Mau* (J.C. Carothers)
1954 *Report of the Committee on African Wages* (Chairman F.W.Carpenter)
1954 *A Plan to Intensify the Development of African Agriculture in Kenya* (R.J.M. Swynnerton)

Bibliography

Other publications

1. Books

Aaronovitch, S. and K., *Crisis in Kenya*, (London 1947).

African Land Development Board, *African Land Development Board in Kenya 1946-55: Report by the African Land Development Board*, (Nairobi 1955).

Allan, W., *Studies in African Land Usage in Northern Rhodesia*, (Rhodes-Livingstone Papers, No. 15, Oxford 1949).

Andaya, B.W. and L.Y., *A History of Malaysia* (London 1982).

Asad, T. (ed.), *Anthropology and the Colonial Encounter* (London 1973).

Austin, D., *Politics in Ghana, 1946-1960*, (Oxford 1964).

Barnett, D.L. and K. Njama, *Mau Mau From Within*, (New York 1966).

Bell, J.B., *On Revolt: Strategies of National Liberation*, (Cambridge, Massachusetts 1976).

Bennett, G., *Kenya: A Political History*, (Oxford 1963).

Bernard, F.E., *East of Mount Kenya: Meru Agriculture in Transition*, (Munich 1972).

Berque, J., *French North Africa: the Maghrib between Two World Wars*, (London 1967).

Blundell, Sir Michael, *So Rough a Wind* (London 1964).

Brett, E.A., *Colonialism and Underdevelopment in East Africa: the Politics of Economic Change, 1919-1939*, (London 1973).

Bromley, R. and C. Gerry, (eds), *Casual Work and Poverty in Third World Cities*, (Chichester 1979).

Buijtenhuijs, R., *Essays on Mau Mau: Contributions to Mau Mau Historiography*, (Leiden 1982).

Cagnolo, C. *The Akikuyu*, (Nyeri 1933).

Cliffe, L. and J.S. Saul, *Socialism in Tanzania*, vol. 1, (Nairobi 1972).

Cohen, A.B., *British Policy in Changing Africa*, (London 1959).

Crowder, M., *West Africa under Colonial Rule*, (London 1968).

Darwin, J., *Britain, Egypt and the Middle East: Imperial Policy in the Aftermath of War, 1918-1922*, (London 1981).

Dewey, C. and A.G. Hopkins, *The Imperial Impact: Studies in the Economic History of Africa and India*, (London 1978).

Farson, N., *Last Chance in Africa*, (London 1949).

Fisher, J.M., *Anatomy of Kikuyu Domesticity and Husbandry*, (London 1964).

Frost, R.A., *Race Against Time: Human Relations and Politics in Kenya before Independence*, (London 1978).

Gallagher, J.A., *The Decline, Revival and Fall of the British Empire: the Ford Lectures and Other Essays*, (Cambridge 1982).

Gallagher, J.A. and G. Johnson and A. Seal (eds), *Locality, Province and Nation: Essays on Indian Politics, 1870-1940*, (Cambridge 1973).

Gann, L.H. and P. Duignan (eds), *African Proconsuls: European Governors in Africa*, (London 1978).

Gertzel, C., *The Politics of Independent Kenya, 1963-1968*, (London 1970).

Ghai, Y.P. and Y.P.W.B. McAuslan, *Public Law and Political Change in Kenya*, (Nairobi 1970).

Goldsworthy, D., *Colonial Issues in British Politics 1945-1961: From 'Colonial Development' to 'Wind of Change'*, (Oxford 1971).

—— *Tom Mboya: the Man Kenya Wanted to Forget*, (London 1982).

Gregory, R.E., *Sidney Webb and East Africa*, (Berkeley 1962).

Gupta, P.S., *Imperialism and the British Labour Movement, 1914-1964*, (London 1975).

Gutkind, P.C.W., R. Cohen and J. Copans (eds), *African Labor History*, (London 1978).

Hailey, Lord, *An African Survey*, 1st edition, (Oxford 1938).

—— *Native Administration and Political Development in British Tropical Africa*, (Nendeln/Liechtenstein 1979).

—— *Native Administration in the British African Territories*, 4 vols. (London 1950).

—— *Native Land Tenure in Africa* (printed for the Colonial Office, London 1945).

—— *An African Survey*, (revised edition, London 1957).

Hake, A., *African Metropolis: Nairobi's Self-Help City*, (London 1977).

Harlow, V., E.M. Chilver and A. Smith (eds), *History of East Africa*, vol. 2, (Oxford 1965).

Harris, J.E. (ed.), *Recollections of James Juma Mbotela*, (Nairobi 1977).

Hennings, R.O., *African Morning*, (London 1951).

Bibliography

Hillmer, N. and P. Wigley (eds), *The First British Commonwealth: Essays in Honour of Nicholas Mansergh*, (London 1980).

Holland, R.F., *European Decolonization 1918-1981*, (London 1985).

—— and G. Rizvi, (eds), *Perspectives on Imperialism and Decolonization: Essays in Honour of A.F. Madden*, (London 1984).

Hollis, A.C., *The Nandi* (Oxford 1909).

Hughes, L. (ed.), *An African Treasury* (New York 1960).

Humphrey, N., *The Kikuyu Lands: The Relation of Population to the Land in South Nyeri*, (Nairobi 1945).

Humphrey, N., *The Liguru and the Land: Sociological Aspects of Some Agricultural Problems of North Kavirondo*, (Nairobi 1947).

Iliffe, J., *A Modern History of Tanganyika*, (Cambridge 1979).

Jeffrey, R. (ed.), *Asia: the Winning of Independence*, (London 1981).

Jones, N.S. Carey, *The Anatomy of Uhuru*, (Manchester 1966).

Kaggia, B., *Roots of Freedom, 1921-1963*, (Nairobi 1975).

Kennedy, P., *The Realities Behind Diplomacy: Background Influences on British External Policy, 1865-1980*, (London 1981).

Kenyatta, J., *Facing Mount Kenya: the Tribal Life of the Gikuyu*, (London 1953).

Kimambo, I.N., *Mbiru: Popular Protest in Colonial Tanzania*, Historical Association of Tanzania, Paper No. 9, (Nairobi 1971).

Kirk-Greene, A.H.M., *A Biographical Dictionary of the British Colonial Governors: Africa*, (Stanford 1980).

Kitching, G., *Class and Economic Change in Kenya: the Making of an African Petite-Bourgeoisie*, (London 1980).

Lambert, H.E., *Systems of Land Tenure in the Kikuyu Land Unit*, (School of African Studies, University of Cape Town, Paper No. 22, February 1950).

—— *Kikuyu Social and Political Institutions*, (London 1956).

Leakey, L.S.B., *Defeating Mau Mau*, (London 1954).

—— *The Southern Kikuyu before 1903*, 3 vols., (London 1977).

Lee, J.M., *Colonial Development and Good Government*, (Oxford 1967).

—— and M. Petter, *The Colonial Office, War and Development Policy*, (London 1982).

Leys, C., *Underdevelopment in Kenya: the Political Economy of Neo-Colonialism, 1964-1971*, (London 1975).

Little, K., *West African Urbanization: A Study of Voluntary Associations in Social Change*, (Cambridge 1970).

Louis, W.R., *Imperialism at Bay: the United States and the Decolonization of the British Empire, 1941-1945*, (Oxford 1977).

Low, D.A. and A. Smith (eds), *History of East Africa*, 3 vols., (Oxford 1976).

Madden, F. and D.K. Fieldhouse (eds), *Oxford and the Idea of Commonwealth*, (London 1982).

Maguire, G.A., *Towards Uhuru in Tanzania: the Politics of Participation*, (Cambridge 1969).

Maina wa Kinyatti, (ed.), *Thunder from the Mountains: Mau Mau Patriotic Songs*, (London 1980).

Mathu, M., *The Urban Guerrilla*, (Richmond, British Columbia 1974).

Middlemas, K., *Politics in Industrial Society: the Experience of the British System since 1911*, (London 1979).

Mitchell, P.E., *African Afterthoughts*, (London 1954).

Moore, S. Barrington, Jr., *The Social Origins of Dictatorship and Democracy* (Boston 1966).

Morgan, D.J., *The Official History of Colonial Development: Origins of British Aid Policy, 1924-1945*, (London 1980).

—— *The Official History of Colonial Development: Developing British Colonial Resources 1945-1951*, (London 1980).

Mosley, P., *The Settler Economies: Studies in the Economic History of Kenya and Southern Rhodesia, 1900-63*, (Cambridge 1983).

Mungeam, G.H., *British Rule in Kenya, 1895-1912: the Establishment of Administration in the East African Protectorate*, (Oxford 1966).

Munro, J. Forbes, *Colonial Rule and the Kamba: Social Change in the Kenya Highlands, 1889-1939*, (Oxford 1975).

—— *Africa and the International Economy, 1800-1960*, (London 1976).

Murray-Brown, J., *Kenyatta*, (New York 1973).

Mwangi, M., *Kill Me Quick*, (London 1973).

Bibliography

—— *Going Down River Road*, (London 1976).
Newman, *The Ukamba Members Association*, (Nairobi 1974).
Ngugi wa Thiong'o, *Detained: A Writer's Prison Diary* (London 1981).
Ogot, B.A., (ed.), *Hadith*, vol. 2, (Nairobi 1970).
Ogot, B.A., (ed.), *Hadith*, vol. 3, (Nairobi 1971).
—— (ed.), *Hadith*, vol. 4, *Politics and Nationalism in Colonial Kenya*, (Nairobi 1972).
—— (ed.), *Hadith*, vol. 5, *Economic and Social History of East Africa*, (Nairobi 1975).
—— (ed.), *Hadith* vol. 7, *Ecology and History in East Africa* (Nairobi 1979).
Owen, E.R.J. and R.B. Sutcliffe, (eds), *Studies in the Theory of Imperialism*, (London 1972).
Palmer, R. and N. Parsons, (eds), *The Roots of Rural Poverty in Central and Southern Africa*, (London 1977).
Parkin, D., *The Cultural Definition of Political Response: Lineal Destiny among the Luo*, (London 1978).
Pearce, R.D., *The Turning Point in Africa: British Colonial Policy, 1938-1948*, (London 1982).
Perham, M., (ed.), *Ten Africans*, (London 1936).
—— *Colonial Sequence, 1930-1949*, Vol. I (London 1967).
—— *East African Journey: Kenya and Tanganyika, 1929-30*, (London 1976).
Peristiany, J.G., *The Social Institutions of the Kipsigis*, (reprinted London 1964).
Ranger, T.O., *Peasant Consciousness and Guerrilla War in Zimbabwe*, (London 1985).
Ricklefs, M.C., *A History of Modern Indonesia*, (London 1981).
Roelker, J.R., *Mathu of Kenya: A Political Study*, (Stanford 1976).
Rosberg, C.G. and J. Nottingham, *The Myth of 'Mau Mau': Nationalism in Kenya*, (New York 1966).
Rosen, I. and F. de F. Stratton, *A Digest of East African Criminal Case Law* (Durban 1957).
Rotberg, R.I., *The Rise of Nationalism in Central Africa: the Making of Malawi and Zambia, 1873-1964*, (Cambridge, Massachusetts 1965).
Rotberg, R.I and A.A. Mazrui (eds), *Protest and Power in Black Africa*, (New York 1970).
Routledge, W.S. and K., *With a Prehistoric People: the Akikuyu of British East Africa*, (reprinted, London 1968).
Sandbrook, R. and R. Cohen (eds), *The Development of an African Working Class: Studies in Class Formation and Action*, (London 1975).
Seal, A., *The Emergence of Indian Nationalism: Competition and Collaboration in the later Nineteenth Century*, (Cambridge 1968).
Shanin, T. (ed.), *Peasants and Peasant Societies*, (London 1971).
Shepperson, G.A. and T. Price, *Independent African: John Chilembwe and the Origins, Setting and Significance of the Nyasaland Native Rising of 1915*, (Edinburgh 1958).
Singh, M., *History of Kenya's Trade Union Movement up to 1952*, (Nairobi 1969).
Sorrenson, M.P.K., *Land Reform in the Kikuyu Country: A Study in Government Policy*, (Nairobi 1967).
Spencer, J., *KAU: The Kenya African Union*, (London 1985).
—— *James Beauttah: Freedom Fighter*, (Nairobi 1983).
Stichter, S.B., *Migrant Labour in Kenya: Capitalism and African Response, 1895-1975*, (London 1982).
Storry, R., *Japan and the Decline of the West in Asia, 1894-1943*, (London 1979).
Swainson, N., *The Development of Corporate Capitalism in Kenya, 1918-1977*, (London 1980).
Swynnerton, R.J.M., *A Plan to Intensify the Development of African Agriculture in Kenya*, (Nairobi 1954).
Thomas, H., *John Strachey*, (London 1973).
Thorne, C., *Allies of a Kind: the United States, Britain, and the War Against Japan, 1941-1945*, (London 1978).
Tignor, R.L., *The Colonial Transformation of Kenya: the Kamba, Kikuyu and Maasai from 1900 to 1939*, (Princeton 1976).
Tosh, J., *Clan Leaders and Colonial Chiefs in Lango*, (Oxford 1978).
Trapnell, C.G. and J.M. Clothier, *The Soils, Vegetation and Agricultural Systems of North-Western Rhodesia*, (Government Printer, Lusaka 1937).
Van Onselen, C., *Chibaro: African Mine Labour in Southern Rhodesia, 1900-1933*, (London 1976).
Van Zwanenberg, R.M.A., *Colonial Capitalism and Labour in Kenya, 1919-1939*, (Nairobi 1975).
Von Albertini, R., *Decolonization: the Administration and Future of the Colonies, 1919-1960*, (New York 1971).

Bibliography

Wachanga, H.K., *The Swords of Kirinyaga: the Fight for Land and Freedom*, (Nairobi 1975).
Wasserman, G., *Politics of Decolonization: Kenya Europeans and the Land Issue, 1960–1965*, (Cambridge 1976).
Wolf, E.R., *Peasants*, (Englewood Cliffs, New Jersey 1966).

2. Articles

Abrahams, P., 'The Blacks', in L. Hughes, (ed.), *An African Treasury*, (New York 1960), pp. 50–62.
African Studies Branch of the Colonial Office, 'Local Government Reorganisation in the Eastern Provinces of Nigerial and Kenya', *Journal of African Administration*, vol. 1, no. 1, January 1949, pp. 18–29.
African Studies Branch of the Colonial Office, 'A Survey of the Development of Local Government in the African Territories since 1947', Supplement to the *Journal of African Administration* vol. 4, no. 1, January 1952, pp. 1–83.
Anderson, D.M., 'Depression, Dust Bowl, Demography and Drought: The Colonial State and Soil Conservation in East Africa during the 1930s', *African Affairs* vol. 83, no. 332, July 1984, pp. 321–43.
Anderson, D.M. and D.W. Throup, 'Africans and Agricultural Production in Colonial Kenya: The Myth of the War as a Watershed', *Journal of African History*, vol. 26, 1985, pp. 327–45.
Anyang'-Nyong'o, P., 'The Development of a Middle Peasantry in Nyanza', *Review of African Political Economy*, no. 20, January–April 1981, pp. 108–20.
—— 'What the "Friends of the Peasantry" are and How they Pose the Question of the Peasantry', *Review of African Political Economy*, no. 20. January–April 1981, pp. 17–26.
Atieno Odhiambo, E.S., ' "Seek Ye First the Economic Kingdom": A History of the Luo Thrift and Trading Corporation (LUTATCO), 1945–1956', in B.A. Ogot, (ed.) *Hadith 5: Economic and Social History of East Africa*, (Nairobi 1975), pp. 218–56.
Bennett, G., 'Settlers and Politics in Kenya, up to 1945', in V. Harlow, E.M. Chilver and A. Smith (eds), *History of East Africa*, vol. 2 (Oxford 1965), pp. 265–332.
Berman, B.J., 'Bureaucracy and Incumbent Violence: Colonial Administration and the Origins of the Mau Mau Emergency in Kenya', *British Journal of Political Science*, vol. 6, pp. 143–75.
Bowles, B.D., 'Underdevelopment in Agriculture in Colonial Kenya: Some Ecological and Dietary Aspects', in B.A. Ogot, (ed.), *Hadith 7: Ecology and History in East Africa*, (Nairobi 1979), pp. 195–215.
Brett, E.A. and S. Gilliatt and A. Pople, 'Planned Trade, Labour Part Policy and U.S. Intervention: the Successes and Failures of Post-War Reconstruction', *History Workshop*, no. 13, Spring 1982, pp. 130–42.
Bujra, J.M., 'Women Entrepreneurs of Early Nairobi', *Canadian Journal of African Studies*, vol. 9, no. 2, 1975, pp. 213–34.
Cell, J.W., 'On the Eve of Decolonisation: the Colonial Office's Plans for the Transfer of Power in Africa, 1947', *Journal of Imperial and Commonwealth History*, vol. 8 no. 3, May 1980, pp. 235–57.
Cliffe, L., 'Nationalism and the Reaction to Enforced Agricultural Change in Tanganyika during the Colonial Period', in L. Cliffe and J.S. Saul, *Socialism in Tanzania*, vol. I, (Nairobi 1972), pp. 17–23.
Cowen, M.P., 'The Agrarian Problem: Notes on the Nairobi Discussion', *Review of African Political Economy*, no. 20, January–April 1981, pp. 57–73
Darwin, J., 'British Decolonization since 1945: A Pattern or a Puzzle?', in R.F. Holland and G. Rizvi, (eds), *Perspectives on Imperialism and Decolonization: Essays in Honour of A.F. Madden*, (London 1984), pp. 187–209.
Ehrlich, C., 'The Uganda Economy, 1903–1945', in V. Harlow, E.M. Chilver, and A. Smith (eds), *History of East Africa*, vol. 2, (Oxford 1965), pp. 395–475.
Fosbrooke, H., 'Public Opinion and Changes in Land Tenure', Special Supplement on Land Tenure to the *Journal of African Administration*, October 1952, pp. 28–36.
Frost, R.A., 'Sir Philip Mitchell: Governor of Kenya', *African Affairs*, vol. 78, no. 313, October 1979, pp. 535–53.
Furedi, F., 'The African Crowd in Nairobi: Popular Movements and Elite Politics', *Journal of African History*, vol. 14, no. 2, 1973, pp. 275–90.
— 'The Social Composition of the Mau Mau Movement in the White Highlands', *Journal of

Bibliography

Peasant Studies, vol. 1, no. 4, (1973), pp. 486-505.
—— 'The Development of Anti-Asian Opinion among Africans in Nakuru District, Kenya', *African Affairs*, vol. 73, no. 292, July 1974, pp. 347-58.
—— 'The Kikuyu Squatters in the Rift Valley, 1918-1929', in B.A. Ogot (ed), *Hadith 5: Economic and Social History of East Africa*, (Nairobi 1975), pp. 177-94.
Gadsden, F., 'The African Press in Kenya, 1945-52', *Journal of African History* vol. 21, no. 4, 1980, pp. 515-35.
Gordon, D.F., 'Mau Mau and Decolonization: Kenya and the Defeat of Multi-Racialism in East and Central Africa', *Kenya Historical Review*, vol. 5, no. 2, 1977, pp. 329-48.
Hailey, Lord, 'The Land Tenure Problem in Africa', Special Supplement on Land Tenure to the *Journal of African Administration*, October 1952, pp. 3-7.
Hennings, R.O., 'Some Trends and Problems of African Land Tenure in Kenya', *Journal of African Administration*, vol. 4, no. 4, October 1952, pp. 122-34.
Holland, R.F., 'The Imperial Factor in British Strategies from Attlee to Macmillan, 1945-63', in R.F. Holland and G. Rizvi, (eds), *Perspectives on Imperialism and Decolonization: Essays in Honour of A.F. Madden*, (London 1984), pp. 165-86.
Horowitz, D., 'Attitudes of British Conservatives towards Decolonization in Africa', *African Affairs*, vol. 69, no. 274, January 1970, pp. 9-26.
Hyam, R., 'The Colonial Office Mind, 1900-1914', in N. Hillmer and P. Wigley, *The First British Commonwealth: Essays in Honour of Nicholas Mansergh*, (London 1980), pp. 30-55.
Iliffe, J., 'The Creation of Group Consciousness among the Dockworkers of Dar-es-Salaam, 1929-1950', in R. Sandbrook and R. Cohen, (eds), *The Development of an African Working Class: Studies in Class Formation and Action*, (London 1975), pp. 49-72.
Johnson, D.H., 'Evans-Pritchard, the Nuer, and the Sudan Political Service', *African Affairs*, vol. 81, no. 323, April 1982, pp. 231-46.
Jones, A. Creech, 'The Place of African Local Administration in Colonial Policy', *Journal of African Administration*, vol. 1, no. 1, January 1949, pp. 3-6.
Kamunchulun, J.T.S., 'The Meru Participation in Mau Mau', *Kenya Historical Review*, vol. 3, no. 2, 1975, pp. 193-216.
Kanogo, T.M.J., 'Rift Valley Squatters and Mau Mau', *Kenya Historical Review*, vol. 5, no. 2, 1977, pp. 243-52.
King, K.J. and R.M. Wambaa, 'The Political Economy of the Rift Valley: A Squatter Perspective', in B.A. Ogot, (ed.), *Hadith 5: Economic and Social History of East Africa*, (Nairobi 1975) pp. 195-217.
Kipkorir, B.E., 'The Educated Elite and Local Society: The Basis for Mass Representation', in B.A. Ogot, (ed.), *Hadith 4: Politics and Nationalism in Colonial Kenya*, (Nairobi 1972), pp. 250-69.
—— 'Mau Mau and the Politics of the Transfer of Power in Kenya, 1957-1960', *Kenya Historical Review*, vol. 5, no. 2., 1977, pp. 313-28.
Kirk-Greene, A.H.M., 'Margery Perham and Colonial Administration: A Direct Influence on Indirect Rule', in F. Madden and D.K. Fieldhouse, (eds), *Oxford and the Idea of Commonwealth*, (London 1982), pp. 122-43.
—— 'On Governorship and Governors in British Africa', in L.H. Gann and P. Duignan, (eds), *African Proconsuls: European Governors in Africa*, (London 1978), pp. 210-257.
—— 'The Progress of Pro-Consuls: Advancement and Migration among the Colonial Governors of British African Territories, 1900-1965', *Journal of Imperial and Commonwealth History*, vol. 7, no. 2, January 1979, pp. 180-212.
—— 'The Thin White Line: the Size of the British Colonial Service in Africa', *African Affairs*, vol. 79, no. 314, January 1980, pp. 25-44.
Kosmin, B., 'The Inyoka Tobacco Industry of the Shangwe People', in R. Palmer and N. Parsons (eds), *The Roots of Rural Poverty in Central and Southern Africa*, (London 1977), pp. 268-88.
Lee, J.M., 'Forward Thinking and War: the Colonial Office during the 1940s', *Journal of Imperial and Commonwealth History*, vol. 6, no. 1, October 1977, pp. 64-79.
Listowel, Earl of, 'The Modern Conception of Government in British Africa', *Journal of African Studies*, vol. 1, no. 3, July 1949, pp. 99-105.
Lonsdale, J.M., 'Some Origins of Nationalism in East Africa', *Journal of African History*, vol. 9, no. 1, 1968, pp. 119-46.
—— 'European Attitudes and African Pressures: Missions and Government in Kenya between the Wars', in B.A. Ogot, (ed.), *Hadith 2*, (Nairobi 1970), pp. 229-42.

Bibliography

—— and D.A. Low, 'Introduction: Towards the New Order, 1945-1963', in D.A. Low and A. Smith (eds), *History of East Africa*, vol. 3, (Oxford 1976), pp. 1-63.

McCracken, J., 'Experts and Expertise in Colonial Malawi', *African Affairs*, vol. 81, no. 322, January 1982, pp. 101-16.

McWilliam, M., 'The Managed Economy: Agricultural Change, Development and Finance in Kenya', in D.A. Low and A. Smith, (eds), *History of East Africa*, vol. 3, (Oxford 1976), pp. 251-89.

Maguire, G.A., 'The Emergence of the Tanganyika African National Union in the Lake Province', in R.I. Rotberg and A.A. Mazrui, (eds), *Protest and Power in Black Africa*, (New York, 1970), pp. 639-70.

Maina wa Kinyatti, 'Mau Mau: the Peak of African Political Organization in Colonial Kenya', *Kenya Historical Review*, vol. 5, no. 2, 1977, pp. 287-311.

Mair, L., 'Anthropology and Colonial Policy', *African Affairs*, vol. 74, no. 295, April 1975, pp. 191-5.

Masefield, G.B., 'Farming Systems and Land Tenure', Special Supplement on Land Tenure to the *Journal of African Administration*, October 1952, pp. 8-14.

Meek, C.K., 'The Amsterdam Land Tenure Symposium', *Journal of African Administration*, vol. 4, no. 3, July 1952, pp. 113-14.

—— 'Some Social Aspects of Land Tenure in Africa', Special Supplement on Land Tenure to the *Journal of African Administration*, October 1952, pp. 15-21.

Miles, J., 'Rural Protest in the Gold Coast: the Cocoa Hold-Ups, 1908-1938', in C. Dewey and A.G. Hopkins, (eds), *The Imperial Impact: Studies in the Economic History of Africa and India*, London 1978), pp. 152-70.

Mukaru-Ng'ang'a, D., 'What is Happening to the Kenyan Peasantry?', *Review of African Political Economy*, no. 20, January-April 1981, pp. 7-16.

—— 'Mau Mau, Loyalists and Politics in Murang'a, 1952-70', *Kenya Historical Review*, vol. 5, no. 2, 1977, pp. 365-84.

Muntemba M. 'Thwarted Development: A Case Study of Economic Change in the Kabwe Rural District of Zambia, 1902-70', in R. Palmer and N. Parsons, (eds), *The Roots of Rural Poverty in Central and Southern Africa*, (London 1977), pp. 345-345-64.

Nelson, N., 'How Women and Men Get By: the Sexual Division of Labour in the Informal Sector of a Nairobi Squatter Settlement', in R. Bromley and C. Gerry, (eds), *Casual Work and Poverty in Third World Cities*, (Chichester 1979), pp. 283-302.

Newton, S., 'Britain, the Sterling Area and European Integration, 1945-50', *Journal of Imperial and Commonwealth History*, vol. 13 no. 3, May 1985, pp. 163-82.

Njonjo, A.L.N., 'The Kenya Peasantry: A Reassessment', *Review of African Political Economy*, no. 20, January-April 1981, pp. 27-40.

Ogot, B.A., 'Politics, Culture and Music in Central Kenya: A Study of Mau Mau Hymns, 1951-1956', *Kenya Historical Review*, vol. 5, no. 2, 1977, pp. 275-86.

—— 'The Revolt of the Elders: An Anatomy of the Loyalist Crowd in the Mau Mau Uprising, 1952-56', in B.A. Ogot, (ed.), *Hadith 4: Politics and Nationalism in Colonial Kenya*, (Nairobi 1972), pp. 134-48.

O'Hagan, D., 'African's Part in Nairobi Local Government', *Journal of African Administration*, vol. 1, no. 4, October 1949, pp. 156-8.

Omosule, M., 'Kiama Kia Muingi: Kikuyu Reaction to Land Consolidation Policy in Kenya, 1955-59', *Transafrican Journal of History*, vol. 4, nos. 1-2, 1974, pp. 115-34.

Palmer, R., 'The Agricultural History of Rhodesia', in R. Palmer and N. Parsons, (eds), *The Roots of Rural Poverty in Central and Southern Africa*, (London 1977), pp. 221-54.

Pearce, R.D., 'Governors, Nationalists and Constitutions in Nigeria, 1935-1951', *Journal of Imperial and Commonwealth History*, vol. 9, no. 3, May 1981, pp. 289-307.

Pedler, F., 'The Contribution of Lord Hailey to Africa', *African Affairs*, vol. 69, no. 276, July 1970, pp. 267-75.

Philip, A.J., 'Nutrition in Kenya', *East African Medical Journal*, July 1943.

Phimister, I., 'Peasant Production and Underdevelopment in Southern Rhodesia, 1890-1914', in R. Palmer and N. Parsons, (eds) *The Roots of Rural Poverty in Central and Southern Africa*, (London 1977), pp. 255-67.

Rathbone, R.J.A.R., 'The Government of the Gold Coast after the Second World War', *African Affairs*, vol. 67, no. 2, 1968, pp. 209-18.

—— 'Businessmen in Politics: Party Struggle in Ghana, 1949-57', *Journal of Development Studies*, vol. 9, no. 3, 1973, pp. 391-401.

Bibliography

Robinson, R.E., 'The Relationship of Major and Minor Local Government Authorities', *Journal of African Administration*, vol. 1, no. 1, January 1949, pp. 30–3.
—— 'The Progress of Provincial Councils in the British African Territories', *Journal of African Administration*, vol. 1, no. 2, April 1949, pp. 53–68.
—— 'Non European Foundations of European Imperialism: Sketch for a Theory of Collaboration', in E.R.J. Owen and R.B. Sutcliffe, (eds) *Studies in the Theory of Imperialism*, (London 1972), pp. 117–142.
—— 'The Moral Disarmament of African Empire, 1919–1947', *Journal of Imperial and Commonwealth History*, vol. 3, no. 1, October 1979, pp. 86–104.
—— 'The Journal and the Transfer of Power, 1947–51', *Journal of Administration Overseas*, vol. 13, no. 1, 1974, pp. 255–258.
—— 'Andrew Cohen and the Transfer of Power in Tropical Africa, 1940–51', in W.H. Morris-Jones and G. Fischer, (eds), *Decolonization and After: the British and French Experience*, (London 1980), pp. 50–72.
—— 'Sir Andrew Cohen: Proconsul of African Nationalism', in L.H. Gann and P. Duignan, (eds), *African Proconsuls: European Governors in Africa*, (London 1978), pp. 353–63.
Rowlings, C.W., 'An Analysis of Factors Affecting Changes in Land Tenure in Africa', Special Supplement on Land Tenure to the *Journal of African Administration*, October 1952, pp. 21–8.
Saul, J. and R. Woods, 'African Peasantries', in T. Shanin, (ed.), *Peasants and Peasant Societies*, (London 1971), pp. 103–13.
Seal, A., 'Imperialism and Nationalism in India', in J. Gallagher, G. Johnson and A. Seal, (eds), *Locality, Province and Nation: Essays on Indian Politics, 1870–1940*, (Cambridge 1973), pp. 1–27.
Singh, M., 'The East African Trade Union Congress, 1949–50: the First Central Organisation of Trade Unions in Kenya', in B.A. Ogot, (ed) *Hadith 4: Politics and Nationalism in Colonial Kenya*, (Nairobi 1972), pp. 233–249.
Spencer, I.R.G., 'Settler Dominance, Agricultural Production and the Second World War in Kenya', *Journal of African History*, vol. 21, 1980, pp. 497–514.
Spencer, J., 'Kenya African Union and Mau Mau: Some Connections', *Kenya Historical Review*, vol. 5, no. 2, 1977, pp. 201–24.
Stevens, R.A., 'The Application of English Local Government Principles in Africa', *Journal of African Administration*, vol. 1, no. 2, April 1949, pp. 68–73.
Stichter, S.B., 'Trade Unionism in Kenya, 1947–1952: the Militant Phase' in P.C.W. Gutkind, R. Cohen and J. Copans, (eds), *African Labor History*, (London 1978), pp. 155–74.
—— 'The Formation of a Working Class in Kenya', in R. Sandbrook and R. Cohen, (eds), *The Development of an African Working Class: Studies in Class Formation and Action*, (London 1975), pp. 21–48.
—— 'Workers, Trade Unions and the Mau Mau Rebellion', *Canadian Journal of African Studies*, vol. 9, no. 2, 1975, pp. 253–75.
Tamarkin, M., 'Mau Mau in Nakuru', *Kenya Historical Review*, vol. 5, no. 2, 1977, pp. 225–41.
Throup, D.W., 'The Origins of Mau Mau', *African Affairs*, vol. 84, no. 336, July 1985, pp. 399–433.
Trapnell, C.G., 'Ecological Methods in the Study of Native Agriculture', *East African Agricultural Journal*, vol. 2, 1937, pp. 491–4.
Van Zwanenberg, R.M.A., 'History and Theory of Urban Poverty in Nairobi', *Journal of Eastern African Research and Development*, vol. 2, 1972, pp. 165–203.
Were, G.S., 'Politics, Religion and Nationalism in Western Kenya'. in B.A. Ogot, (ed), *Hadith 4: Politics and Nationalism in Colonial Kenya*, (Nairobi 1972), pp. 85–104.
Westcott, N.J., 'Erica Fiah: An East African Radical', *Journal of African History*, vol. 22, 1981, pp. 85–101.
—— 'Closer Union and the Future of East Africa, 1939–48: A Case Study in the Official Mind of Imperialism', *Journal of Imperial and Commonwealth History*, vol. 10, No. 1, 1981, pp. 67–88.
Wipper, A., 'Elijah Masinde – a folk hero', in B.A. Ogot, (ed.) *Hadith 3*, (Nairobi 1971), pp. 157–91.

Index

Index

Wyn Harris, 158, 160; warnings of African opposition from settlers, 27, 56
Mombasa, general strike (January, 1947), 173–4; immigration during 1940s, 8, 171
Moon, Trevor, Provincial Agricultural Officer, Central Province, 142; condemns anti-terracing campaign, 153; converted to cash crop production, 205; opposes Brown's policy
Moore, Sir Henry, as chief secretary and governor of Kenya, 23; career of; 278–9
Morgan, D.L., career of, 279
Mortimer, Sir Charles, appointment as Member for Health and Local Goverment, 38; attitude towards squatters, 92; career of, 279
Moyne, Lord, end of trusteeship era, 33
Muchuchu, Job, commercial farmer, 215; muhirig'a administration's reliance on, 71–2, 203; Creech Jones impressed by, 81; organisation of compulsory labour, 5, 76; origins of system in Murang'a, 79–81; to counteract soil erosion, 63, 76, 79–81, 143
Mullins, A.C.M., career of, 279
multi-national corporations, as agents of economic development, 46–7
Murang'a, acreage terraced, 79–81; agricultural development plan, 212–13; Beauttah and Ng'ang'a as business leaders, 75; chiefs, 146–64; opposition to terracing, 6–7, 35; peasants' revolt, 5, 139–64; political significance of peasants' revolt, 245; use of muhirig'a, 79–81

Nairobi, administration of, 174–5; African Advisory Council, 176–7; by-laws to control influx, 192–3; centre of militancy, 8, 171; charter day boycott 193–4; crime, 9–10, 171–3, 177–8; discontent, 171, 192–6; emergency food stocks, 173; general strike (May 1950), 10, 194–6; growth of political protest, 192–6; housing, 171–2, 178–88; housing shortage, 9, 238–9; inflation, 8, 188–90; influx of ex-squatters, 243; Mau Mau oath centre, 171; myth of de-tribalisation, 175–6; over-crowding, 171–2, 178–85, 190; policy, 174; population growth, 8, 9, 171, 178–85, 188; support for Mau Mau, 11; tribalism, 191–3; tribunals, 176
Naivasha, squatter policy of district council, 7, 91, 95–7, 102; squatter resistance, 110–13, 129
Nakuru, squatter policy of district council, 7, 96, 102; squatter resistance, 110–11
Nandi, squatter resistance among, 110–12, 242–3, 247
Nanyuki, grass fires, 224
Ng'ang'a, Andrew, arrested, 224; political

exclusion of, 239; secretary of Murang'a KAU, 75; thwarted business activities, 75
Njuri Ncheke, authority of, 211–12; organisation of compulsory labour, 5, 63
Northey, Sir Edward, as governor of Kenya, 23
Nyanza District Council, squatter policy, 96
Nyeri, coffee cultivation, 5; Humphrey's report on, 63; Mau Mau activities (February 1952), 11; Mau Mau, growing support for, 224; opposition to destocking, 35

oathing, development at Olenguruone, 120
Odede, F.W., career of, 279
O'Hagan, Desmond, career of, 279–80; district commissioner in Murang'a, 79–81; supports terracing campaign, 151; relations with KAU and KCA, 161–2; role of chiefs in terracing, 153–4
Ohanga, B.A., career of, 280
Olenguruone, administration failure at, 124–6; agricultural policies, 126–8; climate and terrain, 123–4; Cohen's attitude towards, 126–7; eviction, 130–4; growth of Kikuyu opposition, 128–34; legal case, 130–31; links with squatters, 8, 113; Maher's policies, 126–8; in Mau Mau *nyimbo*, 134; origins of Kikuyu residents, 8, 121–3; petition to Kenyatta, 129–30; resistance to agricultural regulations, 8, 120–34
O'Rorke, M.S., excluded from policy meeting, 229; reports on Mau Mau, 225, 229
Osborne, agricultural development plan in Murang'a, 212–3; career of, 280; introduction of muhirig'a system in Murang'a, 79–81; relations with Chief Parmenas, 150

peasants revolt, Murang'a, 5; disillusionment with muhirig'a campaign, 80–81; political significance of, 245
Penfold, Cecil, career of, 280; police intelligence, 227–8
Perham, Margery, relations with Mitchell, 33
Pole-Evans, I.B., agricultural report, 64
police, intelligence, 227–8
politicians, government's attitude towards, 3; subversive of 'Merrie Africa'; 4
Potter, Henry, as acting governor, 11; career of, 280–1; warns Colonial Office, 231–2

Rankine, John, career of, 281; failure to react to Mau Mau, 227; relations with Mitchell, 36–7

302

Index

Rennie, Gilbert, career of, 281; early career in Ceylon, 43; negotiations of Closer Union, 49; relations with Mitchell, 36 resident labour, 7
Rimmington, Philip, criticises Maher, 143
Robinson, Ronald, criticism of moral disarmament theory, 237; view of decolonisation , 17–18
Roddan, G.M., deputy director of agriculture, 206
Ryland, R.D.F-H., career of, 281

Scott, Lord Francis, career of, 281–2
second colonial occupation, 4; disruption of the reserves, 11; expansion of administration and technical departments, 25; political consequences of in Africa, 244–6; role of chiefs, 5
Second World War, guaranteed prices to settlers, 7; prosperity of settlers and squatters, 7
settlers, as agents of economic development, 46; attitude to squatters, 7, 91–9; Colonial Office's fears of, 18–19, 21–5; contacts with the Conservative rightwing, 21; control squatter policy, 92, 93–6; coup d'etat by, Whyatt's view, 231; demand action against Mau Mau, 225–6, 231; demands for self-government, 39, 41; division between cereal farmers, planters and ranchers, 7, 95–9; divisions in the Trans Nzoia, 99, 106–8, 112; economic gains during the war, 21–2; fears of African competition, 4, 36, 92–5; fears of Kikuyu squatters, 92–100; influence on the Executive Council, 45–6; influence on Mitchell, 37–8; opinions of Sir Arthur Dawe, 23–4; opinions of Viscount Cranborne, 22–4; political embarrassment, 237–8; political gains during war, 2, 22–4; political influence contrasted with Rhodesia, 249–51; South African expansion, 22–4; squatters and Mau Mau, 233
Singh, Makhan, arrest of, 10, 194–6, 243, 248; career of, 282; influence on Nairobi militants, 10
Smuts, Jan Christian, policy towards Kenya, 24 soil conservation, 4, 63–81; in Murang'a, 139–64
South Africa, hegemony of, 2, 22–4
Soysambu, squatters at, 97; strike to coincide with Creech Jones's visit, 129
squatters, Abaluhya, 242–3, 247; base of Mau Mau, 11; contrasted with the Ndebele, 241–2; *Dini ya Jesu Kristo*, 113; economic effects of Second World War, 7, 94–5; fate of, 3; growth of squatter resistance, 110–13; incomes, 102–4; Kikuyu Highlands Squatters Associa-

tion, 111; links with Olenguruone, 8; Nandi, 242–3, 247; policy of Naivasha District Council, 7, 91, 95–7, 102, 129; policy of labour department, 100–6; opposition to Naivasha order, 91–5, 102; opposition to White Highlands' policy, 41, 52; Resident Native Labour Ordinance (1937), 94–5, 101; resistance in the Secretariat to Labour Department, 108–10; resistance among Abaluhya and Nandi squatters, 111–3; at Soysambu estate, 97, 129; visit Mitchell at Government House, 111
Stanley, Oliver, reaction to Mitchell's agricultural policies, 68
Strachey, John, attitude to Empire, 19–20
Swynnerton Report, contrasted with Humphrey, 69; agrarian reform, 142; appointment of, 206

Tempany, Sir Harold, career of, 282; criticisms of Kenya's agricultural policy, 39
terracing, acreage protected in Central Province, 66, 79–81, 205–6, 216; acreage protected in Murang'a, 151; compulsory labour, 4–5; growth of Kikuyu discontent in early 1950s, 203, 216–7; origins of muhirig'a system in Murang'a, 79–81; peasants' revolt in Murang'a, 6–7, 139–64; reforms too late, 209; switch to bench terraces, 215–6
Thornley, Colin, career of, 282; early career in Tanganyika, 43
Thuku, Harry, career of, 283
Tomkinson, opposes cash crop production, 203–4
Trans Nzoia, squatter policy of district council, 7, 96, 100, 106–8; concern at growth of squatter resistance, 111–3; divisions among settler farmers, 100, 106–8
tribunals, and increasing social differentiation, 9, 140–1; enforces terracing campaign, 151, 153; in Nairobi, 176
Troughton, J.F.G., career of, 283; early career in Kenya, 43–4

Uasin Gishu, squatter policy of district council, 7; model for Trans Nzoia, 107–8; 112
Ukambani, 'D Day', 68; declining maize yield, 66–7; ecological crisis in 1930s, 64; eviction of Olenguruone Kikuyu to B1 Yatta, 133; reliance on Kikuyu maize, 65–6
unemployed, support for Mau Mau, 11
United Nations' Organisation, Colonial Office attitude towards, 16; appeals from the KAU, 26

303